文
景
———
Horizon

徐梵澄 全集

孙波 主编

孔学古微

徐梵澄 著

李文彬 译　孙波 校

上海人民出版社

主编的话

　　徐梵澄（1909 年 10 月 26 日—2000 年 3 月 6 日），原名徐琥，字季海，湖南长沙人。幼塾就学于近代湘中巨子王闿运（湘绮）之再传弟子，其师杨度、杨钧辈，尝讲汉魏六朝古文。后进新式小学，开国领袖毛泽东为其地理老师。再后入教会所办之雅礼中学，接受全面现代教育，并得到了良好的英语训练。1926 年春，遵父命考入湘雅医学院。1927 年春，自作主张转入武汉中山大学历史系，开始发表文章，谋求自立。1928 年春，又考入上海复旦大学西洋文学系。同年 5 月，因聆听鲁迅讲演并作记录，遂与鲁迅通信，从此结下了深厚的师生情谊。1929 年 8 月至 1932 年 7 月，梵澄赴德留学修艺术史专业，分别就读于柏林大学和海德堡大学，其间为鲁迅搜求欧西版画，并自制作品寄与恩师，其作品为中国现代版画最早之创作，被业界誉为"第一人"者。回国以后，寄寓上海，为《申报·自由谈》撰写杂文和短篇小说，并受鲁迅之嘱，有规模地翻译尼采著作，包括《尼采自传》（良友公司 1935 年），《朝霞》（商务印书馆 1935 年），《苏鲁支语录》（含《人间的、太人间的》节译，生活书店 1936 年），《快乐的智识》（商务印书馆 1939 年）和《葛（歌）德自著之〈浮士德〉》（商务印书馆 1939 年）。又译出《佛教述略》（英译汉，上海佛教协会 1939 年）。

抗战爆发后，梵澄随国立艺专前往湘西，复又辗转昆明。1940 年底，艺专回迁至重庆，梵澄遂入中央图书馆，独自编纂《图书月刊》，并授课于中央大学。值 1945 年抗战胜利，梵澄加入中印文化交流计划，于年底飞赴印度加尔各答之桑地尼克丹的泰戈尔国际大学，任教于该校之中国学院，尝讲欧阳竟无唯识思想，并编辑《天竺字原》(佚失)。1950 年，梵澄赴名城贝纳尼斯（今名瓦拉纳西）重修梵文，其间译出印度文学经典《薄伽梵歌》和《行云使者》(迦里大萨)。1951 年春，梵澄又入南印度琫地舍里（今名本地治理）之室利·阿罗频多（Sri Aurobindo）学院，并受院母密那氏（Mira）之托任华文部主任。1950 年代，是梵澄于印度韦檀多学古今经典的译介期，古典有《奥义书》(梵译汉)五十种，今典有阿罗频多的《神圣人生论》,《薄伽梵歌论》,《瑜伽论》(学院版，六册，1957 年、1958 年、1959 年、1960 年),《社会进化论》(学院版 1960 年) 和《伊莎书》,《由谁书》(学院版 1957 年)，皆英译汉；以及院母的《母亲的话》(学院版，四册，1956 年、1958 年、1978 年)，为法译汉。1960 年代，是梵澄于中国传统学术菁华的宣扬期，其以英文著译《小学菁华》(学院版 1976 年),《孔学古微》(学院版 1966 年),《周子通书》(学院版 1978 年) 和《唯识菁华》与《肇论》。1970 年代，是梵澄将中、西、印三大古典文化思想之玄理整合的会通期，其标志乃为疏释室利·阿罗频多《赫拉克利特》之《玄理参同》(学院版 1973 年)。

1978 年底，梵澄回国。1979 年春，入中国社会科学院世界宗教研究所任研究员，直至 2000 年春殁世。此一末期，先生隐然有着确立中国精神哲学之努力的倾向，他的工作成果也不断被推向社会：1984 年，《五十奥义书》(中国社会科学出版社)和《神圣人生论》(商务印书馆)出版；1987 年，《肇论》(中国社会科学出版社)和《安慧〈三十唯识〉疏释》(梵译汉，中国佛教文化研究所)出版；1988 年，《异学杂著》(浙江文艺出版社)和《老子臆解》(中华书局)出版；1990 年，《唯识菁华》(新世界出版社)出版；1991 年，《周天集》(英译汉，生活·读书·新知三联书店)出版；1994 年，《陆王学述——一系精神哲学》(上海远东出版社)出版。先生故去以后，《薄伽梵歌论》于2003 年面世(商务印书馆)；又由编者所辑《徐梵澄文集》十六卷于 2006年推出(上海三联书店)。

纵观先生一生，注重非在某一学，如印学、西学或中学，尽管其治思于各家研讨极为深湛，要其着力所在仍为精神哲学，正如他自己所言："最是我所锲而不舍的，如数十年来所治之精神哲学。"这一端头是依鲁迅("立人""改造国民性")启始，这一线索是从希腊古哲赫拉克利特(永恒之"变是")和德国近哲尼采(精神之回还)，到印度古"见士"(由"无明"见"明")和近代"圣哲"阿罗频多(自性高栖，有为人生，终与"至上者"合契)，再回吾华儒家，并以中国文化为本位(变化气质，转化人生与社会)，收摄、重冶三家并塑模自家学说之雏形。于此可问：先生的尝试成功与否？或许"成功"不见！又有可说者，这是一"渊默而雷声"之事，影响或在久远的将来，它是浑融在中华民族未来希望之曙色中的，并渐行渐起，直趋"午昼"(阿罗频多语)。再问：到了"午昼"又如何呢？一个更高远的、更阔大的目标在上，即"超心思"之域，也可以称之为"精神道"。50 年前，国内"文革"尚未消歇，只身寄寓南印度一海隅的梵澄就发出了其深情的期待，他说："将来似可望'精神道'之大发扬，二者（哲学与宗教）双超"（《玄理参同》学院版）。复问："'精神道'之大发扬"为何种境界？乃光明倾注天理流行矣！

先生著、译述，除佚失和未采者，文集之收录约合 650 余万字。据他本人的想法，全部文字可分为三个部分，他说："编拙稿成集，细思只合分成三汇。属'精神哲学'者一，则《薄伽梵歌·序》等皆收。属'艺术'者一，则论书画者收之，当待大量补充。属'文学'者一，则自诌之俚句，及所译文言诗，并诗说者属之，犹待大量补充。"（《梵澄先生》，上海书店出版社 2009 年）其中三汇之"艺术"者和"文学"者，极为粲然，可入乎美学畛域，编者无似，读者自鉴。此就"精神哲学"者略说，这一宗学问在我国古代属内学、玄学，也即形而上学，有伦有序而不违逻辑，立义黏柔而超乎知识，故"从此一学翻成西文，舍哲学一名词而外，亦寻不出恰当的称呼。"（《陆王学述》）

那么，当解"精神"二字，与寻常概念不同，他以人"型"（the Ideas）来打比方的：

> ……而人，在生命之外，还有思想，即思维心，还有情感，即情感心或情命体。基本还有凡此所附丽的身体。但在最内中深处，还有一核心，通常称之曰心灵或性灵。是这些，哲学上乃统称之曰"精神"。但这还是就人生而说，它虽似是抽象，然是一真实体，在形而

> 上学中，应当说精神是超乎宇宙为至上为不可思议又在宇宙内为最基本而可证会的一存在。研究这主题之学，方称精神哲学。这一核心，是万善万德具备的，譬如千丈大树，其发端初生，只是一极微细的种子，核心中之一基因（gene），果壳中之仁。孔子千言万语解说人道中之"仁"，原亦取义于此。（《陆王学述》）

这"精神"，在徐先生的语境中，也被称为"知觉性""力""气"，即一超乎现象的基本力，在黑格尔或叫作"自然"；亦被称为"心灵""性灵"，即那"极微细的种子"，在柏拉图或叫作"灵魂"。前说好比大树之整个，后说有似其发芽破土的"种子"，二者是一事。又可表之：在本原性东西（宇宙之树）之内的一种自由（心灵或仁）。

先生所治之精神哲学，又分次第，初赫拉克利特和尼采，中诸《奥义书》和《薄伽梵歌》，后阿罗频多和儒家。初则赫氏与尼采之思想，不为"大全"，其精神只行进在半途，盖因赫氏不言"本体"，只说一永恒的"变是"，尼采否定"上帝"，只认一不歇的"心思"力。中则诸典，因受"空论"和"幻论"的消极影响，其真精神泯漠不彰垂二千余年。后则阿罗频多，欲挽沉滞，力振国运，重铸韦檀多哲学，并以《薄伽梵歌》为经，以诸《奥义书》为纬，教示其人民：以工作实践化除私我，以瑜伽精神奉献上帝。而阿氏之学，又与我国宋明儒家心学一路符契，梵澄说："鄙人之所以提倡陆、王者，以其与室利·阿罗频多之学多有契合处。有瑜伽之益，无瑜伽之弊。正以印度瑜伽在今日已败坏之极，故室利·阿罗频多思有以新苏之，故创'大全瑜伽'之说。观其主旨在于觉悟，变化气质，与陆、王不谋而合。姑谓为两道，此两道有文化背景之不同，皆与任何宗教异撰。亦与唯物论无所抵牾，可以并行不悖。"（《梵澄先生》）

又说先生之勤力，中年以后主要当在印度古典和阿罗频多诸书。其中翻译《薄伽梵歌》有句，"盖挥汗磨血几死而后得之者也"（佛协版"序"）；又有翻译《神圣人生论》曾云："'母亲'的精神力量是巨大的，我能够把室利·阿罗频多那样精深的《人生论》翻出来，没有精神力量支撑是不行的。"（《梵澄先生》）其自著之书，《老子臆解》也是颇费了不少心神，曾与友人说道："这是'狮子搏兔'的工作，是用过全身气力的，几十年来断断续续，不知费了多少功夫。"（《徐梵澄传》）对于这些文字的研读，仿佛有见一条基线，引向那本深而末茂的幽隧、高山而仰止的化境……于此可想，入蹊者定会兴味无尽，昭晰者必能疑窦释然，因为那是一注"神圣之泉"（阿罗频多），"没有汲桶放下去不能汲满着黄金和珠宝上来"（尼采）！而先生的自著文字，皆是简洁、雅健、灵犀、深锐，其中传映着他优游涵泳、从容论道的儒者气象，使人读来每每如沐春风而怡然自适，如饮醇醪又不觉自醉。

然而，说到自己的工作，他尝言："我的文字不多，主要思想都在序、跋里了。""我的英语文字多于文言文字，文言文字多于白话文字。"惜乎在本次文集的编辑过程中仍未能如意尽收，可知其一生有多少劳作皆付之东流了，这又是人生无可奈何之事。好在"基线"昭然，于是可问：先生为什么要去印度并且一滞就是 33 年呢？回答：是为了实现鲁迅的理想，即挹取彼邦之大经大法。百余年前，鲁迅就已明示："凡负令誉于史初，开文化之曙色，而今日转为影国者，无不如斯。使举国人所习闻，最适莫如天竺。天竺古有韦陀四种，瑰丽幽瓊，称世界大文。其摩诃波罗多暨罗摩衍那二赋，亦至美妙。"（《摩罗诗力说》）故先生去国，译出经典是首要任务，因为"若使大时代降临，人莫我知，无憾也，而我不可以不知人，则广挹世界文教之菁英，集其大成，以陶淑当世而启迪后人，因有望于我中华之士矣"（《薄伽梵歌论》案语）。

诸《奥义书》乃韦檀多学之经典，韦檀多乃韦陀之终教，为刹帝利族所擅，其陈说巫术祭祀少，探讨宇宙人生多，被称为韦陀之"知识篇"，与婆罗门族所执之"礼仪篇"相对。大致公元前 750 年后，战事稍息，农耕始稳，刹帝利支配力扩大，王庭成为教学的中心，王者成为主宰者，一转婆罗门"祭祀万能"之外求，诉诸内中"心灵"之醒觉，迈出了寻求普遍性的步伐，憧憬最高者、最广者、最完善者，也即"真理"者——"大梵""上帝""逻各斯""道""太极"等等。德哲雅斯贝尔斯将其称为人类的"轴心期时代"。诸《奥义书》首推《伊莎书》与《由谁书》，是为其体系之两柱石。《伊莎书》主旨在：**揭示宇宙本然之大经大法，乃彰显大梵圆成之境。**此是为入道者说法。《由谁书》所表在：**由用达体，描述求道之过程，只止于"阿难陀"之境。**此是为普通人说法。前者可看作精神哲学，后者应当作精神现象学。尤其《伊莎书》，其密接韦陀之根本，反映古韦陀圣人之心理体系，即精神实用者也。徐先生指出：阿氏"疏释"之简约一卷，"而韦檀多学之菁华皆摄。有此一卷，即是书古今余家注疏皆可

不问。"（前记）

阿罗频多为印度近世韦檀多学之集大成者，其学说又可以称之为"大全瑜伽论"。1972 年，阿氏百年诞辰，院母为其出版全集，煌煌然三十巨册。徐先生采译最重要者，乃其中四部，分属世界观者《神圣人生论》、人生观者《薄伽梵歌论》、修为观者《瑜伽论》和历史观者《社会进化论》。四者实"而一而四、而四而一"之论。设若以《薄伽梵歌论》为寻常本（俗谛义），后二者则皆为其系论；如果以《神圣人生论》为超上本（真谛义），余三者则又皆为其系论。《瑜伽论》补白"从成熟的低地（身体）出发"（康德），《社会进化论》注目集团、民族、国家的命运。四者或可一言以蔽之，曰：神圣人生本体论！于此足觇先生印学工作的重要性。我们说，他在这方面的贡献至少表现在二个方面：第一，于《薄伽梵歌》和《五十奥义书》之雅言风格的翻译与经典范式的注释——是基础性的；第二，于阿罗频多博大与精深之思想的介绍与显扬——是方向性的。阅读徐先生的文字，需要跳出寻常知觉性加以体会，或许我们能得出这样的结论：一方面，他造就了一种属于自己的思维风格和语言风格；另一方面，他指出了一个新的哲学工作的方向。

时光迅迈，陵谷替迁，《徐梵澄文集》出版已然 17 年了，先生示寂也 23 年了。这期间国家发生了多大的变化，何可计量？回想起上世纪 90 年代初，先生曾在街头看到一拨拨的农民工穿着西服，于是高兴得像小孩似的回来逢人便讲；又在 90 年代末，他尝与友人聊天，感慨地说道："南水北调如果成功了，南方没有水灾，北方也不干旱，那中国就是天堂了。"

《徐梵澄传》如今，这梦想已经一步一步地变成现实。若果他在天有知呢，会对我们再说点儿什么？也许，他会勉励我们要把这一和平的局面再坚守"一世"（30 年），或"两世""三世"……"子曰：'善人为邦百年，亦可以胜残去杀矣。'""子曰：'如有王者，必世而后仁。'"（《论语·子路篇》）他会希望我们将中国人和平发展的理想推及全世界。因为我们无论多么强大，其根柢都是以"文教"立国的理念，它保证了吾华族"宜尔子孙绳绳兮"之不竭的国运。今兹文集分期再版，正为长久，因为先生的目光始终是发到前方的。而前方正是我们的期许，也是现代文明世界所有人的期许，即"人类同一"的世界。虽然，这"期许"从未在人类社会实现过。然而，正如先生所言：

> 直至今日，这理想仍然只是理想，然而无论这一理想有多广大，却并非不可企及，仍属物理世界，终将实现于有限未来的某一刻，为一普遍真理的最终胜利。（《孔学古微》）

孙 波　写定于癸卯雨水日　2023 年 2 月 19 日

目录

CONTENTS

孔 学 古 微

序

几年前，国际教育中心希望我能开设介绍儒学的讲座，囿于彼时情形，终未如愿。然而我一直未曾忘却此事，后又觉得，与其开设讲座，不如写本小书，略述儒学大义及其殊胜之处，或许会有更长久的参考价值。

我们知道，如果一部学术著作无有关乎永恒或重大的真理，通常逃不脱被人抛弃、漠视或遗忘的命运。人类写过读过的书不计其数，做过听过的讲演也不可胜数。但是，任何心智成熟的成年人如果严肃且诚实地回忆，还能记得多少呢？只有少数异常聪慧的头脑才能记住大量往昔的细节，即便如此，仍然有许多事物被遗忘了，消失在灰暗的空虚之中。遗忘是最自然不过的事，人类不断地进步，每当知识积累到繁复不堪，以致妨碍前行时，其中的道理无论大小，都会一同泯灭。这事并非不幸，在某种程度上甚至还十分有益，正如一个人不能也不需要在记忆中保存孩童时所学的一切一样。虽然如此，我们回顾过去，从被遗忘的文化遗产中搜寻知识，以新的眼光重新评估甚或使用这些知识，总不会毫无益处。总而言之，本书所讨论的古代知识，大多数东方学者仍然十分熟悉，现代人已基本认其为过时了，但大略浏览一番，也是会有所收获的。

室利·阿罗频多 (Sri Aurobindo) 曾与弟子讨论斯宾格勒的著作《西方的没落》，在谈话中提及中国，我冒昧引述如下：

> 弟子："非常奇怪，斯宾格勒没有注意到民族的复苏和重新觉醒。"
>
> 室利·阿罗频多："是的，比如中国。中国在非常古老的时代就已经有了城市。那是一个非常奇特的民族，一直受到侵扰，又总是保持不变。如果你研究一下千年前的中国历史，你会发现他们处在动乱之中，却仍然保持着自己的文化。
>
> 鞑靼王焚烧他们的书籍，试图毁灭他们的文化，但是没有成功。现在的动乱结束后，再过两千年，他们仍然会和今天一样，对此我不会有任何惊讶之感。那正是这个民族的特点。"[1]

当今世界很难找到对中国历史有如此清晰洞见的思想家了，这是多么精要且对我们中国人具有启发性的评论呵！过往的历史显示出中国人非常保守，在某种程度上完全可以说，中国人之所以能够战胜所有的内乱和外

---

1. A. B. Purani 撰录：《室利·阿罗频多夜谈录》，第 112—113 页。

侵，主要是因为我们在两千五百年的历史中一直坚守着儒家的道路。公元
6世纪上半叶，曾经有人试图用佛教统治一个大帝国，但是失败了。除此
之外，道家是这个民族心思中的巨大暗流，但从未显著地浮上表面。

今天，我们想象所及，只能是与人类一同进步前行。在上文的谈话中
还提到了一个理论，认为人类历史一直处于以五百年为周期的轮回之中
[2]，实际上这一理论所出甚古，可溯至亚圣孟子。孟子所说的轮回并非指
首尾相接的圆周，显然他是从古代历史中推演出这样的结论，每五百年会
出现一位真正爱好和平的君主，同时会有圣人将其时的一切安排妥当。（参
见赵岐注《孟子》）孟子认为，从黄金时期到他所处的时代已经有七百多年
了，却仍然没有理想的王国出现。孟子知道他自己就是那一众杰出人物中
的一个。孟子心中的楷模，或说他最敬佩、最愿效仿的老师就是孔子。翻
阅中国历史，我们可以见到中华民族一直处于动乱之中，如无内乱，便有
外侵。外侵大多来自北部或西北部的游牧部落，匈奴、鞑靼、蒙古人，因
于贫困，因于艳羡古代中原文化辉煌的物质财富，故而不断入侵，成为最
持久的困扰。然而一旦中国重获和平，文化就会立即复苏，随即繁盛。中
国历史上持续最长的和平时期是周代，长达八百年（公元前1046—前256年）。
此后亦有黄金时代，废除死刑长达几十年，国内监狱空无一人，那是没有
内忧外患的时代。

伟大的汉代历史学家司马迁，东方的希罗多德，曾计算出从周公（殁
于公元前1104年）至孔子间隔五百年，从孔子到他的时代也是五百年。司马
迁十分珍视并自豪于自己生在这样的节点或时会上，从而可以跟随先贤的

脚步，完成有益于人类的特殊使命，他留于后世的巨著《史记》，堪称不让孔子之作。《史记》纪年结束于公元前 97 年，司马迁虽非圣人，但《史记》却是一部不朽的著作。《史记》记有"天运"信仰，"天运"与星象相关，也与人关系密切，三十年一小变，一百年一中变，五百年一大变，三次大变为一纪，经历三纪，方才变化完备。这其中或许暗示了一种循环变革的观念，虽然这种循环观念并非我们所理解的首尾相接的圆形，但是至少显示出人类的进步并不是一条无限伸展的直线。

我们知道，所有民族或个体生命的历史都充满了接连不断的上升期和下降期。其中有一个共通的特征，即在最悲惨无望、绝倒无助的时刻，会有"光"突然出现，有圣人降世。在印度，称之为"降世应身"（Avatar）；在中国，则称之为应天命而生的"圣人"。《诗经》中有暗示，古代中国人也相信降世应身，曾提到有神降自高山，遂生两位贤人。我们无法确知这样的信仰是否得到广泛接受，其中涉及古人如何理解"天"和"神"，实属另一宏大主题，暂且不论。总之，孔子正是出生在这样的时代。

孔子的生平及其时代背景后文会有详述。实际上，西方人对本书的主题并不陌生。从 17 世纪开始，更早可至 1580 年，意大利耶稣会传教士利玛窦（1552—1610）来华，受聘于皇室，在北京生活了多年。自此不久，西方世界就对中国文化渐有所知。了解中国的西方人一定要知道中国文化的高峰期和典型代表，正如信奉基督教的东方人一定了解耶稣的生平和事业

---

2. 《室利·阿罗频多夜谈录》，第 110 页。

一样。法国大革命之前一百年,《论语》《大学》和《中庸》的拉丁文译本就已经在巴黎出版,之后不到五十年,杜赫德(Du Halde)百科全书式的著作《中华帝国全志》在巴黎出版(1735 年)。在西方文化界,每当一部东方著作译为任何一种西方语言——这是十分艰辛的开荒工作——其他语言的译本便会接踵而至。如今这样的译本数量众多,尽可随意取用。读者可以比较不同版本的译文,经过一番努力,然后获得正确的理解。误译是不可避免的,自古以来中国学者对经文就有不同的解说,学派之间的偏见亦无法避免。通过这种方法,即便不懂中文的读者也可以获得中文经典的核心观念。本书涉及的大多是人们常常提及却又略显注重不够的主题,我将这些主题放置在历史背景中讨论,并参考其他文化。我不想让读者负担大量的中文音译名,也不愿仅为造出一座古代教义的高台而堆砌学究式的枯燥概念。本书之所以采用简明、非学究式的表述方式,只是为了使读者易于理解。

我还想在开端处向读者提及一点,如果仅从外部来看,儒家学问无法引起兴奋、惊奇甚或有趣之感。对于已经习惯于各种强烈刺激的现代人如此,对于古代人亦是如此。相较于世界上其他伟大的思想体系,儒学自身较少色彩和激烈性。在儒学中,我们见不到埃琉西斯(Eleusis)、涅槃、十地或逝去灵魂所往的三十三重天。关于生命有体,儒学中没有超上飞鸿(Paramahamsa)、菩萨或超人,但是有君子。关于人类活动,儒学未曾教导无为、苦修、弃绝或禁欲,亦无炼金术、长生丹,不能驱魔祛邪,更无治病良方。儒学中确实有"超上之道",但没有全能的宙斯,没有六天创造世界的上帝，没有被逐出伊甸园的亚当和夏娃。阿祇尼（Agni）、因陀罗（Indra）、阿黎耶门（Aryaman）以及韦陀众神殿中的所有神祇都不存在，更不用说阿胡拉玛兹达（Ahuramazda）和安格罗曼纽（Angromainyous）了。[3] 流行的观念认为儒学在本质上是世俗的，或以为儒学仅为一堆严格的道德训诫或枯燥的哲学原则。事实却恰恰相反，儒学在本质上是极具精神性的，亦有难以逾越的高度和不可量测的深度，有极微妙精细处乃至无限的宽广性与灵活性，甚或遍在之整全性。

身处现代世界，我们怀疑一切，欲以科学精神检验并重估一切旧物。虽然以上的评述皆是传统之论，读者或仍疑其有夸张过誉之嫌。孔子所处时代距今已有两千五百多年了，以中国人口之众，难道就从来没有如我们一样头脑聪慧者挺身而出，来质疑孔子的学说，并挑战他作为中华民族至圣先师的权威吗？然而时至今日，却从未有人怀疑过孔子的精神性。什么是"精神性"呢？室利·阿罗频多的定义值得我们体味：

> 神圣的完善，在我们上面长存；而在人，在知觉与行为中化为神圣，澈内澈外过一种神圣生活，乃是所谓精神性；一切较微小的意义加于这名词者，皆是未适合地揣摩或欺骗。

这是一遍在的真理，而我们见到孔子正是这一真理的典型印证。如果

3.　阿胡拉玛兹达和安格罗曼纽是古波斯琐罗亚斯德教之善神与恶神。——译者注

将孔子视为婆罗门意义上的降世应身，我希望再次引用"神圣母亲"的话：

> 在永恒的变是之中，每一位降世应身都是未来更加完美之实现的宣告人和前行者。

在儒学中寻找不到起于后世的诸多学说和理论，但这不妨碍儒学的畅行，随着时间的推移，给予孔门教义甚或孔子本人的赞誉愈加多了起来。印度人认为圣言（Aryavada）是知识的来源，在中国亦是如此。总有一些教义，我们无须仔细审视便可信从。重估孔子的学说是正当的且有益的事情，但是我们首先应当以孔子所处的时代及其历史背景来理解他的思想。我们甚可超越自己的祖先，虽然能否做到这一点至今仍可怀疑，然而在人类精神寻求的永恒提升之路上，我们实无必要将标示古人行迹的丰碑夷为平地。

其主要原因正在人性之中。人类的心思总是趋向新奇与惊异，因此而有进步。自佛教传入中国，在其完全被容纳转变之前，曾吸引这个民族中最优秀的智识头脑几近六百年之久。源出中国本土的道教虽然不似佛教那般光彩夺目，也是极具魅力的，同样在若干世纪间吸引了无数的天才人物，影响时间之长甚或过于佛教。而儒教的地位却一如既往，经世未曾动摇或颓败过。或有疑问，为何诸多聪慧人物会转向"异端"如佛道二教？答案是，儒教平和而冷静，无法牵曳住炽烈的性情，此类人物自然较易转入其他宗教。这答案对于旧儒学来说或许恰当，然而肇始于宋代（960—

1279）的新儒家却幸运得多了。时至今日，宋代儒学仍然占据主流。我不倾向于称儒学为宗教，称为信仰或许更恰当。然而，如果这世界上有所谓的国家宗教，在中国，只有儒教负担得起这个称谓。即便是今日的中国，亦曾兴起研究孔子思想的极大热潮，并且持续了三年有余。

有一则发生在元代（1271—1368）的逸事或有助于阐明儒教的特点。[4] 读者需要明了一点，自公元 4 世纪初起，三种"宗教"在中国并存而不悖。首先是儒教，其外部为哲学，而内部核心是一宗教信仰；其次是佛教，中国人视之既非宗教亦非哲学，仅为一"法"，如以欧洲视角理解"法"，仍可称之为宗教；再次是道教，有宗教一面和哲学或说形而上学一面，两方面差异巨大。纵观历史，普通中国人对待宗教的宽容态度，是世界上任何其他民族都无法比拟的。为争取皇权的支持，教间冲突固然不断，佛道之间尤其如此。皇帝的偏爱可以引出王公大臣的资助，其教义可以更加便利地在民众中传播。元文宗图帖睦尔在位时（1328—1332），有高僧为帝师，由中国西部至京都，文宗命一品以下官员骑白马迎于郊外。朝臣皆依命跪地俯身，向帝师献酒，帝师不为之动，端坐庄严有似佛像。国子监祭酒鲁斿举杯对他说道：

"帝师，您是佛陀的弟子，天下僧人的老师，我是孔子的弟子，天下儒生的老师，让我们不必拘此礼节吧。"

众人皆惊。但帝师微笑起身，与鲁斿共饮而毕。

.

4. 参见《新元史》卷二十一。

之后，文宗问鲁衜，三教之中，谁为最优，鲁衜答道："佛教如黄金，道教如白玉，而儒教可比之为稻谷。"

文宗问道："如此，儒教最为卑贱？"

鲁衜答道："黄金白玉固然贵重，无之亦无妨，而稻谷则一日不可离也！"

文宗叹道："说得好！"

我们在史书中读到这则故事时，会发现对于一位头脑朴质的外族君主，如此切实的比喻极易理解且具说服力。这比喻阐明了儒家教义对于维护生命的重要性，无论个人还是群体在生命中遇到的所有困惑，都可以在其中寻出答案。现代文明已经行进至这样一个地步，生命问题是如此复杂，以致找不出任何满意的解答，苦难如此沉重，以致否决任何救愈之可能。如果将这些困难归约为一简单的程式，无论对个人还是对群体，问题的核心仍是如何寻到一种适宜且幸福的生活方式。如果此言确实，我们仍可从儒学的源泉中汲取多多。另有一则故事，一位蒙古太子曾说起，佛教僧人讲授佛学，他可以很容易地理解，而中国老师讲授儒学，他却很难明白。这是很自然的事，因为佛教的基本教义相对简单。虽然佛教戒律已经发展成为一套极其复杂且精细的系统，束缚压抑人的生命活力，原初却是十分简易的。第一戒是"不许杀生"。幸抑或不幸，儒教中没有这样的戒律。儒教对待事物的方式颇为不同，但与佛教归指不异。最终我们会发现，即使有如此基本且重要的戒律，也是相对的真理，不为绝对。或许一位现代作家和思想家对这一观念的理解最好，他说，"黄金法则"就是"没有黄金法则"。在中国，我们称之为"道"。

在精神之域，养护生命且生命须臾不可离者，可称之为"神"(Divinity)。印度人则妥当地视其为"彼"或"大梵"。虽然孔子被封为至圣先师，神圣应身，但他本人极少谈论这一主题。关于"精神"的物质或物理方面，或说其人文方面，我们倾向于认为那是高度发展和文化了的生命，也可视其为文化本身。"文化"在汉语中的意思是，依照人性中的菁华而使人转化和完善。大体而言，中华民族三千年的历史命运端赖于两位圣人的塑造，时至今日我们仍然享其余泽，也可称他们为文化领袖。首先是周公，其次是五百年后的孔子。如果将中国历史和生活在中国之外的亚洲西北部、中亚和东南亚的民族历史相比较，"文化"的含义就会更加明显。生活在这些地区的民族古时被称为"蛮夷"，现在看来，这称谓并非全无道理。日本和西藏是两个对比明显的例证。日本在古时全般接受了儒教，并生发出自己的文化，然而在西藏却并未有之。任何去过西藏的旅人都能见到这个民族现在的文化水平。西藏的憾事暂且不论。

依泛神论的看法，宇宙间万事万物皆具神性。但是我们倾向于认为文化比其他一切事物都更具神性。如上文提及，可以视文化为"精神"之人文方面。"精神"之超越性在万物之上，漠视人的生死乃至世界之兴衰存亡，却又内在地与我们的生死和这个世界紧密相连。依照严格的逻辑原则，这似乎是一个悖论，然实为真理，或是超越了逻辑的真理。中国古代儒家贤圣及其弟子和践行此道者，大都着重人文，着重此世或精神之文化层度，用力于转化人类的低等自性，塑造其品格，擢升人至更高层度。其影响遍布极广，恒长持久，中国文化因此发展与繁盛。从根本上讲，如果没有这一发展，我们仍旧处在原始阶段，一切有关于"神"的概念也将不会形成。关于另一层度，我们或许可以称之为精神之精神，虽然从未公开传授，但是几乎所有名副其实的圣人都曾对"其"有过这样或那样的认识。这从来不是一件众所周知的事，只有仔细分辨圣贤的言行，才能有所知晓。古代圣哲或多或少都会言及体悟，之后却都归于缄默了。

一般而言，很难用一本小书的篇幅讨论儒学这样庞大的主题，但却不妨一试。但是，研究和写作任何主题，欲不加主观批判，实非易事。写作者应当排除一切偏见或成见，无好无恶，必须客观地处理其所书写的主题，就事论事。然而即使写作者仅仅陈述事实，仍会不自觉地在文句和书写方式中融入自己的意见，读者亦会不自觉地受到影响。作者或许自信公正，实际上却很难做到。更妥当的方式，也就是本书所取的方式，让读者阅读原典文字，形成自己的看法。但这样做，就不能避免大量引用原文，读者最终可能对基本观念或整体图景茫然无所得。这是第一个困难。

另外，汉语的结构与一般欧洲语言差别很大，因而思考形式也不同。中国人现在仍然可以很容易地理解古汉语，其间的差别远小于古今希腊语。然而有一普遍问题，某些汉语词没有对应的英译词，只能人为造作，在英语读者看来自然十分古怪。能令译者毫无遗憾的译文少之又少，与原文意思完整对应、无增无减的译文几近天赐，赞赏之余，终是为数不多。除此之外的译文则如雾中赏花，风姿虽在，却总似轻纱笼面。这是第二个困难。

由此可知，为何写作这样一本小书是一项艰辛的劳作，而且注定难以完美。因此，我希望读者能循着引文阅读原书，如有可能，最好翻阅原典。这意味着全面研读中国古代文化，至少需要阅读孔子编撰的"六经"，如此才能对孔学大义有更深入的了解。即是说，读者需要阅读和记忆大约43万字，这对于中国古代学者来说，并不算难事。如今已有更科学和更先进的方法来解读文本了，但是同样艰辛的付出或许仍然不可避免。

第一章

孔子生平

公元前 5 世纪，即耶稣降生前五百年，世间伟人迭出，他们以一生之短，而有不朽之名，为尘世留下极其有益的影响，为人类价值的创建做出丰厚的贡献。时至今日，我们仍然生活在他们的泽惠之中。据说萨摩斯的哲人毕达格拉斯活到公元前 497 年，印度的佛陀乔达摩大约在二十年后涅槃。虽然这些记载可能并不精确，偏差亦不会很大。生平同样略显模糊的老子也生于同一时期，并且曾是孔子的一面之师。墨子出生在几十年之后，苏格拉底（公元前 469—前 399）、希波克拉底（公元前 460—前 370）、柏拉图（公元前 428—前 348）都属于同一时期。孟子（公元前 372—前 289）比柏拉图年轻，二人同样长寿且才智相当。他们全都活到了心智成熟的晚年，尤其是"现代医学之父"希波克拉底，更是在世近百年。这些圣中之圣，哲中之哲，为何同时出现于东西方，十分难解。我们或可接受室利·阿罗频多的说法：他们都属于"上界之神圣力家族"，或如中国传统称之为"应天命而生"。文艺复兴时期有一理论依稀透露出相同的观念，认为世界的德性从一个国家转向另一个国家，首先从亚述移至波斯，然后到米底，依次传递。

这些圣哲中，只有孔子一人之名未曾有任何战争、流血和迫害行于其下。墨家思想以利他为核心，甚爱和平，然而自墨子之后只传了几代，遂近消亡。其中有一个主要原因，就是此派的杰出领袖都甘愿为其所追求的社会改革事业舍弃生命，于是其学说同其性命一样损失大半了。相较于世界上的其他宗教而言，儒教最少血腥和破坏性，更未曾以创造之意而行破坏之事。

拥有确切历史记载的圣者之中，孔子绝非最无名望，却唯独最无传奇色彩。即便在基督教外也尽人皆知的耶稣，一生中也有将近二十年的时间不见于任何记载。司马迁的《史记》中仍存有孔子的传记，不仅详细记录了孔子所说的话和所做的事，另有一篇专门记述诸弟子中之著名者，为一综合传记。同为儒家学派哲学家的孟子和荀子合属一篇。《史记》还专以一篇记述了精通儒学经典的汉代学者及其家学传承。中国文字历经了两千年也未曾有什么变化，我们仍可以像阅读现代报纸一样轻松地阅读大量的古典文献。

然而困难亦在于此。我们的研究工作不缺少文献资料，除《史记》之外，其他文献资料可谓数量巨大。然而，向不熟悉中国古代文化的英语读者清晰明白地解说孔子和儒家思想，并非易事。读者首先要弄清楚诸侯的国名，公侯伯子男爵的姓名和头衔，宗族和家族的名称，山川、河流和关口的名称，还有依不同编年方式表述的日期和年代。不了解这些知识，就无法获得清晰的认识。事实证明，这确实是难以逾越的障碍，而且没有替代的办法。为使读者不被细枝末节所累，我只会大致勾勒出孔子的生平。毕竟，对我们来说，最重要的是主要原则、哲学思想以及孔学教义之大体。亦如老子曾对孔子说过，"子所言者，其人与骨皆已朽矣，独其言在耳。"

孔子生于鲁国，位于现在的中国山东省境内。孔子的祖先是宋国贵族后裔，宋是商朝皇族所居之国，商朝亦称殷朝（公元前 1600—前 1046）。孔子的曾祖父是宋国贵族，为躲避内乱移居鲁国。孔子的父亲叔梁纥在鲁国官居高位，是一名力大过人的武将。孔子的母亲颜征在也出身贵族。叔梁纥娶颜征在时年事已高，婚后五年生孔子，三年后叔梁纥去世。孔子 3 岁无父，24 岁时母亲去世。

按公元纪年，孔子生于公元前 552 年 9 月 28 日，现在这一天在中国被定为教师节 5。古代学者早在公元 3 世纪就已经对孔子时代的日期做过精确计算，依照现代历法，似是无疑。孔子卒于公元前 479 年，享年 74 岁。

顺便提及，"孔子"在英语中通常译为 Confucius，源于拉丁文对"孔夫子"的音译。"孔"是姓氏，"夫子"是"老师"的意思。"子"是对人的尊称，亦如现在对知名人士的尊称。如此称谓还有老子、庄子、墨子等等。孔子的名为"丘"，是"小山"的意思。孔子的字是"仲尼"6。孔子出生前，他的母亲曾去一座名为"尼丘"的山上祈求生子，孩子出生后，为了纪念，取名为"丘"。"仲"是"第二"的意思，而山的名字"尼"也一同放在了"字"里。后世对孔子的崇敬致使他的名字近乎成为禁忌，出现"丘"字时，则代以读音不同的"某"字，表示不明确的指代。

至此为止，一切都很平常。孔子出生时是普通人的形状，出生前没有天使报喜，出生时天无异象，出生后身上也没有任何特殊的标记，不似佛陀乔达摩出生时曾有十二好相。并不是在中国从来没有过这样的传说，孔子出生前及其在世时都有过类似传说，例如曾有一女孩出生时，掌中有字；另有一男孩出生时掌中有字，长大后颇有名声。但是，异相多与后世英雄的出生相关。或在生子时，或在受孕前，其母有梦，或得见异象，然而这些英雄大都不是十分伟大的人物。曾有记载称，孔子的头顶四周高，中间凹，也就是说他的头骨形状特殊，这记载极可能是真实的，却根本算不上是神圣标记或吉祥之相。

孔子19岁时娶宋国丌官姓女子为妻，两年后生下一子。孔子的儿子出生时，鲁昭公送给孔子一条鲤鱼，于是孔子给儿子起名为鲤，字伯鱼，伯就是"最大"。值得注意的是，孔氏家族的血统在过去两千五百多年间一直未曾中断过。孔氏家族目前已传至第七十七代，其中有一人是著名的大学教授。颜氏家族也以同样的传统生活至今。对世袭血统有如此确实记录

.

5.　1985年，第六届全国人大常委会第九次会议通过了国务院关于建立教师节的议案，确定了每年9月10日为教师节。1997年之前，香港地区的教师节定于每年9月28日；台湾地区自1952年就确定9月28日为教师节。——编者注

6.　现在广泛使用的"名"（一个汉字）是正式名字，而日常普遍使用的"字"（两个汉字，极少情况下也用一个汉字）是表示礼貌的称谓。

的例证，如今在世界其他地方已经很难找到了。

在玩耍中领头的孩子长大后多能成为卓越的领袖。孔子儿时喜欢玩弄礼器模样的器物，模仿各种祭祀仪式和其他礼仪。这些作为可能源于其成长的贵族家庭环境。当时的贵族教育基于传统的礼仪训练，旨在强健体格，启蒙心智。孔子青年时精力充沛，教养良好，成年后身高九尺六寸，时人称其为巨人。（周朝使用十进制，1 尺大约相当于 22 厘米。）孔子力大过人，据说可以举起沉重无比的悬城门，这可能部分源于父母的遗传，部分源于经常的训练。孔子未曾以此显名，因为他的兴趣不在于此。读者或可注意到，大概除了商羯罗和罗摩克里希那之外，世界上从未有伟大的宗教领袖体质羸弱。他们几乎全都体格强健，有能力承受世上任何他们认为应当且值得承受的苦难。穆罕默德俊美出奇，身形健硕，更是无须多论。孔子擅长射箭，古代的仪典上有许多仪式并饮酒，孔子在仪典上表演射箭时，人们争相前往观看。

可以想见，孔子的父亲去世后，这一支的孔氏家族在经济上一直颇为拮据。孔子曾为鲁国贵族工作，负责管理国家谷仓，谷物称量公平精准。孔子还曾负责管理公地，牲畜繁殖丰盛。然而我们可以确信，孔子精通诗文，或者用现在的话说，孔子在 20 岁之前就已经对古代礼仪知识非常熟悉了。当时鲁国有一个大夫临终前嘱咐自己的儿子要向孔子求学，并称孔子是自己的老师。这位大夫说，据他所知，孔氏几代祖先都是贤德的圣人，孔子身为圣人之后，虽无权位，但必为圣达。大夫的儿子遵从父亲遗愿，同另外一位公子南宫敬叔前往孔子处学礼。不久后，南宫敬叔向鲁昭公表明，自己想与孔子一同拜访周朝王室，即当时已经衰弱不堪的中央政府。昭公为他们准备了一辆车、两匹马和一名随从。此行目的是学习古礼，他们在周都见到了掌管王室典籍的老子。据说孔子由周都返回鲁国后，向其求学的弟子渐渐多了起来。

我们确实可知的是，孔子从 23 岁起开始为师，自此而后直至生命结束，身边一直有众多弟子追随。他教授过的学生有 3000 人，其中著名者有 72 人，或说有 77 人。孔子说过"有教无类"[7]，还曾说过"自行束脩以上，吾未尝无诲焉"[8]。只有当孔子在朝为官时，他身边的学生才有所减少，而且这一情况也并不十分确定。"有教无类"是一件十分特别而且了不起的事。这种做法完全不同于古代婆罗门，他们认为精神知识的传授只限于再生者。这就难怪现代人称赞孔子是颇具民主精神的教育家了。

只有大致了解孔子所处时代的政治背景，才能恰当地理解孔子中年的政治生涯。孔子生活在周朝后期，即"晚周"。孔子编订史书《春秋》，记述"晚周"前期 242 年历史（公元前 722—前 481），史称"春秋时期"。这是最混乱的时代。

---

7. 参见《论语·卫灵公篇第十五》，第 39 章。（译者按：为方便读者查阅引文，中译文所标《论语》篇章数依据中华书局版杨伯峻译注《论语译注》，因篇章分割不同，会与英文所标篇章数目略有差异。）

8. 这段文字另有英文译为"我不会拒绝教授那些已束起头发、衣着得体的人"，指"超过 15 岁的人"。

公元前 770 年，由于西北蛮族的入侵，周朝将原在陕西的都城向东迁到了洛阳。西周王朝随着都城的陷落而寿终正寝。我们知道，在欧洲，罗马帝国大约崛起于公元前 753 年，约略在西周都城陷落二十年之后。而周朝的命运颇似罗马，在西方陷落后，继续存活在东方。然而与东罗马帝国不同的是，东周中央政府的权力从此逐渐衰弱，虽然在之后的两个多世纪里仍然保留着古旧的传统，维持着统摄诸侯国的威望和尊严。

前文提到，春秋时期是中国历史上最混乱的时代。中华民族的生命力处于良好的约束和规范之中已经四百余年了，春秋时代正是一个生命力磅礴爆发的时代。如果西周是经典时代，与之对比鲜明的春秋时期则是浪漫的反叛。今天，人们喜欢将这一时期和随后的战国时期（公元前 475—前 221）一同赞誉为自由与解放的伟大时代，旧制度土崩瓦解，中国文化进入史无前例的繁荣期，出现各种哲学流派，有"百家"之称（当然实际上不满百家），远超后世，与古希腊哲学流派遥相呼应，思想内容也颇为相类。然而，如果没有发生于前的经典时代，没有和平与统一的西周时代，如果中华民族的文化之力未曾经过四百余年的规范和蓄存，我们无法想象会有这样的思想迸发期出现于后。不积大水无以成洪流，或说，种优土沃才会花开奇艳。

中国古代学者曾用类似现代统计学的方法统计过发生在春秋时期的大事。春秋时期有 15 个主要的诸侯国，还有一些存在时间极短的小采邑。东周王室共有 12 位正式的王或君主，实际有 14 王，因有一王在位不足一年便死去，另一王死于孔子之后。其他统计数字如下：

鲁公	12 位
大战	23 次
诸侯讨伐	213 次
侵掠 9	60 次
霸主	5 位
诸侯结盟	109 次
特盟（鲁往他国 4 次，他国来鲁 5 次）	11 次
诸侯会谈	97 次
齐桓公执牛耳之会	11 次
齐桓公兵车之会	4 次
围城	44 次
侵入国都	27 次
战败迁都	10 次
灭国	30 个
弑君	36 位
亡国	52 个
自然灾害	52 次
日食（视为凶兆 10）	36 次

9. 战斗开始前，通常以击鼓为号，若军队潜行掠境，不击鼓，即为侵掠。

10. 36 次日食记录中，有 34 次可以用现代计算方法验证；另外 2 次无法验证，或是由于史官记录失误。

地震	5 次
山崩	2 次

还记有霜灾、旱灾、火灾、蝗灾、台风、
洪水等其他不寻常的自然现象

孔子生活在春秋末年，他编写的史书《春秋》正是记录春秋时期之事。有现代学者怀疑《春秋》一书作者并非孔子，因此我有必要对这部史书略作说明。

"春秋"即四季中的春秋二季，《春秋》一书是记录鲁国大事的史书。孔子对《春秋》做过修改编撰，删除了其中不值得存留的内容，正因如此，《春秋》作者之名自古以来归于孔子。所以从根本上说，这部书当然并非孔子创作。早在公元 11 世纪，大学者王安石，亦是一位失败的社会经济改革家，曾讽刺《春秋》为"断烂朝报"。《春秋》确有破烂残缺之处，例如书中至少有两处句子只有两个字。然而王安石如此评价《春秋》可能另有原因，也许他对这部书没有学术兴趣，或者因为他曾试图为《春秋》写注，但已有同代人写了非常出色的注释，便心生嫉妒。如果有充足的材料和证据能够证实《春秋》的作者并非孔子，那绝对不失为一个伟大的发现。

我们还应当知道，在那个时代，诸侯大国都有自己的编年史。晋国的编年史名为《乘》，"乘"是"车辆"的意思。车能载人而不论人之好坏，喻为国史记事而不论事之好坏。楚国也有史书，只是名称不同而已。因此,《春秋》仅是鲁国的编年史,记录每年发生的大事。祭祀和军事行动是那个时代的国家大事,最重要的仪式一般在春耕之前或秋收之后举行。封建之初,周公封于鲁,为褒奖周公伟绩,鲁国可行天子礼乐。所以,鲁国因保存有最完善的西周礼乐而闻名。[11]诸侯国设置史官一职并非周朝的先例,史官设置可以追溯到更为古老的朝代。孔子老年时(后文会有详述)研究本国编年史,用我们现在的说法就是"编辑"了鲁国史。《诗经》也是同样性质的书,其中没有一首诗是孔子的创作,而是他依照自己的标准,从三千多首民歌、诗歌和祭颂中选取值得保存并可在仪式上配乐演唱的305 首,集成一书。

如果编撰诗集需要依据标准,编撰史书就更应该有所标准。史书避不开对人物事件的判断和评价,赞誉或指责、欣赏或贬视。其标准则基于撰史人的生命观和宇宙观,中国人称之为"大义"。这样的"大义"体现在书写语言或技巧之中,言中之意不必直接说出,却可以清楚明白。读者可以从书写内容和行文方式中读懂"大义"。有古代注释家认为,《春秋》蕴含着深奥的机密,为了不让公众知晓而有意隐匿,其实不然。实际上所有学者都知道,许多"大义"仍然存在,虽然有些已经过时,有些会令外国人不高兴。如果我们正视这些"大义",《春秋》的作者如果不是孔子,也一

---

11. 实际上,各诸侯国都有自己的音乐和舞蹈,但鲁国的音乐舞蹈采取了周朝王室的风格,寓意高尚,风格华丽。不同等级的贵族使用不同的礼仪,诸侯不能使用天子的礼仪。

定是同孔子一样伟大的圣人。然而，现代学者似乎未能发现这样一位无名的圣人。

《春秋》至汉代有五家注释，其中三家较为出众，文本仍在。另外两家已经消亡，一家因观点无人赞同，一家因最初便无文本存世。如果拥有五家注释之多的《春秋》是一本名为孔子所作而实出无名的伪书，那是极难想见之事。如果《春秋》真是伪书，孟子和庄子对《春秋》的引证就全都是伪造的或篡改的，不然这两位圣哲都被同一个错误的传统蒙蔽了。这都是极不可能的事。

问题的关键并不在于《春秋》真正的作者是谁，而在于这本书的权威性。自孔子以后，《春秋》获得极大的尊崇，曾经左右许多朝代的命运。《春秋》中有许多历史教诲成为古人构建国家内外政策的重要例证。如果现代学者能够充分证明《春秋》并非出自孔子——当然，没人做得出这样的证明——那么书中所有精粗之思想、大小之原则，以及历史例证之权威性，将如纸牌屋一样坍塌。然而事实并非如此简单。我们将来是否会用《春秋》中的道理建构出一个国家是另外一回事，但是这些道理的确曾在历史上产生过很大的影响，这是不可否认的事实。回到《春秋》作者的问题上，我们可看几段《孟子》中的文字：

> 世衰道微，邪说暴行有作，臣弑其君者有之，子弑其父者有之，孔子惧，作《春秋》。《春秋》，天子之事也。是故孔子曰："知我者其惟《春秋》乎！罪我者其惟《春秋》乎！"[12]

　　昔者禹抑洪水而天下平，周公兼夷狄、驱猛兽而百姓宁，孔子成
《春秋》而乱臣贼子惧。[13]

　　孟子曰："王者之迹熄而《诗》亡，《诗》亡然后《春秋》作。……
其事则齐桓、晋文，其文则史。孔子曰：'其义则丘窃取之矣。'"[14]

　　这三段文字清晰明了，从内容、风格和上下文上判断，绝非他人篡改
之词。事实上，孟子夸大了《春秋》一书在当时的影响力。但是历史表
明，《春秋》对后世教益之巨，孟子所言终非虚夸之词。

　　除孟子之外，还有其他可以引证的古代哲学家。

　　《春秋》文字寓褒贬、正名分，即古语所说的"微言大义"，这是在孟
子之前就已公认的事实。我们还可引证《庄子》中的几段文字。后世视庄
子为道家人物，而庄子轻视儒家学说。《庄子》书中有关孔子的故事大体
皆为道家后人的杜撰，不可作史实看待。然而，《庄子》第二篇中有一处
提到"春秋"，说到"春秋"的"经世"和"先王之志"（志即是记录），并说
圣人讨论这些话题但不争辩。既然提到"经世"，便可知《春秋》并非毫无
深意的编年史。从人文主义的角度看，如果一部编年史没有贯穿其中的书

　　　·

12. 《孟子·滕文公章句下》，第9章。（译者按：《孟子》篇章数目依据中华书局
　　 版杨伯峻译注《孟子译注》。）

13. 同上。

14. 《孟子·离娄章句下》，第21章。

写原则，就不是严格意义上的历史书写。如果历史什么也不能教给我们，就不是有意义的历史。即使现代的科学或技术手段也必定有所指向。《庄子》最后一篇指出"春秋以道名分"。这一篇可能并非庄子所作，而是出自惠子之手。惠子是庄子的好友，死于庄子之前。这句对《春秋》的评论被广泛接受，因孔子曾谈论"名分"之事。然而我们或可怀疑，这段文字是由某位汉代学者故意插入《庄子》。《荀子·劝学篇》也曾提到《春秋》的"微言大义"。《荀子·大略篇》中有如下文字：

> 《春秋》贤穆公，以为能变也（"能变"即是"能纠正自己的错误"）。

荀子晚于孟子，但他对《春秋》的看法一定与孟子相同。这句话正是对《春秋》"微言"的解释。自班固开始，汉代以及之后的历史学家都认为"孔子没而微言绝，七十子终而大义乖"。司马迁在其自传中也解释过孔子编撰《春秋》的原因，历史学家之卓越者如司马迁，如果他所绍继的仅是一虚假的传统，这是我们实难想象的事。我们似不必再否定孔子之作《春秋》，更不必为《春秋》另寻作者了。

当然，学者对《春秋》中若干褒贬词汇的含义仍有疑问。《春秋》文风短简，褒贬评价仅区别于一二字之间。考虑到《春秋》记述 242 年历史仅用了 18 000 字，如此文风或许实难避免。我们只需要考虑两点。

第一，在中国，有给予过世者谥号的传统。谥号是单字或双字的称谓，此称谓在中国具有重大意义。犹如在古埃及，死去的人渡过冥河接受检验，评判生前所为之善恶，以此决定能否享受国葬。中国贵族十分看重死后的谥号，活着的时候就对此耿耿于怀。这有些类似欧洲"骄傲的昆塔"和"公平的腓力"这样的称谓，但谥号的意义要远甚于此。功绩或德行出众的普通人死后也会被授予谥号。简单说，谥号就是间接授予家族后人的荣誉，是对生者莫大的激励。这一传统一直延续到 20 世纪初。由此可见，《春秋》以一二字褒贬人物功过是非的传统并非始于孔子。

第二，古代史官于历史书写的权威要远大于统治者本人。中国历朝历代都有两名史官默立在君王两侧，记录君王每日的言行。值得注意的是，在位的君王不可以阅读史官对自己的记录，只有他的继承者在他死后才可阅读。君王可独裁，史官可获死，但君王在位期间的编年史却不可阅读。这一传统源于孔子之前。及至孔子时，诸侯国的史官对褒贬词汇的使用都极其严肃谨慎。发生在春秋时期的一件事可以为证：齐国大臣崔杼密谋杀害了齐国的独裁暴君，史官即刻写道"崔杼弑其君"。崔杼听后大怒，立刻下令杀了这名史官。被杀史官的弟弟也是史官，听到哥哥被杀，前去接替哥哥的职位，同样写下"崔杼弑其君"，也被杀掉。而史官的三弟赶来，也写下同样五个字，崔杼没再杀害史官的三弟。另有史官听到崔杼杀史官之事，即刻抱着竹简赶来，路上有人告诉他，被杀史官的三弟已经记下了事实，他才返回。由此事可以看出古代史官的尊严，以及他们对待自身职责或说历史真相之忠实。孔子编撰《春秋》当然是继承了这一古老的传统。据说，即使孔子最喜爱也最具有天赋的弟子也无法更改这本书中的任何一个字。

孔子是否有意依此改变已然分崩离析的社会呢？或许没有。虽然孔子生活在一个不幸且动乱的时代，诸侯国内部多已瓦解殆尽，但孔子仍期冀理想的君王之治，因此他奔走四方以求获用于诸侯，为的是发挥才智，实现理想。孔子不断地寻求服务于君王的机会，又不断地失败。及至晚年退隐之时，除去编写《春秋》和其他书籍之外，已无他事可为。而这是极其艰巨的工作，首先在规正名份，其次在价值辩护。孔子希望后人能凭借他所留下的遗产实现其高远的理想。而此时，他所能把控的仅有一支笔而已。

因此，《春秋》为孔子所作，似乎已无任何异议。然而仍有一个经久未决的争论，即《春秋》应归于"经"还是归于"史"，"经""史"固然不同，而学者之倾向多为后者。后文论及孔子晚年的工作时，还会论述这一问题。

第二章

孔子生平 (续)

《史记》中记有老子给予孔子的临别赠言，这赠言对孔子个人品格的形成产生了十分重要的影响，其言如下：

> 吾闻富贵者送人以财，仁人者送人以言。吾不能富贵，窃仁人之号，送子以言，曰："聪明深察而近于死者，好议人者也。博辩广大危其身者，发人之恶者也。为人子者毋以有己，为人臣者毋以有己。"

这段简单直白的道德义务教诲想必对孔子影响极大，孔子日后所获"无我"之德性定是得益于此。孔子完全摆脱了四种品性的束缚，"自我"[15]

.

15. 《论语·子罕篇第九》，第4章。另参见本书"末章"。

（非"自我主义"）是其中之一。如果"无我"是达至精神圆满所应具有的基本德性，其教诲首出于老子，后由孔子提倡。

《史记·老子韩非列传》中还有一些确实可信的记载，我们可以清楚地看到，孔子和老子对一些基本精神原则的看法都源自"仁"，在此暂且不论。

孔子对这次会面的印象值得一读：

> 孔子去，谓弟子曰："鸟，吾知其能飞；鱼，吾知其能游；兽，吾知其能走；走者可以为罔，游者可以为纶，飞者可以为矰。至于龙吾不能知，其乘风云而上天。吾今日见老子，其犹龙邪！"

孔子周都之行收获颇丰。此时，周朝王室已经衰败不堪，鲁国的状况也相差无几。鲁在晋楚之间，晋在其西北，楚在其西南，晋楚两国都想称霸诸侯，相与为敌。鲁与其中一国结盟或示好就会受到另一国的攻击。临近东南[16]还有同晋楚一样强大的齐国。齐国施于鲁国的压力甚或友爱，都令鲁国痛苦不堪。鲁昭公与季孙家族的季平子发生争执，引发内乱。昭公出其不意将季平子围在家中，而"三桓"[17]却联合起来对付昭公。经过一天的战斗，"三桓"救出季平子，驱逐了昭公，昭公逃至齐国。诸侯国曾多次会谈，设法送昭公回鲁，甚至以武力威胁恐吓季平子，但一切努力都以失败告终。鲁国权柄已于过去五代之间渐落于季孙家族。鲁公只是名义上的君主，或说最高祭司，主持例行的祭祀活动，仪式中的一国之尊。鲁昭公在流亡中死去，生前一直有一群忠臣追随左右，维持着国君应有的奢华排场。鲁国内政混乱，孔子也离开鲁国，去了齐国。其时孔子 35 岁（公元前 517 年），在齐国勾留大约两年。

孔子在齐国的生活仍有若干记载，他在齐国受到齐景公的礼遇。五年前，景公与大臣晏婴访问鲁国时见过孔子，他们之间有过这样的对话：

> 景公问孔子曰："昔秦穆公国小处辟，其霸何也？"
>
> 对曰："秦，国虽小，其志大；处虽辟，行中正。身举五羖，爵之大夫，起累绁之中，与语三日，授之以政。以此取之，虽王可也，其霸小矣。"
>
> 景公说。[18]

孔子在景公身侧，有依才获用的机会。正是在这段时间里，孔子学习了仍然在齐国演奏的古韶乐，他评价韶乐是尽善尽美的音乐，而武乐则尽美而不尽善[19]。孔子听了三个月的韶乐，竟然忘记了肉的味道。韶乐是古代帝王舜创作的音乐，拥有完美的旋律和蕴意。孔子感叹道："不图为乐

16. "东南"似为"东北"之误。——译者注

17. "三桓"指鲁国大夫孟孙氏、叔孙氏、季孙氏三家，均为鲁桓公之后，遂称"三桓"。——译者注

18. 《史记·卷四十七·孔子世家第十七》。

19. 《论语·八佾篇第三》，第 25 章。

之至于斯也。"[20]

孔子对音乐这样的雅事如此专注，以致三月不知肉味，对此我们无须赘述。齐国的贤德之人为此对孔子称赞不已。

景公问孔子执政之事。孔子回答：

"君君，臣臣，父父，子子。"

景公曰："善哉！信如君不君，臣不臣，父不父，子不子，虽有粟，吾岂得而食诸！"[21]

景公再问执政之事，孔子回答："政在节财。"景公听后非常高兴，准备任用孔子，欲将尼谿的田地赐给孔子做永久封地。

由于晏婴的阻拦，景公取消了封地的念头。《史记》记载了晏婴的话：

夫儒者滑稽而不可轨法；倨傲自顺，不可以为下；崇丧遂哀，破产厚葬，不可以为俗；游说乞贷，不可以为国。自大贤之息，周室既衰，礼乐缺有间。今孔子盛容饰，繁登降之礼，趋详之节，累世不能殚其学，当年不能究其礼。君欲用之以移齐俗，非所以先细民也。[22]

景公觉得晏婴的话有道理，再见孔子时，极力表现出尊敬之意，却再也不问有关礼的事情了。有一次景公说："我无法像对待鲁国权势最大的季氏那样对待孔子。"然而，景公也不能像对待最无权势的孟氏那样对待孔子。于是景公对待孔子，只当他位于季氏与孟氏之间了。

　　依史实推断，齐景公一定多少赏识过孔子，孔子也帮助景公进行过一些政治改革，或者对贵族做过些启蒙工作，使他们有了更高的理想。齐国的大臣因此想要摆脱孔子，试图加害于他。景公得知后，感叹道："我老了，不能实现他的理想了。"孔子听后，返回鲁国。

　　阅读这段历史时，我们会发现鲁国的政治状况非常复杂。孔子42岁时，鲁昭公客死他乡，昭公的弟弟即位，即鲁定公。定公五年，驱逐昭公的季平子也死了。鲁国最有权势的季孙家族由季平子平庸的儿子继承。曾经显赫的季孙氏也逐渐权势衰弱，受制于自己的家臣，而家臣又受制于自己的仆人。各种职权皆在某种程度上被僭越，政府体系运行偏离正轨，全国近于无政府状态。孔子所能做的就是与政治保持相当的疏离，继续自己公共教师的生涯。

　　关于孔子，有这样一个故事，其中孔子应答幽默，自命不凡，却无讥讽。

　　阳货，又名阳虎，是季孙氏的家臣。阳虎实力强大后，预谋叛乱篡鲁。孔子在《春秋》中斥责阳虎是从鲁国宗庙"盗窃宝玉大弓"的强盗，然而未提他的名字。我们要说的这个故事在《论语》和《孟子》中皆有记

20.《论语·八佾篇第三》，第13章。

21.《论语·颜渊篇第十二》，第11章。理雅各将最后一句话译为"即使国家有收入，我又如何能够享用啊？"。

22.《史记·孔子世家》。——译者注

载。我们先看一下《孟子》中的记载：

> 阳货欲见孔子而恶无礼，大夫有赐于士，不得受于其家，则往拜其门。阳货瞰孔子之亡也，而馈孔子蒸豚；孔子亦瞰其亡也，而往拜之。[23]

这个故事并没有就这样结束。《论语》中这样记载：

> 阳货欲见孔子，孔子不见，归孔子豚。孔子时其亡也，而往拜之，遇诸涂。谓孔子曰："来！予与尔言。"曰："怀其宝而迷其邦，可谓仁乎？"曰："不可。""好从事而亟失时，可谓知乎？"曰："不可。""日月逝矣，岁不我与。"
>
> 孔子曰："诺。吾将仕矣。"[24]

孔子洞明世事，或许早已预见这个篡位者的下场，阳虎叛乱失败后，于公元前502年逃往齐国。孔子此时50岁，一直思虑着如何实现自己的理想。鲁国臣子公山不狃邀请孔子会面，孔子有意赴会。弟子子路知道后，很不高兴地对孔子说："末之也已，何必公山氏之之也？"

孔子回答："夫召我者，而岂徒哉？如有用我者，吾其为东周乎！"[25]

公山拥有小规模武装和一小块土地。即便如此，孔子仍有志于在这一小块土地上创建另一个东周，期望为那个时代带来和平。孔子最终还是没有去。孔子说："苟有用我者，朞月而已可也，三年有成。"[26]

孔子所说不假。鲁定公任命孔子为中都宰，一年之后，四方之人都来学习孔子的治理方法，并奉为标准。孔子又由中都宰升为司空，由司空升为大司寇。因此，孔子成了鲁国的首相。公元前 500 年，齐鲁两国在夹谷会盟，孔子出任鲁国相礼。

关于这次会盟的记载多有夸张，古代学者对于孔子在外交上获得的胜利表示怀疑。各种历史文献对这次会盟的记录略有相异，然而，这是孔子从政生涯中最精彩的一幕。综合不同文献的记载，会盟大体情形如下：

赴会之前，孔子对定公说："臣闻有文事者必有武备，有武事者必有文备。古者诸侯出疆，必具官以从。请具左右司马。"定公采用了孔子的建议，左右司马随同一起参加了这次会盟。

而另一边，齐国佞臣犁弥对齐景公说："孔丘知礼而无勇，若使莱人以兵劫鲁侯，必得志焉。"景公依从了这一诡计。

.

23. 《孟子·滕文公章句下》，第 7 章。

24. 理雅各将两个答复都翻译成孔子的回答。实际上，孔子见到阳虎，听了他的一番议论后，只回答了最后一句话。理雅各的翻译中有一处小失误：阳虎送给孔子的猪不是"烤"猪，而是"蒸"猪。正如那篇名文所论，"烤猪"实际上可能是国外的发明，至于"蒸猪"，就要另作研究了。然而，我们可以确定的是，无论读者认为素食是神圣抑或不神圣的事，孔子都不是素食主义者。见《论语·阳货篇第十七》，第 1 章。

25. 《论语·阳货篇第十七》，第 5 章。

26. 《论语·子路篇第十三》，第 10 章。

齐鲁两国君主连同各自的大队随从来到了夹谷。会盟地点已经建好了三阶的坛位。鲁定公与齐景公简单寒暄之后，一同登上坛位，以同等身份行礼，互换酒杯饮酒。

此时，齐国有司上前大声请示："请奏四方之乐。"景公准许。

乐人拥到前台，这是一群居于海边的莱人，手持枪剑矛戈，挥舞旌旗。孔子立刻登上坛位，停在第二阶上，一挥宽大的衣袖，大声说道："吾两君为好会，夷狄之乐何为于此，请命有司！"有司命令乐人退下，但乐人并未散去，孔子直视两侧的景公和晏婴，景公心有惭愧，挥手撤下了乐人。

真实事件至此结束，其他记载都是后人附会，不可信。会盟达成的协议有利于鲁国，协议规定齐国退回曾经侵占鲁国的三块土地。而鲁国要与齐国结成军事同盟，无论齐国何时出兵国界之外，鲁国都应派出三百战车协同支援。之后，鲁国得到了归还的土地，却未曾为此同盟派出过战车。双方庄严盟誓，一切依礼而行。

景公随后邀请鲁公赴宴，而依当时的情形，鲁公无力答谢。由于会盟结果有利于鲁国，任何多余的交涉和商讨都可能引起无法掌控的混乱。于是孔子拒绝了邀请，并告知齐国大臣，宴会必将劳扰司仪，而且珍贵的礼器不能搬出堂室，娱悦客人的美乐不能在室外演奏，如果没有这些华美的仪式，宴会显得过于简陋。依照当下的条件，定将违背礼制。景公听到这些理由后，觉得孔子所言皆在情理，于是取消了宴请。[27]

.

27. 出自《论语》的引文均采用理雅各和《哈佛经典》的译文。后者的译文读起来
更通畅一些，形式上符合原文简短的行文方式，但不似原文文风庄重。为各取
所长，作者对部分文字做了调整，并未完全依赖于其中任何一种译文。作者认
为，译文应当完全忠于原文，由读者自己体会文意。

第三章

周游列国

在希腊神话中，如果某人具有超常的能力，就会招来神的嫉妒，注定命途多舛。这事并不一定确实，然而历史上多有此类例证，功德卓越之人不能久居其位，是一惯例。因世间总有黑暗势力企图遮蔽他们的光辉。孔子56岁开始为鲁国之相，自此时起，鲁国发生了悄无声息的巨大变革和进步。三个月之后，孔子处置了一个叛乱的臣子，颓废的社会风气顿时为之一变。商贩无欺，男女分行于路，道不拾遗，四方来客舒适无怨。不幸的是，这理想的政治和社会秩序并未持续太久，对此艳羡或实为嫉妒的并不是神，而是邻旁的国家，其中尤以齐国为甚。鲁国的兴盛引起了齐国的恐慌，齐景公施以计谋，迫使孔子辞去官位。鲁君多日不听政，又不顾祭奠之礼，孔子方才离去，开始周游列国，共计14年。

诸侯国中，孔子最先到卫国。卫国邻近鲁国，以多君子而闻名。卫灵公询问孔子在鲁国领取多少薪禄，当得知孔子在鲁国年俸六万粟时，也给出同样的年俸。孔子在卫国停留了十个月，卫国贵族对他疑心重重，造谣中伤，实现政治理想更是遥不可及。于是孔子离开卫国，前往陈国。

前往陈国的路上，经过匡城。孔子的车夫是个鲁莽的乡下人，用马鞭指着城墙上的豁口说："昔我入此，由彼缺也。"孔子的身形与阳虎有些相似，当地人听到这话，错把孔子当成了曾经出兵侵害他们的阳虎，于是拦下孔子一行人，将他们整整围困了五天。

孔子最喜爱的徒弟颜渊此前走散，恰在这时赶了上来。孔子对颜渊说："吾以汝为死矣。"

颜渊回答："子在，回何敢死？"[28] 这回答是弟子对老师的尊敬，却一语成谶，颜渊 42 岁时去世，其时孔子 71 岁。

围困加剧，弟子们越发忧惧。为了驱散弟子们的焦虑，孔子说：

> **文王既殁，文不在兹乎？**
>
> **天之将丧斯文也，后死者不得与于斯文也，天之未丧斯文也，匡人其如予何？** [29]

弟子中有人想硬闯出去，被孔子制止。孔子抚琴歌唱如故。匡人最终

·

28. 《论语·先进篇第十一》，第 22 章。
29. 《论语·子罕篇第九》，第 5 章。

弄清了孔子的身份，放他离去。

孔子随后前往蒲城。在蒲城留居一个月后，返回卫国。

卫灵公有夫人南子，南子年龄比灵公小，貌美出众。南子因得灵公宠信，权倾一时。虽如此，聪明的南子对国中贤人不失尊敬。孔子返回卫国后，住在一位退休的大臣家里，主人德高望重。南子使人送信给孔子，说："四方之君子不辱欲与寡君为兄弟者，必见寡小君。寡小君愿见。"因无此先例，孔子拒绝了南子的邀请。但孔子又不得不前往南子处表示谢意。孔子入门，灵公夫人坐在帷幕之后不得见，孔子向帷幕施礼。帷幕内的夫人可以见到外面的情景，鞠躬两次回礼，身上珠珮玉饰相击作响，真切可闻。此次会面非常正式，孔子离开，并未生出其他事情。然而，孔子最勇敢的弟子子路却很不高兴，觉得老师的做法不当。孔子说："予所不者，天厌之！天厌之！"[30] 这事发生时，孔子 57 岁。

孔子在卫国停留了一个多月。一次，卫灵公和夫人南子乘车驶过街道，一宦官随后，而孔子在宦官之后。这极可能是南子有意为之，欲驱使孔子离开卫国。孔子以此为辱，说："已矣乎！吾未见好德如好色者也。"[31] 孔子离开卫国，经过曹邑，前往宋国。

进入宋国时，孔子和弟子在一棵大树下演习礼仪。宋国将军桓魋厌恶孔子，想要杀他，拔掉了那棵大树。孔子起身离开，弟子催促快走，孔子回答："天生德于予，桓魋其如予何！"[32] 之后，孔子与弟子前往郑国，过郑国，至陈国。

陈是小国，境遇并不好过鲁国和卫国。孔子留住不久，吴国侵扰，掠去三邑。陈国弱小，北有强晋，南有悍楚，两国争霸，征伐不断，陈国则两面受敌。孔子在陈国居住三年有余，未尝安宁，说道："盍归乎来！吾党之小子狂简进取，不忘其初。"[33]孔子说的是那些留在家乡，没有同他一起周游列国的弟子。[34]

孔子离开陈国，再次经过蒲城。正巧蒲人叛离卫国，将孔子拦住。孔子有弟子公良孺，人高力大，以私车五乘追随孔子。公良孺愤怒地说："吾昔从夫子遇难于匡，今又遇难于此，命也已。吾与夫子再罹难，宁斗而死。"遂与蒲人拼死相战，蒲人惊恐，对孔子说："苟毋适卫，吾出子。"孔子应允，双方盟誓。孔子一行离开后，直奔卫国。能言善辩的子贡问孔子："盟可负邪？"孔子回答："要盟也，神不听。"

卫灵公知道孔子返回卫国，非常高兴，亲自到城门外迎接。灵公问："蒲可伐乎？"孔子回答："可。"

灵公说："吾大夫以为不可。今蒲，卫之所以待晋楚也，以卫伐之，无乃不可乎？"

．

30. 《论语·雍也篇第六》，第28章。

31. 此段在《论语》中出现两次，分别是子罕篇第18章、卫灵公篇第13章，显然是由两名弟子分别记下。

32. 见《论语·述而篇第七》，第23章。

33. 《孟子·尽心章句下》，第37章。

34. 这段记载在《史记》中出现两次，文字略有不同，有学者怀疑两段文字实为一段，古代抄写错误而分为两段。但是，同样的话是可能在不同处说了两次的。

孔子回答："其男子有死之志，妇人有保西河之志，吾所伐者不过四五人。"

卫灵公答应伐蒲，却并未行动。灵公年老，已厌倦政事，不能任用孔子这样的大人物。不久，孔子再次离开卫国。

中牟的长官佛肸叛离晋国，邀请孔子，孔子有意前往。

子路问："昔者由也闻诸夫子曰：'亲于其身为不善者，君子不入也。'佛肸以中牟畔，子之往也，如之何？"

孔子回答："然，有是言也。不曰坚乎，磨而不磷；不曰白乎，涅而不淄。"

"我岂匏瓜也哉，焉能系而不食？"[35]

孔子虽然这么说，却并未前往。

我们总能在枯燥的历史记载中发现虽无教益却颇为有趣的逸事。卫国是个很有文化的小国，国内君子众多，大都默默无闻，却十分关心时事。孔子在卫国时，一次正在击磬，有人背负草筐经过门外，说：

"有心哉！击磬乎！"

既而曰："鄙哉！硁硁乎！莫己知也，斯己而已矣。'深则厉，浅则揭。'"

子曰："果哉！末之难矣。"[36]

孔子准备前往晋国，拜见晋国大夫赵简子，行至黄河东岸，得知晋国两位贤臣窦鸣犊、舜华被杀。他看着河水，感叹道："美哉水，洋洋乎！丘之不济此，命也夫！"

子贡上前问："敢问何谓也？"

孔子说："窦鸣犊，舜华，晋国之贤大夫也。赵简子未得志之时，须此两人而后从政；及其已得志，杀之乃从政。"

"丘闻之也，刳胎杀夭则麒麟[37]不至郊，竭泽涸渔则蛟龙不合阴阳，覆巢毁卵则凤皇不翔。何则？君子讳伤其类也。夫鸟兽之于不义也尚知辟之，而况乎丘哉！"孔子于是折返，休止在陬乡，作琴曲《陬操》哀悼两位贤大夫。而后再次返回卫国。

卫公询问孔子用兵策略，孔子回答："俎豆之事则尝闻之矣，军旅之事未之学也。"第二天，卫公与孔子对谈时，眼睛望着天上的飞雁，不看孔子。次日，孔子离开卫国[38]，再至陈国。是年夏，卫灵公去世（公元前493年）。

翌年夏，鲁国国都发生大火。孔子在陈国听到这一消息，问道："灾必于桓釐庙乎？"确切消息传来后，果然是这两座祖庙被火烧毁。是年秋

.

35. 这段对话记载于《论语·阳货篇》第7章，由司马迁收入《史记》。"匏瓜"是天上的星名，《史记·天官书》亦有记载。"系"在天上"而不食"。理雅各翻译为"我可是那味苦的匏瓜！只能挂在一旁，无法食用？""味苦"是理雅各依据旧注添加的。原文仅为"我可是匏瓜吗！只能挂在一旁，无法食用？"。

36. 见《论语·宪问篇第十四》，第39章。

37. 麒麟是中国的祥瑞之兽，祥瑞之鸟是凤凰。

38. 《论语·卫灵公篇第十五》，第1章；《史记·孔子世家》。

天，鲁相季桓子病倒，坐在辇车上巡视鲁城，感叹道："昔此国几兴矣，以吾获罪于孔子，故不兴也。"转而对身旁的儿子康子说："我即死，若必相鲁；相鲁，必召仲尼。"几日后，桓子去世，康子主政。葬礼结束后，康子准备召回孔子。大臣公之鱼说："昔吾先君用之不终，终为诸侯笑。今又用之，不能终，是再为诸侯笑。"康子问应该任用何人，大臣回答："必召冉求。"于是派信使召用冉求。

冉求是孔子中意的弟子，与孔子一同周游列国。冉求准备启程时，孔子说道："鲁人召求，非小用之，将大用之也。"又说道："归与！归与！吾党之小子狂简，斐然成章，不知所以裁之。"[39] 子贡听到后，知道孔子有心回鲁，送别冉求时对他说，如果他被委以高位，应立刻召请夫子回鲁。

次年，孔子离开陈国，来到亦是小邦的蔡国。适逢蔡国内乱，蔡公被臣子射杀，楚国由南面入侵。秋天，齐景公去世。翌年，孔子由蔡国至叶邑。

叶公请教治理之方。孔子回答："近者悦，远者来。"[40]

叶公告诉孔子："吾党有直躬者，其父攘羊，而子证之。"

孔子说："吾党之直者异于是，父为子隐，子为父隐。直在其中矣。"[41]

叶公向子路询问孔子，子路没有回答。孔子听到后，说："由，尔何不对曰'其为人也，学道不倦，诲人不厌，发愤忘食，乐以忘忧，不知老之将至'云尔。"[42]

孔子离开叶邑，回到蔡国。这期间发生两件事，值得一提。

有两个农夫，一个身高，一个面凶，满身泥水，在田间劳作。孔子经过，觉得二人是隐者，遣子路前去询问渡口。

高个农夫问道："夫执舆者为谁？"子路回答："为孔丘。"

又问："是鲁孔丘与？"

子路答："然。"

高个农夫于是说道："是知津矣。"

子路转而询问凶面的农夫，后者问道："子为谁？"子路回答："为仲由。"

农夫又问："是鲁孔丘之徒与？"

子路答："然。"

农夫对子路说："滔滔者天下皆是也，而谁以易之？且而与其从辟人之士也，岂若从辟世之士哉！"说完继续挥锄劳作。

子路将对话转告孔子，孔子怃然说道："鸟兽不可与同群，吾非斯人之徒而谁与？天下有道，丘不与易也。"[43]

还有一次，子路与孔子走散，遇见一位老者，用木棍肩负草筐，子路上前询问："子见夫子乎？"

．

39. 《论语·公冶长篇第五》，第 22 章。可译为"（他们）不知如何裁剪"。

40. 《论语·子路篇第十三》，第 16 章。

41. 同上，第 18 章。

42. 《论语·述而篇第七》，第 19 章；《史记·孔子世家》。

43. 《论语·微子篇第十八》，第 6 章。两位农夫被叫作长沮（字面意为"高个满身是泥的人"）和桀溺（"面相凶狠、满脚泥水的人"）。在如此短暂的对话里，很难获知他们的名字。所以长沮和桀溺并非真是他们的名字。

老者回答："四体不勤，五谷不分，孰为夫子！"说完，放下木棍，开始割草。

子路拱手立在老者身前，微微施礼。

老者留子路过夜，杀鸡，煮小米，款待子路，还引他见了自己的两个儿子。

第二天，子路赶上孔子，讲了昨天发生的事情。孔子说："隐者也。"派子路再去拜访，发现老者已经离开了。[44]

是时（公元前491年），吴国侵犯陈国，楚国出兵相救。楚公听说孔子在陈国与蔡国之间，派使者邀请孔子前往楚国。孔子应邀准备出发。关于这件事情，《史记》中有一段并不可靠的记载，说是陈国和蔡国的大夫在一起商议，很怕孔子前往楚国，因为孔子是一位贤人，如果楚国任用孔子，必定使楚国更强，会威胁到陈国和蔡国，自己的官位也会不保，于是派兵将孔子一行人全部围住。此事之不可信，因为陈国邻近楚国，蔡国邻近吴国，陈蔡相与为敌，两国大夫不可能为了一个未来的假想敌相会商讨。其他史书仅是记载了七天之前，孔子一行人用光了补给，但是所有史书都没有说明为何如此。许多弟子都虚弱不堪，相继病倒，而孔子仍如常谈话，吟唱，弹琴。《论语》中的记载[45]颇有可说者：

> 在陈绝粮，从者病，莫能兴。
>
> 子路愠见曰："君子亦有穷乎？"
>
> 子曰："君子固穷，小人穷斯滥矣。"

子贡色作。

孔子曰："赐，尔以予为多学而识之者与？"

曰："然。非与？"

孔子曰："非也。予一以贯之。"

孔子知弟子有愠心，乃召子路而问曰：

"诗云'匪兕匪虎，率彼旷野'。吾道非邪？吾何为于此？"

子路曰："意者吾未仁邪？人之不我信也。意者吾未知邪？人之不我行也。"

孔子曰："有是乎！由，譬使仁者而必信，安有伯夷、叔齐？[46]使知者而必行，安有王子比干？"[47]

子路出，子贡入见。

孔子曰："赐，诗云'匪兕匪虎，率彼旷野'。吾道非邪？吾何为于此？"

子贡曰："夫子之道至大也，故天下莫能容夫子。夫子盖少贬焉？"

．

44. 《论语·微子篇第十八》，第 7 章。

45. 《论语·卫灵公篇第十五》，第 2 章。

46. 伯夷、叔齐是商末的贤人，是在孔子之前最受尊敬的两个人。两人是兄弟，同为中国东北方小国孤竹国国王的儿子。国王将王位传给弟弟叔齐，而叔齐拒绝接受本应属于哥哥的王位。伯夷也拒绝了，于是两人一同隐居。周武王出兵攻打暴君商纣时，伯夷、叔齐出面阻拦。两兄弟最终饿死，也不愿活在周朝。（《论语·公冶长篇》第 22 章，《史记·伯夷列传第一》）

47. 王子比干是商朝亡国之君纣王的贤臣，因不断阻拦纣王的暴政而被杀。

孔子曰："赐，良农能稼而不能为穑，良工能巧而不能为顺。君子能修其道，纲而纪之，统而理之，而不能为容。今尔不修尔道而求为容。赐，而志不远矣！"

子贡出，颜回入见。

孔子曰："回，诗云'匪兕匪虎，率彼旷野'。吾道非邪？吾何为于此？"

颜回曰："夫子之道至大，故天下莫能容。虽然，夫子推而行之，不容何病，不容然后见君子！夫道之不修也，是吾丑也。夫道既已大修而不用，是有国者之丑也。不容何病，不容然后见君子！"

孔子欣然而笑曰："有是哉颜氏之子！使尔多财，吾为尔宰。"[48]

显然，必定有某种外部原因阻断了他们的行程，在这种艰难的情况下，孔子派子路向楚国求援。楚君立即派兵护卫孔子往楚国。楚君虽为子爵，却称昭王，昭王热情欢迎孔子，还准备以七百里地封孔子。[49]但楚令尹子西不同意，他这样说服昭王：

"王之使使诸侯有如子贡者乎？"

曰："无有。"

"王之辅相有如颜回者乎？"

曰："无有。"

"王之将率有如子路者乎？"

曰："无有。"

"王之官尹有如宰予者乎？"

曰："无有。"

"且楚之祖封于周，号为子男五十里。今孔丘述三五之法，明周召之业，王若用之，则楚安得世世堂堂方数千里乎？夫文王在丰，武王在镐，百里之君卒王天下。今孔丘得据土壤，贤弟子为佐，非楚之福也。"

楚昭王被说服，没有封地给孔子。同年秋天昭王死，孔子返回卫国。

孔子在楚国时，遇到一狂士，狂士对孔子做了一番评价，此事如下：

楚狂接舆[50]歌而过孔子曰：

"凤兮凤兮，何德之衰！

往者不可谏兮，来者犹可追也！

已而已而，今之从政者殆而！"

孔子下，欲与之言。趋而去，弗得与之言。[51]

·

48. 颜回是孔子最得意的弟子，但是最贫穷。

49. 这里用"mile"（英里［编者按：5280 英尺］）翻译中文"里"，而 1 里（500 米）实际只有约 1640 英尺。

50. 或以为狂士名叫"接舆"，实际上可以译为"在车附近"，因为在路上偶遇，很难留下姓名。

51. 《论语·微子篇第十八》，第 5 章。

是时，卫出公与其父争位。孔子的许多弟子久在卫国为官，有人怀疑孔子支持在位的出公，反对出公流亡在外的父亲。冉有问："夫子为卫君乎？"子贡："诺，吾将问之。"

> 入，曰："伯夷、叔齐何人也？"
> 曰："古之贤人也。"
> 曰："怨乎？"
> 曰："求仁而得仁，又何怨？"
> 出，曰："夫子不为也。"[52]

这是孔子最后一次去卫国。他曾说过："鲁卫之政，兄弟也。"[53] 两国的远祖是周武王的兄弟。可以这样理解，鲁国与卫国保存了周朝的大部分传统，其他国家则多少存留了野蛮的习俗，如秦国与楚国。鲁卫两国保持着同样高度的文化，但此时卫国政局不稳。卫公已在位十七八年，有意任用孔子。

> 子路曰："卫君待子而为政，子将奚先？"
> 子曰："必也正名乎！"[54]
> 子路曰："有是哉，子之迂也！奚其正？"
> 子曰："野哉由也！君子于其所不知，盖阙如也。名不正则言不顺，言不顺则事不成，事不成则礼乐不兴，礼乐不兴则刑罚不中，刑

罚不中则民无所措手足。故君子名之必可言也，言之必可行也。君子
于其言，无所苟而已矣。"[55]

次年，冉求率领鲁国军队与齐国在郎地开战，获得了决定性的胜利。
季康子问冉求："子之于军旅，学之乎？性之乎？"

　　冉求曰："学之于孔子。"

　　季康子问："孔子何如人哉？"

　　对曰："用之有名；播之百姓，质诸鬼神而无憾。求之至于此道，
虽累千社，夫子不利也。"

　　康子问："我欲召之，可乎？"

　　对曰："欲召之，则毋以小人固之，则可矣。"[56]

．

52. 《论语·述而篇第七》，第 17 章。

53. 《论语·子路篇第十三》，第 7 章。

54. 这次问答暗与卫国时局有关。其时，卫出公由南子扶持在位，大夫孔文子忠于
　　南子，而子路是孔文子的家臣。子路很可能希望孔子辅佐出公，但孔子并无此
　　意。子路对孔子见南子一事不悦，认为两人会面，必会谈起扶立卫君之事，夫
　　子既然不赞同南子扶立出公，又何必与南子会面，或说服南子改变主意。但这
　　仅是猜想，相关文献记载过于简略，无法确证以上说法。

55. 《论语·子路篇第十三》，第 3 章。

56. 《史记·孔子世家》。——译者注

孔子此时正在卫国，卫国大夫孔文子向孔子请教密谋攻伐之事，孔子称自己不懂，客气地拒绝了。会面之后，孔子立即吩咐预备车马，准备离开，并说道："鸟能择木，木岂能择鸟乎！"孔文子坚持挽留。此时，季康子所派信使携带召函和重金到达。周游列国14年的孔子返回故土鲁国。其时，孔子69岁。

第四章

儒学大义

　　至此，我们所见到的孔子是游走各地的政治家，试图获得权力，以期实践高上的理想，或希冀在地上营建"天堂"。但不幸的是，孔子未能成功，他的失败并非源于自身的弱点或不足，而是因为时代的动乱不堪。孔子不是只失败了一二次，而是所有努力都以落空而告终。难道上天有意如此安排吗？或许的。以世俗标准看，孔子的后半生可算是悲剧，然而此后半生实为孔子收获最丰、对人类贡献最大的时期。总而言之，孔子的一生是极大的成功，唯一，完整，神圣。

　　或有人问：为什么孔子不投奔当时的周王呢？答案很简单，周王虽然在名义上仍是最高君主，名为"天子"，然而此时治域狭小、权力空虚。即使仅存的一点权力也被几位大臣僭越瓜分了。这种情况下，显然已经无事可为。然而，当天子将祭祀用的牲肉作为赐福分给诸公时（这与印度分享赐福的习俗完全相同），诸公仍然依礼接受。周王有时会向大诸侯国发布命令，例如修缮都城的城墙，这样的命令都会被妥善执行。周王颁布的法令文书通常文字优美庄严，符合天子的身份，但是无人认真对待，只被视为形式而已。

我们可以从前一章的引文中看出，孔子在性命攸关的时候，多次谈到自己与"天"的关系，并且十分确信"天"赋予他的德性。他以某种方式确知自己在这世上的责任和理想。正因如此，他才不畏惧死亡，即使在死亡将近之时，也是如此。孔子曾说过这样一段话：

吾十有五而志于学，三十而立，四十而不惑，五十而知天命，六十而耳顺，七十而从心所欲，不逾矩。[57]

这段话文辞简短，异常坚定。欲要正确理解这段话，需知道孔子在评价自己时，总是怀有谦虚和谨慎的态度。翻看孔子留下来的言辞，我们很容易推想出，孔子的言说并非其教义之全部，相较于没有说出的部分，其所言说或许极为微少。孔子不同于其他宗教领袖，他从未向聚合之众甚或群集之弟子发表演说，从未向公众宣讲自己的思想。而且，他说的话并未被全部记录下来。随着记诵者的亡去，大部分口传记录都在一两代之后佚失了。记录下来的内容十分简短，某种程度上也缘于古代书写材料的限制，纸张还没有出现，而在丝织品和竹子上书写也并非易事。《论语》极有可能是由孔子弟子的弟子记录下来的。其中有多处简短的记录，只记下了孔子说的话，而说话的原因和弟子们的讨论却没有了。我们只能参照孔子之全部教义及其时代背景来理解这些段落。

宋代（960—1279）和明代（1368—1644）有所谓的新儒家，他们虽然对印度韦檀多哲学一无所知，却认为孔子弟子所学即是"它"（It）的知识而已，相当于婆罗门对"彼"（Tat 或 That）的高上知识。关于这一点，孔子经常提及的"乐"也可以对应于"真、智、乐"中的"乐"。孔子是否觉悟到了"真、智、乐"呢？即使孔子没有觉悟到这一高上知识，也丝毫不会影响他的伟大，然而面对这个问题，我们很难给出否定答案。我们可以暂时搁置形而上学的立场，转而从历史角度来解释这些文字。

查尔斯·艾略特（Charles W. Eliot）主编的《哈佛经典》圣书卷中有一位不具名的译者为这段文字提供了另一种译文，比较而言，此译文稍有无关紧要的差别，很难判断孰优孰劣。正如晚年的托尔斯泰为研读《新约》而开始学习希腊文，欲完全理解经典文字，学习并精通其原初语言是必须要做的事。

说孔子"志于学"，是指学习有关于"礼"的传统知识，例如祭祀礼，其性质既为世俗，亦为精神，终究是有关世间与超世间之关系。在孔子的时代，人们相信"天"在上，所有逝去的祖先都在"他"之侧，所有祭祀都献给"他"。时至今日，这仍是中国的正统信仰。所谓"志"，义为"心之所往"，即"志向"。而我们需要明白，15 岁的孩子不会有与"神圣

---

57. 《论语·为政篇第二》，第 4 章。

者"合一的志向。经过 15 年的学习，他已经在知识上有所"成就"，即为"立"。也就是说，此时的孔子对于世间的事物，或者说对于生命和宇宙已经有了明确的看法。

孔子 40 岁时已经没有困惑了。即是说，他不再怀疑内中的信念，或说，不再因外部的境况而疑惑或动摇自己的信念了。又经过十年的内中努力，他开始知得"天命"，或依宗教的说法，知得"上帝的约命"（此处不可说"律法"），或"神圣意志"。

我们很难探究孔子在 50 岁之后的内中成就。朱熹是注解孔子的大家，他讲解这段话时，说到"五十而知天命"，就不往下讲了。他颇为幽默地说自己还没到 50 岁，无法知道圣人在 50 岁时的状况。这显然是谦虚之词。然而，即便是一位普通学者已经 50、60 或者 70 岁了，因经历不同，也还是无法恰当地解释这段话。有一点似乎是确定的，孔子在 50 岁时，或者更早，已经开始知得上天对他的约命，所谓"知得"，是指心思与内中的确信。我们可以大胆地推断，不仅孔子可以如此，其他人乃至整个人类最终都会如此。对于孔子来说，知得某事通常是知其全体。我们大可认为，孔子在 40 至 50 岁之间（或者至迟 50 岁时），内中经历了大的明悟，绝非仅是一次预见或启示，或是对真理的隐约窥见，而一定是与超上者的直接交流或合一。或如孔子自己所说，"与天地合其德"[58]，以瑜伽的方式表述，便是与上帝和自然合一。直至生命结束之前，孔子的行动和言语都已稳固并整合在其中了。只有在获得这样的内中成就之后，孔子将"真理"传播于人类的事业才会成为他生命交响曲的主旋律。只有在此明悟之中，所有构成人类苦难与不幸之二元矛盾，如生死成败、美誉责难，才会不是问题。而这一定是孔子寻求全般结合于"一"的结果。后文会讨论孔子的弟子对于"一"的解释。

从外部看，儒学与其他世界观体系有一个主要的区别。"道"在宇宙中为一，这一点非常明了，无须阐释。但是"道"的表述，培育和传播的方式会有不同。我们知道，道教、佛教和基督教，或还包括伊斯兰教，都从社会底层兴起，然后在大众中平面式地广泛传播，依次触发个体之灵魂，恰似马拉松火炬依次传递，而儒家则更趋向于层级或纵向。几乎所有中国古代的儒者都是如此行事，我大胆地认为中世纪的教皇也是如此。他们都从最上层开始，直接在皇室中产生影响，如旱季的雨云，笼罩整个国家，将甘露洒满大地。面对数量巨大的人口，这可能是最直接和最简易的方法。而后世，几乎所有哲学流派都努力成为"官学"，儒家教义尤其如此。因为儒学作为人类之基本原则，其教育对象是在国家教育机构内学习的贵族子弟。

自然中有一基本的物理法则，某物以一种方式起始或成功，也必会以这种方式结束或失败。无论我们认为儒学是宗教，还是简单地视其为伦理法则，它都要以政治力量传播自己，只要这力量在，就可实行，这力量垮

---

58. 出自《易经·乾卦文言》："夫大人者，与天地合其德，与日月合其明，与四时合其序，与鬼神合其吉凶。"《易经》有贝恩斯（C. F. Baynes）译本。《孟子》赵岐注有言："行与天合"。

掉，就随之失败。然而，有一个微小的区别须加以说明。因为儒学与政治联系紧密，问题转化为政府是否采纳儒学作为执政方向的指导原则。而儒家并不会将某种信条或教义强加于任何现存的政治力量，并依赖其传播自己的思想。历史表明，几乎所有朝代都或多或少地采用了儒家的学说来治理国家，只是程度不同而已，而儒学没有因为任何一个朝代的消亡而消亡。

我们可以从另外一个角度看待这一问题，儒学中有永恒不灭的真理，自有其合理性和持久性，经得住时间之轮的碾压和挤抑。然而儒学并非是降临世间的新"福音"。孔子在中国被视为圣人，这缘于他伟大的综合事业，或说，他将三代文化的精髓进行了完美的复合，并赋予了新的生命。作为文化的保持者，这综合工作是孔子最重要的成就，而孔子却并未添加任何新的东西。我们可以在这伟大的成就中发现儒学之大义。如果将从古至今的中国文化史分成两段，孔子正好处在此两段之间的连接点上，在他之前是大演绎，在他之后是大归纳。或做一现实的比喻，一匹漂亮的丝绸束结于中间，所有的丝络都汇聚于此，又以此为起点，完好地发舒出去。

研究儒学需要寻出儒学之大义，即中心原则。对于我们来说，相较于圣人一己之所得，圣人的教诲更显重要。即使不存在这样的原则，我们也要从其整体构架中阐明出这原则。这是一种颇为实用的态度，为持事节俭之计，似乎还必不可少，当讨论的主题如此据有精神性时，就显得更为重要了。而且我们确实找到了这样的原则。

"仁"字一直是令翻译家颇为烦扰，并且消耗注释家大量精力的一个字。"仁"字的结构很简单：右边是"二"，左边是代表"人"的偏旁，表明"仁"的意思有关于人与人之间的关系。在日常语中，"仁"字还有果"核"的意思，例如杏仁或桃仁，其中保存着植物的生命原则。"不仁"义指"麻木"或"漠然"，还常用来描述某种痿痹病。

经典中出现"仁"这个中心原则的所有段落都是活泼生动的，丝毫没有神秘或含糊之感，而这个词的英译却大多拙劣，窒碍原义。例如，理雅各将"仁"译为"virtue"（美德），这会使英语读者产生错误的印象，以为如此伟大的精神导师不过是板着面孔宣讲道德规范的教师。而"virtue"在汉语中有另外一个对应字"德"，常与"道"字连用，如老子的《道德经》可以直译为"The Classic on Virtues"。《哈佛经典》圣书卷中，"仁"被简单地译为"love"（爱），更生动，却略显肤浅，也没有传达多少含义。因为"love"在汉语中也有另外的对应字。"仁"还被翻译为"benevolence"（善行）和"beneficence"（仁慈），相对于原义，这两个英文词的含义太过狭窄；还有译为"compassion"（同情）或者"lovingkindness"（慈爱），与原义较近些，含义却更显窄。"sympathy"（怜悯）太过浅陋，"humanity"（博爱）含义足够宽广，但却浮表。总之，英语中没有与"仁"完全对应的词汇。

我们需要的不是完美的译词，也不是任何定义，而是正确的描述。肯定地说，"精神之爱"非常接近"仁"的含义，但这爱并不只针对个人。"仁"是一宇宙原则，汉语中称为"天地之心"，宇宙的大和谐以之显现和遍漫。"神圣恩典"也非常近似，然而其背后有恩典的施加者，而"仁"则更显其非人格性。"仁"可以被看作普降"神圣恩典"的"彼"（That）。以太阳和阳光作类比，"仁"即是太阳本身；但是没有阳光的太阳，如何还是太阳呢？如果我们一定要用"爱"这个字，也只能在"神圣母亲"的定义下使用：

爱是直接源自"唯一者"的巨大震动……[59]

换个说法，"仁"就是"神圣之爱"。"神圣圆成"也十分接近，或说，自存于人类之上的圆成。如果称之为某种圆成状态，那这正是所有人类都努力趋向的一种状态，进入这种状态的人即为神圣。向下趋近人的层面上，"仁"包含着各种善，如平和、非暴力、慈爱、善行、同情、博爱和爱等等，还有其他无数美德，如孝、顺、忠、诚、信，以及对礼仪、礼貌、正义、正直、谦虚和谦逊等的热爱。总之，"仁"在上，亦在内，是宇宙存在的根柢。

经过以上阐述，我们或可继续推敲各种译文，从中寻出恰当的译词。《论语》共 20 篇，除去零星涉及之处，约有 54 章讨论"仁"。（顺便提及，英译《论语》20 篇，共 489 章，内容完整。但不同中文版本的《论语》分篇略有差异，章数也就不同。文本问题过于烦琐，不再细说。）孔子对"仁"的反复提及，正如其对"仁"的反复强调，显示"仁"在孔学中的核心位置。而且"仁"是孔子极少谈及或阐述的三个问题之一，其他两个问题是"命"和"利"，由此可见"仁"的神圣义与庄严义。

然而，"仁远乎哉？我欲仁，斯仁至矣。"[60] 这是孔子在说自己的经验。

显然，"仁"就是"神圣之爱"。作为宇宙原则，"仁"不可能离我们很远。人在转念之间就可以拒绝冷漠枯燥的生活，付出并得到爱，只要人觉醒于"仁"，"仁"便就在眼前了。即使在日常生活中，人在举手之间，就能觉醒，做到公正，善良，亲切。还有另一段话表明同样意思：

　　有能一日用其力于仁矣乎！我未见力不足者。盖有之矣，我未之见也。[61]

　　然而在人的水平上，远不能"要有光，就有了光"；欲在"神圣之爱"中圆成，须付出艰辛的努力，甚至舍弃生命。有人问孔子："伯夷和叔齐是什么样的人呢？"孔子说，他们是古时的两位贤人，他们"求仁得仁"，所以没什么要抱怨的了。这两位贤人为了追求"仁"，竟至饥饿而死。因生命已经献给高上且神圣的理想，便没有任何悔恨，内中已至圆成。他们死去时，心思全然宁静于圆满福乐之中。在中国历史上，于变革时期欣然赴死者无数，尤其在旧王朝崩落时为最甚，究其缘由，区区一"仁"字而已。对于多少具有些德性的普通人，又当说些什么呢？"仁"实非人人可及也。

·

59. 整段为："爱是直接源自'唯一者'的巨大震动，只有极纯洁和强大者才能接受和显现它。"

60. 《论语·述而篇第七》，第 30 章。

61. 《论语·里仁篇第四》，第 6 章。

见《论语》所记：

> 孟武伯问："子路仁乎？"
>
> 子曰："不知也。"
>
> 又问。
>
> 子曰："由也，千乘之国，可使治其赋也，不知其仁也。"
>
> "求也何如？"
>
> 子曰："求也，千室之邑，百乘之家，可使之为宰也，不知其仁也。"
>
> "赤也何如？"
>
> 子曰："赤也，束带立于朝，可使与宾客言也，不知其仁也。"[62]

对话中提到的人都是孔子的高足，多有贤德才能，如有机会，皆能成事。没人比老师更了解自己的弟子了，孔子不认为他们已经做到了"仁"。只有极度贫困的弟子颜渊，安于一箪食，一瓢饮，住在简陋的巷子里，以肘为枕，却不改其乐，孔子如此称赞他：

> 回也，其心三月不违仁，其余则日月至焉而已矣。[63]

一次，另一个穷困的弟子原宪问孔子：

> "克、伐、怨、欲不行焉，可以为仁矣？"

子曰："可以为难矣，仁则吾不知也。"[64]

子张问曰："令尹子文三仕为令尹，无喜色；三已之，无愠色。旧令尹之政，必以告新令尹。何如？"

子曰："忠矣。"

曰："仁矣乎？"

曰："未知，焉得仁？"

"崔子弑齐君，陈文子有马十乘，弃而违之。至于他邦，则曰：'犹吾大夫崔子也。'违之。之一邦，则又曰：'犹吾大夫崔子也。'违之。何如？"

子曰："清矣。"

曰："仁矣乎？"

曰："未知，焉得仁？"[65]

然而，历史上有几位贤人，孔子认为可以有"仁"之称，因为他们的事功使"彼"（It）显于世间。

·

62. 《论语·公冶长篇第五》，第 8 章。

63. 《论语·雍也篇第六》，第 7 章。

64. 《论语·宪问篇第十四》，第 1 章。

65. 《论语·公冶长篇第五》，第 19 章。

子路曰："桓公杀公子纠，召忽死之，管仲不死。"曰："未仁乎？"

子曰："桓公九合诸侯，不以兵车，管仲之力也。如其仁！如其仁！"66

子贡曰："管仲非仁者与？桓公杀公子纠，不能死，又相之。"

子曰："管仲相桓公，霸诸侯，一匡天下，民到于今受其赐。微管仲，吾其被发左衽矣。"67

"岂若匹夫匹妇之为谅也，自经于沟渎而莫之知也。"68

如此可见，为国家带来和平的政治家，因其政绩，也可称"仁"。远至殷商，微子避去，箕子为奴，比干因谏而死。孔子说："殷有三仁焉。"69

子贡曰："如有博施于民而能济众，何如？可谓仁乎？"

子曰："何事于仁，必也圣乎！尧、舜其犹病诸！夫仁者，己欲立而立人；己欲达而达人。能近取譬，可谓仁之方也已。"70

现在，依照"仁"这一伟大原则，我们可以看一下孔子如何看待自己。他曾坦白且谦虚地如是说：

子曰："文莫，吾犹人也，躬行君子，则吾未之有得。"71

子曰："若圣与仁，则吾岂敢。抑为之不厌，诲人不倦，则可谓云尔已矣。"公西华曰："正唯弟子不能学也。"[72]

子曰："君子道者三，我无能焉：仁者不忧，知者不惑，勇者不惧。"

子贡曰："夫子自道也。"[73]

.

66. 《论语·宪问篇第十四》，第 16 章。

67. "披发左衽"是蛮族习俗。中国古人穿衣扣于中间或右侧，头发总是束起。

68. 《论语·宪问篇第十四》，第 17 章。

69. 《论语·微子篇第十八》，第 1 章。

70. 《论语·雍也篇第六》，第 30 章。

71. 《论语·述而篇第七》，第 33 章。

72. 同上，第 34 章。

73. 《论语·宪问篇第十四》，第 28 章。

第五章

儒学大义（续）

人类的爱充满了焦虑。从负极的意义上说，没有爱，就没有焦虑。各种教义体系都曾教导去除尘世之爱。这是虚无主义的倾向，为寻求安宁，最后诉诸大"空"，快乐和痛苦都在其中息止。而孔子的教导却是指向积极和绝对之事。回顾前文所讲之一切，对于"仁"，还有什么比"神圣之爱"更适宜的称谓呢？无论我们有没有意识到，"神圣之爱"正是我们所有人赖以生存的根基。

显而易见，即使不信仰宗教，人也可以是精神性的。不仅僧侣和先知可以拥有这"爱"，伟大的政治家也可以。管仲只是一位出色的政治经济家 74，一个有能力的外交家，一个生活奢华的人，然而他可以被称为"仁"。因为他使齐国拥有了半个世纪的和平，使古代文化得以保存。商代的微子、箕子和比干也受到同样的赞许，他们都践行尘世之路，直至牺牲生命。伯夷、叔齐也是如此。我们是否应当思及几位当代的领袖人物呢？如亚伯拉罕·林肯、孙中山和甘地。他们将神圣之爱带到世间，因此可称他们为伟人。通常理解，牺牲生命可以是大事，也可以是小事，可轻如鹅毛，可重如泰山。问题在于为何种目的？目的或可不同，但可以确定的是，那一定不会是因为某种个人或私我的理由，那只能是为了"神圣之爱"。所以孔子说：

> 志士仁人，无求生以害仁，有杀身以成仁。[75]

我们知道，自我保存是人类与生俱来的本能，教人自愿放弃生命并非易事。但孔子并非教人如何死，而是教人如何生。

> 子曰："民之于仁也，甚于水火。水火吾见蹈而死者矣，未见蹈仁而死者也！"[76]

如果"仁"之于生命的重要性可与水火相较，那么，同样可视"仁"为寻常之事，为人人皆可践行的道路。为了在神圣之爱中圆成，人可以舍

·

74. 这里须提及的是，《管子》并非管仲所作，只是伪托。

75. 《论语·卫灵公篇第十五》，第 9 章。

76. 同上，第 35 章。

弃自己的生命，但是神圣之爱并不要求生命损毁在圣坛之上。与之相反，神圣之爱维持着生命，赋予其意义，将其携至圆成，驻于永恒生命之中。神圣之爱常被比作春天，温带的春天在冰天雪地之后来临，蓝天之下，草长花开，而死亡常常被比作秋天或冬天。人的心灵能否如春季明朗的天空一样广阔、温暖和恩慈呢？

至于"永恒生命"，那是瑜伽之事，是精神或彼岸之寻求，寻求死后的天堂或各种解脱。这不仅是佛教徒或其他宗教徒，也是道教徒最关心的主题。如果我们依照室利·阿罗频多对"瑜伽"作更宽广的解说，即"一切生命皆是瑜伽"，那么儒学之"道"对此亦有可说，已在其中矣。依秉性不同，寻求者或倾向于智识之道，或倾向于敬爱之道。于是有智识瑜伽（Jnana-Yoga）与敬爱瑜伽（Bhakti-Yoga）之别，然两途在终点合一，修智识之道者也可以是修敬爱之道者，反之亦然。人在外部气质上各不相同，有人天生聪慧、机敏，有人不如此，却有慈爱之心。而后者更易于笃行此道。我们再看孔子如何说：

知者乐水，仁者乐山；知者动，仁者静；知者乐，仁者寿。[77]

另一处：

子曰："知及之，仁不能守之，虽得之，必失之。知及之，仁能守之，不庄以莅之，则民不敬。……"[78]

显然，孔子也对这两种不同气质的人作了区分，正对应于古印度的两种不同道路。而永恒生命应在神圣圆成中获得。进而可见：

樊迟问仁。

子曰："爱人。"

问知。

子曰："知人。"[79]

孔子并未说明为什么要爱人。但是"仁"本身不就是原因吗？我们需要在这源头活水上附加任何武断的理由吗？在瑜伽的义度上，说"爱是存于人中的神性"，即是说并非只爱人或人类，而是爱一切存在中的"自我"。这正是一个转折点，韦檀多哲学由此向内，儒者由此向外。我们可以确认，同为儒家人物的孟子觉得了"自我"（the Self 或 Atman）。如果采取严格的历史学视角，仅凭文字记载判断，我们无法全然确定孔子是否也觉得了"自我"。向外之路转向道德伦理领域，扩展至处于同一平面上的大众；向内或向上之路转向在上的神性，转向形而上学之域，个人得以纵向提升。然而儒者会问，"如果个人圆成只是为了自己的救赎，而非为了全体，那

.

77.　《论语·雍也篇第六》，第 23 章。

78.　《论语·卫灵公篇第十五》，第 33 章。

79.　《论语·颜渊篇第十二》，第 22 章。

么有何用处呢？"儒学向外转的努力旨在社会进步，大众成长，最终以至人类整体之拯救。这使我们想起"地狱不空誓不成佛"的菩提萨埵。

同样的问题总是得到不同的回答，如孔子曾说："中人以上，可以语上也；中人以下，不可以语上也。"[80] 孔子弟子三千，才质自然不同，教导之语自然也区别很大。

> 樊迟问知。
>
> 子曰："务民之义，敬鬼神而远之，可谓知矣。"
>
> 问仁。
>
> 曰："仁者先难而后获，可谓仁矣。"[81]

即是说，在"仁"这一原则中，行事不必问结果，但却不能忽略"民之义"。《薄伽梵歌》的信徒最能理解这一教诲。

同一弟子再次询问同样的问题：

> 樊迟问仁。
>
> 子曰："居处恭，执事敬，与人忠。虽之夷狄，不可弃也。"[82]

我们很容易在这里看出向外的转向。

知识水平高的人通常以心思（mind）理解事物，而仁爱的人通过心（heart）领会事物。后者可能拙于言语，但其聪明并不逊于前者。如下：

子曰："刚、毅、木、讷近仁。"[83]

子曰："巧言令色，鲜矣仁！"[84]

司马牛问仁。

子曰："仁者，其言也讱。"

曰："其言也讱，斯谓之仁已乎？"

子曰："为之难，言之得无讱乎？"[85]

或曰："雍也仁而不佞。"

子曰："焉用佞？御人以口给，屡憎于人。不知其仁，焉用佞？"[86]

如今，言语同写作一样，也是一门值得学习的技艺。但在古代中国，

.

80.　《论语·雍也篇第六》，第21章。

81.　同上，第22章。

82.　《论语·子路篇第十三》，第19章。

83.　同上，第27章。

84.　《论语·学而篇第一》，第3章。

85.　《论语·颜渊篇第十二》，第3章。

86.　《论语·公冶长篇第五》，第5章。

没有需要演说的公共集会，也没有产生德摩斯梯尼（Demosthenes）或西塞罗（Cicero）这样的人物。逻辑学家和公共演说家晚至战国才出现。因其常常惑人良知，文己之非而移祸于人，遂受普通人群的轻蔑。然而言语也是孔门四科之一。孔子曾提到：

> 有德者必有言，有言者不必有德。仁者必有勇，勇者不必有仁。[87]

理雅各在翻译这段话时，遇到了一个问题。他用"virtuous"翻译"德"，这是正确的。然而他一贯用"virtue"翻译"仁"，但此时已用于"德"，为了避免重复，便只好用"men of principle"翻译"仁者"，这就不太准确了。

"勇"是另外一种德性，通常指行动之人，践行行业瑜伽之路。儒家并未区分这三种道路，但这三种卓越的德性在儒家总是分别对应于三类人。两宗完全未曾交会的古代学问正是在此处契合，两者对一普遍真理有着完全相同的表述。然而在儒家，这教导不能分开领受，此三种道路必须协和互补，以塑成一神圣人格。因此，心向"神圣之爱"的人仍要获取智性知识，需要行动时，应当勇于完成。我们可读到：

> 好仁不好学，其蔽也愚。[88]

> 子曰："当仁不让于师。"[89]

（这句话有英译为"When love is at stake, yield not to an army"，将"师"译为"军队"［army］是不正确的，尽管"师"确实有"军队"的含义。"师"在这句话里是"老师"的意思。古文中"让于师"连用时，从未有过"军队"的含义。如果没有这个错误，这段英译文就其简洁而言，是非常出色的译文。）[90]

显然，践行仁爱之路的人也应当有知识，否则可能会落至愚蠢。孔子与弟子有这样的对话：

宰我问曰："仁者，虽告之曰：'井有仁焉。'其从之也？"

子曰："何为其然也？君子可逝也，不可陷也；可欺也，不可罔也。"[91]

此处略有疑问，君子和仁者有什么区别呢？显然是没有的，如下：

子曰："君子而不仁者有矣夫，未有小人而仁者也。"[92]

87.　《论语·宪问篇第十四》，第 4 章。

88.　《论语·阳货篇第十七》，第 8 章。

89.　《论语·卫灵公篇第十五》，第 36 章。

90.　参见《宋史·卷二百八十二·列传第四十一》，王旦传。

91.　《论语·雍也篇第六》，第 26 章。

92.　《论语·宪问篇第十四》，第 6 章。

不必详加讨论，我们即可认定，此处"君子"即是"仁者"。但通常后者相对于智者而说，前者相对于小人而说。我们还可读到：

子曰："唯仁者能好人，能恶人。"[93]

（此句有英译文将"好"和"恶"译为"love"和"hate"，实际译为"like"和"dislike"更妥当。）

子曰："苟志于仁矣，无恶也。"[94]

子曰："富与贵，是人之所欲也；不以其道得之，不处也。贫与贱，是人之所恶也；不以其道得之，不去也。君子去仁，恶乎成名？君子无终食之间违仁，造次必于是，颠沛必于是。"[95]

由此可以看出，高上意义上的爱与普通意义上的爱之间有巨大的分别。用心于通常意义上的爱，可能引生出错误的行为。因为如此行为的人仍然游弋于情命之中，如果这种爱得不到回报或受到抵触，任何存于我们自性之中，与爱相反对的元素都会立刻起而反抗。而儒家教导的是"神圣之爱"，在本质上，乃属绝对而纯粹精神之事。"神圣之爱"不求取任何回报（尽管可能得到一切的回报），因此不会产生恶，因其本身超出了所有的恶。这精神之爱是"超人类"（superior-manhood）的本质，这样的人从外表看来无疑是"君子"，但是我们可说，在其内中，他亦是卓绝的精神求道者。

所以，终极且重要的是内中之努力。我们发现，孔子的弟子每次问起相同的问题，都得到不同的答案。精神之爱并非指向一两个人，而是指向宇宙中所有的人和所有的事物。

> 颜渊问仁。
>
> 子曰："克己复礼为仁。一日克己复礼，天下归仁焉。为仁由己，而由人乎哉？"
>
> 颜渊曰："请问其目？"
>
> 子曰："非礼勿视，非礼勿听，非礼勿言，非礼勿动。"
>
> 颜渊曰："回虽不敏，请事斯语矣。"⁹⁶

"礼"在英文中常被译为"propriety"或"courtesy"，这两个英文词都不能相应。但是有关"礼"的细节问题，无须在这里过多讨论，我们暂可接受现存之译文。不过，"courtesy"一词确实太过浮表，完全不达义。中文的"礼"字具有更深广的含义。关于礼，现存有三大部经典，内容涵盖全部古代文化。

.

93. 《论语·里仁篇第四》，第 3 章。

94. 同上，第 4 章。

95. 同上，第 5 章。

96. 《论语·颜渊篇第十二》，第 1 章。

仲弓问仁。

子曰："出门如见大宾，使民如承大祭。己所不欲，勿施于人。在邦无怨，在家无怨。"

仲弓曰："雍虽不敏，请事斯语矣。"[97]

迎宾、行祭是礼所涵盖的内容。这些仪式，无论英文译为"propriety"，还是"courtesy"，都与仪式中演奏的音乐紧密相关。而且礼和乐都共同根基于仁。孔子曾说：

人而不仁，如礼何？人而不仁，如乐何？[98]

但是推己及人并不容易做到。

子贡曰："我不欲人之加诸我也，吾亦欲无加诸人。"

子曰："赐也，非尔所及也。"[99]

同样的道理，孔子曾再次说给子贡：

子贡问曰："有一言而可以终身行之者乎？"

子曰："其恕乎！己所不欲，勿施于人。"[100]

　　由此可见，儒家具有比佛教更为宽广的道德规范，因为前者的道德感知范围更广，远超有限的形式。不杀生、不妄语是非常简单的教义，是佛陀定下的戒律，但是仍然没有触及问题的根柢。儒家仅说，应以自我为量度。如果你不喜欢别人对你说谎，那么你也不应对别人说谎；或者，如果你不想被杀，那么你也不应杀人。将这一同情之感推及至一切有体，即是恕道。积极地说，如果你希望自己免于痛苦，那么也应使他人免于痛苦。这是最简单最直接的道路，扩充至个人行为，远比"你不应当如何"这样的诫命更加整全。因此，即使贤若孔圣之子贡，也不能肯定自己拥有了这样的德性。从根本上说，"恕"仍然根基于"神圣之爱"。如果"神圣之爱"得以完全舒展，那么自然会生出互感或体谅和同情，进而所有的这些道德考量则全为不必要的了。

　　所有道德体系中都有一普遍的教义，即"自制"，这可追溯至刻在特尔斐阿波罗神庙上的箴言"认识你自己"。但是声称一日克己复礼，天下归仁，似乎只不过是修辞而已，不然就过于夸张了。然而，这句话应该放到彼时的历史背景中去理解。我们知道，将这一切付诸实践的人应该是"大人"，通常是君王或统治者，这区别于普通意义上的"君子"，因为儒家之

·

97.　《论语·颜渊篇第十二》，第 2 章。

98.　《论语·八佾篇第三》，第 3 章。

99.　《论语·公冶长篇第五》，第 12 章。

100.　《论语·卫灵公篇第十五》，第 24 章。

学本为官学。可以想见，如果掌控权力的统治者转心趋向这一原则，影响会扩充至所有的人，世人自然会将仁德归于他们。即便如此，必有大的内中努力，才能达至。经过极艰苦的内中奋斗，达至一点，自然向外扩展。这是几乎所有精神之师的共同经验。在形而上学的义度上，这好似又回到出发点——后世称颜回为"复圣"——实际上是圆形运动中的螺旋式上升。回到原点，但是上升到更高的层度，视野大开，觉察到必须要对天下众生有所作为了。

然而，即使有志于此，被尊为仁者，欲成就若干积极之事业并非易事。大众通常是具有惰性的群体，任何提升或转变都伴随着巨大的迟疑，而大众同时又是具有智识的群体，聪慧不逊于全知之神。大众转化之路必将是渐进而且漫长的。即使经由高等知觉性者的创造，已经形成和平、善意、和谐，即仁爱的普遍氛围，反对因素的彻底消除仍需要长久的时间。所以有如下之言：

子曰："'善人为邦百年，亦可以胜残去杀矣。'诚哉是言也！"[101]

子曰："如有王者，必世而后仁。"[102]

依照古义，一世是三十年。真正的君王就是能够创造这种仁爱氛围的人，但是这样的君王并不常出现。历史经验告诉我们，仁爱的扩充不能在短时间内实现。我们在这里可以看到儒家教义的不同之处，其所企望的天堂或乌托邦建在此世，"神圣之爱"扩充至所有人，胜残去杀，仅余福乐。因此儒家教义中没有死后灵魂得救，或入天堂，或入涅槃。且不论儒家是否可以称为宗教，儒家教义之核心即是如此。儒家所教如此，弟子彼时所学，后世所学亦如此。请看如下文字：

> 有子曰："君子务本，本立而道生。孝弟也者，其为仁之本与！"[103]

> 子曰："弟子入则孝，出则弟，谨而信，泛爱众，而亲仁。行有余力，则以学文。"[104]

> 子曰："志于道，据于德，依于仁，游于艺。"[105]

> 子贡问为仁。

.

101. 《论语·子路篇第十三》，第 11 章。

102. 同上，第 12 章。

103. 《论语·学而篇第一》，第 2 章。

104. 同上，第 6 章。

105. 《论语·述而篇第七》，第 6 章。

子曰："工欲善其事，必先利其器。居是邦也，事其大夫之贤者，友其士之仁者。"[106]

曾子曰："士不可以不弘毅，任重而道远。仁以为己任，不亦重乎？死而后已，不亦远乎？"[107]

同样的问题也可问于基督徒，进而还可问："这担负不正如耶稣肩上的十字架一样吗？"

106. 《论语·卫灵公篇第十五》，第 10 章。

107. 《论语·泰伯篇第八》，第 7 章。

第六章

六艺

仁或神圣之爱是儒家教义的核心。或是因为"仁"是内在于所有人类灵魂之中的启明之光，能够与在上的伟大"启明者"相融合，是一条向所有人敞开的道路。如果"仁"并非先天内具于人，那么一定是后天强加于人，如此则一切通向"仁"的途径都成了人为的造作，一切起于内中的生长、发展或自然发华遂为不可能，"仁"也就因此不再是一条敞开的道路了。这敞开的道路最终一定要通向"神圣者"（Divinity），"神圣者"本身虽然仍是秘密，但这秘密属于光明，非属于黑暗。正因如此，孔子是一位精神导师，而非道德说教者。表面看来，儒家教义简单，没有任何深奥的内容。孔子很少提及对终极者或在上者的觉悟。孔子曾说：

"予欲无言。"

子贡曰："子如不言，则小子何述焉？"

子曰："天何言哉？四时行焉，百物生焉，天何言哉？"[108]

子贡曾说：

夫子之文章，可得而闻也；夫子之言性与天道，不可得而闻也。[109]

我们应当知道，孔子所知所想的大部分内容并未传于弟子，他的言语和教导也只有一部分，也许只是很小的一部分被记录下来并保存至今，而且也只涉及精神之文化层面，其他则永远留在沉默之中了。即使这公开的部分也是他所不愿讨论的，例如有关"神圣之爱"的话题，如果不是弟子一再追问，那么孔子还是会保持沉默。[110] 所以，我们仍然缺少关于这个问题的详细论述。且不论孔子这样伟大的精神导师，即使任何有过内中体悟的普通人也知道语言的限度，超越语言的层面虽然并非不能传达，却也无法表述。再进一步说，升至某个境界，语言不仅无用，而且是不必要的了。假使有人与"仁"为一，如天或上帝，万物在其中各顺其性，生长

---

108. 《论语·阳货篇第十七》，第 19 章。

109. 《论语·公冶长篇第五》，第 13 章。此段亦可理解为"夫子之性与天合，不可得而闻"。亦是汉儒相承之说。

110. 《论语·子罕篇第九》，第 1 章。——译者注

增殖，语言又有何用呢？孔子曾站在河水边说道："逝者如斯夫，不舍昼夜。"宇宙万物与季节或时间一同变化，当人到达"不变"的一点，便沉默了。我们不必在这里探讨古希腊哲学家赫拉克利特的变化理论，只问这是否同于某些现代思想家所谓的"合一"？于"永在"之中，不仅语言，就是"时间"也消失了。

孔子对于超上问题保持沉默，外在的原因一定是因为弟子们年纪太轻了，无法理解老师的内中思想。孔子与众弟子的年龄平均相差 35 岁。[111]面对这样一群未经世事的年轻弟子，天命或者人性的话题自然少有议论。颜渊一定最理解孔子，却英年早逝，不然定能继承老师的衣钵。孔门讲授的内容通常为六艺四科。

古代儒门之状况与印度的师徒传统非常相似。弟子拜师后，终生奉其为师。老师对弟子的教育、精神乃至身体修为，甚至生死，都负有责任。弟子的成就会带给老师荣耀，弟子的劣行或枉死则是老师的羞辱。孔子有两三个弟子使他终生蒙羞。弟子要将全部身心奉给老师，一举一动都要经由老师指点。当然，弟子是自由的，但遇到大事必先询问老师。师徒好似父子，而且比父子更加亲密，因为依照中国的传统，即使父亲是老师，也不能教授自己的孩子。这里蕴含着深刻的心理原因，孔子就是一例：

陈亢问于伯鱼曰："子亦有异闻乎？"

对曰："未也。尝独立，鲤趋而过庭，曰：'学《诗》乎？'对曰：'未也。''不学《诗》，无以言。'鲤退而学《诗》。

　　"他日又独立，鲤趋而过庭，曰：'学《礼》乎？'对曰：'未也。''不学《礼》，无以立。'鲤退而学《礼》。

　　"闻斯二者。"

　　陈亢退而喜曰："问一得三，闻《诗》，闻《礼》，又闻君子之远其子也。"[112]

　　如果伯鱼没有碰巧遇到孔子，可能就任自玩耍了。最近有欧洲作家注意到中国父母对于孩子的容忍和溺爱，是否普遍如此不可知。但这古老传统的源头可以追溯至此，中国的父亲对儿子总是保持着礼貌的克制。孟子曾经解释过，也许只有这样才能更好地保持自然的爱。老师可以严苛，但是父亲不能。这里没有"重生"的问题[113]，因为弟子可以依照自己的意愿或者老师的意愿拜投其他老师，后者的情况，就如同父亲将儿子交付给老师一样。一个人一生中可以有若干老师，弟子与每位老师的相互责任几乎

　　·

111.　孔子最出色的30多位弟子中，公孙龙小孔子53岁；伯虔和另外几名弟子小50岁；公西赤小42岁；颜幸小46岁；有子小43岁；樊迟小36岁；商瞿小29岁；澹台灭明小39岁；子张小48岁；子夏小44岁；子贡小31岁；冉求小29岁；颜渊小30岁；只有子路最年长，小孔子9岁，然而子路是军人，死于卫国王位争斗之中。由此可见，孔子周游列国时，随行的实际上是一群年轻人。（参见《史记·卷六十七·仲尼弟子列传第七》）

112.　《论语·季氏篇第十六》，第13章。

113.　依印度传统，拜师是弟子的重生。——译者注

都是伴随其一生的。

热爱树木的人最大的快乐就是看到自己种下的树苗长大成材，教育者最大的快乐就是看到自己的学生成为善良有为的公民。孔子的弟子之后大多都服务于诸侯国，老师的名声也随弟子传播到各处。可以想见，在某种意义上说，孔子的政治影响力非常大。孔子周游在外时，弟子们首要的职责就是尽己所能为老师服务。印度的老师（Guru）如果有很多弟子，在森林期时一定也会经历同样的情感，虽然他们周游的性质不同于孔子。老师会很高兴见到弟子以其所学而有所成就，如不满意弟子所为，则会逐其出门。有逸事如下：

> 子之武城，闻弦歌之声。夫子莞尔而笑，曰："割鸡焉用牛刀？"
>
> 子游对曰："昔者偃也闻诸夫子曰：'君子学道则爱人，小人学道则易使也。'"
>
> 子曰："二三子！偃之言是也。前言戏之耳。"[114]
>
> 季氏富于周公，而求也为之聚敛而附益之。
>
> 子曰："非吾徒也，小子鸣鼓而攻之，可也。"[115]

如上可见老师与弟子之间的关系。

我们接下来讨论孔门所教的科目。在周代，教授知识有六个基本门类，称为六艺。在孔门，六艺指六部经典，稍后我们会详细讨论。六艺分别是礼、乐、射、御、书、数。

以现代眼光看，数学是一门科学，但在古代是一门技艺。我们需要知道，古代学生与现代学生在智力上并无太大差别，老师首先教授基本知识，再逐步讲授高等知识。数学作为一门实用科学十分复杂，涉及房屋建造、各类家具器皿的制作、田地测量等等。所以数学还会包括基本的平面、球面几何知识，以及一些基本物理知识。数学知识还包括计算日期，如日食、月食、夏至、冬至，而这些属于特殊学问，只由高等学生学习。孔子之前的三代时期，天文事务由专门机构负责。这里顺便提及一事，古人比我们现代人具有更高的天文学知识，只是我们不恰当地称其为占星术而已。农民和牧民比居住在大城市里的居民更了解星辰和季节的变化，因为他们的生活与大自然直接相关。欲了解古代数学知识，可以参考三部有关"礼"的经典。而《九章算术》，据称成于公元前 2700 年的黄帝时期，实为后世的伪托。

"书"实际上是一门技艺，现在称为书法。因其有关于文字、发音、字义以及不同书写方式的学习，可视其为字源学。古人在竹子上书写，将竹片经火微烤，除去绿色，表面涂漆，再用皮绳捆绑，这都需要一定的技术和经验。这是保存人类知识的唯一途径，这一技术可算是独立的技艺。

"射""御"在今天属于体育，古时亦然。这两门技艺都有关于特定的

114.《论语·阳货篇第十七》，第 4 章。

115.《论语·先进篇第十一》，第 17 章。

仪式，只是早已废弃。古代战车和货车的构造不同于后世，古代的仪式也不再举行了。《庄子》《列子》《吕览》中，仍然可以读到有关射箭和驾车的技艺，记述得十分精彩，弓、箭和手臂好似一机械装置，又或马匹、御手和战车几乎为一有生命的身体或一有机整体。现存经典《周礼》中，可见到弓、箭、车、轮的制造方法。18世纪的学术研究辅以现代考古发现，可以提供有关这些物件的准确信息。驾驶技术包含关于马的知识，在汉代发展成为专门的相马术，以最优良的马为模型铸成铜像。而在今天，这些只会引起学术研究方面的兴趣了。"射""御"最初的用意就是训练身体，例如拉开强弓，通常在弓弦上挂重物以度衡力量，或者驾驭六匹马六个缰绳的车，这对力量有很高的要求。对于这种训练来说，打猎或战斗是次要的目的。作为普通体育教育的一部分，这两门技艺并非仅仅为了增强肌肉力量，如希腊罗马世界的运动员所为，而是为了培养具有高度文化修养的武士，因为这两项技艺与"礼"密切相关。

中国的古乐未能流传下来，这很不幸。"礼坏乐崩"这句话出现在汉武帝的诏书中，时为公元前124年6月。自那时起，历朝历代的学者和乐师都曾努力恢复古乐，每次恢复都有新的发现，但是古乐的重建无论如何不能算是完全成功。即便到了今天，仍然有学者致力于此，完美的成就只能期待于将来了。古乐器的重造可以求助于考古发掘或者古代文献记载，乐理可以研究（尤其是有关心理学的部分），但演奏能否与周代相同呢？

根本问题是，无论古代或现代音乐、经典或浪漫音乐，虽不一定在不断进步，但一定都在不断变化。周代之初，商王的宫廷乐师带着乐器失散四处，到周公重建音乐时，已有了很大的不同。[116] 这次重建几乎全部局限于宫廷音乐，演奏于宫廷庆典、宗祠祭祀或军队之中。这可称作经典音乐，至少经历了七八百年的变迁。与此相伴的还有普通百姓的音乐，可能不够精致，但一定很流行。这流行音乐也被称作"俗乐"，它不断吸收异域的元素，一直存活至今。

孔子之时，经典音乐仍在，音乐教育从未被忽视过。教学童以歌以舞，弹奏各种乐器，通常以金属、石头、皮革、蚕丝、树木、竹子等自然材质制成。[117] 大司乐掌管国学教育，监管国家教育政策。君子无特殊缘故，不撤琴瑟，只有为父母服丧之时才会停止。孔子生活之中有关音乐的记载有如下几处：

> 子与人歌而善，必使反之，而后和之。[118]

> 子于是日哭，则不歌。[119]

> 孺悲欲见孔子，孔子辞以疾。将命者出户，取瑟而歌，使之闻之。[120]

.

116. 参见《论语·微子篇第十八》，第 9 章。
117. 参见《周礼·春官宗伯第三》。
118. 《论语·述而篇第七》，第 32 章。
119. 同上，第 10 章。
120. 《论语·阳货篇第十七》，第 20 章。

"礼"为六艺之首，相对来说是幸运的。汉代之前，"礼"处于衰败之中，但是得到了部分的恢复。在现代语言中，"礼"确有"礼节""礼仪""礼貌"之义，但在古代，"礼"的含义更加深广，英文中没有对应词。大体上说，古希腊负责庆典的机构和现代的教会仪式都包含在"礼"中。关于"礼"的内容，需要做三个层面的区分：第一，理论体系或哲学；第二，实践，包括所有礼仪、礼节和得当的举止；第三，物质对象。举一个最简单的例子，送朋友礼物，首先要有原因，其次是送的方式，最后是礼物本身。在理论层面，其中蕴含着深层的心理、伦理，尤其是逻辑因素。在根本上这是一门有关区别的知识，区别正确与错误、高上与低下、真与假、美与丑、区别大众与个体之行为、责任和成就的价值。

古人将"礼"解释为"培育"或者"文化（动词）"（荀子语），旨在获得理想的生活方式。我们的全部存在，丝毫不遗，都在此培育和文化范围之内。细微的情绪、感情和感觉经由音乐教育细心培育，美感在其中起着重要作用。"礼"与"乐"犹如同胞兄弟姐妹一样共同前行。礼乐未曾忽略个人的情命体，而是使其规范，将力量导向正当渠道，使激情不致失控迸逸。全然去除欲望，在大众是不可能的事，应当以和谐的方式予以规范，"欲必不穷乎物，物必不屈乎欲"（荀子语）。

从外部观看，"礼"是得体的行为、礼仪和礼节规范，必须在儿童时期学习，或者换个说法，以理想的生活方式教育儿童。只有圣人如周公可以制定这样的规范，亦如只有梭伦这样的智者才能给雅典人立法。在普罗大众中使用惩罚性或禁止性的法律，行恶事会受到惩罚。而"礼"作为一种规范，悄然地除去了行恶的根源，其在根本上有转化之功，并先行于法律之前。但是，无论这规范的效用在当世，或在仍遵从这规范的后世，有多么广大无边，却都是不甚明显的。在和平与和谐的社会氛围中，犯罪事件很少，但是没有人能统计出有多少犯罪是因为规范之效用而没有发生。毋庸置疑，这种社会氛围的益处是不容否认的，其影响巨大。孔子晚年并没有修编法律条文，这本身就显示出他所做的工作更为重要和根本。

佛教戒律亦教导提撕生命的正确方法，与"礼"非常相似，但是"礼"在本质上更加灵活，更加强调理想生活方式的内中向度，而非外部规范。外部规范会随着时间而变化，但其核心本质却不变，这正是周代各家思想教导的首要之事。有关于此，孔子有如下论说：

> 孟懿子问孝。
>
> 子曰："无违。"
>
> 樊迟御。子告之曰："孟孙问孝于我，我对曰，无违。"
>
> 樊迟曰："何谓也？"
>
> 子曰："生，事之以礼；死，葬之以礼，祭之以礼。"[121]
>
> 子张问："十世可知也？"
>
> 子曰："殷因于夏礼，所损益，可知也；周因于殷礼，所损益，
>
> ·

---

121. 《论语·为政篇第二》，第 5 章。

可知也。其或继周者，虽百世，可知也。"[122]

子曰："夏礼，吾能言之，杞不足征也；殷礼，吾能言之，宋不足征也。文献不足故也。足，则吾能征之矣。"[123]

以上三段文字的英译文中，分别使用了"propriety""manners"和"ceremonies"翻译"礼"。如前所述，"礼"是不断变化的，但其本质不变。"杞"是夏代王族后裔的封国。依据古礼，战胜国不应该灭绝被征服王朝的后裔，应分给他们一处封地，以侍奉其祖先。这一古礼一定是源于"仁"的动机，亦是所有古礼的源出处。殷代后裔也同样得到一块封地，即"宋"。伟大的制度跟随伟大的王朝一同消亡了，记录和书籍也被销毁，能够讲述以往建制的贤人也逝去了，因此孔子认定无误的许多事情都无法得到证实。事实上，夏商两代王者的合法后裔一直存续在后世王朝之中，享有祭祀祖先的职责。

子曰："禘自既灌而往者，吾不欲观之矣。"[124]

这也是"礼"的一部分。禘礼复杂，耗时长，奠酒之后，真正的仪式才开始，而这些皆非鲁公所应为，所以孔子认为剩下的就不值得再看了。孔子仍然遵从周礼，但是在孔子之时，诸侯所行之礼已经逐渐发生了改变。

子贡欲去告朔之饩羊。子曰："赐也！尔爱其羊，我爱其礼。"[125]

每年秋末，周天子派使者向诸侯国颁布来年的历法，使者走遍所有诸侯国大约需要三个月。我们不清楚这历法的具体内容，但历法确定出闰月和每月的第一天。各诸侯国要用羊来款待颁布历法的使者，这是古礼。自周景王起[126]，周王不再派使者前往诸侯国颁布历法了，而鲁国每年依旧献羊。子贡认为，既然此礼已经不存，羊也不用再献了。但孔子以为，如果取消献羊，这一古礼就真的荡然无存了。

子曰："事君尽礼，人以为谄也。"[127]

定公问："君使臣，臣事君，如之何？"
孔子对曰："君使臣以礼，臣事君以忠。"[128]

·

122. 《论语·为政篇第二》，第 23 章。

123. 《论语·八佾篇第三》，第 9 章。

124. 同上，第 10 章。

125. 同上，第 17 章。

126. 大约在襄公二十九年，即公元前 544 年。

127. 《论语·八佾篇第三》，第 18 章。

128. 同上，第 19 章。

子曰："能以礼让为国乎？何有！不能以礼让为国，如礼何？"[129]

子曰："君子博学于文，约之以礼，亦可以弗畔矣夫！"[130]

这句话中的"君子"是古代誊抄者的误写，主语是普通人或任何人。[131]

陈司败问："昭公知礼乎？"

孔子曰："知礼。"

孔子退，揖巫马期而进之，曰："吾闻君子不党，君子亦党乎？君取于吴为同姓，谓之吴孟子。君而知礼，孰不知礼？"

巫马期以告。

子曰："丘也幸，苟有过，人必知之。"[132]

子曰："恭而无礼则劳，慎而无礼则葸，勇而无礼则乱，直而无礼则绞。君子笃于亲，则民兴于仁；故旧不遗，则民不偷。"[133]

子曰："兴于诗，立于礼，成于乐。"[134]

子曰："上好礼，则民易使也。"[135]

子曰："……知及之，仁能守之，不庄以莅之，则民不敬。知及之，仁能守之，庄以莅之，动之不以礼，未善也。"[136]

子曰："君子义以为质，礼以行之，孙以出之，信以成之。君子哉！"[137]

子曰："礼云礼云，玉帛云乎哉？乐云乐云，钟鼓云乎哉？"[138]

宰我问："三年之丧，期已久矣。君子三年不为礼，礼必坏；三年不为乐，乐必崩。旧谷既没，新谷既升，钻燧改火，期可已矣。"

子曰："食夫稻，衣夫锦，于女安乎？"

曰："安！"

"女安则为之！夫君子之居丧，食旨不甘，闻乐不乐，居处不安，

·

129. 《论语·里仁篇第四》，第 13 章。

130. 《论语·雍也篇第六》，第 27 章。

131. 参见《论语·颜渊篇第十二》，第 15 章。

132. 《论语·述而篇第七》，第 31 章。

133. 《论语·泰伯篇第八》，第 2 章。

134. 同上，第 8 章。

135. 《论语·宪问篇第十四》，第 41 章。

136. 《论语·卫灵公篇第十五》，第 33 章。

137. 同上，第 18 章。

138. 《论语·阳货篇第十七》，第 11 章。

故不为也。今女安，则为之。"

宰我出。子曰："予之不仁也！子生三年，然后免于父母之怀。夫三年之丧，天下之通丧也。予也有三年之爱于其父母乎？"[139]

上述引文可使我们对"礼"有一总括的理解。孔子的弟子有子对"礼"的解说也值得一读：

有子曰："礼之用，和为贵。先王之道斯为美，小大由之。有所不行。知和而和，不以礼节之，亦不可行也。"[140]

．

139.　《论语·阳货篇第十七》，第 21 章。

140.　《论语·学而篇第一》，第 12 章。

第七章

《诗》《礼》《乐》

世间最痛苦的事莫过于晚年丧子。孔子回到鲁国之后，退出政治生活，将精力集中在后代人身上。孔子受到诸侯国的尊敬，身边是一群天赋极高的弟子，其中大多数都由孔子亲自教育。对于孔子来说，这是一段平静福乐的圣贤时光。然而在孔子返回家乡的当年，他唯一的儿子去世了。幸而孔子身边还有一个孙子，后来成为伟大的哲学家。这是第一个大不幸。两年之后，孔子最心爱并且期许最高的弟子颜渊也去世了，不间断的内中苦行拖垮了颜渊本就羸弱的身体，或许贫困的物质生活也是原因之一。这一损失对于孔子来说也许更大。翌年（公元前481年），孔子年龄最大的弟子子路在卫国内乱中被杀。子路的悲惨结局，孔子早有预感，当他听到卫国爆发内乱的消息时，就说子路难免赴死，结果言中！这又是一个大不幸。后人评价，因为颜渊，众弟子对老师和同门有了更多的爱；因为胆大耿直的子路，诽谤和亵渎才未能损及老师。伤痛时刻，圣人悲哀不已。我们或许会问：圣人也会流泪吗？会的，孔子恸泣，或许如孩童一般地哭。孔子是作为有血有肉的人而被长久地传颂着。

儒家之名望可比肩于任何古希腊哲学流派，但儒家流布更广。或者更相近于古印度的阿施蓝（Ashram）。孔门在春秋两季分别教授《礼》和《乐》，冬夏教授《诗》和《书》。孔子不经常亲自讲授，而由弟子代授。孔门渐渐壮大至堪比国立大学的规模，然而其卓越程度则更有过之，因为有孔圣在也。孔子殁世后，儒家兴盛之势有增无减。

孔门所授"六艺"是六部经典。这些经典远在孔子之前便存在了，孔子仅做了编订的工作。"今文经"学派有学者认为，六经皆始于孔子，这观点虽不能说完全正确，亦非毫无根据。保存至今的"六经"（实为"五经"）经过孔子修订，但他的工作仅限于编辑和整理。孔子晚年的工作包括：

（1）编订《诗》和《书》

（2）编辑《礼》和《乐》

（3）注释《易经》

（4）修订《春秋》

"六经"中除《乐》佚失之外，其他"五经"一直流传至今，读者自可选读，在此不做详论。中华民族占世界人口三分之一，其两千五百年之历史与此六部经典偕同并行。"六经"源于圣人爱人之心，具有无限且永恒之价值，中国文化之主体集聚于此，其所源出之本很值得我们深究。

但是当我们触及中国经典时、问题变得颇为复杂。几乎所有儒家经典以及其他大部分经典，都经历过严重的毁坏，且残缺不全。第一次毁坏发生在公元前 213 年，秦始皇焚书。除一部分医药、农业、园艺和占卜之书以外，所有民间藏书都被政府收缴并焚毁。虽然后果没有想象的那样糟糕，但这是对古代文化的致命一击。此为中国历史上第一次焚书，但政府藏书保存完好。真正的悲剧发生在公元前 206 年，秦朝都城咸阳陷落。刚刚落成六年，堪比世界奇迹的宏伟建筑阿房宫被夷为平地。叛军洗劫并烧毁咸阳宫殿之前，后为汉朝丞相的萧何搜查宫殿，但只是取走地图和户籍。萧何太过短视，或因过于匆忙，并未顾及官府藏书。不久之后，汉朝建立，国土重归和平，才有搜集古书、撰写新书之事。接着第二次毁坏发生在公元 23 年，第三次在公元 190 年，第四次在公元 307—312 年。除第四次多少是有意为之，其他两次都不似第一次计划周密。之后还有三次小的毁坏发生。[141]

我们见到，一个庞大民族的文化遗产历经一次次毁坏和重建的循环。这不独发生在中国，欧洲迫害基督教时期曾经焚烧"圣经"，印度曾经焚烧佛教书籍，公元 642 年哈里发奥玛下令摧毁了亚历山大城图书馆。甚至在 20 世纪，希特勒烧毁书籍的行为算是这一古老做法的最后回响。书籍是人类知识最出色的保存库，然而只要人类的本质不变，无论多么有价值或有用的书籍，都永远无法逃脱永恒时间的宿命。如何避免这样的历史灾难再次上演，是人类所面临的一个重要问题。

古代农业社会，物质进步或革新缓慢，时间因素从未如今天一样显著，几百年可能悄然逝去。第一次焚书之后，不同派别的孔门教义传统被保存下来，没有太大变化。汉初，有旧时儒生能够背诵经典，凭记忆写出被焚毁的经典。这些经典以当时流行的文字书写，形成所谓"今文经"。[142] 公元前 156 至前 143 年，一次重大发现对中国文化史产生了前所未有的影响。鲁国孔庙墙壁内发现大量古书，古书的年代距孔子时代不远，全部用"古文"书写。这些书籍所用文字已经不再使用，但仍然可以解读，许多古代典籍由此重新出现，并转写为"今文"。这些古书的内容与"今文经"内容大体相符，亦有不同，如解读、注释和篇章段落数量上存在差别。也有部分文字完全无法解读，内容含混模糊，学者对此亦无能为力。儒家学者从此分为今文经学派和古文经学派，各自以为正宗。实际上，两派各有优缺点。然而两方争执不下，一直延续到今天，这也是很自然的事。

国外汉学家不必深究儒家学派之间的细微差别，因为准确翻译一部中国经典已经是极难的事，何况还有很多著作没有翻译。但是大体的了解还是必要的。在今文经学派内部，依传统不同而有分别。以前文大量引用的《论语》为例，《论语》并非六经之一，今文经学派的《论语》分为齐《论语》和鲁《论语》，是《论语》在齐国和鲁国的不同传承。除了内容上的

.

141. 历史表明，对特定书籍采取消极措施进行销毁，基本是无效的，然而积极地收集图书，编纂系列图书，却使许多书籍消亡了，如清王朝在 18 世纪编修《四库全书》时所采取的强权做法。

142. 有关中国经文史，可以参考作者的另一部小书《字源学视角下的汉语言分析》。

微小差别之外，前者有 22 篇，后者只有 20 篇。根据可靠的记录 [143]，曾有古文经《论语》100 篇，汉代删去含混和重复的章节，简编为 30 篇。另外一古文经《论语》在当时只有 21 篇。古文经《论语》和齐《论语》都已佚失，我们现在读到的只剩鲁《论语》，属于今文经学派。然而，我们仍能在汉代郑玄的注释中窥见佚失版《论语》的片段，因为郑玄在注解经典时，广泛引用了当时仍然存在的各版《论语》。原文或阐释中的一字之差常常引出理论上的重大分歧，文本越是神圣或权威，所得结论的差异就会越大，《论语》即是如此。

我们面临的问题比较复杂，必须先对经典有十分全面的了解，才能切实理解孔子修订经典的用意。我们需要了解学派之间的分歧，并且具备一些辨别文献真伪的知识，许多工作前人已经做过，多有定论。伪古书也有其价值，因为其中经常含有可用的历史资料，但是仍要视其为伪书。例如，现存有两本记录孔子言行的书，皆为公元 3 世纪王肃的伪造。其一是《孔子家语》10 卷 [144]，其二是《孔丛子》，连同附录共 20 篇，记有孔子与弟子之间的对话。儒学研究可以参考这些书籍，但是不能以其为确实可信。伪书成因很多，且数量巨大，但伪书作者却不必受到过分地责难。另有《越绝书》，据称作者是孔子弟子子贡，实为汉代的袁康。

考虑以上因素，我认为最安全且最确实的方法是以经典解释经典，完全依靠除去所有注释的可信文本，本书所采用的正是这种方法。其次是汉代注释，如果没有汉代注释，许多文本完全无法解读。今文经与古文经的理论都应公正采用，两派观点各有所长。再附以丰富的古代历史文化知识，经由古代地理学和语文学研究之协助，终能使我们清晰地认识这一伟大教义系统的本来面目。进一步的研究可引向石刻、手写卷（如敦煌的发现），以及宋代印刷的书籍。就目前汉学研究的状况而言，对于国外汉学家来说，石刻、手卷、宋书以及唐代开始大量出现的注疏，可以不必投入太大的精力。

孔子晚年编订的四部书应当整体看待。宋代陆象山认为，孔子修书随心而发，没有过多的思量，事实可能确实如此。诗可歌，与乐相连，乐与礼相伴，舞蹈又在其内。所以，孔子所作《诗》《礼》《乐》之内容实为一体。孔子所作之《易》本质上是形而上学著作，《尚书》与《春秋》是历史。"六经"由此成书，分别为《诗》《书》《易》《礼》《乐》和《春秋》。

我们先看这样一段话：

子曰："吾自卫反鲁，然后乐正，《雅》《颂》各得其所。"[145]

这是在说《诗经》。"雅"与"颂"是王宫或祖庙中举行仪式时所唱的诗，伴以音乐和舞蹈。"各得其所"指在正确的时间和正确的场合。《诗经》

---

143. 汉代王充《论衡》中的记载。书名"论衡"，意即"平衡之论"或"公正之论"，内容颇具实用精神。

144. 《孔子家语》有卫礼贤的德译本，可能还没有英译本。

145. 《论语·子罕篇第九》，第 15 章。

中的诗歌具有很高的文学性。[146] 这些诗歌、礼仪和仪式，首先经由周公规范而形成一优雅且详尽的系统，并付诸实施，至东周逐渐式微。天子的权力逐渐衰败，诸侯强大起来，旧系统最后崩溃了。我们可以在历史故事中清晰地看到这一变化。

公元前 635 年，晋文公平定王室内乱，将已经逃离国都的周天子重新扶上王位。天子重赏晋文公，晋文公要求获得一项特权，这特权在今天看来有些特别，但在当时是十分严肃的事。晋文公请求准许自己死后在陵墓中修建墓道[147]，依照周礼，只有周王的陵墓才能使用墓道。周王十分得体地拒绝了这一请求，说道：

王章也。未有代德而有二王，亦叔父之所恶也。

最终，天子赐给晋文公几块土地作为赏赐。[148]

孔子之世，礼坏乐崩更甚。古代习俗变了，古代礼节也无人遵守。王室权力的衰退伴随着礼乐的崩坏，互为因果。不仅在名义上的中央政府如此，在各诸侯国也如此。诸侯的特权也被等级更低的贵族僭越。我们可以读到孔子说：

八佾舞于庭，是可忍也，孰不可忍也？ [149]

依礼，只有天子才能使用八人方阵的舞蹈，公爵使用六人方阵，大夫使用四人方阵。方阵中每列有八位俊美的男童，堂内奏乐，庭外舞蹈。古礼规定了不同级别的贵族使用固定的礼仪，几乎生命中所有的事情，小至衣服配饰、礼服颜色，皆依等级而不同。因为周公的丰功伟绩，他的封地鲁国可以使用天子礼乐，这是周朝建立时给予鲁国的特殊恩惠。但是，鲁国大夫的权力再大，能在自己的祖庙里使用天子的礼仪吗？再看：

> 三家者，以《雍》彻。子曰："'相维辟公，天子穆穆'，奚取于三家之堂？"[150]

这两句诗出自《诗经》周颂中的"雍"，是周成王献给周文王的诗，在祭奠结束，撤除礼器时使用。这首诗显然与鲁公没有关系，更与鲁国大夫没有关系。从这些例子中，我们可以看出那个时代的基本状况，无知与傲慢僭越在贵族礼仪之上，失礼的行为竟被认作传统，并以之为当然，却无人质疑。孔子表示质疑，却不能改变什么。为了寻求问题的根源，孔子着

.

146. 《诗经》有理雅各之英译本，收在《东方圣书》中。

147. 所谓墓道是指通往地下墓室的拱形通道。君王的棺椁硕重，可通过墓道轻松滑进墓室，之后封闭墓道，用土填满至地面高度，只留一关闭的出口，状似城门。普通埋葬棺椁只是用绳索垂直放入墓室。

148. 其时在鲁僖公二十五年，见《春秋左传》第5卷。

149. 《论语·八佾篇第三》，第1章。

150. 同上，第2章。

手整理诗歌，涵盖所有诵诗和赞词，将音乐和礼仪导向正轨。这不是激进的革命，却有转化之力，其效用在人群中逐渐彰显。孔子编《诗》，皆可歌之以乐。我们读到如下文字：

> 子曰："师挚之始，《关雎》之乱，洋洋乎盈耳哉！"[151]

《诗经》开篇第一首诗名为"关雎"，是一首情诗。如前所述，孔子从三千多首古诗中选择了305首。孔子编订《诗经》时，或从一诗中删除一段，或从一段中删除一句，或从一句中删除一字。孔子曾说：

> 《诗》三百，一言以蔽之，曰："思无邪。"[152]

孔子这样评价《关雎》：

> 《关雎》乐而不淫，哀而不伤。[153]

如此，我们可以大致推想出孔子编订《诗经》的原则。孔子把《诗经》作为自己教育弟子的教材使用，他似乎对于《诗经》的知识格外看重。我们可读到：

> 子曰："小子何莫学夫《诗》？《诗》，可以兴，可以观，可以群，

可以怨。迩之事父，远之事君。多识于鸟兽草木之名。"[154]

　　子谓伯鱼曰："女为《周南》《召南》矣乎？人而不为《周南》《召南》，其犹正墙面而立也与？"[155]

　　《周南》与《召南》属于《诗经》第一卷。"正墙面而立"指无法向前走，就是说，无论一个人知道多少真理，如果不学《周南》《召南》，便无法前进一步。关于《诗经》的应用，还可读到：

　　子曰："诵《诗》三百，授之以政，不达；使于四方，不能专对；虽多，亦奚以为？"[156]

　　这是《诗经》的直接用处。熟识《诗经》，除了可以培养委婉得体的修辞能力之外，还可以察知人性，熟谙礼节规范，知晓行动时机。但是《诗经》的主要目的还在于建立人格。深浸在这文化当中的人应是温柔敦

.

151. 《论语·泰伯篇第八》，第 15 章。

152. 《论语·为政篇第二》，第 2 章。

153. 《论语·八佾篇第三》，第 20 章。

154. 《论语·阳货篇第十七》，第 9 章。

155. 同上，第 10 章。

156. 《论语·子路篇第十三》，第 5 章。

厚，仁而爱人。作为一项特殊教育，当综合的知识分疏出不同的枝系，个人只能精通一两部经典，于是战国之后就形成了若干学派。[157]《诗经》内容庞大，含义深远，不能仅从表面来判断其价值。我们来看下面的对话：

> 子夏问曰："'巧笑倩兮，美目盼兮，素以为绚兮'何谓也？"
>
> 子曰："绘事后素。"
>
> 曰："礼后乎？"
>
> 子曰："起予者商也，始可与言《诗》已矣。"[158]

"巧笑倩兮，美目盼兮，素以为绚兮"三句诗中的前两句出于《诗经》卫风中的"硕人"，第三句则只在此处出现。《左传》从《诗经》中引用诗句 150 多处，对诗句的理解和使用非常微妙精到。此处并非道德化之理解，然而一首爱情诗不能只当爱情诗来看，其含义通常更加丰富。对诗的正确理解，在很大程度上是取决于诗的使用背景。诗义在词句之中，同时又在词句之外。总之，这算作一门颇为高深的学问。

《诗经》在历史中几乎未曾发生过任何变化。因为《诗经》一直传诵不断，不仅书写在竹片或丝绸上，同时也镌刻在人们的记忆中，从而幸免于历次焚书之难。今文《诗经》与古文《诗经》基本上没有任何区别。今文《诗经》分齐、鲁、韩三家，各有 305 首诗和独立的解释传统。三家诗在西汉列于学官，各设博士一名。但是三家《诗》都已亡佚。现只存《韩诗外传》[159]，多记古事古语，从中可见《诗经》应用范围之广，但《韩诗外传》并未对《诗经》内容作系统说明。古文《诗经》有 311 首，较今文经多 6 首，存于《毛诗传》中。《毛诗传》属古文经，因其中所述史实与《左传》符契，政治系统和文化组织与《周礼》相谐，注释与《尔雅》同然。《尔雅》是一部古代词典，编撰者可能是孔子的弟子，在汉代有较大的扩充和增补。

因为乐与诗关系密切，而且官学十分重视音乐教育，孔子对音乐也十分了解。我们有理由相信，中国曾存有丰富的音乐文献。不幸的是，所有古代音乐文献都在书籍浩劫之中或之后的短期内毁坏了。除去司马迁《史记》中的《乐书》和班固《汉书》中的《礼乐志》，现存古代音乐文献只有《礼记》中的《乐记》一篇，《吕览》中有六篇（卷二，第二、三、四、五篇；卷六，第二、三篇），以及其他若干零星记录。佐证资料稀少，以至于有学者开始怀疑《乐经》是否真的存在。有学者认为，古代音乐不作记录，只在学校内由乐师口头传授。而且乐师通常是听觉敏锐的盲人，不善书写。歌词保存在《诗经》中，使用规范记在《仪礼》中，原本没有《乐经》。

然而问题并非这么简单。如果原本只有"五经"，为何会出现"六经"的说法呢？"六经"一词首出于《庄子》，或以为出现"六经"一词的那一

157. 参阅章学诚《文史通义》，此书对汉学家极有益处。

158. 《论语·八佾篇第三》，第 8 章。

159. 《韩诗外传》原为六卷，公元 11 世纪佚失。现存十卷本似是后世不知名者编纂。

章是伪作。但《礼记》经解篇引用孔子之言:"广博易良而不奢,则深于《乐》者也。"《经解》讨论"六经",《乐》与其他"五经"并提。更不用说汉代司马迁在《太史公自序》中提到"六经",并在《史记·乐书》中称,"虽退正乐以诱世,作五章以刺时,犹莫之化。"班固依《史记》进一步说明,汉初乐师记录古乐,但不解其意。依今文经学者的观点,孔子书写的文字都应视为经典,那么《乐经》至少有五篇。

问题至此仍未解决。如果《乐经》确实存在过,那么为什么在先秦古籍中找不到任何引述呢?如果《乐经》根本不存在,那么伪造《乐经》之名又是何意呢?《尚书大传》集自汉代伏生之学,多零章断句,有一处引述《乐经》,但不足为确证。假定存在《乐经》一书,并非全无道理,其中应包括孔子所作"五章",如大多数其他著作一样,其中讨论的应该是音乐之心理,即为大司乐在官学中之所教,大司乐在教授学生时想必也有原则和理论。《乐经》或许逃过了秦朝的禁令或焚毁,因为秦始皇和秦二世都喜欢音乐,或以为音乐无害,但是最终全部损毁于秦末战争。音乐理论总是复杂且难于理解,古今皆是如此,所以这样一部以理论为内容的经典一旦佚失,就不可能像《诗经》一样经口述而恢复了。总之,我们现在所说的六经实际只有五经。

礼乐相随,乐是和谐平等之物,礼亦如此,但更注重差别。孔子期许和平之治,以礼乐成就大和谐,万事万物各归其位,重现周朝初期文化之至美至华。然而在孔子之时,社会习俗已然变化,旧事物逐渐消逝。更有甚者,诸侯悄然毁掉了国内保存的古礼记录和文献,因为他们自己不能遵从这样的礼制，即使不以之为多余或有害，也视之为不便。现存的《周礼》并非周公所作，实际成书应在公元前 3 世纪初，是若干不具名的学者用各种材料编写而成，秦代焚书之后，于汉代重新发现。《周礼》未在汉代列于学官。我们现在仍可见到"五经"之《仪礼》，共 17 篇，今文经与古文经的内容几乎相同。孔子对于"礼"曾有过非常多的讨论和解释，由孔子弟子记录下来，之后发现共有 131 卷，加之汉代的发现共有 214 卷。后经戴德（大戴）删除重复和多余段落，整理为 85 卷《礼记》，现存 40 卷。另有戴德的侄子戴圣（小戴）整理为 49 卷《礼记》，是现在最常使用的版本。因此《周礼》《仪礼》和《礼记》（49 卷）三部经典相互关联，任何研究工作都不可能只取其一。这三部经典亦被收入所谓"九经"或"十三经"。

"三礼"之中，《小戴礼记》最重要。《小戴礼记》记述了古礼及其在三代的变化，还有古礼系统的哲学思想（多以孔子与同时代人对话的形式记载）以及孔子弟子之间的讨论。在现代意义上，可视其为一部文化史。目前几乎所有关于"五经"的学术研究都已经被前人完成，自以为有新的发现，其实前人多半早已涉猎过。然而仍有许多工作可做。"吉、凶、军、宾、嘉"礼和细微繁复的礼节，都以人类的深层心理为根基，这方面的研究仍然未有太多的探讨。

让我们来想象这样一幅场景吧：在中国的大地上，一个寒冬的黎明前，宽大的庭院内燃起一堆篝火，装饰华丽的地面，四处燃着明亮的火把，成排的蜡烛和灯台照亮祭坛，光影投向黑暗中的一切，贵重金石制成并绘满几何图案的祭器，犹显神秘；宰杀献祭的各种动物，连同食物和醇酒陈列于前；各级贵族和官员，身着华丽的深色礼服，或沉默伫立，或深深鞠躬。主祭高声引礼，颂词声声，赞歌不断，器乐间起，有男童着礼服，执礼器，起舞于庭。天子祭拜祖先，以其在帝之侧，祭祀仪式延续若干时辰，在平静和谐的氛围中，依次抬出所有祭器。这庄严的景象与天主教的弥撒或世界上任何其他宗教仪式有什么不同吗？中华民族之魂确乎是在这一刻以其完备的荣耀之感和壮美之姿呈现而出，古代人民以此而文化，以此而转入神圣境界。这亦是周代礼制之一分。

第八章

《尚书》《春秋》

　　《尚书》是孔子为教授弟子而编订的教材。《尚书》原本只是保存在王都的古史、讲稿和演说词的汇编，诸侯国存有副本。鲁国与周天子关系亲近，所以庋藏最多。学者欲要从政，须熟悉历史，遂有讲习《尚书》者。《尚书》最初只是零散资料，不成书，没有确定篇章。孔子首编《尚书》，内容自尧帝至秦穆公，跨越一千七百多年。但是此《尚书》教材的最初形态，我们仍然不了解。

　　"六经"中，古文经《尚书》与今文经《尚书》分歧为最大，牵涉问题最多，最复杂。伪古文经《尚书》有两部，其一出现于汉代，旋即佚失；其二有25篇，至今仍在。伪古文《尚书》作伪精良，一千多年间，虽有聪明学者不断质疑，但仍骗过了读者。伪古文《尚书》由多种古代经文之片段拼凑而成，内容多涉高上的道德理想，精心编补成书，极似真作。署名孔安国的《尚书传》亦是伪作。

秦火焚书，有儒者伏生隐匿《尚书》。汉代初年，年逾九旬的伏生凭记忆恢复《尚书》。伏生所传《尚书》列于学官，其弟子欧阳高为博士。伏生《尚书》与古文《尚书》一同勃兴了几代，直至第四次焚书事件，两者俱亡。之后，上文提到的伪古文《尚书》以及伪《尚书孔氏传》出现。直至18世纪，真本《尚书》28篇才被整理而出，并辑出《伏生大传》，但仍有多半原文佚失。经过多代学者的艰苦努力，才得以拨去长久累积下来的层层废墟，见到这古代建筑的真姿。《尚书》是最难懂的文献，措辞和文风都很晦涩，无论古注还是新解，仍有需要我们做的工作。

以上所述为《尚书》。本书第一章中提到孔子编订《春秋》，亦属同一工作。《春秋》有三传，皆是真作。其一作者为左丘明，与孔子同时或稍后；其二为公羊高，其三为穀梁赤。关于这三位作者还有许多疑问没有解决，可以确定的是他们都生活在汉代以前，穀梁赤是子夏的弟子。不同文献对后两位作者的名字有不同的记载，但皆应是父子相袭的同一传统。《左传》重现于汉代，曾短暂地列于学官，后因没有精通此传的学者而被废弃。首次提请《左传》列于学官时，曾在宫廷学者间引起很大争执。其他两传属于今文经学，皆以阐述《春秋》微言大义而见长，《穀梁传》持论公正而显优，《公羊传》则略显偏颇。《左传》多记述历史事实，文风优雅富丽，后世优秀散文家多有效慕者。孔子所编《春秋》言辞简短，如果没有《左传》为之详述，则多有不可解处；如果没有其他两传，《春秋》大义可能因为同样的原因一直含混不明。所以，《春秋》三传亦是一体，缺一不可。

《春秋》应归入经还是史，本书第一章并未给出结论。与其卷入这一古老的争论，不如用现代视角看待这一问题，或更显公正。依古语，"经"是宇宙内超时间之道义准则，多为道德教训，依其可修身立行；"史"则是往昔之成败教训，依其可谙识得失。[160] 宽泛地讲，一者有关事实，一者有关理论。中国的二十五或二十六史即是文化政治史。"五经"或"九经"中包含形而上学、哲学和伦理学，"十三经"中还包含语文学。依章学诚之说，"六经"皆史。最后可说，《春秋》亦经亦史：是一部历史经典，也是一部经典历史。这仍是模糊的结论，但舍此却无更好的说法了。

虽然《春秋》行文零散，但《春秋》三传却并不零散，可以不必顾虑文献问题。有关《春秋》的内容，仍然有许多问题没有解决，或是没有得到正确的对待。试举两例，为何孔子以公元前 722 年即隐公元年作为《春秋》的起始，以公元前 481 年出现麒麟作为《春秋》的结束呢？如果《春秋》是"断烂朝报"，它的权威何在呢？

如前所述，司马迁在《史记·太史公自序》中清楚地说明了孔子修订《春秋》的真正用意。《春秋》虽然是一部经典历史，但整体上符合孔子的理想和中心原则，孔子编订《礼》《乐》《诗》亦是如此。孔子晚年的工作可以分为几个部分，但其主干只有一个。《春秋》是史书编撰的永恒范本，司马迁也暗自效仿，虽然他并未承认这一点。依照中国传统，历史书

160. 《新唐书·列传第二十七》，璿班传。

写本身就是一种"创造"，是圣人所为。即使孔子也不认为自己是在创制意义上的"创造者"或"作者"。他称自己是"述者"而非"作者"，"信而好古"[161]。换句话说，是保存者，而不是创新者。在东方世界，没有人会称自己是圣人，或许只有狂人才会如此。司马迁在《太史公自序》中记述了自己与上大夫壶遂的对话，表明自己的工作仅仅是编订历史资料而已，没有任何"创造"。并且说明，"如果你将我的工作比之于《春秋》，那就错了。"设若我们相信司马迁的这句话，那我们也错了。可以这么想，如果司马迁无意追随孔子，为什么要讨论这个问题呢？在司马迁所生活与服务的汉武帝时期，政治环境已然有所不同，但史官的权威仍如从前。司马迁这么说仅仅是出于谦逊，避免在嫉妒的君王面前显露武断。他没有明确地说出自己的想法，只在对话中稍做暗示。这一对话并非杜撰，却也不必全然基于事实。我们对鲁隐公的生平继续进行深入的探讨，事情就会渐渐清晰起来。

必须假定孔子不会随意选择一位鲁公作为《春秋》的开端。《尚书》以尧帝为开端，因为尧之前没有文字记录，只有不能作为历史对待的传说。自伯禽封于鲁起，传十二代至鲁隐公之父。自鲁隐公起，至春秋时代结束再传十二代。对这么长的时间跨度作如此划分，必定有其原因所在。首先，在《春秋公羊传》中可见如下文字：

> 《春秋》何以始乎隐？祖之所逮闻也，所见异辞，所闻异辞，所传闻异辞。

这段文字暗示三世划分，但并没有解答《春秋》何以始于隐公，只是说明了历史材料的丰富性或者歧义性，也表明了《春秋》整理史料的必要性。我们不禁要问：三世怎样划分？孔子所处的时代为"亲见"之世？隐公之前已经不是所谓的"传闻"之世了？那么，是经由哪些先祖"亲闻"的呢？有一个武断的划分，以前五公为"传闻"之世，下四公为"亲闻"之世，最后三公为"亲见"之世。历史事实是否如此呢？《春秋》注释家都没能给出确定的答案。

公元3世纪末，《春秋左传》的注释家杜预给出另外一种解释，稍显可信：

> 周平王，东周之始王也；隐公，让国之贤君也。考乎其时则相接，言乎其位则列国，本乎其始则周公之祚胤也。若平王能祈天永命，绍开中兴；隐公能弘宣祖业，光启王室，则西周之美可寻，文武之迹不坠。（《春秋左传序》杜预注）

杜预的解释有时间上的考量，平王在位起于公元前770年，终于公元前722年，同年鲁隐公摄政于鲁。这也合于孔子之意，依种种推断，似乎有可信之处。但终究无法确定，我们只能视之为天才的推断。

《春秋穀梁传》没有讨论这个问题，但是对隐公的批评却很严厉。"隐

---

161. 《论语·述而篇第七》，第1章。

公可以让位千乘之国，但不能践行大道。"

后世有宋代学者认为《春秋》的起始并无深义。这种世代划分没有意义，重要的是《春秋》所包含的义则。另有学者以为，孔子所能得到的历史材料以鲁隐公为最早，所以便以隐公为《春秋》之始。以上两种解说堪称狡黠而大胆，将难题消解掉了。

我们现在考察一下隐公的生平。鲁隐公的母亲是鲁惠公的妃子，隐公的出生虽然合乎法度，但母亲一系却略显模糊。隐公为公子时曾率兵与郑国作战，被俘囚禁，贿赂守卫，得以逃回鲁国。惠公给他选定一位宋国女子为妻，可是当惠公发现这女子美貌过人时，竟将其纳为自己的妃子。这妃子后来生了一个儿子，被惠公提升为鲁夫人。不久，惠公去世，因太子年幼，国君之位一直空缺。鲁人商议决定由隐公摄政。《春秋》三传都没有记载隐公继位。

历史记载，隐公摄政第十一年时，公子翚向隐公献媚说："百姓拥护您，您就正式立为国君吧。我请您允许我替您杀死太子允，您用我做国相。"隐公听后严肃地回答道："先父有遗命，允年幼，我代替他执政。现在允长大了，我正在菟裘营建房屋，准备在那里终老，很快会把政权交还给允。"公子翚被隐公拒绝，担心事情败露，转而向太子允献出同样的计策，太子应许。公子翚趁隐公斋戒备祭时将其杀害。太子允继位鲁君，是为桓公。

司马迁在《史记》中删去了故事的结尾，《春秋左传》中却有记述，公子翚派人包围隐公所在之处，彻底搜查并杀人若干，故事更显完整，历史真相也因此没有被淹没。

如此可见，隐公实为一悲剧式主角。隐公成长历程艰辛，几于囚死，侥幸逃脱。父亲不义，而隐公却谨遵父命，顺从履责。国君之位已经在手，他却不受，善以让位，因此丢掉了性命。《春秋》为何没有记载隐公即位呢？因为隐公一直都想让贤，故而从来就没有正式登上过君位。因此可以推断，孔子编订《春秋》以隐公为始，是因为赞许他的德行。杜预的判断是正确的，但是他的解说并不准确。杜预认为周朝会因此复兴强大等等，这过于夸张了，因为东周自平王起便开始衰败，外部蛮族威胁频繁，内部冲突瓦解不断。期许隐公能完成振兴周朝或延续和平大业，皆是不实之望。

《尚书》开篇赞颂年老的尧指定有德的舜作为自己的继承人，将帝位传给了他。同尧一样，舜也禅位于有德的禹，同样得到史书的称赞。司马迁在《太史公自序》中总结"世家"，使用了 21 个"嘉"字。首嘉吴太伯，为世家第一。司马迁嘉赞太伯弃王权而让位。出于同一德性，伯夷位于列传第一。[162] 以至后代，凡有新王即位，都会作形式上的推辞。即使野心勃勃的英雄豪杰，或者冷血的篡位者，通常也要再三推辞，如此几番之后，才会行祭天之礼，宣布自己是新的君王。说之为伪善亦是确实，但是我们却可在这形式中看到传统习俗的力量，没有人会像拿破仑一样，在加冕仪

---

162. 有宋版《史记》以"老子列传"为第一，这是宋代因袭唐代的缘故。在唐代，老子与皇族同姓而备受崇敬。《史记》原是以伯夷为列传第一。

式中表现得那样直截了当，冒没地夺过了王冠。

无论是阅读东方史还是西方史，我们都会发现，王宫是世界上最不幸的地方，是一切阴谋诡计、堕落和杀戮的温床。为权力、王位和宠信而进行的明争暗夺一天也没有停止过。任何稍有头脑的君王都会意识到达摩克利斯之剑时刻悬在头上。于是，放弃与生俱来的王权，在某种程度上说，也不失为明智之举。

在古代，这是不容易做到的选择，就如在现代，富豪很难放弃自己的财富一样。如果这德行并非出于恐惧、胆怯、懦弱或伪善，而是行之以真精神，理应得到我们最高的赞许。朴素人性中总含有谦让、自我否定和自我牺牲的原素，对行为的影响可算巨大。即使在日常生活中，我们也能在礼貌的举止中得见其踪影，这是野蛮社会与文明社会的分界线。如果这一德性发展至极，许多战争和冲突都可以避免，中国的二十五史或许要重写了。这一定就是孔子编订《春秋》以隐公为始的微言。如果在《春秋》中寻找大义，那么，这就是第一个大义。

《春秋》以哀公十四年获麟结束，其时为孔子殁世前两年。于此，有许多迷信的解说。真实情况是，在鲁国西郊的一次狩猎中，捕获一只罕见的动物，已经受伤，但没有人认识，于是被抬到孔子面前。孔子博识，认得这动物是麟。麟极少出现，消息在国人中传开，以为大事。以孔子明觉的心思判断，以此事作为历史书写的结尾是很自然的事情，可能并无什么深意。有后世评注家认为，或出于孔子的不祥之感或悲伤云云，皆可不论。

关于《春秋》的权威性，可说的是，中国古代学者一直遵从《春秋》

之义制定国策。基督教的《圣经》一直被视作个人和社会行为的指南。可能未曾有任何国策建立在《圣经》之上，而许多战争却因其教义而起，或至少冠以《圣经》之名。《春秋》无关个人行为，是国家治理的标指。每当在叛乱或革命中迷失方向，总会转向《春秋》，以《春秋》为准建立新王朝。《春秋》不似西彼拉神谕，不能预测国家前途，却可以提供正确适宜的行动、形式、规范和例证，供人遵循。新国君都要依赖《春秋》证明其即位的唯一合法性。如果依据《春秋》的标准判定新国君是篡位者，不是合法或正当的君王，那么他就要做好准备，使用武力镇压因"大义"而起或受"大义"支撑的无休止的反抗。此类例证在历史上不胜枚举。

可以举一两个事例，展示基于《春秋》教义而制定的外交政策。在公元前的若干世纪中，中国北部和西北部边疆从未有过长时间的安宁，为防御外敌遂有长城的修建。汉代发生过几次大的入侵，经过无数次艰难争战之后，才将匈奴驱逐离境。公元前 57 年，匈奴内乱，部落之间相互攻伐。有朝臣向汉廷建议，认为这是难得的机遇，可派兵一举将匈奴歼灭，永远消除边患。汉帝询问朝臣萧望之，萧望之也是一位大学者，他回答道：

　　《春秋》晋士匄帅师侵齐，闻齐侯卒，引师而还。

　　君子大其不伐丧，以为恩足以服孝子，谊足以动诸侯。

　　前单于慕化乡善称弟，遣使请求和亲，海内欣然，夷狄莫不闻。

　　未终奉约，不幸为贼臣所杀，今而伐之，是乘乱而幸灾也，彼必奔走远遁。不以义动兵，恐劳而无功。

> **宜遣使者吊问，辅其微弱，救其灾患，四夷闻之，咸贵中国之仁义。如遂蒙恩得复其位，必称臣服从，此德之盛也。**[163]

汉帝听从了萧望之的建议，派遣特使护送单于复位，匈奴内战终止，各部落重归和平。之后，单于朝见汉帝，以王的身份受到接待，亦是萧望之的建议。

因此，《春秋》中的区区片语可以使千年之后的邻族免于大祸。历史总是在重复自己，同样的事情也发生在公元 1048 年的宋代，西夏国君李元昊死，留有幼子，朝政把持在三位将军手中。有人建议宋仁宗应分别授三位将军以官爵，使权力分散，西北边疆才会获得些许安宁。朝廷内部照例展开了一场争论，大臣程琳基于同样的原因，引据《春秋》中同样的内容，建议采取汉代对待匈奴的策略。仁宗采纳了程琳的建议，并取得良好的效果。[164]

以上即是历史实例中之孔门教义，中国人亦在历史实际中依其而行。欧洲学者对此可能十分陌生，但这一切都是真实的历史，而非传说。

.

163. 参见《汉书·卷七十八·萧望之传第四十八》。

164. 参见《欧阳修集·卷三十·墓志四》。

第九章

《易经》

现在，我们来看孔子最后着手编撰的伟大经典《易经》。《易经》是中国的第一经典，是儒道两家的第一经典，可能也是东方的第一经典。孔子晚年非常喜欢读《易经》，经常翻阅，串联竹简的皮绳翻断了三次。自基督纪年起，每年至少出现一本列在《易经》名下的书。不计各种小册短文，有关《易经》的传、注、义、疏、释及论文，现存已有两千多本。几乎每位名副其实的中国学者都读过《易经》，读过之后，自然要写下或长或短讨论《易经》的文章。编撰学者文集，如果有研究《易经》的文章，一定列在文集之首，因为《易经》位列诸经之首。除学者之外，其他社会阶层的人也阅读《易经》。《易经》虽然关涉形而上学，但大多表以具体形象。政治家处理政务，军人指挥战役，医生治疗疾病，工匠建筑房屋、修建坟墓，瑜伽师调息修行，武术家、算命先生，甚至书法家，都会参阅《易经》，并以《易经》为基础创建理论。《易经》在本质上牵涉宇宙，与以往人类知识的所有分支都有关联，所以我们应当向读者简短地介绍一些细节。

从整体看，现存《易经》文本不算零散，但仍有残缺之处。《易经》主要使用于诸侯和君子，我们无法确知《易经》如何逃过了秦始皇焚书的劫难。汉初恢复经典，《易经》列于学官，田何为博士，再传约分为三支，皆属今文经学派。古文《易经》有博士费直，自东汉起兴盛若干世纪。两派《易经》都可追溯至子夏 [165]（其他流派亦如此），最终归至孔子。

《易经》"十翼"应为孔子所作，分别为《彖传》上、下，《象传》上、下，《大传》上、下，《文言》，《说卦》，《序卦》和《杂卦》。

《隋书·经籍志》记载，《说卦》《序卦》《杂卦》晚出，遂怀疑并非孔子所作。至宋代欧阳修怀疑《大传》和《文言》皆非孔子所作。西汉称《大传》，至东汉称《系辞传》或《系辞》。《文言》《系辞》大部分是儒者所作，以"子曰"开始的文字基本是后世讲师加入的可靠引文。因《易经》也用于占卜，《杂卦》和《说卦》是无名占卜师所作。[166]

近几年，渐有西方读者通过译本对《易经》产生了一些兴趣，这值得

·

165. 这里有一个容易忽略的小问题：西汉学者韩婴，字子夏，精通《诗经》，还教授《易经》。而另有一子夏，是孔子的弟子，名卜商。见《清史稿》卷四百八十一，列传二百六十八，臧庸传。

166. 《文言》非孔子所作最有说服力的证据是，《文言》解释乾卦的首段话与《左传》中穆姜所说相同，而其时早于孔子出生 12 年。而且很难证明这段话是由后人窜入《左传》。

我们花费一些篇幅，从中国传统的视角，对这部经典的某些方面做一些概括性的说明。德国汉学家卫礼贤和英国贝恩斯的译本都非常好。通常而言，译文之完美自有其限度。语言终归是难以克服和逾越的障碍，书写方式完全不同的两种语言之间尤其如此，圆凿方枘不能相合。一般来说，诗和韵文是无法翻译的，而《易经》兼含这两种文体，其中有很多对仗工整的韵文。对此只能忽略不计，这属于外部形式，对于我们来说，最重要的是内容。然而《易经》文本并没有完全确定的诠释。对《易经》的语文学研究，尤以清代学者为盛，他们在 18 世纪所做的工作几乎穷尽了这一领域的研究，值得我们钦佩。《易经》的德文译本仅参考了朱熹（1130—1200）的注释，朱熹的注释是用于科考的标准本。朱熹注释最明显的不足是他的模糊性。当然，诠释《易经》这样的古代神秘著作，模糊性的注释也许是最好的方法，可以给未来的研究留出空间，但这样就缺少学术性，也不是真正的科学方法。然而朱熹是一位深蕴经典的伟大学者，说他没有正确理解《易经》是不妥当的。德译本《易经》的遗憾，乃是没有参考朱熹之后的成果。

18 世纪对《易经》的研究主要集中于语文学领域，或说其文字层面，这是我们现在要讨论的四个方面之一。关于《易经》的形而上学问题，先不做讨论。虽然《易经》本质上属于形而上学，但我们倾向于不称其为"哲学"，以现代方法将《易经》整理为一系统化的哲学是非常不明智的做法。正如亚里士多德代表希腊逻辑，乔荼波陀（Gaudapada）和其他论师代表印度逻辑，墨子和其他名家（现在几乎消亡）代表中国逻辑，本质上彼此所论相同，但是形式不同，所以不能以其中之一系统规范其他系统，应当使其各自独立。《易经》也是如此，它的建构如此圆整，内容如此复杂多元，向外扩展出如此多的分歧和对立，我们无法将其规范并纳入适应现代思维的新程式。我们可以全般接受《易经》，以其中的一切为当然，得出自己的结论，或者，我们可以全般忽略或否定它。《易经》虽然源出于远古时代，但仍是具有生命力的知识，它拥有未被现代知识体系破坏的独立程式。

中国的形而上学主要包括三部书：第一部是《易经》，第二部是《老子》，第三部是《庄子》。《易经》研究"有"（Being），以此为基础，进而通过其他两部书研究"非有"（Non-Being），这三部书可以使研究者完整地理解"有"与"非有"。完整地理解"有"与"非有"意味着圆成于"道"，"超上之有"，或以现代语言表之为与上帝合一。这是一条通过心思之上层知觉性而进阶的精神修习之路。可以说，以此成就进而欲求解脱，只不过是顺带之事。

追溯《易经》的历史，我们会发现这部经典由四位作者完成，或者应当称之为四位伟大的思想者，在中国，他们都被称为圣人。第一位圣人是伏羲，最先制作八卦。三条横线上下放置组成一个经卦。横线可以是一条连贯的直线，也可以是两条不相连的短线，有 8 种组合的可能。两个经卦上下放置组成一个重卦，有 64 种组合的可能。有两种不同的说法：一种认为六十四卦也是伏羲所作 [167]；另一说法认为伏羲只制作了八卦。第二位

167. 关于六十四卦的制作者，不同学派有四种不同看法，分属四人：伏羲，神农，禹，文王。

圣人是文王，作卦辞。第三位圣人是周公，作爻辞。第四位圣人是孔子，作十翼。后三位人物的真实性是确定的，关于第一位人物，还有需要讨论的地方。除去周公，《易》也被称为"三圣之书"。

伏羲（也称庖牺）仅是传说中远古时期的部落英雄。我们无法确定伏羲是部族的名字，还是部族首领的名字。合理的推断是，在远古时期一个叫伏羲的人制作了八卦符号，又自然地演化为六十四卦。毫无疑问，八卦符号与古代文字的形成关系密切，因为有三个经卦与三个古代文字相同。进而我们还可以认为，经卦和重卦的简单构成意味着它们早于或同时于文字的使用。文字书写的发明不可能归因于某个人，比如传说中的仓颉，中国文字的多样性意味着它的形成一定有多个源头。即使在组织严整的现代社会中，任何人，无论他有多么大的权力，也很难将自己独自创造的文字系统推行至全社会。合理的解释是，仓颉将在当时已经流行使用的多种文字形制标准化，方便使用，因此才有仓颉造字的传说。经卦和重卦的形成也应是同样的过程。伏羲或文王将已经流行使用于远古时代的抽象符号甚或文字整合为一个系统。在游牧或半游牧半农业社会，这些符号可能都具有实际的意义，如"水在雷上，停留"（卦三），"水在山下，泉"（卦四），"水在天上，等待"（卦五），"水在天下，争冲"（卦六），"地在水上，师"（卦七），"水在地上，结合"（卦八），等等。这些符号刻在地上、树上或崖壁上，向路人指示特定信息。在一块贫瘠的土地上，"井"（卦四十八）这个符号可能指示着附近有井。"坎"（卦二十九）这个符号指示着附近有坑。"损"（卦四十一），"益"（卦四十二），"蹇"（卦三十九），"解"（卦四十），"归妹"（卦五十四），"家人"（卦三十七），等等符号可能具有社会学意义，所有经卦和重卦的原初义都早于后世的神秘义。

随着语言文字的发展，这些符号渐渐不再使用。巫师将存留下来的符号系统全部用于预测。还有另外两套早于《易经》的符号系统，都已佚失，只留下名字，内容都不可知。周文王首先注解《易经》，之后周公也有注解，因此称之为《周易》。

以上是有关《易经》于古代社会学方面的讨论，重要与否不可知。如果我们相信人类的整体进化，相信人类社会的发展过程是从野蛮到文明，那么以上论述便可为正确，后世的解说《说卦》可以看作古代传统的余存。一旦这些在远古时代表示实物或属性的抽象符号不再有实际用处，仅仅成了巫师预言的工具，那么巫师就要对这些抽象符号重新进行合理的解释。古圣之言即为神圣之言，神圣之言则有神力，而巫师可从中得到启示。然而依据《易经》而得出的预言，我们却无法理解其存在的理由。

世界著名的心理学家荣格，80多岁时为《易经》英译本作序言，谈到自己应用《易经》的经验，认为因果概念是西方人的偏见。他说，"一个人越少思考《易经》的理论，他便睡得越好。"整篇序言都在努力说明，不能用现代西方思维强行规范古代东方思想。中国的古代学问并没有忽略因果性，但是不关注偶然，巧合（coincidence）同样是不被注意的问题。他们只是确信某种境况引起某个事件，我们称之为偶然，但是此类境况不可知。巧合可以用相对应的事件完全解释，后文会对这个问题进行详细的讨论。

同一事物在不同层面会表现出不同面相。《奥义书》中对"有之部分"（parts of Being）的分割早在汉代中国就有相似之观念。在中国历史上，与其说《易经》是一个哲学体系，不如说是共同的信仰。因果性在物理层面是有效的，但是在情命层面却并非十分有效，在心思层面就更加无效了。我们仍然承认因果性本身是自明的真理，在不同层度上显示出不同的有效性。有层度在心思之上，须经神秘之路方可到达，在此层度内，我们通常理解的因果性或存或亡。而此层度内的事应当求知于全然觉悟之人，而非专心于物质的科学家。摩西和埃及人的木棍能变成蛇，耶稣能把水变成酒，现代科学家无法解释这些事情，我们简单称之为奇迹。如果有人认为这些事是真实的，我们倾向于认为他可能头脑出了问题，或许需要接受荣格教授的治疗了。当我们不去思考其他层度的事物时，就能够睡得更好。然而我们仍然可以假定在其他层度中存在着因果性，只是"面相"不同而已。

《易经》既不是记述奇迹的书，也不是伪装在神秘主义外衣下的一堆无意义的漂亮文字，更不是供迷信人士占卜用的预言集。如果真是如此，《易经》早就消亡了，因为一本欺世盗名的符号集不可能被智识界世代传承至今。相反，关于《易经》的著作多如牛毛，历史上记载了无数《易经》对人事产生有益影响的例证。基本上没有人怀疑《易经》在四个方面的权威性：第一是其文学性；第二是其形而上学；第三是其艺术性；第四是其神秘性。只有第三方面略显模糊，其他方面都很确定。这里引用《易经·系辞上》中的一段话：

《易》有圣人之道四焉：以言者尚其辞，以动者尚其变，以制器者尚其象，以卜筮者尚其占。[168]

贝恩斯的英译文并不准确。她将"以言者尚其辞"翻译为"我们应当用《易经》之辞指导言语"，虽然字面意思如此，然而实际含义应当是"喜好文字的人崇尚《易经》之辞"。即是说，作为一部由诗和散文构成的文学作品，《易经》具有极高、极珍贵的永恒价值。其中所蕴含的某些原则虽然缺乏科学佐证，却是可证的，若非可证的真理，或可称之为可证的信仰。宇宙广大无边，超出人类心思所及，我们必须承认宇宙中不仅只有现代科学真理。我们通常以此为确定无疑，遂有必要略作阐释，为此目的必须转入形而上学。

依《易经》所论，宇宙由三个根本权能组成，即"天道、地道、人道"[169]。"天"即是"上帝"，与"地"合，即为"自然"，"人"为两者间之一极。再进一步可引出一信念，即人是天地之圆成，可影响天地，因此在某种程度上说，人是宇宙之主。《易经·文言》中有这样一段话：

先天而天弗违，后天而奉天时。天且弗违，而况人乎！ [170]

·

168. 贝恩斯英译本《易经》第一卷，第 337 页。

169. 同上，第 377 页。

170. 贝恩斯英译本《易经》第二卷，第 15—16 页。

"先天"行而不与天相违，即是指征服自然，譬如开垦荒地，驯服野马，为生计而开发自然资源。但是仍然应当让自己顺应天时，即是指在正确的时机采取正确的行动，譬如种植应在春天而不是冬天。这些简单的道理不用太多解释，但是其中有微妙处需要我们注意，站在圆心处，任何指向上的微小变化扩展出去，都会在远处的圆周上产生巨大的差异。"人"自知处于"天""地"之间，为一极，是"天""地"之主宰，同时还知觉到，弥漫于"天""地"之间而无处不在者，正是他自己。以印度"大我"哲学最能理解这一点，新儒家对此也有十分清楚的表述。进而，既然人内中具有神圣自性，即可知觉到自己可以转化为神圣。英译"极"为"entity"，很难达意，汉语"极"本义是"屋脊最高处的正梁"或"顶点"，正如我们说北极或南极，表三者中之尽处。换个说法，人既然是天地间之一极，那么自然是一"先天的"神性存在。

对于畏惧上帝的西方信仰传统来说，这样的信仰似乎荒谬至极。然而，《创世记》中说，上帝以自己的形象创造了人，如果视之为寓言，这不过是用另一种形式表达了同样的观念。如果人具有上帝的形象，那么人与上帝相似。"与上帝相似"这句话如果有任何意义，那一定意味着人可以成为上帝。这一观念实际上暗含在《创世记》中，然而为了免于误读，书写此段文字的古圣明智地停笔于此，因为这书是写给所有人的，而非选定的少数人。寻求上帝的努力一直存在于人类历史中，从埃及法老到希腊罗马世界，从印度天衣派教徒和瑜伽师到沙漠隐士和台柱圣徒，尽管大多近于荒谬，如装扮成传说中的阿波罗（Apollo）、赫拉克勒斯（Hercules）或伊西斯（Isis），或者索性以自己为神，接受崇拜，如战胜大流士之后的亚历山大，这些努力表明了一种信仰，即相信人类有进至神圣、成为上帝的可能。中国人的境况也大体相似，只是在精神世界中更为纯净，没有如此狂热，未曾笼罩在祭坛上焚烧乳香或百牲的浓烟之中。

我们可以见到两种文化之间的差异愈加明显，距离也越来越大。中国人的心思从来都不是无神论的，但其信仰的中心仍然在"人"。因为"人"是宇宙的一极，他一直知觉自己在这个世界中的地位。当公正在社会中得以践行，他便满足了，然后将一切归于上帝。然而他的上帝在某种程度上仍在"人"域之内。若将这一思想推至极限，便可以知道，人以自己的形象创造了上帝，与《创世记》所述相反。以基督教的视角看，这是异端的宗教或信仰，其中没有"原罪"概念，没有对神谴的恐惧，也没有对上帝的爱，没有对天堂的向往，也没有对地狱的憎恶。如前几章所述，这"爱"属于人自己，需要他践行并且完成。

这是通往中国人心灵的关键，依此方能正确理解《易经》。神圣圆成是在人的限度中完成的终极圆成，历史告诉我们，人之限度为无限。以人类活动表之，可引出希腊所谓的"大度"（megalopsychia）和"大方"（megaloprepeia），多见于古人及其成就中。这也可以解释为什么佛教较易进入中国，且不论佛陀与孔子的教诲中有许多相谐之处，因为佛教也强调人的自持。基督教（包括犹太人的宗教）曾两次传入中国，两次都失败了，每次尝试都只持续了几十年，目前正在进行的这次传教活动是第三次，历时仍木足百年。基督教过于着重人格神和造物主，着重原罪或死后彼世的荣耀，很难从中国人那里得到积极的回应。虽然一个中国人经过一番努力和自我奋斗之后，最终也会无限谦卑地说："上帝啊，那将完成的是你的旨意，而不是我的。"

在《易经》中，经卦的中间一爻总是代表"人"，"天"在上，"地"在下，或者由重卦的中间两爻表示，即外卦最下一爻和内卦的最上一爻。它总是在中间或中心，处在一个平衡位置，在所有人类活动中起着重要作用。"中"与"和"作为哲学理论源于《中庸》，在音乐中得到最好体现，这会在后面的章节中讨论到（第十三章）。

接下来，由"天""地"可衍生出另外两个原则，暗者为"阴"，明者为"阳"。或可称为二元式一元论，中国人称之为"道"，英译有"the Way""the Path"，或者"the Truth"。阴阳消长为"易"，如白天与黑夜、冷暖季节的相互交替。阴阳的"老""少"之分是相对晚起的程式，至今已有许多世纪。在宇宙的不断运动中，阴与阳或消或长，但不是"老"或"少"，因为"老""少"皆为相对，不确定。发展并非是无限的直线式进程，而是一循环，一者至其极限时便转为自己的对面。领悟、统御和规范两者是"善"，[171] 完成两者是"性"（继之者善也，成之者性也）。虽然这仍是一宇宙原则，但表之以人类层度，便是"仁者见之谓之仁，知者见之谓之知，百姓日用而不知。"

阴和阳在原初义上可指女性和男性。西文曾将"阳"译为"创造者"（the Creative/Das Schoepferische），"阴"译为"接纳者"（the Receptive/Das Empfangende），这两种翻译都不够准确。依照古义，两者之一不能独自创生，只有两者结合才能创造。两者在潜能和量级上是相等的，作为两个独立原则，相互依赖，缺一不可。朱子认为阳总是大于阴，这一说法并无根据，朱子如此论断或是因为他见到天在空间上比地大。"大""小"只能在彼此消长的意义上理解，正如德文"Vergroesserung"（放大）和"Verkleinerung"（缩小）。《易经》之义原是在道德之上，伦理心思在孔子时代进入《易经》，"阴"遂下降至与恶相关了。阴阳在根本上表明性别平等，一者不能离开另一者。甚至在人体之内，无论男性还是女性，完好健康的躯体中阴阳必定是平衡的，缺少任何一方都会导致生命的终结。

接下来，我们讨论"易"这个概念。一般说来，赫拉克利特（公元前525—前475）的哲学中有一种似是的真实性，他认为宇宙处于不断的变化之中，其中没有任何事物是永恒的。他说"人不能两次踏入同一河流"（残篇41，81），或"一切源于一，一源于一切"（残篇59），"神就是白天与黑夜，夏天与秋天，战争与和平，饱食与饥饿"（残篇36）。所有这些观念都可以从《易经》中得到，而且不会陷入玄虚的诡辩之中。同样的观念也出现在印度哲学中，我们不必追究这些观念出现时间的早晚，或者是否曾互相影响。过分强调无常（Anitya）或自然的变化方面，会对生命产生消极的态度，在佛教尤其如此，佛法以无常为四法印之首。而古代中国哲学中的

·

---

171. 此句有德译文 "Als Fortsetzender ist er gut. Als Vollender ist das Wesen."（Tashenauesgabe, *Das Buch der Wandlungen*, S. 276）；英译文 "As continuer, it is good. As completer, it is essence."（*The I Ching*, Vol. I, p.320）；两种译文皆为"接续者是善，完成者是性"，"接续者"（Fortsetzender 或 continuer）一词不能达意。

"变化"理论在发展为思辨哲学之前，转向了"人"。"一切"都在"变化"中，但是"变化"中有"太极"，即赫拉克利特所说的"一"。"太极"生出"两仪"，即阴阳两种基本力量。进而，宇宙中的所有活动都起于这两种力量的运动，扩张或收缩，前进或后退，吸引或排斥，上升或下降，永不停止。是二元，但也是一元。

另一方面，《易经》虽然强调变易，却从未忽略宇宙的静态真实。让我们再以人的视角来讨论这一问题。大乘佛教认为人是变化的"相续"，别无他物，对于人来说，几乎没有任何静态可言。以实际用处言，这一理论有助于破除对自我的执着，因为明白了自己不是真实存在的个体，便可获得解脱。但是在中国的"道"中，人是一基本权能，是真实，可成圣成贤，为神性之人。在宗教维度上，这也是人的解脱。现象世界中的"变化"只是"道"的一面，而"道"自身作为变化的根基是不变的。《易经》从未教导过，宇宙中除了变化的相续，没有任何真实存在。所有经卦和重卦中，每一爻代表一种确定的条件，条件是可变的，而其状态是明确的，如"天"的位置在上，"地"在下。爻的位置和顺序不变。"刚柔相推而生变化。"就是说，相对于确定性和明确性，变化是后天的。变化不会随意发生，而是有其"理"在，"理"有译为"logos""law"或"reason"。总括来说，《约翰福音》中的第一段可作这"理"的最好注释。宋代新儒家的学问即是对这"理"的知识。而至上之理即是万物中之理。《易经·系辞上》中可读到：

易简而天下之理得矣。天下之理得，而成位乎其中矣。[172]

所谓"易简"即"简易","易"有"变易"义，还有"简易"义。关于变易的形式，后世分有"交易""互易""反易""移易""对易"，等等。但"易"的正极义"不易"，以及"不可易"义，属于"易"的原初义。因此，"易"有三个明显的含义：一是变易，指多；二是不易，指稳定、稳固，也指不可易；三是简易，指简单。第三义实为一外部属性，可与第二义共同构成一实用的生命哲学，极有用处。任何行动，行以正确的方法和时间，以其不可易性来衡量，可视为圆成。如果达至圆成，既不必再作调整，也不能再有变化，这定是与"神圣圆成"相协之状态。从根本上讲，圆成应在宇宙中所有存在状态之理中寻，而不能只在外部现象中求，因后者总是在变化中。进而，持握某一原则或一原则之若干要点，并以此应对生命中的各种危机和无尽的兴衰起伏，是获得至上结果的关键。将这种态度简化为一程式，即以不变应万变。其中有安宁和恒定，有简易和幸福。所谓"易简之善配至德"（《易经·系辞上》）。继续推论可至老子哲学，在此不论。

这篇简单的文字将近结束，室利·阿罗频多在《柏格森笔记》中的一段话可以引在这里作为有益的说明：

在我们的经验世界中，矛盾常是互补的，彼此依存的。变易的可

172. 铃木大拙因为误读而将这句话错译为，"经由变化（？）和选择（？），而得宇宙之理。获得宇宙之理后，圆满（？）位于其中。"（参见《早期中国哲学小史》英文本，第17页）

能必有赖于可从其变易之状态；但是这一状态的存在仅是作为暂停的一步，变易之相继道路上的一步，或是变易在其创造的道路上转入另一步前所暂停的那一步。在这关系背后是二元的永恒状态与永恒运动，在这二元背后的东西既不是状态，也不是运动，而是包含两者为其两面者——"它"可能就是真正的实在（Reality）。

中国学者称"它"为"理"。"阴阳不测之谓神"（《易经·系辞上》），"理"存于阴阳之中，同时也超越阴阳，所以古注称之为"不测"。

第十章

《易经》(续)

在东方，《易经》所受之关注一直经世不衰，近时亦引起西方人的兴趣，诸多原因中，必是因其有占卜之用。人类对未来一无所知，可预知未来的知识，自然会引起极大的关注和好奇。然而中国智识界从未十分注重对任何事物的前识。但是《易经》的占卜有所不同（占卜亦只是《易经》圣人四道之一），所以仍在中国经典中占有尊贵的位置。孔子曾说，"洁静精微，则深于《易》者也"，但是这一知识的缺点是"其失也，贼"，这缺点是必须除去的。

西方人遇到大的疑惑或挫折，常在《圣经》中寻找指引。在东方，《易经》也有同样的功用，只是这指引需要通过计算寻得。柏拉图在《裴德罗篇》中将这种预言归于"明智"之类，另有"狂喜"或"热烈"形式的预言。每个民族的历史上都有各种形式的预言、先知和神谕。不必说希腊罗马世界，苏格拉底和柏拉图这样伟大的心灵都相信神谕。神谕大多有关于将来之事，因为现在和过去或多或少都已知晓。但是，祭司、术士或先知的神谕似乎没有定则，其所预示亦无共通之特点，虽然大体皆可归之为宗教。古印度的裸形者（Nirgranthas）将魔法程式画在地上。吉普赛占卜师现在用扑克牌作预言，甚或应验，却没有写下任何基本原则，只依经验口耳相传，充斥着欺诈和骗局。《易经》则完全不同，有确定的原则，表之以一组符号，占卜时需要经过确定的计算。《易经》有其独特的系统，若非本性神秘之故，或可称其为"科学"了。

《易经》用数字计算。以现代眼光看，数字和算术本身没有任何哲学可言，依附于数字的思想也十分武断和外在。黑格尔在《小逻辑》中说，"赋予各种数字和计算以重要意义不过是幼稚的消遣，而且还是智力不足的表征。"但是古代中国人认为数字不乏其内在价值。1 是阳数或奇数；2 是阴数或偶数。然而，1 不是一个数字。2 不是一个数字，因为 2 还可以是 1 的正极或负极面。当已经有 1 时，"一与言为二"（庄子语）。孔子在《易大传》中也提到"言"与"意"不同。当有 1 和 2 时，自然出现 3。至此，我们见到第一个严格意义上的"完成之数"。5 包含一个主阳数 3 和一个主阴数 2。而且 5 在中间，5 之前是 1，2，3，4；5 之后是 6，7，8，9；5 被称为"数之祖"。洛水是黄河的支流，"洛书"出自洛水。"洛书"可能成于生活在洛水河畔的居民之手，5 在"洛书"中也居中。"洛书"的内容并不神奇，算得上是"幼稚的消遣"。然而"数之祖"5 正对应毕达哥拉斯理论中以 5 为"婚姻"之数，或是因为 5 是主阴数与主阳数相合之故。如果以

2 和 3 为一对，1 的第一个变化始于 7，因为 1 加 5 是 6，而 7 是 2 与 5 之和。《列子》）9 是数字的末尾，10 再次为 1。如果以阴阳二元原则组合数字，两者都有极限（也称为"老"，即可能变为相反），于是主阳数 3 以 9 为极限，主阴数 2 以 6 为极限，皆乘以"完成之数"3。相乘表示成长至极处，乘以相等之数不仅表示潜能或能力上的相等，亦表示程度之相等。以现代语言表述，在这样一个相对二元的宇宙观中，阳可代表空间，阴可代表时间，在空间上 9 比 7 多，或大，或"老"，但在时间上 8 比 6 "少"，因为在时间序列上，8 比 6 出现得晚。所以，重卦中的卦爻只用 6 和 9 两个数字表示，64 重卦中，阴阳爻数相等，各为 192 爻。这既不是真正的哲学，也不是神秘主义，然而作为表征数字的方便之法，又两者兼而有之。

深入了解之后，我们会发现《易经》中实有一机械程式，不无满足智识好奇心的魅力。但其中没有任何哲学表述，也不存在任何程度的神秘主义。《易经》占卦，需要 50 根蓍草，使用时只用 49 根。古法用蓍草，用卵石或其他物件也可。49 根蓍草随机分成两份，从右边一份中取出一根。然后以 4 根为一组分别数左右两份蓍草。结果可得：左边一份余下 1 根，或 2 根，或 3 根，或 4 根；右边一份对应余下 3 根，或 2 根，或 1 根，或 4 根。此为第一变。合两边余下的蓍草，加上最初取出的 1 根，总为 5 根或 9 根。9 为双，因其中含有两个 4 根；5 为单，因其中只有一个 4 根。将余下的蓍草放置一边，重新合并两份蓍草，再随机分为两份，重新数过。同样的过程重复三次。在第二变与第三变中，左边一份余下 1 根，或 2 根，或 3 根，或 4 根；右边一份余下 2 根，或 1 根，或 4 根，或 3 根。加上最初取出的

1 根，为 4 根或 8 根，4 为单，8 为双。三变成一爻。余下蓍草归总，只有四种可能：

(a) 3 单　　　 = 13 = 老阳

(b) 2 单 1 双　 = 17 = 少阴

(c) 2 双 1 单　 = 21 = 少阳

(d) 3 双　　　 = 25 = 老阴

如此重复 18 次，从最下一爻向上排列至最上一爻，得一重卦。《易经》中该重卦下的文字即是所得占辞。老阴与老阳爻变化之后，还可以得出另一重卦，两个重卦下的文字皆为占辞。从这两个重卦中，还可得出两个经卦，第一个重卦中的第三爻至第五爻，第二个重卦中的第二爻至第四爻。这些都在考虑之内，可谓范围广大。

　　在中国，古时的单数和双数观念与现代不同。3 近似圆周率，被视为圆；4 的平方根是 2，被视为方。"天圆地方"并非物理之天为圆，地球为方，而是天地之道为"圆"（球形），为"方"（正立方体）。（参见《大戴礼记》）表之以现代语言，"天"或"精神"无所不包，无所不在，自为一，故为球形。"地"表示物理自然，其多种多样的真理或物理法则为方，"人"亦在其中，无所逃遁。好似直线，表面，边缘，因此为限制。在计算中，3 为全取，4 取其平方根。于是我们再次见到数字 6，7，8，9，如下表：

	余下蓍草数	数过的蓍草数
(a)	3 单 =3×3=9	36=4×9
(b)	2 单 =2×3 1 双 +2=8	32=4×8
(c)	2 双 =2×2 1 单 +3=7	28=4×7
(d)	3 双 =2×3=6	24=4×6

至此，我们不得不钦佩中国古人的聪慧才智，构造出这样的数字系统，以阴阳爻表现抽象数字符号化的两种力量的前进与后退、联合与分离等等。用简单至极的八卦系统表示宇宙中的所有变化，虽为不可能，然其用意如此，这又是一个加于一种方法之上的另一种更简单的数字表征方法。不幸的是，这种数学智识并没有发展成为任何高等或科学数学，而只是停滞于原始的占卜工具上。只重视神谕和占卜，那么科学自然就不会兴盛了。

下面我们来讨论《易经》的使用。"《易》之兴也，其于中古乎？作《易》者，其有忧患乎？"（《易经·系辞下》）依据传统，人们只有遇到疑惑时才使用《易经》占卜。龟甲上的神谕一般用于询问外出打猎时是否会下雨，这是商代的习俗。"中古"是指起于周初的时代。这时已经个再询问简单粗鄙的问题了，只有重大时刻才会占卜，要在《易经》中寻求适宜的指导，并做出正确的行动。我们经常在生活中遇到两难之境，需要做出选择。疑惑意味着至少有两种选择，好坏差别不大，所以无法选择。如果方向已定，自然也就不需要使用《易经》了。《易经》中经常出现"吉""凶"二字，英文翻译为"good fortune"和"misfortune"，更字面的翻译可以是"auspicious"和"inauspicious"，或者"toward"和"untoward"。严格来讲，算命的性质与此完全不同，我们没理由相信，圣人和伟大的思想家关心盲目的命运胜过关心正确的道路与行动。

另外，《易经》是君子或大人之书，而非小人之书。"君子"一词在《易经》上卷中出现了 58 次，下卷中出现了 47 次，《系辞》中出现了 21 次。可以想见，君子占卜通常会有不同的性质，至少他们并不十分关心个人的"吉"或"凶"，答案中的同一个字可能在另一义度上被理解，不同于寻常的解释。即便如此，普通人仍然可以找占卜师算一算，他或她在远方的爱人何时归来，家人的病能否痊愈。依照传统，可以用《易经》占卜这些问题。只要占卜师对问题感兴趣，问询者心意诚恳，就很可能得到应验的结果。因此，结果应验与否很大程度上有赖于对待占卜的态度。

在传统中，为琐事使用《易经》，也不算亵渎，甚至可以用《易经》作为娱乐。但是，精通此道并能准确预知的人会为此付出严重的代价。这似乎是宇宙中的一个机械法则：不可揭露未来之事。古希腊神话意味深长，发生在这块遥远的土地上的事情可以为相同的现象提供例证。拉奥孔预知木马诡计，正要说出，却当下被蛇缠死了。拉奥孔预知诡计，并非经由任何神秘或超自然的途径，然而即便如此，还是不能说出。由此可见，古希腊智慧表述出了相同的道理。在中国社会中，占卜师、算命先生地位低下，名声最大、能力最强者常常死于非命，不得善终。我们或可怀疑这事实中是否含有真理，但无数经验表明其确实无疑。知晓未来者似乎只能是在上的全知全能者，任何企图从他手中夺取知识的人必受惩罚。若果有人因恩典而获得些许知晓未来的权能，确信其结果（占卜师并非全属此类），那情况自然就不同了。

即便如此，计算蓍草或卵石，为何与遥远空间或时间之外的事情相关联呢？我们或可遗弃整个《易经》系统，罔顾其事实，以之为迷信。大可让"君子"们去思虑，或让百姓为之操心好了。然而神秘主义者认为，《易经》只是神秘的计算。这如何可能？在神秘之域为可能。如此，理性主义者则又斥之为迷信。我们可从历史角度作一稍客观的分析，如果《易经》占卜可以被思维的心思解释清楚，那么这一切早就应当被解释清楚了，这门技艺也不会流传至今。反之，如果思维的心思对此完全无法理解，那就不会出现众多解释《易经》的书籍，甚至《易经》这本书也早就消失了。然而《易经》的深奥教义世代传承至今，其秘密却不曾被大众知晓。据说传授《易经》前，弟子要向老师发誓保守秘密，只传给他们选定的下一代弟子，不然会遭天谴。现代术士认为，不能教授没有能力操控神秘权能的人，老师可能因此失去自己的权能。这几乎是同一道理的另一种说法。然而我们同样有理由认为，精通占卜术的人自己并不了解其中的道理，就像优秀的钢琴演奏者可能不一定通晓乐理或者钢琴的制造史和构造一样。他们依据特定的计算说出特定的预言，却不明白结果为何如此。

我们必须先接受许多事，才能理解占卜的理论或原则。对于明晰的思维心思来说，这不可能是科学真理，只能是共同的信仰。这些信仰中可能有真理在，但无须所有的人接受。首先，我们必须接受宇宙中存在"前定"。水在地上会流经确定的路径，到达确定的地点，在其流动的环境中，必定如此。这可类比于一个人的一生。某种程度上，过去决定现在，现在决定未来。因此，依据过去和现在预知未来并非完全不可能。我们必须接受，占卜进行的那一刻，问题的答案已经确定了。或有哲学家将前定的源头溯至"第一因"，而《易经》的伟大之处正在于此，它不独赖万事皆已注定的宿命，而是将人引至正确的行动和态度。

还有一种与此信仰相关的推断，认为物理层之外存在一微妙层，未来将要发生的一切都已经在微妙层之中完成了，只是还未显现。人的意识通过某种方法能够投射或穿透至微妙层，预测未来并非不可能。许多先知曾经做到，他们的预言都已应验。我们不知道他们是如何做到的，而《易经》的方法是使用一组确定的符号。

易学传统认为，主要的问题并不是预见未来，而是弄清事物的根本或真实。我们必须改变通常的时间观念。在数学中，例如计算日月食，计算过去的日期和计算未来的日期在道理上是相同的。《易经》用符号表示生命的基本原素，放在不同的公式中决定结果，过去或未来皆如此。如果抛弃通常的时间观念，"对未来的记忆"在语言上并不矛盾，在推理上也不违逻辑。[173]

其次，我们必须承认宇宙中的万事万物为一有机整体，处在一平衡的和谐中。中国文化的有益之处或许正是在这里显示：人们被教导要谨言慎行，以防破坏宇宙的和谐。[174] 通常而言，任何"有害或损伤天地和谐"的粗语卑行都是有罪的，这是极严厉的责难。阴阳二元统一原则构成整个有机整体，如果阴阳各为独立的权能，那么两者之间互相变化，运动不止。如果行动和运动停止，那么就没有和谐可言了。任何现象的数据无论多么复杂多样，最终都由这两种力量规范。我们人类存在于这两个原则的大和谐之中，却知觉不到它们的存在。

依此种观念，宇宙中的所有事物都彼此相联，我们的每一行为，无论多么微小，都会对其他人产生直接或间接的效果或影响，反之亦然。这一相互关系甚至在物理层面也是可以想象的。我走在花园中，一只苹果从树上掉下来，会对我发生影响，因为苹果掉下的那一刻，我所在氛围的内中条件改变了，或者说，其内中平衡改变了，正如重力点发生了变化。在某

.

173. 此处有必要介绍室利·阿罗频多的定义："可以认为，时间是行动中的知觉性工作在永恒中，空间是自我伸展中的意识。"（《夜谈录》，第98页）另一处："时间自显为人类努力之敌人或朋友，抵抗，中介或一工具。但它实常为灵魂之工具。……对神圣者来说，为一工具。"（《瑜伽综合论》，第76页）

174. 典型的例证就是，不在鸟兽繁殖的春季出去打猎。甚至死刑犯也只在平和的冬季择时处决。

种意义上，我们可以说，世界上没有任何相互隔绝的事物，所有事物如果不是在严格意义上的相互依赖，也都是相互关联的。一般而言，在精神领域中，空间可以是另外的样子，空间中的距离异于通常。某件有益或有害的大事在物理层面发生之前，神秘主义者常常已经意识到了。这也是可以理解的，因为相互关联包括行动、运动或静止物体之间复杂的交互。或可作一类比，音调的变化改变了共鸣，引进新种植物或昆虫改变了旧植物的命运。在这一大和谐中，力量的作用与反作用从未停止过，只是此时加入了人类的意志而已。如果其为觉悟的心灵，那么便是神圣意志，因为觉悟的心灵与"他"的意志无异，觉悟者依此行事。占卜师不会认为自己是在此大和谐之外，提问者亦是如此，两者都是互相作用的力量，也与力量相互作用。他的职责实际上只是"知晓"，但是"知晓"任何事已经是完成了的行为。他可以采取进一步行动，但是通常止步于仅仅将获得的知识告诉对方。因此，最终我们发现，人的命运是可以改变的。

至此，我们似乎是将一个假设建立在另一个的假设之上，好似空中城堡，没有坚实的理性基础。然而，这一系统并非如我们认定的那样毫无理性，其坚实的基础仍是知觉性。最为重要的是提问者和占卜师之间的心理条件，或者在占卜进行的那一刻他们之间的心理氛围。双方必须真诚，占卜师尤其不能用意，需要近乎机械地计数，勿使喜好或厌恶左右其心思。也就是说，心思混合体不能干扰占卜，高等知觉性须独自指出决而未显的答案。基本上只有高等知觉性在起作用，真诚即是要求心思全力集中于一点。剩下的过程仅是如何有效地解释《易经》占辞，这更多地有赖于占卜师的世俗经验和灵感。

一般说来，《易经》占卜总能得到不可思议的结果，而且从未产生过任何危害社会或个人的恶果。正如"技艺"需要天才，历朝历代都有精通此"技艺"的天才，且成就惊人。我们可从中国的"官史"中引述几个例子：

（晋）公子亲筮之，曰："尚有晋国。"得贞屯、悔豫（"屯"为第三卦，"豫"为第四卦），皆八也。筮史占之，皆曰："不吉。闭而不通，爻无为也。"

司空季子曰："吉。是在《周易》，皆利建侯[175]。不有晋国，以辅王室，安能建侯？我命筮曰'尚有晋国'，筮告我曰'利建侯'，得国之务也，吉孰大焉！

震，车也。坎，水也。坤，土也。屯，厚也。豫，乐也。[176]车班外内，顺以训之，泉原以资之，土厚而乐其实。不有晋国，何以当之？

震，雷也，车也。坎，劳也，水也，众也。主雷与车，而尚水与众。车有震，武也。众而顺，文也。文武具，厚之至也。

175. "利建侯"有英译为"It furthers one to appoint helpers"，还有译为"It furthers one to install helpers"，皆不准确。

176. "震"是第三卦的内卦，也是第十六卦的外卦，"坎"是第三卦的外卦，"坤"是第十六卦的内卦。所以这里出现了"震""坎""坤"三卦。

故曰《屯》。其繇曰:'元亨利贞,勿用有攸往,利建侯。'主震雷,长也,故曰元。众而顺,嘉也,故曰亨。内有震雷,故曰利贞。

车上水下,必伯。小事不济,壅也。故曰勿用有攸往,一夫之行也。众顺而有武威,故曰'利建侯'。

坤,母也。震,长男也。母老子强,故曰《豫》。其繇曰:'利建侯行师。'居乐、出威之谓也。

是二者,得国之卦也。"[177]

占卜结果成真。

南蒯(鲁国大夫的家臣)之将叛也……枚筮之,遇《坤》之《比》,曰:"黄裳元吉。"以为大吉也,示子服惠伯,曰:"即欲有事,何如?"

惠伯曰:"吾尝学此矣,忠信之事则可,不然,必败。

外强内温,忠也。和以率贞,信也。[178] 故曰'黄裳元吉'。

黄,中之色也。[179] 裳,下之饰也。元,善之长也。中不忠,不得其色。下不共,不得其饰。事不善,不得其极。

外内倡和为忠,率事以信为共,供养三德为善,非此三者弗当。

且夫《易》,不可以占险,将何事也?且可饰乎?

中美能黄,上美为元,下美则裳,参成可筮。犹有阙也,筮虽吉,未也。"(《左传·昭公十二年》)

惠伯的话最终应验，南蒯叛乱失败。

如上述两例，汉之前还有许多有关占卜的记载。司马迁身为史官，想在自己的历史著作中保存人类活动的所有分支，《史记》中的《日者列传》《龟策列传》[180]专门记载占星师和占卜师。时至汉代，这门"技艺"似乎繁荣起来，支派甚多。据班固《前汉书》记载，传《易》者有十三家，但其中不都行占卜之事。阴阳哲学为其中一支，与占星术相关。研究这一主题必得参考《前汉书·五行志》[181]，因其主要处理天人关系的问题。汉代著名学者董仲舒、刘向、刘歆（刘向之子）都是天人关系信仰的极力鼓吹者，历史学家班固也深受其影响。然而《易经》占卜从来没有像宗教一样神圣，受人膜拜。《易经》占卜常被视作游戏，汉武帝曾在宫中以《易经》取乐，猜测器皿中所藏之物。大学者东方朔（亦是倍受喜爱的喜剧人物）每猜必中，一次是只蜥蜴，另一次是些蘑菇。[182]人们不以《易经》为神奇，以之为寻常。《易经》并未引出科学的发现，也未曾在中国人的思维中生出任何哲学系统。

177. 见《国语·晋语》。三家分晋发生于基督纪年之前，不可与晋代混淆，晋代的历史后文会有提及。

178. 这句话得自第八卦"比"，外卦为"坎（水）"，内卦为"坤（地）"。

179. 在古文献中，"黄"含义多为"吉"。

180. 卷一百二十七，日者列传第六十七；卷一百二十八，龟策列传第六十八。

181. 卷二十七，五行志第七上、中之上、中之下、下之上、下之下。

182. 《汉书·卷六十五·东方朔传第三十五》。

范晔《后汉书》为从事此"技艺"的 34 人作传，并收为一篇[183]，排在第一位的是任文公，最后一位是王和平。其中还有医师，魔术师，印度称为赫他瑜伽师，隐士或具超自然力者。这些人使用的"术"大多本于《易经》。

紧接汉代的三国时期（220—265），此类奇人亦不罕见。陈寿在《三国志·魏书》中集奇人传记为一篇[184]，其中有著名的占卜师管辂，记载详细。另有虞翻，所著《易经》注非常有名，《三国志·吴书》中有虞翻的传记[185]。继这四部史书之后，历代官修史书中多有此类文字。若翻译成欧洲语言，供公众评判，非有若干书册不能尽收。

聪慧的读者在阅读历史时，不免怀疑此类记载多有杜撰的成分。历史书写有一准则，允许委婉的说辞，但绝不容忍造假，官修史书通常都遵循严格的规范。即便如此，仍不免有些许不实之处。然而史籍记载中出现如此多的奇事和智者，不可能全为虚假。其中有一通则，此类智者多出现在最坏最不安稳的时代。他们受众人敬仰，占卜出的预言大多应验，已成为社会中一通常"技艺"。下文录出一篇载于《晋书》（266—420）的传记[186]，表明占卜术并非君子或贵族阶层独有：

> 隗炤，汝阴人也。善于《易》。临终，书版授其妻曰："吾亡后当大荒穷，虽尔，慎莫卖宅也。却后五年春，当有诏使来顿此亭，姓龚，此人负吾金，即以此版往责之，勿违言也。"炤亡后，其家大困乏，欲卖宅，忆夫言辄止。期日，有龚使者止亭中，妻遂赍版往责

之。使者执版惘然，不知所以。妻曰："夫临亡，手书版见命如此，不敢妄也。"使者沈吟良久而悟，谓曰："贤夫何善？"妻曰："夫善于《易》，而未会为人卜也。"使者曰："噫，可知矣！"乃命取蓍筮之，卦成，抚掌而叹曰："妙哉隗生！含明隐迹，可谓镜穷达而洞吉凶者也。"于是告焅妻曰："吾不相负金也，贤夫自有金耳，知亡后当暂穷，故藏金以待太平，所以不告儿妇者，恐金尽而困无已也。知吾善《易》，故书版以寄意耳。金有五百斤，盛以青瓷，覆以铜柈，埋在堂屋东头，去壁一丈，入地九尺。"妻还掘之，皆如卜焉。

183. 卷八十二，方术列传第七十二上、下。

184. 卷二十九。

185. 卷五十七，吴书十二。

186. 卷九十五，列传第六十五。

第十一章

夫子赞

司马迁曾游历孔子故乡，称自己几难离去。其时在汉，已是孔子殁世后400余年了。司马迁在《史记》中简略地记述了孔子殁世前几日的情形（参见《孔子世家》），大略如下：

孔子病，子贡请见。孔子方负杖逍遥于门，曰："赐，汝来何其晚也？"孔子因叹，歌曰：

"太山坏乎！

梁柱摧乎！

哲人萎乎！"

因以涕下。谓子贡曰："天下无道久矣，莫能宗予。夏人殡于东阶，周人于西阶，殷人两柱间。昨暮予梦坐奠两柱之间，予始殷人也。"后七日卒。孔子年七十三，以鲁哀公十六年四月己丑卒。（以现代历法计算，孔子终年 74 岁。）

鲁哀公写了一篇祭文。

　　孔子葬鲁城北泗上，弟子皆服三年。三年心丧[187]毕，相诀而去，则哭，各复尽哀；或复留。唯子贡庐于冢上，凡六年，然后去。弟子及鲁人往从冢而家者百有余室，因命曰孔里。鲁世世相传以岁时奉祠孔子冢，而诸儒亦讲礼乡饮大射于孔子冢。孔子冢大一顷。

　　故所居堂、弟子内，后世因庙，藏孔子衣冠琴车书，至于汉二百余年不绝。高皇帝过鲁，以太牢祠焉。诸侯卿相至，常先谒然后从政。

司马迁的记述真实不妄。孔里经后世不断重建扩建，存留至今，访拜者每年数以千计。在亚洲，孔学传播广远，说汉语的地方便有孔子的影响在。世人对孔子敬重有加，《孟子》中记载：

公孙丑与孟子对谈：

　　·

187.　依古礼，弟子不必为老师服丧。三年之丧实为死后 25 个月，此处所提"心丧"起于孔子，因为弟子尊孔子如父。此礼于老师不似于父母一样为义务。

宰我、子贡善为说辞，冉牛、闵子、颜渊善言德行，孔子兼之，曰："我于辞命，则不能也。"然则夫子既圣矣乎？

（孟子）曰："恶！是何言也？昔者子贡问于孔子曰：'夫子圣矣乎？'孔子曰：'圣则吾不能，我学不厌，而教不倦也。'子贡曰：'学不厌，智也；教不倦，仁也。仁且智，夫子既圣矣乎？'夫圣，孔子不居，是何言也？"

（公孙丑）"昔者窃闻之：子夏、子游、子张皆有圣人之一体，冉牛、闵子、颜渊则具体而微。敢问所安？"

（孟子）曰："姑舍是。"

（公孙丑）曰："伯夷、伊尹何如？"

曰："不同道。非其君不事，非其民不使；治则进，乱则退，伯夷也。何事非君，何使非民；治亦进，乱亦进，伊尹也。可以仕则仕，可以止则止，可以久则久，可以速则速，孔子也。皆古圣人也，吾未能有行焉。乃所愿，则学孔子也。"

（公孙丑）"伯夷、伊尹于孔子，若是班乎？"

（孟子）曰："否！自有生民以来，未有孔子也。"

（公孙丑问）"然则有同与？"

曰："有。得百里之地而君之，皆能以朝诸侯，有天下；行一不义，杀一不辜，而得天下，皆不为也。是则同。"

（公孙丑）曰："敢问其所以异。"

曰："宰我、子贡、有若，智足以知圣人，汙不至阿其所好。宰我曰：'以予观于夫子，贤于尧、舜远矣。'子贡曰：'见其礼而知其政，闻其乐而知其德，由百世之后，等百世之王，莫之能违也。自生民以来，未有夫子也。'有若曰：'岂惟民哉？麒麟之于走兽，凤凰之于飞鸟，泰山之于丘垤，河海之于行潦，类也。圣人之于民，亦类也。出于其类，拔乎其萃，自生民以来，未有盛于孔子也。'"[188]

另一处，孟子说：

昔者孔子没，三年之外，门人治任将归，入揖于子贡，相乡而哭，皆失声，然后归。子贡反，筑室于场，独居三年，然后归。他日，子夏、子张、子游以有若似圣人，欲以所事孔子事之，强曾子。曾子曰："不可，江、汉以濯之，秋阳以暴之，皜皜乎不可尚已。"[189]

孔子弟子以师礼侍奉有若之事，《史记》记载有所不同。有若比孔子小43岁，形貌与孔子相似。孔子弟子中有人以师礼侍奉有若。一次，弟子问有若：

"昔夫子当行，使弟子持雨具，已而果雨。弟子问曰：'夫子何以

.

188. 《孟子·公孙丑上》，第 2 章。
189. 《孟子·滕文公上》，第 4 章。

知之？'夫子曰：'诗不云乎？"月离于毕，俾滂沱矣。"昨暮月不宿毕乎？'他日，月宿毕，竟不雨。

　　商瞿年长无子，其母为取室。孔子使之齐，瞿母请之。孔子曰：'无忧，瞿年四十后当有五丈夫子。'已而果然。敢问夫子何以知此？"

　　有若默然无以应。弟子起曰："有子避之，此非子之座也！"（《仲尼弟子列传》）

古代圣人似乎有先知能力，尤能预测天气，否则难成圣人。古信史有如下记载：

　　二十二年春，臧武仲（鲁国圣人）如晋，雨，过御叔。御叔在其邑，将饮酒，曰："焉用圣人！我将饮酒而己，雨行，何以圣为？"穆叔闻之曰："不可使也，而傲使人，国之蠹也。"令倍其赋（以惩其傲慢）。（《左传·襄公二十九年》）

孔子引《诗经》作答，本是玩笑，只是弟子未懂。孔子的幽默总是以安适、满足和冷静的态度在生活中显现。孔子的预想应验，表明他确有预知能力，只是不曾展露，也没有传授于弟子。

　　外部形貌的相似与内中相似毫无关系。孔子弟子三千，出类拔萃者是颜子（亦称颜渊或颜回），而非有若。颜子一生贫困，以他的天赋，本可服务于衰败中的鲁国，这在他不是难事。鲁国是颜子的祖国，用现在的话说，这是"救国"，但是他没有这样做。他也可以写出有益于他人的书，这在他也不是难事，他也没有这样做。他还可以收授弟子，但是他也没有。即便如此，同门对他敬重仍仅次于孔子。读如下文字，可略知颜子言貌：

> 子谓子贡曰："女与回也，孰愈？"
> 对曰："赐也何敢望回？回也闻一以知十，赐也闻一以知二。"
> 子曰："弗如也。吾与女弗知也。"[190]

> 哀公问："弟子孰为好学？"孔子对曰："有颜回者好学，不迁怒，不贰过。不幸短命死矣。今也则亡，未闻好学者也。"[191]

> 颜渊喟然叹曰："仰之弥高，钻之弥坚。瞻之在前，忽焉在后。夫子循循然善诱人，博我以文，约我以礼，欲罢不能。既竭吾才，如有所立卓尔，虽欲从之，末由也已。"[192]

> 子曰："回也，非助我者也，于吾言无所不说。"[193]

190. 《论语·公冶长篇第五》，第 9 章。
191. 《论语·雍也篇第六》，第 3 章。
192. 《论语·子罕篇第九》，第 11 章。
193. 《论语·先进篇第十一》，第 4 章。

颜渊死。子曰："噫！天丧予！天丧予！"[194]

颜渊死，子哭之恸。从者曰："子恸矣！"曰："有恸乎？非夫人之为恸而谁为？"[195]

颜渊死，门人欲厚葬之，子曰："不可。"门人厚葬之。

子曰："回也视予犹父也，予不得视犹子也。非我也，夫二三子也！"[196]

假使颜子死于孔子之后，孔子定会传衣钵于他，同门对有若的敬重便可适宜地施于颜子，这是十分合理的猜想。颜子会依随孔子的脚步，教示自己的弟子。孔门正统遂得以延续，或许体量略逊宽广，中国文化史定会生出别样美丽的花实。颜子是极具天赋的圣者——学为圣者必须有天赋，或以现代语言说，具有特殊的精神能力——一切世俗担当对他而言都不重要（例如供职于官府，收徒，或著书，等等）。只有孔子知晓颜子的内中成就。孔子恸哭不已，因为他失去了无可替代的传承者。《庄子》所记颜子言行真假难定，然而颜子确实为凝心与冥想这一脉教义提供了最好的诠释。与此同时，后人依然重视并传授着克己和自制的原则。自宋代起，孔子被尊为"至圣"，孟子为"亚圣"，颜子为"复圣"，正因其克己而复于礼。

如前所述，弟子服丧已毕，各自散去，前往诸侯国，或为官，或为师，其中以子夏为最长寿。公元前 407 年子夏去世时，正与魏文侯讨论古乐，终年 101 岁。"六经"主要经由子夏传授于后学。可以想见，孔子亲手修订的文字在其时代就极具重要性，逐渐形成以"子曰"开头的经典。印度佛教中冠以"如是我闻"的文字亦形成于佛陀入般涅槃之后。精神教义之洪流在传承中分为不同支流，是再自然不过的事了，然而却只能称之为哲学的支脉。其中一支以孔子弟子子游和孔子之孙子思为代表，传至孟子始至其极，以理性主义自立，仍以精神性为根本。另一支以子夏、曾子为代表，至荀子始至繁盛，现代学者认为近于经验主义。两支儒学奠定了宋代新儒家的根基，后者亦分两派，各自又再分，传承各异。后文会有详细论述。论述孔子至此为止，引《论语》作为结尾：

卫公孙朝向于子贡曰："仲尼焉学？"子贡曰："文、武之道，未坠于地，在人。贤者识其大者，不贤者识其小者。莫不有文武之道焉。夫子焉不学？而亦何常师之有？"

叔孙武叔语大夫于朝，曰："子贡贤于仲尼。"

子服景伯以告子贡。子贡曰："譬之宫墙，赐之墙也及肩，窥见室家之好。夫子之墙数仞，不得其门而入，不见宗庙之美，百官之

194. 《论语·先进篇第十一》，第 9 章。
195. 同上，第 10 章。
196. 同上，第 11 章。

富。得其门者或寡矣。夫子之云，不亦宜乎！"

叔孙武叔毁仲尼。子贡曰："无以为也！仲尼不可毁也。他人之贤者，丘陵也，犹可逾也；仲尼，日月也，无得而逾焉。人虽欲自绝，其何伤于日月乎？多见其不知量也。"

陈子禽谓子贡曰："子为恭也，仲尼岂贤于子乎？"

子贡曰："君子一言以为知，一言以为不知，言不可不慎也！夫子之不可及也，犹天之不可阶而升也。夫子之得邦家者，所谓立之斯立，道之斯行，绥之斯来，动之斯和。其生也荣，其死也哀，如之何其可及也？"[197]

197.《论语・子张篇第十九》，第 23—25 章。

第十二章

颜子和曾子

欲要知晓儒学精义，必先了解孔子不断失败而又成就非凡的一生，以及彼时的政治环境，前文已略有记述。孔子的思想塑造了中华民族的命运，对中国历史有着巨大的影响。儒学代代相传，不断演进，孔门弟子着重各有不同，然而儒学大义历久不衰。如一宏伟建筑，总需修补扩建，才能免于老化与残破，但其基本形制从未改变，抑或不可改变。原初的大与美一直保持着，如同高耸的金字塔在沙漠中划破寥寂的地平线，宁静，永恒。

孔门教义的演变牵涉几代弟子后学。孔子的生命是一整体，他的所有言行，无论大小，皆已成为后世的模范或标准，弟子后学与之相比自然稍显不及。后世之师多以言为教，孔子则以其全部生命有体为教。然而，作为孔门教义的倡导者，孔子弟子及其追随者皆能践行其原则，不致违离过甚。

孔子殁世后，儒分八家。八家之儒同出一源，侧重有别。关于这个问题，古文献记载略显零散，但足以供研究之用。我们的讨论将只限于四位影响深远的大儒。

第一位是"复圣"颜渊。我们对颜渊所知甚少，可靠的文字只能凑足一两页纸。除去已经引述过的文字，这里再作一些补充：

　　　子曰："贤哉，回也！一箪食，一瓢饮，在陋巷，人不堪其忧，回也不改其乐。贤哉，回也！"[198]

　　　子曰："语之而不惰者，其回也与。"[199]

　　　子谓颜渊曰："惜乎！吾见其进也，未见其止也！"[200]

颜子在物质上非常贫困，却似乎一直很快乐。他愉悦在真理之中，有恒常之喜悦。宋代考试曾以"颜子所乐何事"为题作文。时至今日，这仍是一个难答的题目。除非答者已经获得恒常的喜悦，否则很难作出恰当的答复。更难的是如何获得这恒常的喜悦。然而有一件事确定无疑，那就是

198.　《论语·雍也篇第六》，第11章。

199.　《论语·子罕篇第九》，第20章。

200.　同上，第21章。

即使没有教授过许多弟子，没有写过 101 卷书，没有做过 1001 次讲演，只要有真实的内中觉悟，也能在两千五百多年的历史中享有盛名。这觉悟犹如悦乐之甘露，在这悦乐之中，财富和名望皆微不足道了。我们可问，如果弟子已经如此，老师则将如何呢？

我们无法确定庄子或其他人是否真的受过颜子的影响，但他们所走的路径基本相同，这是无疑的。无需过多的外部学习或书本知识，经过不断坚定的内中努力，个人可以逐渐获得某种程度的明悟，虽然最终的明悟仍需依靠恩典。书是一定要读的，然而有一个古老的问题：在我们的历史刚刚开始的尧舜时代，那时的圣人读什么书呢？颜子为后世学者开辟了一条道路：从外部来看，他具备完好的儒家德性；然而，在内中，却是简朴至极的道家境界。似乎只要保持"与天地精神往来"《庄子》），知识便可以自为显现。宗教中的所有外部分别消失了。史家立传，将他们归于道家，还是归于儒家，是件不易抉择的事。

第二位是曾子，孔子的另一位弟子。《论语》第一篇第 4 章就记录了曾子的话：

> 曾子曰："吾日三省吾身，为人谋而不忠乎？与朋友交而不信乎？传不习乎？"[201]

然而孔子认为曾子"鲁"。[202]"鲁"是笨的礼貌说法，笨与愚同义。然而没有人能忽略"鲁"之大用，"鲁"能负重担，行远途。在日常生活中，聪明和机警通常会受到表扬。其实如果应用正确，"鲁"也值得称赞，因为"鲁"意味着坚持、集中和耐性。大多数有成就的人并非所有方面都优秀，过于聪明或机敏的人往往最终收获甚少，或一无所获。其中原因可能是，机敏之人的神经能量很容易被强烈的反应耗尽。想要获得最后的成功，改变顽固自性所需要的是大力，而不是快速。孔子认为曾子"鲁"，然而曾子却成了圣人。

《论语》中涉及曾子的文字不多，除去上文所引（本书第五章结尾处），还有可读的文字：

子曰："不在其位，不谋其政。"曾子曰："君子思不出其位。"[203]

曾子的话出自《易经·艮卦象传》。是说心思能量应该导向正确的通道，不能浪费，这时常是每一位智识者都面临的难题。

子曰："参乎！吾道一以贯之。"曾子曰："唯。"

子出，门人问曰："何谓也？"

曾子曰："夫子之道，忠恕而已矣。"[204]

·

201. 《论语·学而篇第一》，第 4 章。

202. 《论语·先进篇第十一》，第 18 章。

203. 《论语·宪问篇第十四》，第 26 章。

204. 《论语·里仁篇第四》，第 15 章。

孔子对子贡也说过同样的话。曾子以"忠恕"理解孔子的"吾道一以贯之"。显然这只是曾子的解释。"一以贯之",字面上理解是"遍在之一或彻底之全"。这意思是,在"一"之中的整全和统一。对于"一"的解释无法穷尽,通常意义上可以理解为个人有体之整全,言行合一。于此最后一句话,理雅各曾有英译文,自然反映了他的理解。"忠",英文有译为"faithfulness",然而"loyalty"或者"truthfulness"似乎更确切。"恕"有译为"forgiveness",亦有译为"considerateness"。然而"恕"含义更宽广,意指原谅和宽恕他人对自己犯下的所有过错和不当。但这只是从负极意义上谈。从正极角度讲,可理解为将爱和善扩展至他人,例如像爱自己父母一样爱所有老人,像爱自己孩子一样爱所有孩子。

孔子之道异常广大。对"一"的解说,我们不能妄称这是定论,或别无他论可寻。如果同样的问题问于颜渊,他可能会给出不同的答案。但在日常生活中,忠恕二字足以指导个人的普通行为。严格讲,践行"忠恕"之道是一项艰巨的工作,尤其"恕"道,更是需要极大的仁爱。"道"广大且艰难。

关于曾子的文字还有:

> 曾子曰:"以能问于不能,以多问于寡;有若无,实若虚,犯而不校,昔者吾友尝从事于斯矣。"[205]

马融注释以为"吾友"一定是指颜子。《大戴礼记》中有一段文字也可提供佐证，曾子十分敬重颜子。

曾子曰："可以托六尺之孤，可以寄百里之命，临大节而不可夺也。君子人与？君子人也！"[206]

曾子曰："士不可以不弘毅，任重而道远。仁以为己任，不亦重乎？死而后已，不亦远乎？"[207]

曾子临终之言亦有教益：

曾子有疾，孟敬子问之。曾子言曰："鸟之将死，其鸣也哀；人之将死，其言也善。君子所贵乎道者三：动容貌，斯远暴慢矣；正颜色，斯近信矣；出辞气，斯远鄙倍矣。笾豆之事，则有司存。"[208]

曾子有疾，召门弟子曰："启予足！启予手！《诗》云：'战战兢兢，如临深渊，如履薄冰。'而今而后，吾知免夫！小子！"[209]

205. 《论语·泰伯篇第八》，第 5 章。
206. 同上，第 6 章。
207. 同上，第 7 章。
208. 同上，第 4 章。
209. 同上，第 3 章。

注释者对最后一段文字多有误解。曾子临终前把弟子叫到床边，嘱托他们，要在自己去后将四肢摆放整齐，因为这是礼之一部分。而且，通常古人殁世前应有男人在侧，因为女人时常无法理解男人的遗言，抑或伪造遗愿。有注释家认为，曾子要弟子掀开被子，查看自己的手足是否在生前受到损伤，这种解释并不准确。依儒家教义，物理身体全然得之于父母，应当仔细看护，任何损伤和疾病都会引起父母的伤痛。人们以此为"孝"。曾子所引《诗经》词句是他对待生活的总体态度。

汉语中，称对父母的爱为"孝"，这可能引起一些西方读者的误会。西方人与东方人一样爱自己的父母，但自古代起，东方人对这个问题就有很深入的讨论。人类文化从根本上讲有两个来源：一是源于心，如情感；一是源于脑（mind），如理性。伟大的建筑，如泰姬陵，乃源于爱。伟大的工程，如大运河，是源于理性的成就。人类的所有建制都源于这两种主要的力量。爱本身是神圣的，在理性之上。但是，如果爱在人的层度上错误地受制于理性，爱将会降为平庸之物，甚至会成为反面。在人中，爱的最基本形式是对父母的爱，尤其是对母亲的爱。其中有一内在的本能力量，如果导向正确之通道，可成为巨大的权能。中国古代教育利用这一原初动力，成就了一系伟大的文化。无须说，正是同一动力产生了天主教的圣母玛利亚崇拜和印度的"神圣母亲"崇拜。

曾子对"孝"了解最深。在深入讨论之前，先看一下曾子对"孝"的理解：

曾子曰："吾闻诸夫子：人未有自致者也，必也亲丧乎！"[210]

曾子曰："吾闻诸夫子，孟庄子之孝也，其他可能也；其不改父之臣与父之政，是难能也。"[211]

曾子曰："慎终，追远，民德归厚矣。"[212]

　　曾子的话要放到中国古代文化中看，才能完全理解。中国古代社会以大家族居多，一家三代（也有五代，甚至七代）共同生活，类似小部落。这样的家族系统固然有很大的不足和缺点，无须讳言，但是也有很大的好处和优点。以现代眼光看，这样的家族是一种原子形态的社会主义公社，家族成员无论男女老少都为共同利益各尽所能。家族形成一个大的经济体，为成员提供住处、饮食、衣服以及其他用品和设施，单独生活则无法获得这些资源。家族系统有自然的等级结构，年龄与辈分最长者在重大的决定中拥有最大的威信。如果家族状况良好，年长者能享受舒适的生活，这在现代社会中很难见到。家族生活的组织原则比较简单，即每个成员都应该孝顺自己的父母，仅此而已。

　　　　·

210.　《论语·子张篇第十九》，第 17 章。

211.　同上，第 18 章。

212.　《论语·学而篇第一》，第 9 章。

孝顺父母是指儿女应当履行自己的责任，不复杂也不困难，只要做好几件基本的事即可：第一，尊敬与顺从自己的父母，指出父母的不当时要委婉，父母年老体弱或者生病时，要尽心照顾。这是爱的自然结果，而爱是最主要的本能力量。第二，要在成熟的年龄结婚——男人的成熟年龄是30岁，女人20岁——至少生一个儿子，以延续家族的血统。最后，父母去世后，必须守孝25个月，守孝期间要过纯净简朴的生活，最好停止一切奢侈的享乐，反省自己。这是非常明智的传统，个人在守孝期间有着足够的空间和时间，在悲伤和痛苦中回归自我。依照惯例，无论你正在从事多么重要的工作，甚至在军队或官府中（如正准备出征的将军或者正在进行重大决策的大臣），只要得知自己的父亲或母亲去世，就必须放弃工作，立即回家参加葬礼，建造坟墓。这是个人生命进程中的一大停顿，每个人一生中至少要遇到两次。个人因此有机会从纷繁的生活中退出，客观地思考一下过往的一切，并重新规划未来。25个月跨度为三年，为父母守孝又称"三年之丧"。三年不短，但也不长，三年之后，每年只要依礼祭奠即可。

这一习俗的主要用意，在于将个人对父母的爱提升为伦理规范，以期塑造良好的人格。为了家族利益，个体性会受到些许抑制，但绝不同于现代极权国家忽略或抹杀个体性。在某种程度上，家族是社会的堡垒，如果家族培养出良好的成员，他在社会中就是良好的个体。这不同于古希腊，国家第一位，个人第二位。在中国，国家第二位，家族第一位。在家族中，个人仍然是第一位。自中世纪起，对君王的忠诚变得同样重要了。不能在战场上勇敢作战，便被视为"不孝"。做优秀的公民会为父母带来荣耀，为了能够成为尽职的儿子，就要做优秀的公民。大家族因此得以稳固，大国亦因此保持稳定。

从心理上讲，家族的安乐并不完全取决于物质上的丰富，却更在于和谐，而和谐最易得于血亲之间。这一伦理原则超越了穷富，因为穷人从爱子那里得来的喜悦与富人是相同的。我们不必在这里详细地讨论，因为有一部经典名为《孝经》，其内容便是孔子与曾子讨论这一主题的对话。他们主要讨论了如何以"孝"治理国家，探讨从君主到普通人的责任。孝的理论有其优点，恰好能弥补立法者无法解决的漏洞。文明社会无疑需要法制，但是无论多么完美的法律，总有缺点和不足。古人将法律比作只能抓住小虫子的蜘蛛网。许多古代学者都幻想过一个乌托邦国家，人们像大家庭一样居住在一起，只需要最基本的几条法律。

《孝经》有两个版本，古文经版有22章，今文经版只有18章。两个版本在汉代都有很好的注释。但是公元722年，唐玄宗亲自注释今文经版《孝经》，颁布天下，旧本《孝经》渐被废弃。宋代朱熹勘定古文经版《孝经》，删掉222个字，将《孝经》分为经1章，传14章。元代吴澄又以今文经版《孝经》为底本作《孝经章句》，分传1章，经12章。唐代流行过郑玄注《孝经》，著名历史学家刘知几和其他学者疑其为伪造，但现已佚失。奇怪的是，18世纪在日本发现另一版本郑玄注《孝经》，则是伪上作伪了。

另一部非常重要的儒家经典《大学》，其作者归于曾子。《大学》原是《礼记》中的一篇（卷十，第42篇），自宋代起独立成书，列为"四书"之一。

《大学》中属于"经"的文字是孔子所教，曾子转述；属于"传"的文字有
十章，是曾子解释孔子所教之言，由曾子弟子记录。《大学》有三个版本：
古文经版，章节间似乎不相关联，内容则有其次序；石刻版，章节顺序不
同，但也有明显窜自《论语》的文字；标准版，宋代程颢（1032—1085）和
程颐（1033—1107）勘定，朱熹注释。标准版问世后一直流行至今。新儒家
大师王阳明（1472—1529）也勘定过《大学》，与标准版微异。自宋代至今，
学者对《大学》一直争论不休，几个简单术语的解释，未能达成共识。《大
学》经文只有 207 个字，传自孔子，如下：

> 大学之道，在明明德，在亲民，在止于至善。
>
> 知止而后有定，定而后能静，静而后能安，安而后能虑，虑而后
> 能得。
>
> 物有本末，事有终始。知所先后，则近道矣。
>
> 古之欲明明德于天下者，先治其国。欲治其国者，先齐其家，欲
> 齐其家者，先修其身。欲修其身者，先正其心。欲正其心者，先诚其
> 意。欲诚其意者，先致其知。致知在格物。
>
> 物格而后知至，知至而后意诚，意诚而后心正，心正而后身修，
> 身修而后家齐，家齐而后国治，国治而后天下平。
>
> 自天子以至于庶人，壹是皆以修身为本。
>
> 其本乱而末治者否矣。其所厚者薄，而其所薄者厚，未之有也。
>
> 此谓知本，此谓知之至也。

我们可在其中见到几乎近于球形视觉的儒学。通过培育一完整的人格，扩充至全世界的和平之治，得出包含八个条目的实践哲学体系。我们可将这一体系视为八层球体，层层相套，犹如镂空的象牙球。个体之内中有体位于最中心，向外发出照射的光熙，穿透心思、情命和身体，映在外部环境上，如家族、国家和天下。现代人或以为这不是实践哲学，因为个体与社会之间存有巨大的鸿沟，难以逾越。但是我们知道，个体与社会之间还有另一个纽带，即家族。如果将家族理解为上文所述的部落，那么这纽带便容易理解了。

但是，问题的关键在于如何理解第一个条目"格物"。关于"格物"的解释至少有 18 种之多。曾子没有解释"格物"，原意已不可求。或许在古代，"格物"之义十分简单，无须解释。我们也无法确知"格物"的原初义是否如此丰富，以致有 18 种解释。或许"格物"只有一义："物"是指"事物"，"格"指"捍御""量度""来""至"，等等。

我们只讨论三种解释：第一义最古老，最权威；第二义最流行，传播最广；第三义是"去除"。第一义源自汉代经学家郑玄，"格"指"来"，"物"指"事"。郑玄认为，如果一个人非常了解善，就会有善物来，非常了解恶，就会有恶物来。这与孔子所论"吾欲仁，斯仁至矣"相合。依此同样可说"吾欲恶，斯恶至矣"。此义最古，不足之处在于，人必须在物至于己之前，具有理解善物或恶物的知识，而这与经文"物格而后知至"的表述顺序相反。否则依据世俗生活之经验，这一解说十分正确。

第二义，朱熹释"格物"为"研究事物"。他的解释如下：

　　所谓致知在格物者，言欲致吾之知，在即物而穷其理也。盖人心之灵莫不有知，而天下之物莫不有理，惟于理有未穷，故其知有不尽也。是以《大学》始教，必使学者即凡有天下之物，莫不因其已知之理而益穷之，以求至乎其极。至于用力之久，而一旦豁然贯通焉，则众物之表里精粗无不到，而吾心之全体大用无不明矣。此谓物格，此谓知之至也。（《大学章句》）

　　依现代眼光看，这是科学家与哲学家相结合之工作。不断研究事物可使人心思纯净、心灵净化吗？这转变似乎没有心理学之必然，也没有逻辑上之连续。事物的知识能否如朱熹所说，通过"今日格一物，明日格一物"而穷尽，也是值得怀疑的事。王阳明曾经依照此法"格"竹子。他将心思集中在竹子上，冥思苦想三天之后病倒了，终于放弃。

　　第三义源自宋代历史学家司马光。司马光认为"物"是指外部对象，所有可欲的东西，如音乐、女人和打猎等等。而"捍御"这些东西，就是要在主观上消除对这些东西的欲望。也就是说，即使想要获得普通知识，在某种程度上也要抑制情命欲望。然而这种解释仍是徘徊在心思层度。各大宗教都曾教诲，只有当接受者完全去除情命欲望时，真正的知识才会降临。此理古今皆然。

　　有相反观点认为，《大学》的教诲对象是邦国中的年轻学者，多是王子或国内具有特殊才能的学生，而不是隐士或僧人。但是我们也要知道，正是因为他们日后将掌握权力，年轻时才需要接受此种教育。东南亚亦有相同的观念，时至今日，贵族子弟都要出家为僧，过一段修行生活，然后还俗为官。古希腊之"秘法"似乎也有类似的修行方式。无论如何，年轻的贵族子弟生活在奢侈的环境中，节制物欲是很不错的修行规范，待到日后执政时，民众与他们都会因此减少若干不必要的危险。然而《大学》中没有任何严酷的训练或宗教戒律，教导年轻人去除物欲，是为获得知识。这是一条中庸之路，其中没有任何极端的措施，为了人格培育之故，情命体乃应受到精心的养护。

第十三章

子思

　　《大戴礼记》与《小戴礼记》中还记有孔子与曾子的其他对话，这些对话集成一书《曾子》。《曾子》在汉代有 18 篇，后有 8 篇佚失，现存 10 篇。著名注释家阮元（1764—1849）曾为此书作注，虽有名家注释，《曾子》的读者却不多。

　　儒家还有一部几乎所有学者都读过的经典《中庸》，这部经典无论从哲学甚或心理训练角度看，都极具重要性。《中庸》原是《礼记》第 31 篇，宋代独立成书，位列"四书"之一。《中庸》主要记载孔子之言，编者是子思，孔子的孙子。《中庸》西文译名众多，如 *Juste Milieu*，*L'invariable Milieu*，*Medium constans vel sempiternum*，*The Constant Medium*，*The State of Equilibrium and Harmony*，*The Doctrine of the Mean*，等等。

　　从字源上讲，"中"有"射中目标"的意思，从而有"正确"之义。所有第二义如"中心""中间""平等"皆出于此。"庸"意为"用"或"常"。"中庸"指不偏于任何一侧，保持在中间，为常，即不变。恒常而不可变者为"道"。浅近地说，可表述为"正确恒常之道"。

对《中庸》的诸多理解中，有些虽不为全错，然实属多余。因此在正式讨论之前，很有必要做些澄清工作。常有人声称自己在生活中不走极端，走中间道路，以大众标准为量度。此类人努力使自己维持在平均水平上，不太好，也不太坏。然而这并不是中庸的真正含义。还有一种误解，认为中庸即是做一半，留一半，不坚持到最后，安于略微的不完美。艺术家常在艺术创作中故意搁置，读者或鉴赏者通过这未完成的部分，依想象力获得更高层次的完美，但是中庸并非此义。艺术中的不完美应当视为未表达的完美，未完成的部分应视为已完成。如果中庸的教义是正确恒常之道，那么艺术之不完美也应属于"正确"。

在日常生活中，行事不走极端总是明智的选择。《易经》乾卦上九爻辞有言"亢龙，有悔"。行事极端会有厄运，最终耗尽自己。《易经》"文言"说，"亢"是指一个人"知进而不知退，知存而不知亡，知得而不知丧"，于是才会"有悔"。但后文又说，"其唯圣人乎！知进退存亡而不失其正者，其唯圣人乎！"（《乾卦文言》）

同样显而易见的是，折中或妥协并不一定是正确的选择。有现代学者争辩，如果建造一座一万英尺高的大坝，必须要做到极端，一个蚂蚁洞都不能留下，不然水会渗透蚂蚁洞，渐渐扩张，最终摧毁整个大坝。这种情况下，我们必须做到完美，而不能让完美只存在于想象之中。因此问题就不再是是否要做到极致，而是以正确的方法，在正确的时间和正确的地方，做出正确的事情。这就是《中庸》的主题。

我必须再次强调，本书阐述问题的基本方法是"以经解经"。宋代大儒陆九渊声称"六经皆我注脚"，我们毫不怀疑他说这话的胆量。那是对同时代烦琐解经方式的矫正，学者为无穷无尽、细如毫发的经典注释工作耗尽毕生精力，却所获甚少。然而陆九渊对待经典的态度也值得商榷。一个人必须首先在别处获得了觉悟，或者已经建立了自己的哲学，然后才能成功地以经典为注脚。事实上，有所觉悟的学者大有人在，却未曾直接道明这一点。大多数（如果不是全部）经典都是任人取用的资源，无尽且慷慨。强加虚妄之义或扭曲原意迁就一己，都是对待经典的不公之举。正确的阐释始终有限，牵强的解说和理论却无穷无尽。本书尝试搁置所有注释，直接面对经典。采用这种方法，则需要解说者对大部分经典已经有了妥当的理解，切入点相对较高，亦相对可靠。

《中庸》开篇写道：

天命之谓性，率性之谓道，修道之谓教。

这是儒家真正的正统教义，人类本性得之于天（或上帝）之授命，为纯善。人类得此本性之善，有责任扩充至极。这一简明教义贯穿整个中国历史。毫无疑问，本性是指精神本性，人中之神性。《孟子》中亦有相同看法。我们无法否认，人性可分为高等自性和低等自性，在印度哲学称为萨埵性、剌阇性和答摩性。除高等自性或萨埵性之外，其余都不必为善。但在儒家，本性与习性相对。人的本性先天为善，但后天的习性可能为恶。战国时期的儒者荀子认为，人性为恶，善在人为，故人需要教化。汉代的杨子认为，人性是善与恶的复合。这三种理论只是对同一问题选择了不同的着眼点加以强调：最后一种理论仅是认为人性具有不同等级的善；第二种理论强调人类的低等自性，正统儒家称之为习性；第一种理论指向高等灵魂或君子的精神本性。中国古代教育几乎全部用力于对君子的培育。

"道"在英文中译为"Tao""Path"，还常译作"Truth"。[213] 践行与真理相应之道，即是指发现、显现和培育此真理。《中庸》紧接上文写道：

道也者，不可须臾离也，可离非道也。

印度韦檀多学者读到这段文字可能会说，这与我们的"自我"（Atman）非常一致。这世界上除了"自我"与"大梵"之外，还有什么不能须臾离开呢？我们都是"彼"，我们都在"彼"之中，我们怎么可能须臾离"彼"，而须臾也是"彼"。道家也会认为，这"道"是完全相同的，不独为儒家所有。宋明新儒家也会称之为"理"。觉悟者在一切之中见上帝，当如何表述上帝呢？他们同样会说，上帝不可须臾离。接下来《中庸》写道：

---

213. 理雅各译为"the Path (of duty)"，即"（责任之）道"，此修饰词实无必要。

> 是故君子戒慎乎其所不睹，恐惧乎其所不闻。
>
> 莫见乎隐，莫显乎微，故君子慎其独也。[214]

君子所不睹或所不闻者，是在上之"彼"（That），"彼"超越我们的听觉和视觉感官，但并不因此而隐或微。对"彼"的正确态度应是保持警觉和敏锐，怀以无声的崇敬，无时无刻不处于祈祷或沉思之中。当我们说"彼"时，似乎以其为非人，为中性，但是无论我们祈祷、冥想或沉思的对象是"彼""她"或"他"，都无任何区别。同样，当我们说"在上"时，只是一种表述方式。传统上我们说"如其在上，如其在左右"。因此人在独处时，总是处于警醒状态，此"如"或"神圣存在"总是在场，人独处时不再是一个人。用现代语言表述，这三段文字是在讨论人所具有的神圣自性和上帝遍在以及以奉献方式崇敬上帝的正确态度。

接下来的一段文字关涉心理学，讨论微观世界（人）的平衡与和谐，及其与宏观世界（宇宙）的相协。

> 喜怒哀乐之未发，谓之中；发而皆中节，谓之和。中也者，天下之大本也；和也者，天下之达道也。
>
> 致中和，天地位焉，万物育焉。

《中庸》第 1 章至此结束。后 10 章内容皆是引孔子之言解释第 1 章。第 12 章为子思之言。之后 8 章内容杂有孔子之言和子思之言。第 21 章至

第 33 章（末章）为子思之言，偶引孔子之言及《诗经》，然而后者居多。

值得我们注意的是，上段文字中同时提及"怒""哀"与"喜""乐"。似乎并不认为"怒"和"哀"是完全负面的情绪，需要去除。后世学者有称，"孔子家儿不知骂，曾子家儿不知怒"，但是这说法或为后出。这段文字中有一句或许需要做些说明，"发而皆中节"原意指"合于节拍"，如在音乐中。即是说情感自然外发，合宜，节制，或如理雅各的表述"in due degree"（适度），而非疯狂的爆发。音乐合于节拍即是说在正确的时间击打。不必完全去除愤怒和悲哀，但是要有所节制。历史告诉我们，愤怒在某种程度上是健康的，正当的表露可以治愈某些疾病。悲伤总是有害，但悲伤也可使人保持清醒，净化生命力的涌动，有助于成长。无论如何，对于一个人在精神道路上的成长，皆为必要。（我们可从此看出儒家与佛教的细微差别，在佛教中，怒是三毒之一，需要完全去除。）

儒家对"乐"的态度略有不同。据统计，"乐"字在《论语》中出现45 次，而"苦"字一次也没有出现。孔子的弟子们曾经表述或经历过精神之极乐。宋代学者曾以看似难解的语式说："乐此学，学此乐"，或"学即学此，乐即乐此"。韦檀多学者会说"此"是"彼"，"乐"即是"梵悦"（Brahmananda）。真理在根本上一定相同，表之以不同系统，外部表征可能完全不同。而"苦"是之后经由佛教进入古代中国人的知觉性中的。这并

---

214. 理雅各的英译文属于直译，他认为此段文字对英语读者来说很难理解。然而本书作者并不如此认为。

不是说古代中国人比后人更快乐，而是中国人更注重生命中积极的一面，以其能增长生命之力，进至更大的悦乐和觉悟，不注重以负极的趋向得涅槃求解脱。

"中"的心理状态并不容易获得。英文有"思维"(mind)和"心"(heart)的区别，在中文则是同一字。"中"原意指"安于中心"。那是一种清明或觉悟的状态，人在此状态中觉得"思维"与"心"安于其整体存在的中心，无法言表，纯净并充满光明。传统上将这一状态描述为"理"在此人内中之显现，这"理"很容易被误解为"理性"(Reason)。眼睛是灵魂之门，老师能通过眼睛敏锐地察觉到弟子的状态。我们通常说，此人的精神存在投向了前方，其他人能够毫无差错地辨识出这种精神状态。在这状态中没有激烈的情感和感觉的劳扰，喜、怒、哀、乐的涌动仅在表层游走。取而代之的只有更深沉、更平静、更安定的无限悦乐，可称为"阿难陀"(Ananda)。

"和"英译为"和谐"(harmony)，指活动。必先有活动和外部表征，才能谈"和"。表之以音乐则很容易理解。音乐确然可以无声，但音乐本身以和谐为其灵魂。如果音乐没有和谐，便只是一聚无序的声音和音符而已，不再是音乐。即使只有一个音符，其与自身的一组震动也是和谐的，人的活动也是如此。高度发展的心思可以指导个体依照特定的原则行为，但其有体的其他部分或可跟随，或可不跟随，仍为自我矛盾或不和谐，整个有体仍是不和谐。然而一旦精神有体进至前方，情况就完全相反了。整个有体始为一真整体，可以自然而然地依照特定的原则行动，无须劳费许多心思力量。当精神有体退至后方，或失去所谓"中"时，常为模糊不清；然而这不清可以使其为清，正如太阳不会永蔽于乌云一样。人中之神圣性，至善之本性如此显露，以"和"称之最为恰当。正是在此处，室利·阿罗频多精神哲学与古代中国哲学几乎完全相应。

和谐无处不在，在人中，亦在宇宙中。如老子所说，婴儿不停地啼哭一日而不至于沙哑，正因其中有超上之和谐在。如果个人致此中和，依此扩充至个人之外在环境，则上下万物得其正位，天地得其和。这不仅是一主观品能，而且径直是一客观影响。这一影响，无论为大为小，所施为远为近，皆有赖于其辐射中心的权能，及其显露程度。如果人本身不"中"或不"和"，便不能控制外部境况，甚至难以存活。同样，若无此中和，我们无法想象任何有生命或无生命之物能在这宇宙中存在。举一例，牛的叫声在我们听来可能为刺耳，然此声音在牛群中必为一和谐。这是一普遍真理。如果石头失其"中"，就会无止境地向下落，直至再次落到某处，成为静止。此进程始于一中心，一球形的中心，逐渐扩充自己，直至其影响伸展至所有方向。

《中庸》引孔子的几段话足以佐证这一原则：

> 仲尼曰："君子中庸，小人反中庸。君子之中庸也，君子而时中；小人之中庸也，小人而无忌惮也。"

> 子曰："中庸其至矣乎！民鲜能久矣！"

子曰："人皆曰予知，驱而纳诸罟护陷阱之中，而莫之知辟也。人皆曰予知，择乎中庸而不能期月守也。"

子曰："回之为人也，择乎中庸，得一善，则拳拳服膺而弗失之矣。"

子曰："天下国家可均也，爵禄可辞也，白刃可蹈也，中庸不可能也。"

"中庸"是哲学问题。在古代中国，中庸完全规范在"礼"中，何时应做何事有十分详细的规定，应当依此行事。子思对此一定有十分透彻的理解，他的解说方法独特而且全面。他认为行事符合自己的位置、境况或环境，即为中庸。人可以安足在自己的命运之中，但又不盲目地顺从于命运，最重要的是等待天命（或上帝之命）。人在愉悦中坚定地依规范行事，且更为自制、自醒。这是一种更深层意义上的墨守成规，但是伴随着内中更坚定的确信。我们还可读到：

君子素位而行，不显乎其外。

素富贵，行乎富贵；素贫贱，行乎贫贱；素夷狄，行乎夷狄；素患难，行乎患难；君子无入而不自得焉。

在上位，不陵下，在下位，不援上。正己而不求于人则无怨。上不怨天，下不尤人。

　　故君子居易以俟命，小人行险而徼幸。

　　子曰："射有似乎君子；失诸正鹄，反求诸其身。"

　　这段文字对中庸的解释最为得当。射箭之喻是指以中"道"射中靶心。这与"中间"或平庸毫无关系。此外，行事合于某人的位置，是指与普遍模式保持恒常的一致，其含义要远宽广于仅仅履行自己的职责，因为有些职责可能并非自天而命。君子当行之事是什么呢？后文将其综括为治理国家，因为君子教育即为使其能"尊贤""亲亲""柔远人"等等，并明白其缘由和效用。这些问题属于政治哲学，在此不作详述。人类文化（动词）有一心理学基础，《中庸》对其阐述最为明晰，古代文字无有可比拟者，此基础即是"诚"。我们来读如下文字：

　　诚者，天之道也；诚之者，人之道也。诚者不勉而中，不思而得，从容中道，圣人也。诚之者，择善而固执之者也。

　　博学之，审问之，慎思之，明辨之，笃行之。

　　有弗学，学之弗能弗措也；有弗问，问之弗知弗措也；有弗思，思之弗得弗措也；有弗辨，辨之弗明弗措也；有弗行，行之弗笃弗措也；人一能之，己百之。人十能之己千之。

　　果能此道矣，虽愚必明，虽柔必强。

自诚明，谓之性；自明诚，谓之教。诚则明矣，明则诚矣。

诚者，自成也。而道，自道也。

诚者，物之终始。不诚无物。是故君子诚之为贵。

诚者，非自成己而已也，所以成物也。成己，仁也；成物，知也。性之德也，合外内之道也，故时措之宜也。

唯天下至诚，为能尽其性；能尽其性，则能尽人之性；能尽人之性，则能尽物之性；能尽物之性，则可以赞天地之化育；可以赞天地之化育，则可以与天地参矣。

其次致曲，曲能有诚，诚则形，形则著，著则明，明则动，动则变，变则化，唯天下至诚为能化。

至诚之道，可以前知。国家将兴，必有祯祥；国家将亡，必有妖孽；见乎蓍龟，动乎四体。祸福将至：善，必先知之；不善，必先知之。故至诚如神。

故至诚无息。不息则久，久则征，征则悠远，悠远则博厚，博厚则高明。

博厚，所以载物也；高明，所以覆物也；悠久，所以成物也。

博厚配地，高明配天。悠久无疆。

如此者，不见而章，不动而变，无为而成。

唯天下至诚，为能经纶天下之大经，立天下之大本，知天地之化
育。夫焉有所倚。

肫肫其仁！渊渊其渊！浩浩其天！

苟不固聪明圣知达天德者，其孰能知之？

　　《中庸》对"诚"的阐释简洁明了，开始即点明一事实，"诚"是宇宙
万物存在的根基。当"诚"在个体中达到极致，当个体进入圣者之域，便
可转化事物。当下世界环境中，我们无法期望民族国家之间的外交关系中
存在这种"诚"，然而这是解决冲突的唯一法门，而且某种程度上，"诚"
时常也是存在的。"神圣母亲"曾不止一次地指出，"诚"是瑜伽之路上唯
一的"救护"。我们还发现，"诚"是个体心理圆成的第一条件。这是何等
的正确！东方西方，古代现代，教授着同一真理，这是何等令人惊奇。至
于转化问题，"神圣母亲"还曾说："当你真的改变了，你周围的一切也就
改变了。"[215]

．

215.　参见《母亲的话》第三卷，第 98 页。

第十四章

孟子

  《中庸》余下的内容论及"人"或"君子"的最高成就，以及在地上建立神圣治域。自汉代起，传统上称之"天人之学"。这知识中没有对彼世或此世天堂的许诺，只有精神之治的理想立于后人之前，在组织完善的人群中，将和平、幸福、文化和转化带给一切有体。这理想就是"建诸天地而不悖，质诸鬼神而无疑，百世以俟圣人而不惑"（第29章）的道。相较于这种理想，后世高举的崇高价值，如一神论、英雄主义、慈善、博爱和人文主义等等，自然相形见绌。那王国不属于神，而属于神性之人，宇宙中最高上的转化有体。

  《礼记·礼运篇》讨论"大同"，对这理想之物质层度有具体的描述，近时学者多有引用：

> 大道之行也，天下为公。选贤与能，讲信修睦，故人不独亲其
> 亲，不独子其子，使老有所终，壮有所用，幼有所长，矜寡孤独废疾
> 者，皆有所养。男有分，女有归。货恶其弃于地也，不必藏于己；力
> 恶其不出于身也，不必为己。是故谋闭而不兴，盗窃乱贼而不作，故
> 外户而不闭，是谓大同。[216]

这是所有人都曾梦想却无人能够许诺的乌托邦，相较于现世，那是一个充满欢乐的世界。只有以此为基础，人类文化才能繁荣，才会出现无数稀世的天才。如果人类忽视大同理想，那么，福祉就只关涉特殊阶层或选定的少数人群，而人类的救赎或社会的进步就只能是空谈了。人类同一是现代文明世界中所有人的期许。这是出于现代思想吗？显然不是。基督降生前四百年，就已经有人这么构想了。问题是这理想可曾实现过吗？历史告诉我们，曾有"小康时代"部分地实现了这一理想，但仅限于某地或某国，区域或大或小，时间或长或短，尤其当精神性人物存居于其地，他不必官职在身，但有内外卓然的成就，影响至广至远。然而，"大同"却从未在一民族（国家）中实现过。直至今日，这理想仍然只是理想，然而无论这一理想有多广大，却并非不可企及，仍属物理世界，终将实现于有限未来的某一刻，为一普遍真理的最终胜利。

子思之后，我们得有孟子。孟子在宋代列于颜子、曾子和子思之后，

---

216. 张其昀：《中国文化要义》，第 10—13 页。

是第四位伟大的哲学家，被尊为"亚圣"，仅低于孔子。欲了解孟子，仍须关注其所处的时代背景。

孔子殁世后，中国进入战国时代（约公元前476—前221）。曾经的北方强国晋国被三家大夫分割，亦曾是北方强国的齐国被田氏篡夺。南方的楚国吞并了汉水流域的所有小国，虽然仍是强国，却处于衰落之中，不得不联合其他国家一同抵抗刚刚兴起于西北的秦国。吴、越属大国，居于东南，相互征战不断，吴国终被越国吞灭。战国时代纷争不止，各国君主自立为王，被黑暗的政治"游士"阶层摆弄于股掌之间。即便如此，战国时代是一个哲学家的时代，有"百家"之说。秦国以强力统一各国成为一大帝国。秦始皇（公元前259—前210）因焚书坑儒在中国文化史上留下永久的污点，前文对此已有述及。

孟子是鲁国贵族孟孙氏的后裔，据称生于公元前371或372年，卒于公元前289年，正处于战国时代。刘向在《列女传》中曾记载孟子的母亲很有天赋，为了孩子的教育三次迁移住所，这是非常有名的故事。我们不能确定孟子是子思的弟子，还是子思的再传弟子。经现代计算，司马迁《史记》中的年代记录有相互矛盾之处，并不可靠。子思去世的年龄可能比传统记载的62岁要长20岁，然而孟子是他的再传弟子，似乎更为合适。毫无疑问的是，孟子经由子思学派直接从孔子一系传统获得学识。

孟子一生的命运几乎与孔子相同。为了实现其高上理想，周游列国以求任用，欲行王道（Royal Path of Peace），而非其时流行的霸道（Heroic Path of Might）。然而与孔子不二，他也毫无意外地失败了。孟子去过齐国和魏国，多次与两国君主会晤，两国君主尊敬其人，却不用其言。年老以后，孟子与孔子一样别无选择，只能以哲学家的身份收授弟子，其言语被记录并保存下来。孟子还是伟大的数学家，从作品上看，他还精通语文学。

保存至今的《孟子》一书据称出自孟子晚年，许多证据表明并非如此。最重要的证据是，《孟子》一书中多处以"子"称呼孟子弟子，而老师不会如此称呼学生。《孟子·梁惠王篇》中，孟子称梁惠王为"王"十余次之多，然而惠王生前从未自称为"王"，只是死后被尊称为"王"。如果《孟子》是孟子本人所著，则不会出现这样的纰漏。而且，齐宣王攻占燕国的事情，实际上发生在很多年之后。这一系列矛盾表明，《孟子》甚至并非孟子弟子所作，而是其弟子的弟子所作。

《孟子》在宋代被列入"四书"，是中等教育的教科书，也是科举考试用书，所以古代学者都十分熟悉，甚至现代学者也不陌生。《孟子》为散文体，文风朴实清晰，虽有几段文字文义不清，仍属易读。全书七卷，每卷分上下，共 259 章，35 226 字。公元 2 世纪，赵岐在为《孟子》注释所作序言中，提到他所用的《孟子》为 261 章，共 34 685 字。缺失章数或由分章不同所致，多出的字数可能源于文字篡入。他还提到在《孟子》七卷之外，另有四卷，通过文风和内容判断，定为伪作无疑，因此他没有为这四卷作注释，之后这四卷也佚失了。汉代著作中仍有各种引自《孟子》的零星文字，不见于今本《孟子》，但内容都不甚重要，这里不作讨论。

《孟子》主涉政治哲学。孟子的理想与孔子相同。其时诸侯凭借封地自立为土，一转而变为绝对独裁体制，自然相互争冲。依此情势，孟子提出王道。历史证明，就孟子所处的时代环境而言，这也是一条容易践行的路；"故事半古之人，功必倍之。"《孟子·公孙丑上》以现代眼光看，孟子的学说极具民主色彩。这里只略引几段文字为例：

（孟子）曰："国君进贤，如不得已，将使卑逾尊，疏逾戚，可不慎与？

左右皆曰贤，未可也；诸大夫皆曰贤，未可也；国人皆曰贤，然后察之。见贤焉，然后用之。左右皆曰不可，勿听；诸大夫皆曰不可，勿听；国人皆曰不可，然后察之。见不可焉，然后去之。

左右皆曰可杀，勿听；诸大夫皆曰可杀，勿听；国人皆曰可杀，然后察之。见可杀焉，然后杀之。故曰，国人杀之也。如此，然后可以为民父母。"[217]

孟子曰："民为贵，社稷次之，君为轻。"[218]

孟子告齐宣王曰："君之视臣如手足，则臣视君如腹心；君之视臣如犬马，则臣视君如国人；君之视臣如土芥，则臣视君如寇雠。"[219]

依以上文字判断，孟子宣扬的是君主体制下的民主精神。然而学者最终为谁效力呢？当然不是诸侯或天子，甚至不是人民或国家——学者永远忠于并为之奉献自己的应该是"道"。孟子达至自己信仰的道路，是神圣的天命或上帝之命，先于孟子的圣人开辟并践行此宽广平坦之路，他坚信后世的圣人也会追随在同样的道路上。孔子不仅为自己的故土效力，而且周游列国，孟子亦如此。对于他们所掌握的真理，我们确信不疑，后世从未有人质疑过他们不忠或不爱国。相反，世人几乎将孔子和孟子的所有言行都视为准则。

我们知道，儒学的中心原则是"仁"，即"神圣之爱"。"亚圣"所授亦是同样的内容，只是略有不同，还有另外一个与此神圣之爱紧密相连而次之的原则——"义"。"义"原在儒学教义之内，但从未被特别注重，因其属于"礼"的范畴，属当然之事，后又含在"中庸"之内。前人从未像孟子这样单独强调"义"。在传统意义上，两个原则构成一个十字形，"仁"是一条下降（或上升）的纵线，"义"是一条向两端伸展的横线。在精神之域中，下降的纵线内含宇宙自性（cosmic nature），个人有体与宇宙的极深处以之同一，即所谓"天地之心"。伸展的横线处于人类层度，尤在心思之域。"义"表理性，但此理性并非纯为智识，而是内含以情命自性（emotional nature）掌握的实在。说到中国人的心思，从古至今都不独是一逻辑家或法家的格局，而是多属儒家的心思，为人文主义。"义"的提出使儒学更加完整、完美，滋长繁盛，所得赞颂名副其实。如丝之经纬，织而成绸。

.

217.　《孟子·梁惠王章句下》，第 7 章。

218.　《孟子·尽心章句下》，第 14 章。

219.　《孟子·离娄章句下》，第 3 章。

今人以"义"为一道德价值，我们须了解孟子如何理解"义"。在孟子的阐述中，"义"与其时的另一个原则"利"直接相对。孟子与梁惠王第一次会面时，就对这两个原则做了明确的阐述，见《孟子》开篇：

> 孟子见梁惠王。
>
> 王曰："叟！不远千里而来，亦将有以利吾国乎？"
>
> 孟子对曰："王！何必曰利？亦有仁义而已矣。
>
> 王曰：'何以利吾国？'大夫曰：'何以利吾家？'士庶人曰：'何以利吾身？'上下交征利而国危矣。万乘之国，弑其君者，必千乘之家；千乘之国，弑其君者，必百乘之家。万取千焉，千取百焉，不为不多矣。苟为后义而先利，不夺不餍。
>
> 未有仁而遗其亲者也，未有义而后其君者也。王亦曰：仁义而已矣，何必曰利？"[220]

汉代著名学者王充认为，"利"通常被理解为"货财之利"，然而"利"还可指"安吉之利"，梁惠王所指或为后者，为自己的国家求"安吉之利"并无不妥之处。然而孟子所重在"仁""义"原则，物质之"货财之利"或"安吉之利"不在他的考虑范围之内。我们还可读到：

> 仁，人之安宅也；义，人之正路也。
>
> 旷安宅而弗居，舍正路而不由，哀哉！[221]

仁，人心也；义，人路也。

舍其路而弗由，放其心而不知求，哀哉！

人有鸡犬放，则知求之；有放心而不知求。

学问之道无他，求其放心而已矣。[222]

宋牼将之楚，孟子遇于石丘。

（孟子）曰："先生将何之？"

曰："吾闻秦楚构兵，我将见楚王说而罢之。楚王不悦，我将见秦王说而罢之。二王我将有所遇焉。"

（孟子）曰："轲也请无问其详，愿闻其指。说之将何如？"

曰："我将言其不利也。"

（孟子）曰："先生之志则大矣，先生之号则不可。

先生以利说秦楚之王，秦楚之王悦于利，以罢三军之师，是三军之士乐罢而悦于利也。为人臣者怀利以事其君，为人子者怀利以事其

．

220. 《孟子·梁惠王章句上》，第 1 章。

221. 《孟子·离娄章句上》，第 10 章。

222. 《孟子·告子章句上》，第 11 章。"心"通常译为"heart"，理雅各译为"mind"，亦属妥当。"学问之道"中的"道"通常译为"means"（方法），而理雅各译为"the great end"（目的），似乎不妥。两个词似乎相差无几，但是推而广之，就会产生巨大差别，因为"学问之道"是说"方法"，而非"目的"；学问之目的另有所在。如此说，会导向对"无"的强调，属于道家教义，而非孟子所论。

父，为人弟者怀利以事其兄，是君臣、父子、兄弟终去仁义，怀利以相接，然而不亡者，未之有也。先生以仁义说秦楚之王，秦楚之王悦于仁义，而罢三军之师，是三军之士乐罢而悦于仁义也。为人臣者怀仁义以事其君，为人子者怀仁义以事其父，为人弟者怀仁义以事其兄，是君臣、父子、兄弟去利，怀仁义以相接也，然而不王者，未之有也。何必曰利？"[223]

宋牼是战国时期的著名哲学家，或年长于孟子。孟子以"先生"称呼宋牼是表尊敬，这在《孟子》中并不常见。以现代眼光视之，宋牼是一和平主义者，《庄子》最后一章中简略叙述了他的学说。宋牼以现实主义原则劝说秦楚二王，说明两国可能会面临的物质损失和破坏等等，即为"无利"。孟子所论则是一永恒真理，更为理想主义，是一"迂回路线"，因不切实际，君主不欣赏。欲向军阀们传播和平福音，以实用精神说服他们或许是最好的方法，告之以将遭受的损失和毁坏等等。而孟子不是一纯粹的和平主义者。即使对于普通价值，他也有不同的看法。如下：

孟子曰："今之事君者皆曰：'我能为君辟土地，充府库。'今之所谓良臣，古之所谓民贼也。君不乡道，不志于仁，而求富之，是富桀也。

'我能为君约与国，战必克。'今之所谓良臣，古之所谓民贼也。君不乡道，不志于仁，而求为之强战，是辅桀也。

由今之道，无变今之俗，虽与之天下，不能一朝居也。"[224]

如果我们极其严肃地对待这些古代观念，一切价值都将被重估。另如下：

孟子曰："有人曰：'我善为陈，我善为战。'大罪也。

国君好仁，天下无敌焉。……"[225]

孟子曰："求也为季氏宰，无能改于其德，而赋粟倍他日。孔子曰：'求非我徒也，小子鸣鼓而攻之可也。'

由此观之，君不行仁政而富之，皆弃于孔子者也，况于为之强战？争地以战，杀人盈野；争城以战，杀人盈城，此所谓率土地而食人肉，罪不容于死。

故善战者服上刑，连诸侯者次之，辟草莱、任土地者次之。"[226]

如上思想即是孟子对孔子教义的理解和发展。相较于同时代的其他学派，孟子思想同属激进，却与流行的观点多相抵牾。孟子思想中包含极明

.

223. 《孟子·告子章句下》，第 4 章。

224. 同上，第 9 章。

225. 《孟子·尽心章句下》，第 4 章。

226. 《孟子·离娄章句上》，第 14 章。

白的道理，历万世而不误，经得起历史事实的验证。孟子思想有不可忽视的影响，在某种程度上可以解释，为什么中国人作为一个民族一直爱好和平，不好战争。

依此思考序列，好政府应由好人组成，但最终还是要依赖君主自身。故曰"徒善不足以为政，徒法不能以自行。"[227]

是以惟仁者宜在高位。不仁而在高位，是播其恶于众也。

上无道揆也[228]，下无法守也，朝不信道，工不信度，君子犯义，小人犯刑，国之所存者幸也。

故曰：城郭不完，兵甲不多，非国之灾也；田野不辟，货财不聚，非国之害也。上无礼，下无学，贼民兴，丧无日矣。[229]

孟子曰："人不足与适也，政不足与间也。唯大人为能格君心之非。君仁，莫不仁；君义，莫不义；君正，莫不正。一正君而国定矣。"[230]

孟子对春秋时期的历史有如下评价：

孟子曰："五霸者，三王[231]之罪人也。今之诸侯，五霸[232]之罪人也。今之大夫，今之诸侯之罪人也。

天子适诸侯曰巡狩，诸侯朝于天子曰述职。春省耕而补不足，秋省敛而助不给。入其疆，土地辟，田野治，养老尊贤，俊杰在位，则有庆，庆以地。入其疆，土地荒芜，遗老失贤，掊克在位，则有让。一不朝则贬其爵，再不朝则削其地，三不朝则六师移之。是故天子讨而不伐，诸侯伐而不讨。

五霸者，搂诸侯以伐诸侯者也。故曰：五霸者，三王之罪人也。五霸，桓公为盛。葵丘之会诸侯，束牲、载书而不歃血。初命曰：'诛不孝，无易树子，无以妾为妻。'再命曰：'尊贤育才，以彰有德。'三命曰：'敬老慈幼，无忘宾旅。'四命曰：'士无世官，官事无摄，取士必得，无专杀大夫。'五命曰：'无曲防，无遏籴，无有封而不告。'曰：'凡我同盟之人，既盟之后，言归于好。'今之诸侯，皆犯此五禁，故曰今之诸侯，五霸之罪人也。

长君之恶其罪小，逢君之恶其罪大。今之大夫，皆逢君之恶，故曰：今之大夫，今之诸侯之罪人也。"[233]

·

227.　《孟子·离娄章句上》，第1章。

228.　此句的英译文参考了赵岐的可靠注释。理雅各将此句译为"当君主没有准则，据以审度自己的执政措施"。

229.　《孟子·离娄章句上》，第1章。

230.　同上，第20章。

231.　"三王"即为夏代之禹王、商代之汤王、周代之文王。

232.　"五霸"即为齐桓公、晋文公、秦穆公、宋襄公和楚庄公。

233.　《孟子·告子章句下》，第7章。

第十五章

孟子（续）

至此，我们见到，这理想治域并不局限于一个国家，而是以和平方式延伸至整个世界，是为仁义之治。早在孟子之前，这就是儒家所珍视的理想，孟子之后一直兴盛至今。前文已述，古希腊政治哲学倡导先国家后个人，而儒家教义则相反。如今，我们或以为，如果社会依照良好的政治体系完善地组织，个体自然会有最好的发展，贡献于公共福利，过上幸福的集体生活，因此以为良好的社会体系最为首要。

有一点需要说明，孟子的学说不是我们所理解的个人主义。因为作为一种哲学思想的个人主义，或者说"私我主义"，是诸子百家中杨子的观点。杨子没有留下任何著作，他的学说主要保存在同代人的引述或辩驳中。杨子可能过于彻底地践行了私我主义原则，或说他太过自私，根本不想让别人因为自己的著作而获益。而我们最终见到，即使良好的社会体系也需要合适的人付诸实践，而合适的人又必须有赖于相应的知觉性状态，才能使自己忠实于特定的原则。然而在古代，政府由诸侯掌控，要先正他们的心，才会如孟子所说，产生良好的结果。现代民主体系中不再有如此多的诸侯王，取而代之的是领导者。以偏于形而上学的方式说，如果期望领导者对被领导者施以有益的影响，能在某种程度上成就和谐的集体生活，仍有赖于充当领导者之个体知觉性的高等状态。

无数历史事实证明，无论多么完善和完整的规章法律（如今名为"计划"），多么出色的体制，都会衰颓，渐至无用。除非有高上之心思以远见，更重要的是，以善意对其不断地维护、更新和改善。善意在古代称为"善心"，神圣之爱（仁）为其宅舍。在此"仁"中存有给予和保持生命的巨大权能。正当地应用这一权能，可为社会乃至个人福乐的不竭之泉。这给予和保持生命的力量即为"天地之大德"，即为"恩典"（Grace）。那就是"人类应居于其中的安适宅舍"，亦即是所有学者的志向所在。我们可读到如下文字：

王子垫问曰："士何事？"

孟子曰："尚志。"

曰："何谓尚志？"

曰："仁义而已矣。杀一无罪非仁也。非其有而取之非义也。居恶在？仁是也。路恶在？义是也。居仁由义，大人之事备矣。"[234]

·

234. 《孟子·尽心章句上》，第33章。

"仁"不离"义"。"杀一无罪"是指以此"而得天下"。"非其有而取之"是指不偷盗,同于佛教五戒之第二戒,在这里是包含在"义"这一更宽广、更积极的原则之中。再看:

> 孟子曰:"霸者之民驩虞如也,王者之民皞皞如也。杀之而不怨,利之而不庸,民日迁善而不知为之者。
>
> 夫君子所过者化,所存者神,上下与天地同流,岂曰小补之哉?"[235]

如此我们知道,知觉性高等状态的变化可以很好地解释转化的影响。扩而言之,可以发现老子所言"不言之教"或"无为之事"确实不虚。然而孟子所重端在个人,即少数领导者或统治者,如果他们能成为仁义君子,那么他们在国中所实行的政策和原则自然是合宜的,社会便可进步、繁荣,无论国人知或不知,皆可安足。所行之事总是处于中心,所以一旦角度稍有偏离,球面上产生的差异就会很大。即是说,问题应在根基处得到解决。

> 孟子曰:"人有恒言,皆曰'天下国家'。天下之本在国,国之本在家,家之本在身。"[236]

我们可深入研究孟子对"君子"这一概念的阐述:

居天下之广居，立天下之正位，行天下之大道；得志，与民由之；不得志，独行其道。富贵不能淫，贫贱不能移，威武不能屈，此之谓大丈夫。[237]

孟子曰："大人者，言不必信，行不必果，惟义所在。"[238]

孟子曰："大人者，不失其赤子之心者也。"[239]

"赤子之心"指一种无邪、质朴、纯洁和真挚的状态，伟大的事物只有以此为基础才能建立。这与耶稣的教诲相同："你们若不回转，变成小孩子的样式，断不得进天国。"

问题转回到了人性，人的本性必为善。

孟子曰："人之所不学而能者，其良能也；所不虑而知者，其良知也。

.

235. 《孟子·尽心章句上》，第 13 章。理雅各此句英译文非常出色，只有很小的词句调整。

236. 《孟子·离娄章句上》，第 5 章。

237. 《孟子·滕文公章句下》，第 2 章。

238. 《孟子·离娄章句下》，第 11 章。

239. 同上，第 12 章。

> 孩提之童无不知爱其亲者，及其长也，无不知敬其兄也。
>
> 亲亲，仁也；敬长，义也；无他，达之天下也。"[240]

明代大学者王阳明以"良知"建立一宗大哲学。这段文字引起许多讨论，最终只能说人性中隐含有善的种子，教育可使其生长并得以醇化。怀中的婴孩受母亲养育，因而爱自己的母亲，这爱可转向任何提供养育的人。孩子长大后，会尊敬长者。然而，如果教师过于严苛，孩子的尊敬可能会转向其他人。因此有学者认为，如果没有后续之培养，这里所说的良知和良能便无甚用处了。

前文已述，人性问题一直是哲学讨论和争论的焦点。告子与孟子同时，他认为人性无所谓善或恶。《孟子》一书中有孟子对告子理论的驳斥：

> 告子曰："性，犹杞柳也；义，犹桮棬也。以人性为仁义，犹以杞柳为桮棬。"
>
> 孟子曰："子能顺杞柳之性而以为桮棬乎？将戕贼杞柳而后以为桮棬也？如将戕贼杞柳而以为桮棬，则亦将戕贼人以为仁义与？率天下之人而祸仁义者，必子之言夫！"[241]

> 告子曰："性犹湍水也，决诸东方则东流，决诸西方则西流。人性之无分于善不善也，犹水之无分于东西也。"
>
> 孟子曰："水信无分于东西，无分于上下乎？人性之善也，犹水

之就下也。人无有不善，水无有不下。

今夫水，搏而跃之，可使过颡；激而行之，可使在山。是岂水之性哉？其势则然也。人之可使为不善，其性亦犹是也。"[242]

告子曰："生之谓性。"

孟子曰："生之谓性也，犹白之谓白与？"

曰："然。"

"白羽之白也，犹白雪之白；白雪之白，犹白玉之白欤？"

曰："然。"

"然则犬之性犹牛之性，牛之性犹人之性欤？"[243]

告子曰："食色，性也。仁，内也，非外也；义，外也，非内也。"

孟子曰："何以谓仁内义外也？"

曰："彼长而我长之，非有长于我也。犹彼白而我白之，从其白于外也，故谓之外也。"

曰："异于白马之白也，无以异于白人之白也。不识长马之长也，

·

240. 《孟子·尽心章句上》，第 15 章。

241. 《孟子·告子章句上》，第 1 章。

242. 同上，第 2 章。

243. 同上，第 3 章。

无以异于长人之长与？且谓长者义乎？长之者义乎？”

曰：“吾弟则爱之，秦人之弟则不爱也，是以我为悦者也，故谓之内。长楚人之长，亦长吾之长，是以长为悦者也，故谓之外也。”

曰：“耆秦人之炙，无以异于耆吾炙，夫物则亦有然者也，然则耆炙亦有外与？”[244]

公都子曰：“告子曰：‘性无善无不善也。’

或曰：‘性可以为善，可以为不善。是故文武兴，则民好善，幽厉兴，则民好暴。’

或曰：‘有性善，有性不善。是故以尧为君而有象，以瞽瞍为父而有舜，[245] 以纣为兄之子且以为君而有微子启、王子比干。’[246]

今曰‘性善’，然则彼皆非与？”

孟子曰：“乃若其情，则可以为善矣，乃所谓善也。

若夫为不善，非才之罪也。

恻隐之心，人皆有之；羞恶之心，人皆有之；恭敬之心，人皆有之；是非之心，人皆有之。恻隐之心，仁也；羞恶之心，义也；恭敬之心，礼也；是非之心，智也。仁义礼智，非由外铄我也，我固有之也，弗思耳矣。故曰：‘求则得之，舍则失之。’或相倍蓰而无算者，不能尽其才者也。……”[247]

孟子论述中使用的推论形式本可发展成为若干思辨哲学，然而事实并未如此。孟子是一位精神导师，纯粹的心思推理哲学在他仅居次位。孟子所教在本质上皆为实用，教人以正道事天。我们可读到：

虽有恶人，斋戒沐浴，则可以祀上帝。[248]

孟子曰："尽其心者，知其性也。知其性，则知天矣。

存其心，养其性，所以事天也。

夭寿不贰，修身以俟之，所以立命也。"[249]

此段文字中的"性"同于《中庸》开篇所述的"性"，即人的神圣自性。告子或其他人对人性的阐述虽然不为全错，但未曾指向此神圣义。双方所论未能得出确定结果，严格讲，在于所论的对象不同。

·

244. 《孟子·告子章句上》，第 4 章。

245. 象是舜的弟弟，总是加害于舜。瞽瞍是他们的父亲，无知且顽固。

246. 纣是暴君，王子比干和微子启都是有德之人。

247. 《孟子·告子章句上》，第 6 章。

248. 《孟子·离娄章句下》，第 25 章。

249. 《孟子·尽心章句上》，第 1 章。此段文字亦有理雅各之英译文，比较之下，我们会发现两者之间的巨大差别。理雅各的译文试图极力忠实于原文，其努力近乎艰辛，甚至将原文的注释翻译过来作为译文之脚注，然而所得之结果虽不能说不可读，但是令人迷惑。其实只要翻译清楚主要之概念，这段文字自然就很好理解了。

稍做些语文学上的辨析将有助于我们的理解。同样的术语也出现在道家经典中，含义略有不同，本书所论以儒家为主，在此暂且不论。汉语的"心"字也有"思维"(mind) 义，因此指整个心思有体，在更高层度上也指"良知"(conscience)。"天"指物理自然，实指更高层度的上帝，或上帝之良知，也可作为"天命"的简称。"天命"也可称为"上帝之命"，狭义可为个人之命运。"生命"(life) 在英文为一字，在汉语为一词，由"生"和"命"二字组成。自汉代起，"生命"在传统上解释为"天以其统帅人之生存及生长者"。除去少数觉悟的灵魂，个人对天命极少自知。即使孔子，也是 50岁时才知天命。然而每个人或多或少都能意识到某种形式的天命。个体都受制于在上之命，上帝塑造或"支配"着个体命运，个体必须服从。但这并不意味着盲目地顺从于无知无光的命运。个体依照自己的良知行事，个体良知在最高层度上与上帝之良知相符，内心没有任何悔恨、怨憎或不安。英文"恩赐"(Blessing) 在中文的含义为"个体道德完满之状态"。个体甚至不应期望从"天"那里得到任何额外的好运。即是说，个体应尽其所能使自己完满，其他则等待天命，或者换个说法，将自己交给上帝。这是正统儒家对待生命的态度，无论个体在生命中遇到何种变故，寿命或长或短，遭遇或幸或不幸，都不应改变面对生命的正确态度。这态度根本上源自对于人性本善的坚信，人应依此而行。

然而教育或培育个人的神圣自性远比相信人性本善要困难得多。我们不禁要问，当如何践行呢？在这里我们第一次遇到"养心"这个词，意指保持知觉性的高等状态。这很容易理解，因为关于这个问题，孟子的教诲与东西方所有圣人的教诲相同。我们可读到：

> 孟子曰："养心莫善于寡欲。其为人也寡欲，虽有不存焉者，寡矣；其为人也多欲，虽有存焉者，寡矣。"[250]

这仍是就否定的方面说，即去除某物。肯定地说，即是培育心和思维中的良知或善。孟子对此有如下阐释：

> 孟子曰："牛山之木尝美矣，以其郊于大国也，斧斤伐之，可以为美乎？是其日夜之所息，雨露之所润，非无萌蘖之生焉，牛羊又从而牧之，是以若彼濯濯也。人见其濯濯也，以为未尝有材焉，此岂山之性也哉？
>
> 虽存乎人者，岂无仁义之心哉？其所以放其良心者，亦犹斧斤之于木也，旦旦而伐之，可以为美乎？其日夜之所息，平旦之气，其好恶与人相近也者几希，则其旦昼之所为，有梏亡之矣。梏之反覆，则其夜气不足以存。夜气不足以存，则其违禽兽不远矣。人见其禽兽也，而以为未尝有才焉者，是岂人之情也哉？
>
> 故苟得其养，无物不长；苟失其养，无物不消。

.

250. 《孟子·尽心章句下》，第35章。此段文字亦有理雅各的英译文，其译文虽不能说是错译，但与原意不相应。

孔子曰：'操则存，舍则亡；出入无时，莫知其乡。'惟心之谓
与？"[251]

这段文字对"养"的重要性做了清晰的阐释。这里的"气"字或需要解释。日夜交替之时，有平旦之气，即如人休息一夜，感觉清爽，体力恢复。英文有译为"沉静"（poise），与文中"夜气"相同。所有人都有这样的经历，以瑜伽方式言之，即是阿祇尼（Agni）之火升起之时。其中包含所有的善。

有一个故事可以说明个人内中有体的培育自然显现于个人之"气"。

孟子自范之齐，望见齐王之子，喟然叹曰："居移气，养移体，大哉居乎！夫非尽人之子与？"

孟子曰："王子宫室、车马、衣服多与人同，而王子若彼者，其居使之然也。况居天下之广居者乎？

鲁君之宋，呼于垤泽之门。守者曰：'此非吾君也，何其声之似我君也？'此无他，居相似也。"[252]

个人内中有体的培育有赖于个人如何生活，即是上文提到的"居"。外部环境影响内中有体，但最终一定是内中有体决定外部生命。我们当然不能说君王的生活会使人成为君王，但人的灵魂内部一定有可安立的伟大之处。

接下来我们要处理的是整个孟子学说中最难理解的一个问题。虽然英文中没有完全对应的译词，但是说清楚这个问题并非不可能，只是阐释的可能性太多，以迂回方式才有可能说得清楚。关于圣人之内中成就这一问题，大致不离一个汉字"气"，英文有译为"air"。"气"也指"生命之气"（vital breath），相当于梵文的 Prana，为一生理实体。我们的身体中有一生命之流游走于整个系统，不同于我们呼出或吸入的空气（air）。我们先看一下物理有体或形式，孟子认为只有圣人才能"践行／完成"其物理有体。如下：

孟子曰："形色，天性也。惟圣人然后可以践形。"[253]

"践形"即是说，无论美丑，人必定不会只是一个空洞的外部形式，一定有内中的内容填充这形式。这内容就是真理，或善或美。在此种人的形式中，所有身体器官的功能在正常状态下都是良好和完善的，其所应用之目的必须与这良好和完善相匹配。在此义度中，形式的彻底完满，韦檀多哲学称之为"梵形"（brahmavarcasam）。不然，欲断定一人，此外部形式或人的形相为最不可靠之依据。我们无须提及苏格拉底的容貌，甚至孔子也

.

251. 《孟子·告子章句上》，第 8 章。

252. 《孟子·尽心章句上》，第 36 章。

253. 同上，第 38 章。

说过自己曾经因为以貌取人而犯过错。

进而，此构成内中有体的"气"，理雅各译为"the passion nature"（情命自性）。

> （孟子说：）夫志，气之帅也；气，体之充也。夫志至焉，气次焉；故曰："持其志，无暴其气。"[254]

充满并鼓动身体的"气"即是情命有体。两者有一细小差别，"气"重在强调有体的运动，而非有体本身。所以称其为"情命体之运动"，更为妥当。通常，世界上严格的宗教戒律有一明显的倾向，即弱化、消减或压制情命体之运动，在儒家看来，却不应如此。相反，纵容和许可情命有体无节制地蔓衍同样也是错误的。"气"需要有"志"（Will）为其统帅。进一步阐释如下：

> （公孙丑问：）"既曰志至焉，气次焉，又曰持其志，无暴其气者，何也？"
>
> 曰："志壹则动气，气壹则动志也。今夫蹶者趋者，是气也，而反动其心。"[255]

公孙丑问的是，既然"志"是主帅，只要注意"志"即可，为什么还要留心情命运动呢？回答是，"志"固然可以引领所有情命运动，但是在某些情况下，情命运动会影响"志"。孟子给出的例子是，人绊倒或跌落时，心思会受到扰乱，或者生出恐惧，开始奔跑。这个例子不算恰当，但我们明白，情命运动确实会影响"志"，并将其降低或转变为欲望。这样的例子在生活中很容易见到。愤怒（气）可改变心思，使人放弃原来的决定，或偏离正常轨道。

接下来的问题有关于孟子的内中成就，如下：

（公孙丑又问：）"敢问夫子恶乎长？"

曰："我知言，我善养吾浩然之气。"[256]

此处有一关键点，这句话中的"气"不能再用"passion nature"（情命自性）来翻译。用"vast"和"flowing"来翻译"浩然"是可以的，或可用"vast-like"，更准确些。但是这个变幻莫测的"气"在这里应当翻译为"atmosphere"。不辞辛苦的译者可以将"浩然之气"译为"vast-like Spiritual Atmosphere"。

首先，我们看一下如何是"知言"。"言"有不同，如果是觉悟之"言"，则需圣人解读。然而孟子所擅长仍在心思层面，他所谓的"言"主要指同

.

254.　《孟子·公孙丑章句上》，第 2 章。

255.　同上。

256.　同上。

时代哲学家所持的不同理论。对于这个问题，孟子有如下解答：

> 诐辞知其所蔽，淫辞知其所陷，邪辞知其所离，遁辞知其所穷。生于其心，害于其政；发于其政，害于其事。圣人复起，必从吾言矣。[257]

这段话的含义非常明了，无需多余的解释。因为无论作者或讲者如何伪装，读者都可以通过文字了解他们的思想和情感。

接下来，我们仔细探讨一下"浩然之气"。

> （公孙丑问：）"敢问何谓浩然之气？"
>
> 曰："难言也。其为气也，至大至刚，以直养而无害，则塞于天地之间。
>
> 其为气也，配义与道。无是，馁也。
>
> 是集义所生者，非义袭而取之也。行有不慊于心，则馁矣。"[258]

如果孟子认为"浩然之气"难言，我们又当如何言之？孟子的阐述虽然简短，仍可使我们有些具体的了解。"直"与"义"实含于更大的"道"即真理之中。"馁"的"退缩"（shrinking）和"衰弱"（emaciation）义都出自原义"饥饿"，所以理雅各译之为"starvation"。由此可知，"浩然之气"产生于"道"的自然生长，与"道"相伴，一直得到"道"的维持——即是说，道"养"浩然之气，使其不至于饥饿。浩然之气充塞宇宙，超出言语表述之外，几乎所有获得内中成就的导师都知晓这个精神事实。那么，如何是"道"呢？"道"为一终极的内中经验，只能证实于相同的内中经验，或更大的经验。除此之外，我们别无可说。中国学者从古至今，都用这段话指导个人之修为。

这里不再赘述孟子思想中与前人完全相同的内容了。道德问题，如父亲如何正确对待自己的儿子，或者天才之于普通人，或导师之于询问者；社会问题，如农业社会的基本经济福利，以及和平治域下的理想状况；哲学问题，如驳斥墨子的利他主义和杨子的利己主义，杀身成仁的重要性，以困境磨炼自身以期担负天之大任；等等，几乎所有学者都熟悉这些著名的文字。这些文字大都明白可解，无须分别阐述，阐明其中任何一个问题都需要不短的篇幅。引用一段有关孟子内中成就的文字，作为本章的结尾。或许不止基督教的先知，即便印度教的圣人（Rishi），都会对这段话点头称许。文字如下：

孟子曰："万物皆备于我矣。反身而诚，乐莫大焉。强恕而行，求仁莫近焉。"[259]

．

257. 《孟子·公孙丑章句上》，第 2 章。

258. 同上。

259. 《孟子·尽心章句上》，第 4 章。

末章

古代儒学在孟子之后停滞了，不再有伟大的人物，直至宋明两代再次萌芽，学派林立，形成所谓新儒家。然而那是另一主题了。

读者阅读至此，或已对孔子的教义以及践行同一道路的儒者有了相当的了解。同时也应知觉到这一主题牵涉甚广，许多困难源于语言的障碍。经典译文中缺少对应词汇，只能选用含义相近者，只有经过语文学的解释，才能有清晰的理解。除语言之外，心思程式本身也是理解的障碍，中国传统思想不同于现代心思，尤其异于西方心思。仅以简单算术为例，中国人用自己的算盘和记忆法则，亦可轻松得出与使用阿拉伯数字计算相同的结果，然而其所使用的系统不同。随着科学知识的增长，人们不再以古代心思程式思考。古旧事物对我们没有了吸引力，大多数人以之为无趣，方法与品味都已不同了。

　　无名学者如我，是否有能力书写这样一本书，首先表示怀疑的是作者本人。一般而言，拥有与圣人相近的内中成就才有能力书写圣人，然而作者不敢如此自恃。有一则古代寓言讲一穷人大谈黄金（"贫子说金"），他的描述可能是正确的，黄金是黄色的，很有分量，等等，但这事仍不免是个闹剧。正相应于道家的一句话："知者弗言，言者弗知。"

　　然而问题要比看起来容易得多。欣赏一件艺术品时，观者无须考虑作品背后的艺术家。当智者都已逝去，他们的文字还在。站在读者的角度看，最重要的是，本书提供的信息是正确的，而且值得阅读。作者尽其所能选择最可信、最权威的信息来源，仔细撷取，给出最忠实于原文的译文，做最少的解释，将思考留给读者。如果有读者能从一两行引文，甚或一两个字之中获得足够真实的益处，那么这本书的全部目的就达到了，作者的劳作就得到了收获。无论如何，本书可视为一本选文集。

　　贝伦森（Bernard Berenson）在《文艺复兴时期的意大利画家》一书的序言中说："你必须仔细欣赏画作，直至融入其中，有一瞬间与之相合。一幅历史悠久、倍受喜爱的画作，如果你爱不起来，欺骗自己说喜爱是毫无用处的。"如果画作如此，古代圣人阐释出的真理更是如此！个人要切身体会这些真理，不仅在一瞬间与之相合，而是永远与之相合。似乎只有如此真诚的方式才能达至高上的体悟。

　　还有一点需要聪慧的读者注意，阅读本书时，一定不要受制于心思结构。神圣母亲对此曾有过非常明确的说明，如下：

以一非常普遍且流布全球的迷信为例，这迷信认为苦行与精神是同一事。如果你说某男人或女人为一精神之人，人们立刻以为这人不进食，或终日枯坐不动，或在一棚屋中过着极度贫苦的生活，或施舍一切所有，不留一物。当你提及精神人物时，一百人中有九十九人的头脑中会立刻升起此种景象：他们用贫穷和弃绝一切享乐或舒适证明自己的精神性。如果你想见到并追随精神的真理，必须抛弃此种心思结构。因为当你诚心立志接近精神生活，你想遇见神圣者，在你的知觉性和生命中实践神圣者；如果你来到一地，非是棚屋，见到一神圣者过着舒适的生活，正常进食，身边围绕着美丽或奢侈的物品，没有将自己的所有分给穷人，而是接受并享受人们赠予他的一切，你当如何？以你固执的心思准则，定会不知所措地大喊，"为什么，这是怎么回事？我本以为自己要见的是一精神之人。"此种错误观念需要打破，并去除。一旦去除之后，你会发现另一事，高出你狭隘的苦行准则许多，一彻底的敞开，有体因此不再受限……260

"抛弃此种心思结构"，正与孔子"四毋"之一在负极方面相合。"子绝四"261，第一为"毋意"，意指孔子不使论断先行，但并不是说他没有逻辑推理能力或想象力。相反，这正表明孔子的智慧。第二为"毋必"，意指孔子不独断，但并不是说他没有好的意见或决定。第三为"毋固"，意指孔子不顽固，但并不是说他不能坚持正路。正是因为坚韧和"毋必"，孔子才能固守于"义""礼"，遂被称为"圣之时者"262，意指能够随时间变化而进步的圣人。第四为"毋我"，意指孔子没有私我，仁爱正是生于此处，但并不是说他没有自我培育的"自我"。第一点中也包含偏见和成见，或许无人能完全免除偏见和成见。不能摆脱心思结构的桎梏，就永远无法扩大视野。我们所重视的一点心思知识常常不过是一聚意见、偏见和成见而已，以致常常阻碍新知识的汲取，固执则使进步为不可能。作为解决之途，儒家如道家一样总是强调"空／无"，只有使心思保持"空"的状态，才能接受别人的意见，或所有的新知识。

如上所见，从外部看，孔子就是这样一位精神人物。他没有过贫穷的生活，而是过着合乎贵族身份的相对富足的生活。《论语·乡党篇》详细地记录了孔子的生活，限于篇幅，在此不作叙述。大体上说，孔子遵照古礼过着非常健康和舒适的生活，在成熟的老年自然地离去。他不似耶稣被钉死在十字架上，不似佛陀归于般涅槃，也不似老子如印度隐士（Vanaprastha）一样遁去。倘如此，孔子就不是一位精神导师了吗？

在印度神话中，佛陀正要进入般涅槃之门前，目光转回，望向人类，所以他被称为大悲者。"慈"（Maitri）与"悲"（Karuna）有什么根本不同吗？又与"仁"有什么根本不同吗？只是孔子的目光一直望着人类，望着后世之人，望着此世，而他的内中视见一直企向天或上帝。孔子曾说："丘之

---

260. 《母亲的话》卷一，第 114—115 页。

261. 《论语·子罕篇第九》，第 4 章。

262. 《孟子·万章章句下》，第 1 章。

祷久矣。"孔子一生从未教导过如何止息和完全消除苦痛。他对生命也从
未怀有过消极的态度。可以想见，孔门弟子愉快地生活在和谐的氛围中，
于不知觉中渐渐转化了自性。我们究竟为何称孔子为圣人呢？孟子作了很
有教益的回答：

> 可欲之谓善。
>
> 有诸己之谓信。
>
> 充实之谓美。
>
> 充实而有光辉之谓大。
>
> 大而化之之谓圣。
>
> 圣而不可知之之谓神。[263]

．

263. 《孟子·尽心章句下》，第 25 章。谈论"人"，又是一个庞大的主题，历史文
     献中有许多可供研究的资料。现代人可能对《庄子》的内容比较感兴趣。最
     近有 James R. Ware 的英译本《庄子》出版（New American Library，1962）。班固
     在《汉书·艺文志》中将著名历史人物归为"九流"。刘劭《人物志》亦值得
     关注。

Confucianism

INTRODUCTION

Several years ago, I was asked to give some talks in our International Centre of Education on the subject of Confucianism. At that time, owing to certain circumstances it was impossible, and those talks never materialized. Still, there remained in my mind a feeling that something was left undone. Instead of giving the lectures, it has occured to me that it would be better to put in the form of a booklet some of the outstanding principles and salient features of Confucianism, so that it could perhaps have a more permanent value for reference purposes.

Nevertheless, we should remember that it is a common destiny of academic works that unless what is said or written is of permanent truth, or of a truth too great to be ignored, it can scarcely escape the usual fate of being put away, neglected or forgotten. Innumerable books have been written and read, endless lectures have been delivered and listened to, but let any one in his ripe age honestly ask himself in serious introspection, how much he still retains in his memory. Only a few exceptionally brilliant minds can recollect a good deal of the past to the minute details, yet even with them much is still forgotten and faded away into a grey void. This forgetfulness is all too natural because mankind is ever progressing and whenever the past accumulation of knowledge becomes too cumbersome to the point of retardation of further progress the truths in it, great or small, are simply sunk into oblivion. This phenomenon cannot be considered as unfortunate and in a way we can say that it is even helpful, just as one cannot and need not retain everything in one's memory which has been learned in childhood. Yet it is always of some use to look back into the past, to regain the knowledge in the cultural heritage which has been lost and to throw it into a new light of the present for revaluation or eventual readoption. So it will not be without gain to review again in some broad lines such an ancient theme generally regarded as out of date now, though still very familiar to most of the scholars in our oriental world.

I remember Sri Aurobindo had once made a casual remark about China as He discussed with His disciples Spengler's *Decline of the West*. Here I venture to quote His words as follows:

DISCIPLE: It is very curious that Spengler misses the fact that there can be national resurgence and reawakening.

SRI AUROBINDO: Yes, take, for instance, China. China has had cities from most ancient times. It is a peculiar race always disturbed and always the same! If you study Chinese history one thousand years back, you will find they were in disturbance and yet they had their culture.

The Tartar king who tried to destroy their culture by burning their books did not succeed. I would not be surprised if, after the present turmoil, two thousand years hence, you find them what they are today. That is the character of the race.[1]

Such a clear insight into Chinese history can rarely be found among the thinkers of the world today, and how pithy a remark it is, yet how instructive to us Chinese! We Chinese were very conservative so far as the past indicates, and in a way we can safely say that we survived every inner turmoil and civil strife and all external aggressions mainly because we kept to the path of Confucianism throughout the twenty and five centuries past. The experiment of adopting Buddhism in ruling a large empire had been tried in the first half of the sixth century A.D., but that experiment failed. Apart from this, Taoism existed in the mind of the race as a strong undercurrent, but never came too prominently to the surface.

Nowadays we can only think of making progress and advance together with the rest of humanity. But the theory that human history has always run in a cycle of five hundred years talked about in the Conversations mentioned above is an old one, spoken of by Mencius, a great sage next to Confucius. What Mencius meant was not exactly a cycle; what he meant, evidently deduced from ancient history, was that every five hundred years there would arise a true peaceful sovereign, and during that period there would be illustrious sages capable of setting everything of the age in good order. (Ref. Commentary by Chao Chi.) Yet it was already more than seven hundred years from the golden period upto his time, as Mencius himself said, and there was as yet no ideal state. But Mencius was conscious himself that he was one of those illustrious men, and his model or the great master whom he admired and emulated most was Confucius. No doubt, our history tells us that the Chinese race was always in a state of disturbance; if there was no internal strife, there was external invasion, mostly coming from the northern or northwestern part of China, and those nomad tribes, either Huns or Tartars or Monghols, driven by poverty and envy of the brilliant material aspect of ancient Chinese culture, gave constant trouble to the population through their repeated incursions. Yet whenever peace again reigned, culture at once began to revive and flourish. The longest period of peace was the Chow dynasty, which lasted for more than eight hundred years (1123–256 B.C.), and henceforth there were equally golden periods when capital punishment was abandoned for decades and jails and prisons were entirely empty throughout the state. These were the times uninterrupted by those two evils.

In the Han dynasty, the great historian Ssu Ma Tsien, the Herodotus of the East, calculated in chronology that it was about five hundred years from the time of the Duke of Chow (died in 1104 B.C.)

---

1. *Evening Talks with Sri Aurobindo* — recorded by A. B. Purani, pp. 112–113.

to Confucius, and it was again five hundred years from Confucius upto his time. He cherished in his pride the idea that he himself was born at that juncture or interval, and therefore following the footsteps of the ancient sages, he had his special mission to fulfil towards humanity, such as to leave to posterity a monumental work comparable to that of Confucius. His *Chinese History*, ended in the year 97 B.C., proved to be a monumental work but he himself was not so great a sage. And it was the belief, as noted down in that *History*, that the Celestial Path, which is connected with the constellations and intimately related to man, undergoes a minor change every thirty years, a medium change every hundred years, and a great change every five hundred years. Three great changes make an era in which changes become generally completed. In such a belief perhaps the idea of a cyclic revolution is implied. It cannot be called an exact cycle as we understand it, but at any rate it does show that human progress does not proceed ad infinitum in a straight line.

Needless to say, there are periods of ups and downs, one following another in every history, in the history of every race or of every one's life. But it is a common feature that it has been at the most disastrous and desperate, helpless and hopeless moments that there has all of a sudden appeared the Light, and a great sage is born. In India people call him an Avatar; in China, a Sage born of Heaven. In the *Book of Odes* there was some suggestion that the ancient people believed also in Avatarhood; in one place it was mentioned that gods descended from the great mountain and two great men were born. Whether that belief was generally accepted or not we cannot definitely say. This involves the problem of the ancient conception of Heaven or God, a subject too great to be treated here. But Confucius was born in such a period.

The life of Confucius and his age will be discussed later; but we can well see that it is no new subject unfamiliar to the West. Ever since the seventeenth century, or even earlier, soon after Matteo Ricci (1552–1610), the Italian Jesuit missionary who visited China in 1580 and stayed under the royal patronage in Peking for many years, Chinese culture became gradually known to the West. If Chinese culture was known, its highest peak or representative could not be unknown, just as people in the East believing in Christianity must have learned about the life and work of Jesus Christ. Just one century before the Great French Revolution, the books of *The Analects of Confucius*, the *Great Learning*, and the *Doctrine of the Mean* were rendered into Latin and published in Paris, and after less than fifty years, Du Halde's encyclopaedic work *The Complete Gazetteer of the Chinese Empire* also appeared (1735 Paris) . The general condition in the cultural field in the West is such that when any oriental work is translated into any of their languages, (a task of ice-breaking, and perhaps back-breaking as well) then other renderings into different languages easily follow one after the other. Such works are now in existence in abundance, and one can make substantial use of them. It is worthwhile to compare different translations of the same texts and thus, through one's own effort, one can approach a correct understanding. Misinterpretations there must be, because in some places our native scholars have since ancient times disagreed in their explanations, and scholastic or sectarian biases are equally unavoidable. Yet in this way one can still get to the core of the idea, even if one does not know the Chinese language. The discussions here are concerned with those things usually talked about but perhaps not sufficiently emphasized, and they are cast in a historical view with broad reference to other cultures of the world. It is not the idea of the writer to burden the reader with a heavy load of Chinese names in transliteration, or merely to give dry and pedantic definitions exalting the ancient doctrines. Things are expressed here in a simple, non-pedantic way merely for the sake of making them more understandable.

It must be noted at the very outset that if we take it outwardly there is nothing in Confucianism exciting or striking or even interesting. It is not only so to our modern world where we are used to all sorts of highly-pitched stimulation, but was so to our ancient people as well. In contrast to other great systems of the world, it is less colourful or drastic. We do not find in it any ideal of Eleusis, or Nirvāṇa, or any of the Ten Bhumis, or any of the Thirty-three Heavens for the departed souls. With regard to the living beings, there is no Paramahamsa or Bodhisattva or any Superman, though the conception of the Superior Man is there. As to human activities, nothing is taught about non-action or Tapasya or renunciation or asceticism; and also nothing about alchemy for the transformation of base metals into gold, or for brewing any sort of elixir vital for prolonging our worldly life. And also there is in it no use of charms for scaring away devils and evils; nor is there any way taught for curing diseases. The Supreme is there indeed, but there is neither that all-powerful Zeus, nor God who created the world within six days together with the blissful couple eventually chased out of His Paradise. Agni, Indra, Aryaman, indeed the whole pantheon of the Vedic gods were not there, nor, needless to say, were Ahuramazda and Angromainyous. Yet, contrary to prevalent ideas, Confucianism was never merely secular in its nature, nor is it merely a set of rigid ethical codes or dry philosophical principles. On the contrary, it is supremely spiritual in its nature, never lacking in insurmountable height and unfathomable depth, in the minutest subtlety, and, what is more, in its immense broadness and flexibility or all-pervading comprehensiveness.

In our modern world we doubt everything and, relying upon our scientific spirit, we want to examine everything of the past and bring it to revaluation. What has just been mentioned may appear as an exaggeration and unjustified eulogizing, though it is a traditional view. Now, more than two thousand five hundred years have elapsed since the time of Confucius; have there not been among such a large population certain wise men, just as clever as we are, who had the brains which we have, who challenged those teachings of his and disputed his authority as a Guru of the race? Yet upto present, no one ever had any doubt about his spirituality. Above all, what do we mean by "spirituality"? Here a definition given by Sri Aurobindo is worth our consideration:

"The divine perfection is always there above us; but for man to become divine in consciousness and act and to live inwardly and outwardly the divine life is what is meant by spirituality; all lesser meanings given to the word are inadequate fumblings or impostures."

The truth here expressed is universal, and we find exactly in Confucius a representative of such a truth. And if we regard him as an Avatar in the Brahmanic sense of the word, I beg also to quote the Mother's words:

"In the eternity of becoming, each Avater is only the announcer, the forerunner of a more perfect future realisation."

Many theories of the later ages we do not find in Confucianism, yet it prevailed, and as time went on, we find praise and admiration increased, not only of his teachings but of the man himself. In India Aryavada is regarded as a source of knowledge, and in China it is no less so. There are teachings which we can safely believe without the need of scrutiny. Revaluation of his doctrines is a thing sound and useful, but first we must understand them in the context of his time or in their historical background. We may proceed farther than our ancients did, although this is still doubtful, but we need not level to the ground those monuments already established as landmarks of the distance they had already covered in the eternal ascent of Man's spiritual searchings.

The chief reason can be found in our human nature. Human mind always tends toward novelty and curiosity. That makes us progress. Ever since Buddhism was introduced into China, it absorbed the best intelligence of the race for nearly six hundred years before it was entirely assimilated and changed into something else. The native Taoism was not the less attractive, and had equally engaged men of great genius for even more centuries than Buddhism, though it never appeared as brilliant. Yet Confucianism stood as it was, unshaken and unshattered throughout the ages. But it was asked why many a good genius could be converted into such "heretic" religions as Buddhism and Taoism. The answer given was that, because Confucianism was calm and nonchalant, it could not grasp in its hold those who had strong temperaments and so they were easily drawn into other religions. That might be true with regard to the old Confucianism; as to the so-called Neo-Confucianism that took shape in the Sung dynasty (960–1277 A.D.) it was more fortunate. It has predominated upto the present day. If there is anything in the world like a national religion—and I hesitate to call it a religion, it can be better put as a national belief—that in China was no other than Confucianism. Even in the country at present, for about three years or more, there has arisen a great tide of interest in the study of the teachings of the Sage.

To illustrate the special characteristics of Confucianism, one simple anecdote from the Yuan dynasty (1277–1367 A.D.) may be given (Vide *New History of Yuan Dynasty*, Vol. 21). But we must bear in mind that three "religions" ran parallel to each other in China from the beginning of the fourth century A.D.: first Confucianism, which is outwardly a philosophy but a religious faith at its core; second Buddhism, which in China is considered neither as a religion nor philosophy, it is simply "Dharma" which can be taken as a religion in the European sense of the word; and third Taoism, which has its religious aspect and philosophical or rather metaphysical aspect trenchantly distinct from each other. Religious tolerance among the common people in China is well known in history, incomparable to that of any other race in the world. But they were not without constant struggles for power in the imperial court, especially between the Buddhists and Taoists, and the side which could best win the emperor's favour could then secure the patronage of the nobility and could have a better chance for promulgation of its doctrines among the populace. It happened that during the reign of Dhu Timur (1328–1332 A.D.) a Royal Buddhist preceptor came from the western parts of China to the capital. It was ordered that all officers of the court from the highest rank down should ride on white horses for the reception on the highroad outside the city wall. In obeying such an imperial order, the great ministers all bowed low before the preceptor, each offering him a goblet of wine, kneeling on the ground. That preceptor remained seated, dignified as a Buddha statue, without a muscle of his face being moved. Then a minister named Lu Chun, a teacher of the national scholars, raised his goblet, addressing him thus:

"Reverend Preceptor, You are the disciple of Buddha and the Teacher of all monks in the world; while I am a humble disciple of Confucius, and the teacher of all scholars under heaven. So let us not observe formalities towards each other."

All those present were amazed. But on hearing these words, the preceptor gave an ample smile, stood up, and finished a goblet of wine with him.

Afterwards, the emperor asked this minister which among the three religions he considered the best, and he said: "Buddhism is like yellow gold, and Taoism, white jade, but Confucianism is comparable to grain."

"Is then Confucianism something cheap?" asked Dhu Timur.

"Gold and jade are indeed precious, yet one can live without them; but with regard to grain, how can one dispense with it for a single day?"

"Excellent!" said Dhu Timur.

When we come across this story in reading history, we see that to a simple-minded foreign prince this concrete analogy was understandable and even convincing. This illustrates the importance of such a teaching for the maintenance of life, which involves the solution of all our life problems, whether of the individual or of the populace. In our modern world, civilization has progressed to such an extent that the life problems have become too complex to find any satisfactory solution and sufferings have become so intense as to defy any cure. Yet resolving all those difficult problems into a simple equation, we find it is still a problem of the discovery of a proper and happy way of living, both for the collectivity and for the individual. If that is true, then we can still derive much from this source. It may be noted, however, that one of the Monghol crown-princes once said that when the Buddhist preceptor taught him about Buddhism, he could easily understand; but when the Chinese teacher taught him Confucianism, he experienced difficulty. This is quite natural because Buddhism is comparatively simple in its elementary teachings. Take, for instance, the Buddhist Shila, or Moral precepts, before they were developed into a great complex and minute network binding and constricting the vitality of man; the fundamental rules were plain to every one. "Thou shalt not kill..." that is the first commandment. Unfortunately or fortunately there is no such rule in Confucianism. Things are treated in a different way, yet they also come to the same end. Ultimately we find that even such a rule, be it so elementary and important, is yet only a relative truth and cannot be absolute. Perhaps a modern writer and thinker best understood this idea in saying that the Golden Rule is that there is no Golden Rule. In its stead, we have the Greater Way (Tao).

Now, in the spiritual field, if we consider that by which we maintain our lives and without which we cannot live for a single day, we can understand it as Divinity. Indian friends can best explain it as That or Brahman. Undoubtedly Confucius was revered as a great sage, a Master of all ages, and a divinity incarnate. But he scarcely talked about this subject. With regard to the material or physical aspect of the Spirit or rather its human phase, we would rather take that as a highly developed and cultivated life which may be held as culture itself. The term for "culture" in Chinese means transformation and perfection of humanity by whatever is excellent in humanity. Generally speaking, we had two great sages in Chinese history who shaped the destiny of the race for the past three thousand years, and nowadays we still enjoy their blessings. We may call them cultural leaders as well: first, the Duke of Chow, and five hundred years after him, Confucius. This is only evident when we compare the Chinese history with those of the peoples outside China, those people in the north-western part and in Central Asia, and those in south-eastern Asia. In ancient times they were called "barbarians", a name which seems now not altogether unjustified. Two examples in striking contrast to each other were Japan and Tibet. Japan in ancient times amply and substantially accepted Confucianism, and developed her own culture, but Tibet failed to do so. Any traveller into Tibet can give a good account of the cultural level on which the people stand now. The Tibetan tragedy we need not bother about here.

In a pantheistic view, everything in the universe is regarded as divine. But we are inclined to regard culture as something divine above everything else. Yet, as said before, it may be regarded as the human aspect of the Spirit, the Spirit which is transcendent ,above all, indifferent to our life and death, even to the construction and destruction of the world, and yet still intrinsically involved in our life and death and in this world. This sounds like a paradox which cannot stand in a strict logical formula, but this is a truth, a truth perhaps too large for logic. Most of our sages in the past who were Confucians, including the disciples and those who followed the same path, emphasized in their teachings this human phase, this worldly or spiritual cultural aspect, and tried to transform the lower nature of men, to build up their character, and to elevate all to a higher level. The influence exercised was usually very broad, enduring and lasting and, because of this, Chinese culture developed and flourished. Fundamentally speaking, without this development we would have remained still in the primitive stage and all our conceptions of divinity could not have come into being. The other aspect which, if we like, may be called the spiritual-spiritual, was never exoterically taught, and yet nearly every sage worth the name had this or that realization of That, a fact which was never publicly known except by a few, unless we deeply examine their sayings and deeds. Great masters and teachers always spoke to a certain extent about realization, but after that they remained silent.

On the whole, Confucianism may be too large a subject to be treated in any miniature form; nevertheless this may be tried. But usually to write a study of any subject without being critical is not an easy task. One is supposed to be free from any bias or prejudice, *sine ira et studio*, and must take the topic quite objectively, viz. to take the subject as it is; yet even in stating mere facts, one's opinions spontaneously respond to the statements and in the way of writing, and thereby the readers are unconsciously influenced. So one cannot be too just in his attitude though one may believe himself to be so. A better way which is adopted here is to let the readers read the original words of the authors themselves thus forming their own opinions. But for that too many quotations would be unavoidable, and in the end a general idea or a view of the whole scope may be incomprehensive or even missing. This offers the first difficulty.

Next, Chinese language is totally different in its construction from the European languages in general. Hence forms of thought are also different. Ancient Chinese is still easily understandable nowadays, much more so than Greek, but it is a very common feature that certain terms have no equivalents in English, and one can only put them in an artificial way which may appear very odd and awkward. There are only a few passages in translations which the writer finds fully satisfactory, having the original sense completely conveyed without anything added or left out. These belong almost to the category of inspired words worth our high appreciation, but they are not many. Otherwise, the translation stands as a flower seen in a mist; the original beauty may still be there, but it looks as if veiled. This offers the second difficulty.

This may explain why and how such a small task of writing a booklet can be a big one, and in the end cannot be totally successful. Therefore it is advisable for the reader to go into the works of those authors himself, and, if possible, to go through the original texts. And that means a study of ancient Chinese culture as a whole. At least the Six Classics edited and compiled by Confucius must be studied so that those principles held by him can be more deeply understood. That means about 430,000 words must be read and committed to memory, a task not too difficult to our ancient scholars. Nowadays, texts are treated in a more scientific and advanced way, but perhaps an effort equally strenuous will be required.

Chapter I

LIFE OF CONFUCIUS

Many great men of the world, who have within the short span of one life achieved immortal fame, leaving their most salutary effects upon earth and contributing so much to the establishment of human values that even nowadays we subsist through their blessings, were born within the same period of about a century, the fifth before Christ. The Samien sage Pythagoras was supposed to have lived upto 497 B.C., and Gautama Buddha in India entered into Parinirvana about twenty years later. Though these dates might not be exact, they cannot be too far from the truth. Lao Tze, whose life was somehow similarly shrouded in mist, was born in the same period, and on a certain occasion he was the teacher of Confucius. Mo Tze was born a few decades later, and Socrates (469–399 B.C.), Hippocrates (462–361 B.C.), Plato (429–348 B.C.) all belonged to the same age. Younger than Plato but equally long lived and of the same calibre was Mencius (Mon Tze 372–289

B.C.). All these men lived to a ripe old age, especially Hippocrates, father of modern medicine, who remained in the world for nearly a hundred years. Why all those sages, greatest among the great and most eminent among the eminent, manifested on earth both in the East and in the West at about the same time is inexplicable, unless we accept the doctrine of Sri Aurobindo that all were a Descent of Divine Forces from Above, or "born of Heaven" as the Chinese tradition goes. A Renaissance theory that the world's virtue shifted from country to country, first from Assyria to Persia, then to Medea and so on gives a faint glimpse of this idea.

Among all these sages, the only one in whose name no war, no bloodshed or other persecution was committed was Confucius. One of the main causes why Mohism, altruistic at its core and exceedingly peaceful in nature, almost died out only several generations after Mo Tze, was that most of the prominent leaders of that school sacrificed their lives for social reforms which they fought for and, together with that sort of voluntary extermination of their lives, their teachings were mostly extinguished. Confucianism compared to other religions of the world proved to be the least sanguinary and the least destructive even for constructive purposes.

Furthermore, among all of them, the least legendary but not the least celebrated of whom we have the most exact historical record was Confucius. Even the life of Jesus Christ, so well known even among non-Christians, has nearly two decades in it unaccounted for. The biography of Confucius is now extant, included in the *Ancient History* of Ssu Ma Tsien. Not only the words and activities of the Sage himself were recorded in detail, but also those of his disciples, all famous men, were noted down in a separate chapter as a sort of collective biography. Mencius and Hsün Tze, both great philosophers of the same school, filled another chapter. The lineage of scholars who were versed in Confucian classics in the Han Dynasty had a special chapter in the same *History*. Since the Chinese language has remained unchanged throughout these last twenty centuries, we can read now the whole bulk of ancient literature as easily as we read our modern newspaper reports.

But difficulty lies here also. We find indeed in our research no lack of materials because, apart from this *Ancient History*, numerous other sources are available, but to present a clear picture of Confucius and Confucianism before English readers unfamiliar with ancient Chinese culture is not so simple a task. Names of feudal states and the names and titles of dukes, marquises, counts, viscounts and barons, and names of clans and families, together with geographical names of mountains, rivers, passes, and then dates and years according to different chronological calculations have to be understood first. Without a correct knowledge of these, a clear impression would be impossible. Indeed, it proved once a great obstacle and unfortunately there is no substitute or better way out. So only a general sketch of the life of the Sage in broad outlines can be given without burdening the reader with too many minute details. Above all, what matters to us most is the main doctrines, the philosophy and his teachings in general. As Lao Tze once told Confucius in an interview: "With regard to what you have just said, these men together with their bones all perished, only their words remain. ..."

Confucius was born in the feudal state Lu, now in the Shantung province of China. His ancestors were descended from a branch of the ruling house of Sung who belonged to the royal family of the Shang dynasty otherwise called the Ying dynasty (1766–1122 B.C.). His great-grandfather, one of the great nobles of the Sung state, immigrated to the state Lu in withdrawing from a certain civil tumult. His father, Shiu Liang Hê, served as a high officer in an administrative district of the state Lu, being also a knight renowned for his great physical strength. His mother, named Chen Tsai, was of the Yen family, also of aristocratic origin. She was married to Shiu Liang Hê in his late years; five years later Confucius was born, and three years thereafter her husband died. Thus Confucius was semi-orphaned when he was only three years old, and his mother died when he was twenty-four.

According to our calendar, Confucius was born on the 28th of September in the year 552 B.C., and this date is now fixed as a festival for teachers in China. Since the third century A.D. scholars have been engaged in the exact calculation of historical dates of that period, and now, in terms of our modern calendar, this seems to be the final correct one. He lived upto 479 B.C., aged seventy-four.

It may be noted in passing that the romanization of the name

Confucius is the usual current style. In Chinese he is called Kung Fu Tze, or else Kung Tze. Kung is his family name and placed first, and Fu Tze simply means "master". Tze is just a complimentary appellation for a man whom we would consider nowadays a respectable and known person. Such examples are Lao Tze, Djuang Tze, Mo Tze, etc. His monosyllabic name is Ch'iu, meaning "hillock" or "mount". His two-worded name is Chung Ni.[2] Before his birth his mother prayed for a son on the Hill Ni, and when the son was born, the name given was Ch'iu in memory of that Hill; and Chung indicated merely the second one, while the name of the hill, Ni, was also retained. Yet so great was the respect of later ages towards this sage that these normal appellations were nearly tabooed, and in meeting his name, the word Ch'iu in a text, it was read as "mou", different from its original pronunciation, meaning something like "so and so."

Thus far it is quite uninteresting, because we see Confucius was born just as an ordinary man. There was no Annunciation before his birth, nor did there appear any brilliant star in sky when the child was born, nor was there any special sign or mark on the body of the child after being born, such as the thirty-two auspicious signs of Gautama Buddha. It is not that such legends never existed in China; some such

---

2. The monosyllabic name, used widely nowadays, is the official name whereas the polite style, usually in two syllables (two words, very rarely also in one word) is employed in ordinary usage.

stories actually existed before and during his time, as a certain girl was born with certain words in her hand, and on another occasion, a boy, who afterwards became a famous man. But they were mostly attached to the births of certain heroes of later ages, and connected with a dream or a special vision of the mother just before pregnancy or when the child was born, and generally these heroes were less-great characters. There was only one record about the physiognomy of Confucius which was most probably a fact, that the crown of his head was somehow hollow in the middle and raised up around, thus he had a peculiarly shaped skull. But that could scarcely be taken as the stamp of any Avatarhood, or as an auspicious sign of the body.

Confucius was married at the age of nineteen to a girl of the Sung family with the surname Ch'i Kuan, and in the next year, a son was born. It happened that on the occasion of this child's birth, the Duke of Lu presented a carp to Confucius, and so the son was named Li — or "carp" —, and for a polite name, styled Pê Yu, or "Fish, the eldest." It is remarkable that the genealogy of this Kung family remained in a lineage unbroken throughout the past 2,500 and more years, and now the descendants in the seventy-seventh generation are living, and one of them is a famous professor in China. Yen's family preserved the same tradition. Such examples of authentic historicity in recording the hereditary lineage can scarcely be found anywhere in the world today.

It is a common feature that certain children like specially to play in a group as leader and afterwards, when they are grown up, they become successful generals. But Kung Tze in his childhood liked to play with symbolic sacrificial vessels, imitating the performance of worship and other ceremonies. It was probable that he learned these things from the environment of his aristocratic family. The general education in those days of aristocratic families was calculated to develop the body and to enlighten the mind with a training based upon traditional proprieties. He reached a robust youth well-educated, and when grown up, was called a giant by his contemporaries because he measured nine Chinese feet six inches in height. (In the decimal measurement of the Chow dynasty, a foot was equivalent to about 22 centimeters.) His physical strength, perhaps partly inherited from his parents, and partly through constant training, was said to be so great that he could raise up the hanging city gate, a very clumsy and heavy thing. But he never signalized himself in that, mainly because his attention was directed to other studies. It may be noted in passing that none of the great religious leaders of the world, with the exception perhaps of Shankaracarya or Ramakrishna, was of frail constitution; nearly every one of them was physically sturdy and strong, capable of bearing the necessary hardships in the physical world which had to be nobly borne for the cause they stood for. Needless to say that Mohammed was exceptionally handsome and well built. Yet Confucius was a good archer, and when he displayed his bowmanship — with rites in ancient days accompanied with some wine drinking and much ceremony — people flocked to see him.

It can be imagined that after the death of his father this branch of

Kung's family remained to a certain extent in economic privation. Then Confucius served in one of the three noble houses as a keeper of state granaries and under his supervision the measurements of grains became just and correct. Afterwards as a guardian of common lands, the cattle breeding of the state prospered prolifically. Yet we must suppose that Confucius was well-versed, or in our modern language, specialized in the knowledge of ancient propriety and rites before he was twenty years of age. A contemporary minister of the state on his death-bed ordered his son to go to Kung Tze for learning and regard him as his master because, as the dying minister said, so far as he knew, the ancestors of Kung for several generations had been all sages of illustrious virtue, and their descendant must be a man of great distinction though he might not come into power. Obeying this will, the son of the said minister went along with another prince to Confucius and learned from his rites of propriety. Afterwards the prince told the Duke of Lu that he wanted to go with Confucius to the Imperial Court of Chow, the then very much weakened central government, and the Duke equipped them with a carriage, two horses, together with an attendant. The purpose of this journey was to study the ancient rites, and on this occasion they met Lao Tze who was the chief librarian of the archives. In returning home after this visit, it is said, his disciples increased in number.

It is a fact well-established that Confucius began his career as a teacher at the age of about twenty-three and had henceforward to the end of his life always a group of disciples following him. The number amounted to three thousand, among whom seventy-two or seventy-seven were the most eminent. Confucius himself said: "In teaching there should be no distinction of classes." [3] Further: "From the man bringing his bundle of dried meat (for my teaching) upwards, I have never refused instruction to any one." [4] — It was most likely that only during his years serving in the ministries of the state that he attracted fewer disciples to himself, but even then this fact is doubtful. That the knowledge could be imparted without social distinction, is a thing unique and remarkable, different entirely from the practise of ancient Brahmins whose spiritual knowledge was confined to the twice-born. No wonder people nowadays praised him for his democratic spirit as an educator.

It is important to get a general idea of the political situation of the period in which Confucius lived before we can properly trace his career as a statesman in his middle age. It was the later part of the Chow dynasty, called "the Eve of Chow" for which Confucius compiled a History entitled *Ch'un Ch'iu*, or *Annals of Spring and Autumn*, covering a period of 242 years (722–481 B.C.). It was of course the worst of times.

Owing to the incursion of a barbarian tribe from the northwestern

---

3. Vide *Analects*, trl. by James legge.

4. This passage permits another interpretation: "Upwards from those who can dress their hair and decorate themselves properly I have never refused instruction to any one," meaning "from those of 15 years of age upwards."

part of China, the royal capital of the Chow dynasty was compelled to be shifted from its original site in Shensi eastwards to Loyang in 770 B.C. The Western Chow thus ended with the fall of its capital. We must remember that in Europe, the first foundations of Rome were laid in about the year 753 B.C., almost two decades after this national catastrophy in the East, yet the case was not unlike the survival of the Eastern Roman Empire after its fall in the West. But unlike the Eastern Roman Empire, the Eastern Chow dynasty became gradually very weakened in its power as a central government, though it still preserved its age-old tradition, and maintained its prestige and dignity over the dukedoms for at least two centuries more.

As said before, this "Spring and Autumn" period was the worst. in the sense that it represented a great outburst of vital forces of the race held in check and well regulated for nearly 400 years. If we take the Western Chow dynasty as the age of Classicism, then in sharp contrast to it, this was a period of romantic revolt. People nowadays praise this age together with the following period of Warring States (481–221 B.C.) as a great period of liberation and emancipation, because old institutions were broken down and Chinese culture especially began to flourish greatly with the the rise of diverse philosophical systems, the so-called "Hundred Schools" — in fact less than a hundred — unrivalled in later ages and running in parallel lines to the famous schools of the Greek philosophers, corresponding to a great extent to their thoughts as well. But we are inclined to believe that if there had been no classical period preceding it, no peace, no centralization, unification, standardization and preservation of the racial together with its cultural strength of nearly four centuries, such a wealth could not have come forth. The storage of water must be very great before it can issue out into large streams. Or, to take another metaphor, the seeds must have been carefully chosen and the soil well-prepared beforehand for the rare and beautiful flowers to blossom.

Let us follow our modern way of making statistics. Ancient Chinese scholars have done the same thing. In this period we find the country divided into fifteen major feudal states together with a number of small fiefs which quickly disappeared. In the Eastern Chow house, there were legally 12 kings or emperors; in fact, 14, but one among them died within less than a year after coming to the throne, and another one died after Confucius. And then:

Dukes in the Lu state	12
Great battles	23
Open attacks with armed forces among states	213
Silent attacks[5]	60
Powerful leaders among feudal princes	5
Convenants among states	109

5. Usually battles were commenced with a loud fanfare of beating drums. In surprise attacks this was abandoned.

Special convenants	11
(including 4 with representatives sent from and 5 with representatives coming to the Lu state)	
Political Conferences	97
Conferences with Duke Huan of the Ch'i state as the leader holding the "ear of the oxen" in an oath	11
Conferences summoned by the same prince accompanied with war chariots	4
Sieges	44
Invasions into states	27
Shifting of the capital of the enemy by armed force	10
Annihilation of small states of fiefdoms	30
Princes (including great dukes) assassinated	36
Fall of large and small states	52
Natural calamities	52
Eclipses (regarded as a catastrophic omen[6])	36
Earthquakes	5
Mountains falling	2
and a number of great frosts, droughts, conflagrations, locust-damages, typhoons, inundations, and other extraordinary natural phenomena, etc.	

Such was the Ch'un Ch'iu period, the last part of which Confucius lived through and for which he wrote or rather compiled the *Annals*. This book needs just a word of explanation here because modern scholars have doubted its authorship.

The term "Ch'un Ch'iu," literally meaning "Spring and Autumn" is no more than a historical record of the Dukedom of Lu, and since ancient times its authorship was assigned to Confucius because he worked on it, elaborated it and deleted those parts which he considered unnecessary or not worth preserving. So fundamentally it was certainly not an original work of his own creation. Far back in the eleventh century A.D., this book was ridiculed by a profound scholar, also an unsuccessful social-economic reformer, Wang An-Shih, as "ragged and fragmented court-papers" (or "reports of the court"). It is true that it is broken and fragmented because at least in two places we find only two words beginning a sentence and nothing following. Yet it leaves room for doubt as to whether Wang put this forth merely as a disinterested academic opinion, or from personal jealousy because his intention of writing a good commentary on it had been frustrated, since a contemporary of his had worked on it and written a nice one. It would be a great discovery indeed if clear evidences and sufficient proofs could be given to support the contention that Confucius was not the author of these *Annals*.

---

6. Among the 36 eclipses, 34 could be verified through modern calculations; two were found to be inaccurate owing to the error in recording by the state historian.

But it must not be forgotten that such Annals were common in the large feudal states in those days; for example that of Tsin state was not called "Springs and Autumns" but "Shen" or "Vehicles". The usage of a vehicle is to convey men, be they good or bad and in this analogy the historical record of a state is to note down every great event, be it a good one or a bad one. There was the same thing in the state Ch'u, called only by another name. Thus the name "Spring and Autumn" (or we may use the plural) meant nothing else than a chronicle in the court of Lu, recording the great events that took place each year. In those days the greatest events of a state meant sacrifices and military services, which had their most important rites held in these two seasons in spring before the planting, and in autumn after the harvest. Lu was a state famous for the preservation of the ancient rites and propriety, and music of the Western Chow dynasty because, at the beginning of the feudal age, the state of Lu accepted from the Imperial Court these two things as a reward for the great merit of its Duke.[7] The establishment of a historian in the dukedom was no new institution in the Chow dynasty but could be traced to even more ancient dynasties. Confucius in his old age (which will be treated afterwards) worked on those Annals of his native land. In our modern terminology, he "edited" them. His *Anthology of Poems*, now translated as the *Book of Odes*, was of the same nature. Out of a number of more than 3,000 folk-songs, poems and sacrificial hymns etc. he selected 305 pieces which, judged by his standard, were worth preservation and could be sung in accompaniment to music played for various ritual performances. He himself wrote not a single poem in this collection.

If a collection of poems had to maintain a certain standard, the more so would a compilation of history. It could not be without its judgments, criticisms, praises and denunciations, appreciations and devaluations — all based upon a philosophical view of life and of the universe which we call in Chinese his "Great Principles." Such great principles were involved in the language or art of writing in which the idea could be clearly understood without being openly expressed. Generalizations could be deduced from what had been written and the way of writing. It was not anything esoteric and intentionally hidden from the public, as some ancient commentators supposed. Actually we still find a good number of such principles in existence, a subject well known to every scholar. If we do not ignore those "Great Principles," some out of date now and some unpleasant to foreigners, then some sage must be found just as great as Confucius to whom the authorship could be assigned. It seems that modern scholarship has not been able to discover such a great anonymous man.

It is very difficult to suppose that the five schools of commentators

.

7. Each state had indeed its music and dances, but those of Lu state could adopt the style of those of the Central Imperial Court, loftier in significance and more splendid perhaps in show. In propriety different ranks of nobility were distinct from each other and the ceremonies held by the emperor or king could not be held by any duke.

of the *Annals* upto the Han dynasty, of which three great commentaries are now extant, (with two schools faded away because one had no exponent and another had originally no written text) were all centered upon a spurious text supposed to he written by Confucius but really by some person unknown. Furthermore, references made by Mencius and Djuang Tze on the *Annals* would all have to be taken as forgeries and interpolations, or else it must be assumed that these sages were equally deceived by an erroneous tradition: both facts being well-nigh impossible.

The kernel of the problem lies not so much in the true authorship but rather in the authority of the *Annals*, an authority that ever since Confucius, commanded the respect and shaped the destiny of many dynasties. Since historical teachings in this book were great, they were taken as examples in outlining the internal or external policy of the state. Now, if it could be sufficiently proved — and unfortunately it could not be — that these *Annals* were not written by the Sage, then the authority of all those historical examples, of all those ideas, gross or subtle, and of all those principles, great or small, would crumble like a house of cards. Yet the fact is not so simple. Whether or not we should adopt these things in future for the building up of a nation is another problem; but that they had actually exercised tremendous influence in the past is an undeniable fact. And to return to the true authorship, let us refer to the *Book of Mencius*:

"(Again) the world fell into decay, and principles faded away. Perverse speakings and oppressive deeds waxed rife again. There were instances of ministers who murdered their sovereigns, and of sons who murdered their fathers. Confucius was afraid, and made the *Spring and Autumn*. What the *Spring and Autumn* contains are matters proper to the emperor. On this account Confucius said, Yes! It is the *Spring and Autumn* which will make men know me, and it is the *Spring and Autumn* which will make men condemn me." [8]

Again:

"In former times, Yu repressed the vast waters of the inundation, and the empire was restored to order. The achievements of the Duke of Chow extended even to the barbarous tribes of the east and north, and he drove away all ferocious animals, and the people enjoyed repose. Confucius completed the *Spring and Autumn*, and rebellious ministers and villainous sons were struck with terror." [9]

And again:

"Mencius said: The traces of imperial rule were extinguished,

.

8. *The Works of Mencius*, Bk. III, Pt. II, Ch. IX, 7, 8.
9. *Ibid*, Bk. III, Pt. II, Ch. X, 2.

and the imperial odes ceased to be made. When those odes ceased to be made, the *Ch'un Ch'iu* was produced. ... The subject of *Ch'un Ch'iu* was the affairs of Huan of Ch'i and Wen of Tsin, and its style was the historical. Confucius said: 'Its decisions I ventured to make.'" [10]

These three passages are clear enough not to need any explanation and, judged by the contents, the style, and the context, they can scarcely be doubted as interpolations made by a foreign hand. Indeed, Mencius exaggerated the effect of this work upon the time, but history shows that the salutary influence it left to later generations was great and ultimately what Mencius said proved to be no hyperbolic description.

Apart from this reference, we may also take other ancient philosophers into consideration.

Even before Mencius it was a general, recognized fact that norms and censures and praises — in ancient language "subtle words" or implied criticisms — were hidden in the work between the lines. We may refer to a few passages from other sources, say the *Book of Djuang Tze*. Djuang Tze, in later ages called a Taoist master, took Confucianism lightly and most of the anecdotes in that book about Confucius were legends generally forged by the followers of his school , which could never be taken as historical facts. Yet in the second chapter (Ch. II, 7) there is a place where this *Annals of Spring and Autumn* is mentioned, in which its "regulation of the world" together with "the records (verbally "will") of ancient kings" was talked about, saying that these were subjects discussed but not debated by sages. By "regulation of the world" we can understand that it was not merely a chronology containing no deep sense. In a humanistic view, a mere chronology without some sustaining principle in it was not taken as a proper history, and a history that teaches us nothing cannot be of any purpose. Even the modern scientific or technical treatment must necessarily lead us somewhere. In the last chapter of the same, it was pointed out that the "*Annals of Spring and Autumn* deals with norms and duties." This last chapter was probably written by Hui Tze, not by Djuang Tze himself, but Hui Tze was a friend of Djuang Tze and died before him. This statement about the *Annals* was generally accepted, because Confucius talked about "norms and duties" in his life time. Yet we may consider even this passage as an interpolation, intentionally inserted into to text by some unknown writer in the Han dynasty. If we refer to *Hsün Tze*, we find the "subtlety" of the *Annals* was once also mentioned (I, 7), and in another place of the same book (XXVII), we find these words:

"In the *Annals of Spring and Autumn*, the Duke Mo (of the Chin state) was esteemed as worthy, as being able to change (i.e. as being capable of correcting his faults)."

Hsün Tze lived after Mencius, but with regard to the *Annals* he

.

10. *Ibid*, Bk. IV, Pt. II, Ch. XXI, 1.

must have had the same opinion. This was exactly an explanation of one point of those "subtle ideas." Furthermore, ever since Pan Kuo (33–92 A.D.), historians in the Han dynasty and in later ages used to say that the "'subtle ideas' (or literally 'words') died out after the death of Confucius, and his great principles became distorted since the seventy and more disciples dispersed." Ssu Ma Tsien in his Autobiography also explained the reason why Confucius had written the *Annals*, and we can scarcely assume that such a celebrated historian merely attached himself to a false and meaningless tradition. Thus it seems to be impossible to deny Confucius, still less to discover another true author of the *Annals*.

But still some doubts remain with regard to the use of one or two words for censure or praise in this history. This history was written in an arid and brief style, the implications of which merely hinged upon the use of one word or two in praise or in blame of someone or some undertaking. Perhaps it could not but be so, considering the fact that great events within those 242 years were covered with only 18,000 words. Here we need only to take two points into consideration.

First, in China there was the custom of honouring or censuring the dead with the appellation of a special name in one word or two, and the choice of such an epithet was considered as a matter of great consequence. It was something like the ancient Egyptian practice of taking their dead across a river and examining and discussing the deeds of their lives, whether they were good or bad, whether they deserved a stately burial or not. Among the Chinese nobles, this posthumous title was a matter of great concern even while they were still alive. It was something like the European expressions "Tarquin the Proud" or "Philip the Fair," but with a much more emphatic bearing. Common people with distinguished merits or virtues were also given such honorific titles after death, in short, it was an honour indirectly bestowed on the descendants of the family and a tremendous encouragement to the living. Such a custom lasted until the beginning of this century. So to praise or to blame some one in his *Annals* with a good or with a bad word was not a new invention by Confucius.

Secondly, the authority of the historians of the court surpassed that of the ruler himself with regard to their writings. In every dynasty the court historiographers noted down daily what was said by the king on the one hand, and what was done by him on the other. They were usually two officers who stood silently on both sides of the king. The thing worth noticing is that what was written about that particular king on the throne could not be read by himself; it could only be read by his successors after his death. The king might be a tyrant, the historiographers could be killed, but the current chronicle could not be read. This was the tradition preserved during the time before Confucius. Upto his time, the history-recorders of each state were extremely cautious and serious in the use of words for censure or for praise. Just to give as an example an anecdote of this period: in the dukedom of Ch'i, a minister conspired and succeeded in killing the duke, a tyrannic despot. So the historian of the court at once wrote: "Ts'ui Chu assassinated his king." Enraged by these words, the minister ordered him to be instantly executed. On hearing this, that historian's brother of the same profession, went to the court and wrote the same words: "Ts'ui Chu assassinated his king," and again he was killed. So the third brother went straight to the court and again wrote these same five words, but this time the minister took no further action. Another historian having heard of this disaster, also took his writing-tablet and went to the court but, when he was informed on the way that the third had written the correct thing, he returned. From such an example we can see how dignified and how faithful to their duty or rather to truth were the ancient history-recorders. Confucius certainly followed such an old tradition in editing the *Annals* of his time, and it was said that even his most gifted and favorite disciples were not able to adjust a single word in this piece of work.

Had Confucius the idea of reforming a decadent society by this? Perhaps not. Yet he lived in an unhappy and unpeaceful time when the dukedoms were mostly rotten at the core, and yet he hoped for the ideal sovereign reign. So he strove to be employed in any of the dukedoms in order to deploy his talents and carry out his ideals. Repeatedly he sought for a chance to serve, and repeatedly he failed. In his late years in retirement, there was nothing left for him to do except merely to write the *Annals* and other literary works. It was a tremendous task: first, in the rectification of names and norms, and next, in the justification of values. His ultimate aim was to leave behind him something to future generations for the realization of his high ideals. A pen was now practically the only means left at his disposal.

Thus it seems that there can be no room for doubt as to the true authorship of this work. But the ancient quarrel still remains as to whether this *Ch'un Ch'iu* or *Annals of Springs and Autumns* should be classified under the category of history or of classics, because these two categories were distinct from each other, though it was always looked upon as pertaining to the latter. That problem will be treated afterwards when we come to the discussion of the work of Confucius in his late years.

Chapter II

LIFE OF CONFUCIUS *(continued)*

The farewell address given to Confucius by Lao Tze, as noted down in the *Ancient History* of Ssu Ma Tsien was indeed instructive and important in the building up of his character. Lao Tze's words are as follows:

"I have heard that men of riches and high rank endow others with wealth, and men of great compassion (Jen) endow others with words. I could not be rich or remain in a high rank, yet stealthily I assumed a fame of being compassionate. So I send you these words: Wise, intelligent and deeply clearsighted men are very near to death, because they like to criticize. And men of broad knowledge, sharp discrimination, extensive capacity always endanger their own lives, because they reveal the evils of others. ... As long as one serves his parents, there should be no longer oneself. As long as one serves his master or king, there should be no longer oneself."

This deontological instruction, so simple and plain, must have helped Confucius greatly in developing afterwards that great virtue of his: selflessness. Ego, (not as in many translations "egoism") was one among the four traits from which he was entirely free. [11] If we consider this virtue as the elementary step towards spiritual perfection, this was first taught by Lao Tze and afterwards by Confucius.

Other discourses recorded in the Biography of Lao Tze in the same *Ancient History* we may take as authentic, and we see well that they dealt with some of the fundamental principles of spirituality, all sprung from the same source of Compassion (Jen). These we need not go into detail here.

The impression which Confucius had of this interview as described in his own words is worth reading; it runs:

After his departure from Lao Tze, Confucius said to his disciples thus:

"Birds, I know they can fly. Fish, I know they can swim. Animals, I know they can run. That which runs can be netted in; that which swims can be drawn up with threads; that which flies can be brought down

11. *Analects*, IX, 4. See Conclusion.

by arrows tied on strings. But with regard to a dragon, I am unable to know its riding on storms and clouds ascending upto heaven. Lao Tze, as I have seen today, was he not like a dragon?"

Thus the trip made to the Imperial Court was very fruitful. At this time, the royal house of the Chow dynasty was indeed much reduced in power, but the dukedom of Lu was no stronger. It was situated between two great rivals, both competing for the leadership of all the states: Tsin in the north-west, and Ch'u in the south-west; an alliance with or inclination towards either meant an attack by its opponent. What was more, the state Ch'i on the south-east was equally as powerful as these two states, and its pressure on Lu or even its friendship was scourging. It happened that the Duke Chao of Lu had a quarrel with the Viscount of the third house of his state, and a civil strife broke out. The Duke succeeded in besieging that Viscount who was taken by surprise in a citadel but, after a day's fight, the forces of those three noble houses combined and chased off the Duke. The besieged Viscount was released and the Duke fled from his country to the state of Ch'i. Afterwards attempts were made by other states to reinstate him in his dukedom and diverse conferences were held, even accompanied by military force, menaces and threats to that Viscount. All were empty and hollow, and all failed. The actual fact was that the real power of the Lu state had been gathering for the last five generations in the hands of that third noble house, and the duke became merely a nominal chieftain, or rather a high priest, performing the routine sacrifices and representing the honours of the state in ceremonies. Thus the Duke Chao died as an exile outside his native country, though accompanied till the end of his days by a group of faithful ministers who maintained every pomp of that highest rank of nobility. In such an internal disorder of political affairs, Confucius also left his native land and went to the Ch'i state. He was then thirty-five years of age (517 B.C.), and he stayed abroad for about two years.

Regarding this period of his residence in the Ch'i state, a few records still remain. He was treated with hospitality in the court of the Duke Ching, because five years previous, when Duke Ching and his minister Yen Yin visited the Lu state, he was made known to them, and one of their discourses still remains:

The Duke Ching of the Ch'i state asked Confucius:

"Formerly the Duke Mo in the western tribes ruled a very small state in a remote place, how could he have become such a leading feudal power?"

To this Confucius answered:

"That state was indeed a small one, but its ambition was great. Though located in a far and remote place, its policies were correct and proper, following the middle path.

"The Duke Mo, having met a talented captive, ransomed formerly at the price of five ram-skins, raised him to a high post and, having talked with him for three days, handed him the reins of a chief minister. In following such a course, the Duke Mo was entitled even to be a great sovereign over the whole country, not to say becoming the overlord among the feudal princes, which was a trivial matter."

The Duke Ching was pleased to hear this.[12]

Now in coming personally to the court of the Duke, he could be employed according to his talents. It was in this period that he learned the ancient music Shao that remained in existence in the Ch'i state. He afterwards said that this music was perfectly beautiful and also perfectly good in contrast to the music of Wu which was perfectly beautiful but not perfectly good.[13] He listened to performances of that music for three months, and during that period he "did not know the taste of meat." Shao was the name of the music made by Shun, an ancient emperor, both perfect in melody and in sentiment.[14] To this, Confucius said: "I did not think that music could have been made so excellent as this." [15]

We need not pass any remark on such a state of concentration on higher things that even the ordinary taste of food is forgotten for a long period. The wise men of the Ch'i state praised him.

It happened that the Duke Ching asked Confucius about government. Confucius replied:

" (There is government.) When the prince is prince, and the

minister is minister; when the father is father, and the son is son."

"Good!" said the Duke, "If, indeed, the prince be not prince, the minister not minister, the father not father, and the son not son, though I have the grain, shall I be able to eat it? " [16]

On another occasion, the Duke Ching asked again about government, upon which Confucius answered: "(Right) Government lies in the proper measure of state-finance." And again the Duke was pleased to hear this. He was then about to appoint him to some ministry, and to endow him with the grainfields of the Ni Valley as his private possession for his permanent settlement.

But this donation did not materialize, owing to the remonstrance of Yen Yin, and his words related in the *Ancient History* are as follows:

"These scholars belonging to the Yu school (that is to say, the school with Confucius as its representative) are fawning and loquacious; they can not be taken as examples or standards. They are self-righteous

---

12. Biography 17, *Ancient History*, Vol. 47.

13. Vide *Analects*, III, 25.

14. Legge's trl., *Analects*, III, 25.

15   *Ibid*, VII. 13.

16. The last sentence has been also rendered by Legge as "although I have my revenue, can I enjoy it?" XII, 11.

and full of pride, and they can never serve as subordinates in any office. Their observance of mourning and funeral rites and ceremonies causing people to become bankrupt in affording grand burials, cannot be regarded as a good custom. As wandering politicians or mendicants, they cannot be loyal to any state.

"Furthermore, since many great sages passed away, the Royal House of Chow declined, and 'rites and music' fell out of use and became obliterated. Now Confucius makes luxurious ornamentations and decorations together with a great complexity of formalities, such as the ceremony in ascending and descending, deportment in swift walking and slow pacing, so much so that even a study of that knowledge of propriety cannot be completed throughout many years or even generations. If you want to employ him to transform the custom of our state, he cannot be an example to the common people."

Moved by these words, the Duke Ching ever afterwards met Confucius with much more courtesy, but stopped asking him anything about "propriety". Once he said also: "I cannot treat him as I would the chief of the most powerful in his state"; and yet he could not treat him as the chief of the first family who had no power. So he treated him in a manner befitting someone between these two.

Judged by historical facts, Confucius must have met some favour with the Duke Ching of the Ch'i state, and he must have brought with him certain reforms to the government or else awakened the nobles to a higher ideal. Thus the ministers wanted to avoid him by involving him in certain intricacies. This was conveyed to the Duke and the Duke sighed: "I am now old, I can no more realize his ideals." On hearing this, Confucius returned to his native state.

As we read the history of this period we find the political situation in the Lu state an exceedingly complicated one. The Duke Chao died an exile when Confucius was aged forty-two, and his younger brother (called afterwards the Duke Ting) succeeded him to the throne. In the fifth year of his reign, the Viscount who deposed the Duke also died, and that most powerful House was inherited by his son, a man of no great talent. So the power of that brilliant viscounty was further weakened usurped by his ministers, and again, by the attendants of those ministers, so that each office was somehow overstepped in its functions and a certain state of anarchism prevailed in which the whole administration strayed from its proper course. What Confucius could do was to withdraw and to keep himself aloof from the political field, and thereby continue his work as a public teacher.

Here we find a story in which Confucius gave an answer pretentious and humorous without being satirical.

Yang Ho, known also as Yang Hu, was nominally the principal minister of the house of the Viscount but afterwards, having gathered much power into his hands, schemed to arrogate the whole authority of the state of Lu to himself and rebelled. He was condemned as the "thief" or "robber" who had "stolen the precious jade and large bow" from the ancestral temple of Lu, so was he mentioned by Confucius in the *Annals* without being named. The anecdote was mentioned by Mencius as well as in the *Analects*, and we read first the section in the *Book of Mencius*:

"Yang Ho wished to get Confucius to go to see him, but disliked doing so by any want of (a proper occasion) propriety. (As it is the rule, therefore, that) when a great officer sends a gift to a scholar, if the latter be not at home to receive it, the scholar must go to the officer's to pay his respects. Yang Ho watched when Confucius was out, and sent him a roasted pig. Confucius, in his turn watched when Yang Ho was out and went to pay respects to him." [17]

But the story does not end there. We read in the *Analects*:

"Yang Ho wished to see Confucius, but Confucius would not go to see him. (On this,) he sent the present of a pig to Confucius, who, having chosen a time when Yang Ho was not at home, went to pay his respects (for the gift). He met him, (however,) on the way. Yang Ho then said to Confucius: 'Come, let me speak with you,' and then he asked: 'Can he be called benevolent who keeps his jewel in his bosom, and leaves his country to confusion? ... Certainly not! (Yang Ho made such a question and answered himself.) (Furthermore) Can he be called wise, who is anxious to be engaged in public employment, and yet repeatedly has lost the opportunity to do so? ... Certainly not. ' (And he himself answered again:) 'The days and months are passing away; the years do not wait for us.'

"Confucius said: 'Yes, I must take office.'" [18]

We can well understand that with his insight into things, Confucius might have foreseen the ultimate failure of this usurper who fled after much struggle in 502 B.C. to the state Ch'i. Confucius was now fifty years of age, he was constantly thinking of realizing his ideals. It happened that on a certain occasion a minister of the state Lu, named Kung-shan Bu-ngu, invited the Master to visit him, and he was inclined to go. His disciple Tze-lu was displeased, and said: "Indeed, you cannot go. Why must you think of going to see Kung-shan?"

The Master said : "Can it be without some reason that he invited me? If any one employ me, may I not make another Chow state in the east." [19]

.

17. *Book of Mencius*, III, Pt. II, Ch. VII, 3.

18. Legge's translation has taken two answers as given by Confucius. In this meeting Confucius actually said only the last sentence after having heard the whole lecture. Here we meet also a slight inexactitude in Legge's translation: the pig sent to Confucius was not a "roasted" one, but a "steamed" one. Ultimately the "roast pig" could be a foreign invention as pointed out in the famous "Dissertation", but a "steamed pig"... it leaves another topic for research. In any case, we see that Confucius was not a vegetarian, divine or undivine as the readers may judge it. *Analects*, XVII, 1.

19. *Ana.*, XVII, 5.

In other words, Confucius had the idea of bringing peace to the times by creating another Chow dynasty, even in a small district which Kung-shan had occupied with a small force. Yet in the end he did not go. On another occasion he said: "If there were (any of the princes) who would employ me, in the course of twelve months, I should have done something considerable, and within three years, perfection could have been reached." [20]

His words proved true, for the Duke Ting appointed him as the governor of the capital, and one year later all the people of the four directions took his measures as standards. From that post he was promoted to the Minister of Finance and again to the Great Chief of Justice. Thus he became the Prime Minister of the Duke Ting. And in the Peace Conference held at Chia Ku in the year 500 B.C. between the states Ch'i and Lu, in which both the dukes presided, he acted as the Chief Secretary of the Lu state.

With regard to this conference, much had been exaggerated and ancient scholars doubted the success in diplomacy achieved by Confucius. Historical accounts of this meeting varied also slightly, yet it stood as a very nice episode in the political life of Confucius. Summarizing the main points narrated in different records, we may get a general idea as follows:

Before going to the meeting, Confucius said to the Duke Ting: "As I have heard, whenever there is a civil undertaking, there must also be at the same time military equipment; and whenever there is some military action, there must be at the same time civil equipment. In ancient days when dukes left their dominions, they were usually accompanied by all officials. So on this occasion, it would be better to have the right and left commanders-in-chief of the army follow in the train." Duke Ting approved of this idea, and those two generals went together on this peaceful mission.

On the other side, a certain sinister politician named Li Mi said to the Duke Ching of the Ch'i state: "That person Kung Ch'iu knows much about rites and propriety, but he has no courage. If during the meeting we let the warlike natives of the Lai district kidnap the duke, we may get what we want." The Duke Ching approved of this black plot.

Thus both dukes, each attended by a large group of followers, came to the appointed place called Chia Ku. A large altarlike pulpit was built beforehand, three steps elevated above the earth. After much courtesy, both dukes ascended the pulpit and performed the ceremonies designated as those of "meeting of nobility of equal rank." Some goblets of wine were offered and exchanged.

Just at this moment, the announcer of the Ch'i state proclaimed aloud: "Now, music performance of the four directions will be offered." And the Duke Ching said: "Be it so."

.

20. *Ana.*, XIII, 10.

Then the music band, composed mostly of the natives of the Lai district near the sea, together with their flags and banners, swords and spears, halberds and lances, swarmed up to the foot of the platform; Confucius instantly ascended, to within one step from the top.

He raised the large sleeves of his robe in a manner of salutation, and said in a loud voice: "Our two kings are having a friendly meeting and discussion, why should the music of the barbarians be displayed here? Please order the announcer to call them off." The announcer gave the command, but the band refused to disperse. Then Confucius looked straight to the Duke Ching and his minister Yen Yin on both left and right. The Duck felt inwardly ashamed and, with a wave of his hand, sent them away.

The real story ends only here, all other accounts of this meeting are imaginations added to the history by people of later ages, all unbelievable. The agreement reached in this meeting was more satisfactory to Lu than to Ch'i. It was concluded that Ch'i should return to Lu the grain-fields of three districts previously occupied and that Lu should then be militarily allied with Ch'i, so that whenever the troops of Ch'i were sent out of the borders of that state, Lu should follow with three hundred chariots for support. In fact, afterwards the three districts were returned to Lu, but on no occasion was any chariot sent out for the support of this ally. An oath was taken, solemnly participated in by both parties and everything was finished in accord with the proper rites.

But then the Duke of Ch'i had the leisurely demeanour of giving a banquet which, judging by the circumstances, could not he reciprocated by the Duke of Lu and, since the case had just been settled somehow more in favor of Lu, any further entertainment or discussion could easily give rise to other unexpected perplexities. So Confucius declined, telling the minister on the other side that it would be too tiresome to those in charge of affairs and, moreover, the precious ceremonial vessels should never be carried out of the hall, and that excellent music for honouring guests could never be played in the open fields. If a banquet were to be given without these nice formalities, it would be too insignificant ; but if given with this equipment, it would be contrary to the rules of propriety. These reasons were made known to the Duke of Ch'i and, being convinced, he cancelled the idea of giving a feast.[21]

.

21. It may be noted here that the English translations of the passages quoted from the *Analects* are taken from Legge and the *Harvard Classics*. The latter affords a happier reading, appears more in conformity with the original in its brevity of expression but often not in its gravity of style. With the intention of making use of the best of each, some adjustment of the wording has been made; there has not been a strict reliance upon either. In the opinion of the author it is always preferable to render the original into an exact translation and let the reader appreciate the ideas by his own approach.

Chapter III

HIS TRAVELS

Greek mythology tells us that if, as a human being, one has achieved certain superhuman feats, he is likely to incur the jealousy of the gods and hence be doomed to certain disastrous fate. That may or may not be true. But as a rule, as we see in many examples in history, people too good or too brilliant in their achievements cannot keep their posts too long, because dark forces in the world usually tend to overshadow them, obscuring that very brilliancy. From the time Confucius became the Prime Minister of the Lu state at the age of fifty-six, he had brought about silently and invisibly great progress and reformation in the state. After three months, he had a rebellious minister put to law, and thereafter the decadent customs of society swiftly changed. Merchants and sellers of goods became more honest, and men and women kept with courtesy to different paths on the streets, and nobody picked up anything carelessly dropped on the highway. Foreign missions and visitors from all directions coming to the state found proper accommodation without any complaint. This state of ideal administration and social order unfortunately did not last very long because it aroused the admiration and indeed jealousy not of the gods, but of the neighbouring states, especially Ch'i, which had a fear of the growing power of Lu. So, by a cleverly designed plan, the Duke of Ch'i indirectly forced Confucius to resign. He took his departure when for days no court was held, and official ceremonies were neglected and no longer attended to. Henceforth he began his travel of fourteen years to different states.

The first of a number of feudal states, large or small, which Confucius visited was Wei, a country very near to the state Lu, famous for having had many Chun Tze or superior men. The Duke of Wei asked what was the emolument for him in his native state, and found that it was sixty thousand measures of grain (a measure was equal to four bushels) per year, so he offered him annually that amount. He stayed there for ten months and, finding that he could not be free from the suspicions of the nobles who tried to slander him — not to speak of being unable to realise his political ideals — he left for the state Ch'en.

It happened that on the way he had to pass a small town K'wang, a small fief. The driver of his carriage, a rustic man, pointed with his horsewhip to an opening on the city-wall, saying: "On the other occasion I entered the town through that entrance." Having heard of these words, the inhabitants mistook Confucius for Yang Ho whose army had formerly done great injustice to them; Confucius had some physical resemblance to that treacherous minister. So they stopped the whole retinue. For five days he was surrounded on every side, unable to proceed farther.

On this occasion, his most beloved disciple Yen Yüan who had fallen behind the group went to rejoin him. Confucius said: "I held thee as dead."

"While our Master lives, why should I presume to die?" Yen Yüan replied.[22] This answer was complimentary to the master but, by the sheer irony of fate, this disciple died at the age of forty-one, when Confucius was seventy-one.

But the chord of encirclement was more tightened by the population, and the master and all his disciples were beset with fear.

Then in dispersing the doubts of his attendants, Confucius said:

"After the death of King Wen, was not the cause of Truth lodged here in me?

"If Heaven (or as we say 'God') wished to let this cause of Truth perish, then I, a future mortal, should not have got such a relation to that cause. While Heaven ('God') does not let the cause of Truth perish, what can the people of K'wang do unto me?" [23]

Then some of his disciples wanted to fight their way out, but they were stopped by the master. He played on his lute and sang as usual, so that finally his identity was made clear and the natives of that district set him free.

Then he went to Pu, another small fief. After having stayed there for one month, he returned to Wei.

It happened that the Duke of Wei had a wife, named Nan-tze, who was famous for her beauty and younger than her husband. She had great influence over the duke and hence wielded much power in her hands. Yet she was clever enough to respect the venerable men of the state. On returning to Wei, Confucius resided in the house of a retired minister, also a man of great virtue. So a message was sent from the court to Confucius, saying: "All superior men of the four directions condescending to come to our state and to cultivate a brotherhood with our duke must first see our humble duchess, and our humble duchess wishes to see Confucius." Confucius declined, because there was no such precedent. Yet he could not but go to pay her his respects. When he entered the hall, the duchess could not be seen, being seated behind a curtain, to which he made his salutation. The duchess who could see from within the curtain, bowed to the ground twice in return, with her armlets and ornaments tinkling, distinctly heard outside. This visit was quite formal and he came out without much ado. But his disciple, the most courageous Tze-lu, was displeased, feeling somehow that his

.

22. *Ana.*, XI, 22.
23. IX, 5.

master had done too much. So the Master said: "Wherein I have done improperly, may Heaven reject me, may Heaven reject me!" [24] This episode happened when Confucius was fifty-seven.

Staying in this state for more than one month, the duke and the duchess once went out driving through the streets in their carriage, taking with them a eunuch as the third one in their company and Confucius as the fourth. It is highly probable that this was a deliberate manoeuvre designed by Nan-tze to expel him from the state. Confucius was ashamed of this humiliation and said: "It is all over! I have not seen one who loves virtue as he loves female beauty." [25] Again he left the state Wei and passing through a small fief, Tsao, he went to a larger dukedom, Sung.

In coming to this dukedom, Confucius and his disciples practiced certain rites under a large tree. The marshal of that state, named Hwan T'ui, disliked this master and wanted to kill him so he uprooted that tree. Then Confucius left the place. His disciples said: "We must hurry!" Upon this he answered: "Heaven produced the virtue that is in me; Hwan T'ui what can he do unto me?" [26] Then the Master with his group of disciples went to Chêng and, passing through that state, came to Ch'en.

Residing in the smaller state which was no better off than Lu or Wei, it happened that the state Wu invaded the country and took away three districts. Situated as it was between the powerful Tsin in the north and the equally powerful Ch'u in the south, which fought constantly for overlordship, this weaker dukedom was always invaded on both fronts. After having stayed there for more than three years and finding no peace, Confucius said: "Let us return! Let us return! The scholars there of my school are ambitious and grand. They are for advancing and progress, yet they cannot forget their early days." [27] By this he meant the group of disciples in his native land who had not followed him along the journey.[28]

Then Confucius left Ch'en, and on the way the passed the district Pu again. It happened that the natives of that district had rebelled against Wei and they stopped the Sage on the way. One of the disciples, Kung Liang Yue, was a tall and brave knight who followed the master with five chariots of his private possession, and on this occasion he said in exasperation: "Formerly I met with our Master the trouble in K'wang, and now I meet again this trouble here. This is my fate. If our Master and I should again meet such a trouble, I prefer to fight

---

24. VI, 26.

25. This passage appeared twice in the *Analects*: IX, 17; XV, 12; apparently noted down by two different disciples.

26. VII, 22.

27. *Menicus*, VII, 37.

28. This passage had appeared twice in the *Ancient History* with slight variations of words, and certain scholars suspected that it was the same passage duplicated through some mistake of the ancient scribes. Yet the same thing could have been said twice on different occasions.

to death." So he fought desperately with the natives. The people were alarmed and they said to Confucius: "If you do not go to Wei, we will let you pass." To this he consented. Then an oath was taken by both parties and the whole retinue was set free. Upon this Confucius headed directly to Wei. His eloquent disciple Tze-kung asked: "Can the oath be disavowed?" "It was an extorted agreement; the gods will disapprove." the Master replied.

On hearing that Confucius was coming to his state again, the Duke of Wei was exceedingly pleased and accorded him a personal reception outside the city-gate. He then asked: "Should the people of Pu be punished?" "Yes." said this state-guest.

"Our ministers said that it was not right, because Pu is the district which our state had kept (as a corridor) for protecting from the aggressors of Tsin and Ch'u. If we attack it, is it perhaps wrong?"

"All the men there have the will to die, and all the women there have the will to guard the front on Si-ho (the district on the west of the River). Those whom I wish to punish are limited to four or five persons."

"Good." the Duke of Wei agreed, yet afterwards no punishment was inflicted. As the duke was old and tired of politics, he could not employ such a big man in his government. And soon afterwards Confucius left again.

And it happened that Pi Hsi, a governor of Chung Mau district revolted against the Tsin state. Pi Hsi invited Confucius to visit him and he was inclined to go.

Tze-lu said: "Master, formerly I have heard you say, 'When a man in his own person is guilty of doing evil, a superior will not associate with him,' Pi Hsi is in rebellion, holding possession of Chung Mau; if you go to him, what shall be said?"

The Master said: "Yes, I did use these words. But is it not said that, if a thing is really hard, it may be really white, it may be steeped in mud without being made dark?

"Am I a bitter gourd! How can I be hung up out of the way of being eaten?" [29]

Though arguing in this way, yet he did not go to that invitation.

In dry history we find sometimes an anecdote that is not greatly instructive yet interesting. Wei was a small state highly cultured and noted for its superior men, who were mostly anonymous yet intimately concerned with the current affairs. It happened that the Master was chiming one day on some musical stones in Wei when a man bearing a straw-basket passed Confucius' doorway and listening, said:

.

29. This dialogue is recorded in the *Analects*, XVII, 7; which has been taken into the *Ancient History* of Ssu Ma Tsien. It is the translation of Legge. Only the last sentence needs some explanation. The "gourd" is supposed to be the name of a star in sky which is also recorded in the *Book of Constellations* of the same *History*; it is "hung up" in the sky "out of the way of being eaten." "Bitter" is the word added by Legge following an old commentary. The original is simply "Am I a (or "the") gourd? How can I be hung up without being eaten?"

"His heart is full who so beats the musical stones!" A little while after, he added:

"How contemptible! What a tinkling note! When one is taken no notice of, he has simply to abandon.

'Deep water must be crossed with the clothes on;

'Shallow water may be crossed with the clothes held up.'"

The Master said: "How determined is he! But this is not difficult." [30]

Then Confucius repaired to Tsin, intending to see Chao Chien-tze, a great minister of that state, and having reached the eastern bank of the Yellow River, he heard the news that Tou Minto and Shun Hua, two great officers of the same state, were being executed. On gazing at the water of the river, he sighed: "How beautiful is this water ... so overflowing! That I shall not cross this river is, alas, my fate!"

Then his disciple Tze-kung went forward and said: "Do I venture to ask what is meant?"

The Master said: "Tou Minto and Shun Hua were both talented and virtuous high officers of the Tsin state. Before Chao Chien-tze attained to power, he needed the help of these two men so that he could enter into government service. After he had attained his purpose, he killed them both."

"As I have heard, if the pregnant womb of animals were ripped open or their tender ones slaughtered, then the auspicious unicorn[31] does not come to the suburbs. If the pond were drained and every fish caught, then the male and female dragons do not cohabit. If the nests of birds were overturned and all the eggs destroyed, then the phoenix does not hover around that land. Why? The virtuous ever shuns the destruction of its own kind. Even birds and animals know enough to avoid unrighteousness, what to say of me?" Then he returned and, resting in a district called Tsou, he composed an elegy in accompaniment to the music of the lute. He came back again to the dukedom of Wei.

The duke of Wei asked Confucius about tactics. He replied: "I have heard all about sacrificial matters, but I have not learned military science." The next day when the duke was talking to him his eyes were looking upwards to the flying swans, not at Confucius. On this Confucius took his departure the next day.[32] And again he went to the state Ch'en. In the summer of the same year the Duke of Wei died (493 B.C.).

In the summer of the next year, it happened that a conflagration broke out in the capital of Lu, while he was still staying in the state Ch'en. Having heard of this, he said: "The fire must have destroyed

30. XIV, 42.
31. The unicorn is one of the auspicious animals in Chinese belief. The auspicious bird is the phoenix. They will not come to any locality where cruelty or inhumanity has taken place.
32. *Ana.*, XV, 1; *Ancient History*, Biography of Confucius.

the two ancestral temples, that of the Duke Huan and that of the Duke Hsi." Later on, detailed information reached him that it was actually so; these two temples were burnt out. In the autumn, the chief minister of Lu, named Chi Huan-tze fell sick and, borne on a comfortable carriage, he was led to have a view of the town. He sighed: "Formerly this state was about to rise in power, but because I offended Confucius it could not rise." And turning to his son named Kan-tze at his side, he said: "After I pass away, you will become minister, and as soon as you come to office, you must call back Chung Ni. " After a few days, Chi Huan-tze died and he was succeeded by his son, Kan-tze. When the funeral ceremony was over, Kan-tze wanted to call back Chung Ni. Then one of his officers, Kung Chi Yue, said: "Formerly our duke employed him in government, but failed to come to an end, so the thing became a scandal among the dukes. And now if we employ him again and yet unable to come to any result, we will be once more ridiculed by all the dukes." Then Kan-tze asked whom should he employ. "We must call back Jan Ch'iu." said the officer. And so a messenger was sent to call back Jan Ch'iu, a favourite disciple of Confucius who accompanied him on the wanderings.

When Jan Ch'iu was about to go, Confucius said: "People of Lu are calling back Ch'iu; it is not that they will employ him in a small office, they are going to employ him greatly." And on the same occasion, he said: "Let us return! Let us return! The children of my school are ambitious and grand. They are accomplished and complete so far, but they do not know how to restrict and shape themselves." [33] His talented disciple Tze-kung knew that the master thought of returning to his native land and, by sending off Jan Ch'iu, he told him that in case he should be employed in the state for any high service, he should at once invite the master home.

The next year, Confucius moved from Ch'en to another small state Tsai. And it happened that this state was in a tumult and its duke was shot by one of his ministers, and the state was invaded by Ch'u from the south. In the autumn the duke of Ch'i died and, in the following year, Confucius moved from Tsai to another fief, Yeh.

The Duke of Yeh asked about government.

The Master said: " (Good government obtained when) those who are near are made happy and those who are far off are attracted." [34]

The Duke of Yeh told Confucius, "Among us here are those who may be styled upright in their conduct. If their father has stolen a sheep, they will bear witness to the fact."

Confucius said: "Among us, in our part of the country, those who are upright are different from this. The father conceals the misconduct of his son, the son conceals the misconduct of his father. Uprightness is to be found in this." [35]

---

33. V, 21. Another translation: " (They) know not what needs fashioning!"
34. XIII, 16.
35. XIII, 18.

The Duke of Yeh asked Tze-lu about Confucius and Tze-lu did not answer him. Confucius heard of this and said: "Yao (the name of Tze-lu), why did you not say to him: He is in his behavior a man who learns about the Path (Truth) without satiety and instructs others without being wearied; who, in his eager pursuit of Truth, forgets his food and who in constant joy forget his sorrows, and who does not perceive that old age is coming on." [36]

Afterwards he left Yeh and moved back to Tsai. Two anecdotes are attached to this period, and they are worth mentioning.

Two farmers, one tall and one grim-faced and both muddy, were at work in the field together when Confucius passed by. Thinking they were recluses, he sent Tze-lu to inquire for the ford.

The tall man said: "Who is he that holds the reins in the carriage there?" "It is Kung Ch'iu." Tze-lu told him.

"Is he not Kung Ch'iu of Lu?"

"Yes," was the reply, to which the tall-muddy rejoined: "He knows the ford."

Tze-lu then inquired of the other grim-faced one, who said to him: "Who are you, sir?" He answered: "I am Chun Yao."

"Are you not the disciple of Kung Ch'iu of Lu?" asked the other.

"I am." he replied; then that man said to him: "Disorder, like swelling flood, spreads over the whole empire, and with whom are you going to change its state? And you, rather than follow one who merely withdraws from this one and that one, had you not better follow those who have withdrawn from the world altogether?" (With this) he went on hoeing.

Tze-lu went and reported their remarks, when the Master (after a long while) observed with a sigh: "It is impossible to associate with birds and beasts as if they were the same with us. If I associate not with people — with mankind — with whom shall I associate? If right principles (Tao) prevailed through the empire, there would be no use for me to change its state." [37]

On another occasion, Tze-lu, following his master, happened to fall behind, when he met an old man carrying across his shoulder on a staff a basket for weeds. Tze-lu said to him: "Have you seen my master, sir?"

The old man replied; "Your four limbs are unaccustomed to toil; you do not plant (separately the five kinds of) grains. Who is your master?" With this, he placed his staff on the ground and proceeded to weed.

Tze-lu joined his hands across his breast and stood slightly bowing before him.

The old man kept Tze-lu to pass the night in his house, killed a

---

36.   VII, 18; *Ancient History*, Biography.

37.   XVIII, 6. The two farmers, Chang-tsue (literally "the tall and muddy man"), and Chieh-ni ("the grim one with muddy feet") were supposed to have these two proper names. It was doubted how these two names could be known in such a brief inquiry of the ford. So they are not given as personal names in this translation.

fowl, prepared millet, and feasted him. He also introduced him to his two sons.

Next day, Tze-lu went on his way and reported "his adventure." The Master said: "He is a recluse, " and sent Tze-lu back to see him again, but when he got to the place, the old man was gone.[38]

It happened that at this time (491 B.C.) Ch'en was invaded by the state Wu, and Ch'u came to its rescue. Having heard that Confucius was staying somewhere between Ch'en and Tsai, the Duke of Ch'u sent a messenger and invited him to his state. Confucius was about to go. Here is a paragraph in the *Ancient History* which seems to be untrustworthy, saying that the great officers of both Ch'en and Tsai were consulting together, fearing that as Confucius was a talented man and a great sage, his employment in Ch'u would then greatly strengthen that large state, and thereby weaken their own states, hence, their own positions would also be endangered, and thus they sent out their soldiers to the wilderness and surrounded his whole retinue etc. This anecdote is unbelievable in so far as these two states, Ch'en and Tsai, were antagonistic to each other, because Ch'en was sided with Ch'u and Tsai with Wu. So it was highly improbable that the ministers of both states could come together for a conference to find out some means for protecting themselves against a future hypothetical foe. Other histories only say that seven days before, Confucius had exhausted his provisions. This fact was given in every history but no one had given the cause. On this occasion many of his followers were fatigued and fell sick, but

Confucius talked, chanted, and played on his musical instrument as usual. A discourse noted down in the *Analects*[39] seems to be instructive; it runs as follows:

When he was in Ch'en, their provisions were exhausted, and his followers became so ill that they were unable to rise.

Tze-lu, with evident dissatisfaction, said: "Has the superior man likewise to endure want (in this way) ?"

The Master said: "The superior man may indeed have to endure want but the mean man, when he is in want, gives way to violence."

Tze-kung, who was by the side, changed his countenance on hearing this.

The Master said: "Ts'ze (the name of Tze-kung), you think I suppose, that I am one who learns many things and keeps them in memory?"

Tze-kung replied: "Yes, but perhaps it is not so?"

"No, " was the answer; "I seek a unity all-pervading."

Confucius, knowing that his disciples were dissatisfied, first summoned Tze-lu and asked him thus:

"It is said in an ancient poem:

'It is neither a rhinoceros nor a tiger,

.

38.   XVIII, 7.
39.   XV, 1.

Following the path in the wilderness. '

Is my Path (Tao) a wrong one; otherwise why am I here (in such a condition) ?"

Tze-lu replied: "May it be that I am not having enough loving-kindness (Jen) toward men, so that people do not trust in me? Or, may it be that I am not wise enough, so that people do not follow me?"

Then Confucius said: "Can it be so? Yao. If people of loving-kindness (Jen) were all trusted in, how could there have been Pê Yi and Sheu Ch'i? [40] If people of wisdom were all followed, how could there have been the Prince Pi Kang?" [41]

Tze-lu went off.

Next, Tze-kung came in.

Confucius asked the same question, saying:

"It is said in an ancient poem:

'It is neither a rhinoceros nor a tiger,

Following the path in the wilderness.'

Is my Path (Tao) a wrong one; otherwise why am I here (in such a condition) ?"

Tze-kung replied: "The Way (Tao) of our Master is the greatest, so the world cannot bear with our Master. Could our Master perhaps condescend a little?"

Then Confucius said: "Ts'ze! A good farmer can plant well, but he cannot be sure of a good harvest. A good worker can be skilled in his craftsmanship, but he cannot please every one. The superior man can cultivate his Truth (Tao), bring forth Its leading principles, systematize or synthesize them or regulate them, but he cannot make himself borne with by others. Now, you do not cultivate your Truth and wish to be borne with by others, Ts'ze! Your aspirations seem to be not too high (literally 'far')."

Tze-kung went off.

Next, Yen Whei (alias Yen Yüan) came in.

Confucius asked the same thing, saying:

"It is said in an ancient poem:

'It is neither a rhinoceros nor a tiger,

Following the path in the wilderness.'

.

40.   The two persons mentioned were ancient worthies of the closing period of the Shang dynasty, being the two most revered persons before Confucius. They were brothers, sons of the king of Ku Chu, a small state in the northeastern part of China. Their father left his kingdom to Sheu Ch'i, the younger, who refused to take the place of his elder brother. Pè Yi in turn declined the throne, so they both abandoned it and retired into obscurity. When King Wu was taking his measures against the tyrant Chau by which the Chow dynasty was afterwards founded, they made their appearance and remonstrated his course, Finally they starved themselves, preferring death rather than life under the new dynasty. (*Ana.*, V, 22; *Ancient Hist.*, Biography 1)

41.   Prince Pi Kang was the great minister of the tyrant Chau, the last king of the Shang dynasty. He was executed because of his repeated remonstrances against those tyrannical measures.

Is my Path (Tao) a wrong one; otherwise why am I here (in such a condition) ?"

Yen Whei replied: "Our Master's Tao is the greatest, so the world cannot bear with him. Nevertheless, when our Master brings it forth and spreads it to the people, what is the harm of not being borne with? Just in being not borne with, there appears the superior man. Indeed, if the Tao were not being cultivated, that would be my shame; but if it were greatly cultivated and yet unemployed, that must be the shame of those who rule kingdoms. What is the harm of being not borne with? Just in being not borne with, there appears the superior man."

Confucius was pleased with this answer, and said:

"Is it so? You, son of Yen's family, I wish you could be wealthy, I would even manage for you." [42]

It is clear that certain external conditions must have made the journey impossible and, in such a difficult position, Tze-kung was sent to ask for relief from Ch'u. The ruler of that state — a baron in rank, but also called the King Jao — sent immediately his soldiers to escort Confucius to his state. After bidding him welcome to the state, the king Jao was about to donate to him a piece of land of seven hundred square miles. (The word "mile" here is used to translate the Chinese word "li", which is only about 1890 feet in English measure.) But the chief minister of Ch'u, named Tze-si, refused to give it. He then argued with the king in this way:

"Is there any one among His Majesty's ambassadors sent to different states like Tze-kung?"

"No." said the King Jao.

"Is there any one among His Majesty's ministers like Yen Whei?"

"No."

"Is there any one among His Majesty's generals like Tze-lu?"

"No."

"Is there any one among His Majesty's governors like Tsai-yü?"

"No."

"And the ancestor of Ch'u, " said the minister further, "was appointed to the government of a baron in a territory of fifty square miles in the Chow dynasty. Now, Kung Ch'iu promulgates the rules and regulations of the Three Ancient Sagekings, and knows the achievements of the Dukes Chow and Shao. If His Majesty should employ him in government, how can our Ch'u state maintain for future generations such a large territory of several thousand square miles? Moreover, King Wen was staying in a small district called Feng, and King Wu, in Kao, and as the rulers of small areas of a hundred miles, they finally became the emperors of the whole country. If now Kung Ch'iu can occupy some land, and with his talented and sagacious

.

42. Yen Whei was the favorite disciple of Confucius, but materially the poorest.

disciples as assistants, this cannot be a blessing to Ch'u."

Thus was the king convinced and he gave up the idea. In the autumn of the same year King Jao died; and Confucius returned to Wei.

While Confucius was travelling in Ch'u, a madman made some impression on him. The anecdote is as follows:

Chieh-yü, [43] the madman of Ch'u as he passed Confucius, sang:
"Phoenix, bright phoenix,
Thy glory is ended!
Think of the future:
The past can't be mended.
Up and away!
The court is to-day
With danger attended."
Confucius alighted and fain would have spoken with him. But hurriedly he made off; no speech was to be had of him. [44]

It happened that at this time there was a quarrel for the throne between the father and the son in the state of Wei, and many of the disciples of Confucius had long been in offices of this state. Someone suspected that Confucius had sided with the son who was already on the throne, against the father who was in exile. Jan-yu said: "Is our master for the ruler of Wei?" T'ze-kung said : "O! I will ask him."

He went in (accordingly) and said: "What sort of men were Pê Yi and Sheu Ch'i?"

"They were ancient worthies," said the Master.

"Did they have any repinings (because of their course) ?"

"They sought for Love and found It, what was there for them to repine about?" the Master again replied.

On this, Tze-kung went out and said: "Our master is not for him." [45]

It was now his last visit to the dukedom of Wei. And once he said: "The governments of Lu and Wei are brothers." (XIII, 7) It was a fact that both of their remote ancestors were brothers, being two brothers of King Wu of the Chow dynasty. It can well be understood that these two states preserved most of the traditions of the same dynasty, different from other states which were partially barbarian in their customs, such as Ch'u or Ch'in. Both these states maintained an equally high level of culture. Yet at this time the political condition of Wei was unpeaceful. The duke of the throne was about seventeen or eighteen years old and had the idea of employing Confucius to govern. So Tze-lu said to the

43. Chieh-yü is here taken as the personal name of the madcap, but in fact it could be translated as "nearby the carriage," as the name of such a person met on the high-way could scarcely be known judged by the circumstances.

44. *Harvard Classics*, XVIII, 5.

45. VII, 14.

master:

"The ruler of Wei has been waiting for you, in order with you to administer government. What will you consider the first thing to be done?"

The Master replied: "If anything is necessary to be done, [46] it is perhaps the rectification of names and words."

"Is it so?" said Tze-lu, "You are wide of the mark! Why must there be such rectification?"

The Master said: "How uncultivated is this Yao! A superior man, in regard to what he does not know, shows a cautious reserve.

"If words and names be not correct, language is not in accordance with the truth of things. If language be not in accordance with the truth of things, affairs cannot be carried on to success.

"When affairs cannot be carried on to success, proprieties and music will not flourish. When proprieties and music do not flourish, punishments, large and small, will not be justly awarded. When large and small punishments are not justly awarded, the people cannot move hand or foot.

"Therefore whatever the superior man does, it must have an appropriate name, and whatever he speaks must be able to be carried out. What the superior man requires is that in his language there may be nothing incorrect." [47]

In the next year, Jan Ch'iu led an army of Lu and fought with Ch'i;

he gained a great victory in a district called Lang. This battle was a decisive one. Kan-tze, the chief minister, asked Jan Ch'iu: "With regard to your military knowledge, have you learned it, or were you originally gifted with it?"

Jan Ch'iu said: "I learned it from Confucius."

Kan-tze said: "What sort of man is Confucius?"

Jan Ch'iu replied: "If employed in government, he will become famous; and no dissatisfaction or resentment will arise if his fame were spread among the people or presented before the gods. That I have come to this path, or even if I were donated with a large land of thousands and thousands of families, our Master is not thereby touched (literally 'benefited')."

Kan-tze then said: "If I wish to invite him, is it possible?"

"If you wish to invite him, then do not let him be stopped by small

.

46. These questions and answers were implicitly connected with the internal politics of the state of Wei. The prince was installed on the throne by Nan-tze, to whom the lord of Tze-lu (Kung Wen Tze) owed his allegiance. Tze-lu most probably expected his master to work for the existing government while Confucius was disinclined. on the other occasion when Confucius went to see Nan-tze, Tze-lu was displeased because he thought that there could have been talks in the interview about the installation, thinking that if the Master was not for her policies, what was the use of going to pay her respects or perhaps to convince her to do otherwise. Yet this is merely an intelligent conjecture. The actual facts noted down were too brief to testify to this with any certainty.

47. XIII, 3.

men in his undertakings. That is then possible." So said Jan Ch'iu.

But at this moment Confucius in the Wei state was consulted about the scheme of a revolt by Wen-tze. Confucius politely declined, saying that he knew nothing. After the meeting, Confucius ordered at once the carriage to be prepared for his departure, saying: "The bird can choose the tree (for perching), but how can the tree choose the bird?" Wen-tze energetically stopped him from going. Just at this juncture, the messenger sent by Kan-tze with a large sum of money as an offering arrived with the invitation. Then Confucius returned to his native land Lu, after fourteen years of wanderings among many dukedoms. His age was then sixty-nine.

Chapter IV

A CENTRAL PRINCIPLE

Thus far we have seen this great sage as a statesman travelling into all parts of the country, trying to secure power in his hands in order to realize some of his high ideals so as to bring about, perhaps, a Paradise on this earth. But unfortunately he failed, and he failed not owing to his own weaknesses or shortcomings, but to the turbulent circumstances of his time. Moreover, he failed not only once or twice or several times, but on every occasion in his life. Had the Supreme so willed it? Perhaps yes. The latter part of his life, judged by worldly standards, was a tragedy, and yet it was the most fruitful period of his achievement and contribution to humanity; and, viewed as a whole, his life was a supreme success, unique, integral and divine.

A practical question arises: why had Confucius not gone to the still existent government of the Chow dynasty? It was plain that the Emperor at that time had no power and his dominion was limited to a very small district, though in status he still maintained the highest reverence of the land, called the "heavenly king," or "Son of Heaven." Even the little remaining power of his kingdom was usurped and shared by several ministers. Evidently under such circumstances nothing could be done. Yet, as sometimes the meat of sacrifices was sent to different dukes as blessings (exactly like the Indian custom of sharing the *prasād*), it was accepted with due formalities. A royal mandate was sometimes issued to several powerful states, ordering for example the building of the city-wall of the capital, and that was also carried out. Usually the language of those imperial decrees was very well-phrased and dignified, suited to the style of a Heavenly King, but it was merely words and not much cared for.

In the discourses quoted in the previous chapter we notice one thing; Confucius talked about his relation with Heaven on several occasions when his life was endangered and was sure of the virtue Heaven produced in him. Thus somehow he was conscious of his mission in the world and the cause he stood for. Merely because of this, there was no fear of death in him, even at the most critical moments. According to his own words we find the following account :

"At fifteen, I had my mind bent on learning.

At thirty, I stood firm.

At forty, I had no doubts.

At fifty, I knew the decrees of Heaven.

At sixty, my ear was an obedient organ (for the reception of truth).

At seventy, I could follow what my heart wished for, without transgressing what was right." [48]

If we seek for a correct understanding of such a passage, so brief and definitely stated as it was, we must bear in mind that when he spoke of himself, he had recourse to modesty and reserve which was his usual way. Through glimpses into this or that saying, we can well conjecture that what was said was not the whole of his teaching and perhaps only a trifle as compared to what was not said. Different from other religious leaders of the world, he had never addressed any great mass of people or even a large assembly of his own disciples, elucidating publicly this or that principle he meant to be made known. Furthermore, not everything said by him was noted down; most of the oral tradition was lost after one or two generations when those who had kept his sayings in memory passed away, and those things written down were brief owing also to the material circumstances in ancient times, as paper was not yet used, and to write on silk or pieces of bamboo was not a simple thing. We find in the famous *Analects*, most probably recorded by the disciples of his disciples, only brief statements mainly made by the Master himself, as the causes together with other discussions of the disciples that occasioned these answers were not given, We can only

---

48.   II, 4.

understand the passages in the context of his teachings as a whole, in the context of the historical background of his time.

Certain scholars of the so-called Neo-Confucianism in the Sung (960–1279) and Ming (1368–1644) dynasties went too far in suggesting that what was learnt by his disciple Yen Yüan and others was simply the knowledge of It, corresponding to the higher Brahman knowledge of Tat (or That), though those scholars had no information at all about the Vedanta philosophy. And, in this connection, as Joy was often talked about by Confucius, it could again be interpreted as the third term in "Sachchi-dananda". Was Confucius no man of such realization? It matters not a whit to his greatness if he had no such realization in that Higher Knowledge, yet it is difficult to answer in the negative. For the moment let us be content to take the historical rather than the metaphysical stand in the explanation of these passages.

Here we copy another translation of the same saying: (Sacred Writings, The *Harvard Classics*, edited by Charles W. Eliot, without the name of the translator.)

"At fifteen, I was bent on study; at thirty, I could stand; at forty, doubts ceased; at fifty I understood the laws of Heaven; at sixty, my ears obeyed me; at seventy, I could do as my heart lusted, and never swerve from right."

Here we find slight variations in the renderings that appear trivial, yet not without significance. We cannot say which is more correct. Here we understand why Leo Tolstoy in his old age began to learn Greek in order to study the New Testament. The original language must be learned and mastered before such sacred texts can be thoroughly understood.

When it was said that his mind was *bent on* learning, it was the study of the traditional knowledge of mostly the so-called Li or Propriety, including ceremonies of sacrifices, both secular and spiritual in nature, which ultimately led to the relationship of the mundane with the supermundane. That Heaven was above, every one in his time believed, and it was to Him that all the sacrifices were offered, next to one's departed ancestors; this is still the orthodox belief in China in the present day. The bent of his mind — in Chinese this word means "whither the mind and heart go" —should be interpreted as his "aspiration", and we must suppose as a boy of fifteen he had not yet the aspiration of becoming one with the Divine. After fifteen years of learning, he became "established" in knowledge, translated here as "to *stand*." This means that he had then a series of definite ideas about things in this world or, so to say, his settled views of life and of the universe.

Upto the age of forty, he had then "no more doubts" ; that is to say, no more doubts about his inner convictions or, in other words, he could no longer be puzzled by external circumstances or shaken in his own faith. And after another ten years of inner effort, he began to know the "decree of Heaven," or religiously put, the "appointment of God"

("*Law*" is not correct here), or the "Divine's Will."

It would be unfruitful to beat about the bush with regard to his inner accomplishments after fifty, as it was a good joke by the famous commentator on him, Chu Hsi, when he stopped once in his lecture at the statement of "at fifty" and proceeded no further. When asked to continue he declined, saying that since he himself was not yet fifty, how could he understand the experience of the sage at that age? Indeed, that is modesty. Yet, even if an ordinary scholar had reached the age of fifty, sixty, or seventy, but with different experiences, even then he could not properly interpret what was said. But this seems to be certain: at the age of fifty, or probably much earlier than that, he began to know the appointment of God in him, and "to know" he meant the assurance both in mind and heart, and we can safely infer that, not only in himself, but also in others and finally in humanity at large. Moreover, for him to know anything meant usually to know from alpha to omega. It is very reasonable to suppose that somewhere between forty and fifty (or the latest at fifty) he had certain great inner Enlightenment which could not be just a vision or a revelation or some faint glimpse of Truth; it must have been a great experience of direct communication or identification with the Supreme, which in his own way of putting it, was "a Union of virtue with Heaven and Earth" [49] — in the Yogic way of speaking, it is simply a Union with God and Nature — that henceforth stabilized and integralized all his actions and sayings until the end of his life. Only after that inner realization, there appeared the "leitmotiv" in the symphony of his life in spreading his Truth to humanity and, in the presence of that, there could be no more the question of life and death, success or failure, praise or blame — in short, of all the contradictory dualities that make up the miseries and sufferings of mankind. This must be then the result of his seeking the allpervading unity and Oneness. Explanations about this Oneness given by his disciples will be treated later on.

It may be pointed out here that outwardly there is one main difference between Confucianism and other different systems of the world. Tao — the Way or Truth — in the universe is one; this is too plain to need any discussion. But the way, or rather, the mode of expressing it, of cultivating and spreading it, may be different. We see that both Taoism and Buddhism, and Christianity, and perhaps Mohammedanism as well, all started from a lower level of society, extended themselves broadly among the mass on a flat plane, kindling one soul after another, just as the torch of the Marathon race was successively transferred. But the Confucian was more hierarchial or longitudinal. Nearly every ancient Chinese master tried the same thing, and I venture to remark

49. This is found in the *Book of Changes*, translated by C. F. Baynes as "The great man accords in his character with Heaven and Earth, in his light, with the sun and moon; in his consistency, with the four seasons; in the good and evil fortune (that he creates), with gods and spirits" (Vide *I Ching*, Vol. II, p. 15.)
"The union of one's action with Heaven (or God)" was spoken of by Chao Chi in his commentary on *Mencius*.

that the Pope in the Middle Ages did no other; viz. they all started from the top, tried to exercise their direct influence first in the imperial court, and then, like a rain-cloud in dry season, overshadowed the whole country and showered the nectar of relief upon the land. Perhaps among such a large population this was the most straight and convenient way. And in later ages, nearly every school of philosophy felt proud in styling itself "the royal learning," or "the imperial knowledge." The Confucian doctrines were the more so because, as the fundamental principles of humanity, they were taught to the children of aristocrats in the state educational centres.

But it is a general mechanical law in Nature that if anything starts or succeeds by a certain means it must necessarily end or fall also with that means. If Confucianism, be it a religion or simply a code of moral teachings, had to propagate itself by the help of political influence, it could do so as long as that influence lasted, but it would also have to collapse with the fall of it. Yet here a subtle distinction must be made. Because these teachings were intimately related to politics, the question resolves itself into their being adopted or not as the guiding principles of orientation of the government. As it was not superimposing a certain set of beliefs or dogmas upon any existent political power and relying upon that for its promulgation, such a problem does not enter into consideration. And history proves that in nearly every dynasty, there was the question of their adoption with only the variation of degrees, and they never perished with any of the ruling dynasties.

We may tackle this problem in another way; it is that within these teachings there is the everlasting and imperishable truth by itself sound and endurable that stood the tests of Time without being crushed under its grinding wheels. Nevertheless, it was no new Gospel that was brought into the world. Confucius, known in China as a sage, was praised for his work of the "great synthesis" or, literally, "gathering together to a great perfection" of all the essence of the culture of the Three Dynasties in the past and breathed into it a new life; and as a conservator, this Synthesis was his first and last achievement. He brought forth nothing new. It is within this great achievement that we find out its central principle. And if we divide the whole history of Chinese culture from the most ancient to recent times, he stood there just at the linkpoint between two halves, a great deduction and a great induction before and after him. Or, to use a material metaphor, a bundle of beautiful silk is tied just in the middle, with all threads gathered at the knot and again, with that as a source, it issued out in good order.

Evidently, if we make a study of Confucianism, we must find out its central principle. What the sage achieved personally can only be of secondary importance to us as compared to what he taught. Even if there is no such principle in existence, we must form or formulate one from its whole fabric. This is rather a pragmatic attitude, indispensable perhaps in the economy of things, and the more important when a subject so spiritual in nature is to be dealt with; unmistakably we do find one.

Here we find only a single word that has baffled every translator, and makes no end to the work of commentators. It is pronounced as Jen in Chinese, and it is very simple in its etymological construction: the word for "two" on the right side is added with a radical or "classifier" for "man" on the left, showing that it is something connected with the relationship between man and man. In the ordinary language it is also used to denote the "kernel" of fruits, such as almond or peach-stones in which the life-principle of the plant is preserved. The opposite to it means then "numb" or "apathetic", used to describe certain diseases of paralysis.

Now the difficulty lies in that all the live passages dealing with such a central principle, vivid and never cryptic or ambiguous by themselves, were simply stifled and smothered by the clumsy translation of this word Jen into "virtue" (done by Legge) which gives the wrong impression to English readers that such a great spiritual master was no more than a stony-faced teacher of ethics. For "virtue" there is another word pronounced as "Teh", which is always used in combination with the word "Tao", — as *Tao Teh Ching* was given as a title to the *Book of Lao Tze*, which means literally "The Classic on Virtues." In the Sacred Writings (*Harvard Classics*) "Jen" is simply translated as "love", which is a little more lively yet too flippant, and does not convey much sense. For "love" there is also another word. "Jen" has been also rendered as "benevolence" and "beneficence", both too small to cover the original idea; and then as "compassion" or "lovingkindness", both nearer to the original but equally incomprehensive. "Sympathy" is a term too shallow, and "humanity" is a word broad enough but superficial. So practically there is no exact equivalent in English.

We must then abandon the hope of finding one word as its exact translation and try to find out its descriptions, but again, not to seek for any definition. Positively, "psychic love" is very near to an exact interpretation, but it pertains not only to the individual. It is a cosmic principle called in Chinese "the heart of Heaven and Earth," that by which the Harmony of the universe manifests and pervades. Divine Grace is another nearer equivalent, but with that there is the One who graces with the Grace, while with this, it is more impersonal; it can be spoken of as That from which the Divine Grace radiates. In the parable of the sun with its rays, it is the sun itself; but what can a sun be without its rays? If we must use the word "love", it can only be in the sense of that as defined by the Divine Mother:

"Love is a mighty vibration coming straight from the One ..." [50]

---

50. The whole passage runs:
"Love is a mighty vibration coming straight from the One, and only the very pure and very strong are capable of receiving and manifesting it." L'amour est une vibration toute puissante émanée directement de l'Un, et seul le très pur et le très fort est capable de la recevoir et de le manifester.

In other words, it is Divine's Love. Yet Divine Perfection is also near, or, we may say, the perfectness that is self-existent on a higher level than the human; and, if we call it any state of perfection, it is that towards which every human being strives, and having attained it he is then divine. Descending more to the human level, it is that in which every goodness is included, such as peacefulness, nonviolence, kind-heartedness, benevolence, compassion, humanity and love, and endless other virtues such as filial-piety, fraternal submission, loyalty, truthfulness, faithfulness, love of propriety, of courtesy, of justice, of righteousness, of modesty, of humility, etc. All in all, Jen is something that is rooted above and within, an entity without which there can be no universe.

With this borne in mind, we may proceed to examine the diverse translations and meditate for a right word where the translator failed. Within the twenty chapters of the present *Analects*, we find no less than 54 passages dealing with this subject apart from other sporadic references. (It may be noted in passing that so far the English translations of these twenty chapters have missed nothing in their division of 489 passages or sections; but the subdivision of each chapter varies in different Chinese editions, and hence, the number of passages also varies. But that textual problem is too complicated to be treated here.) The constant reiteration of this subject no less than the emphasis laid upon it shows clearly its importance as the core of teaching and, what is more, as it was one of the three things which Confucius seldom talked about or elucidated in any detail — treated on a par with the "appointment of Heaven" or otherwise "doom", and "profitableness" or "gain" — its solemnity or sanctity can be seen.

Yet,

"Is Love (Jen) so far a thing? I yearn for Love (Jen), and lo! Love (Jen) is come." [51]

Here Confucius speaks of his own experience. Apparently what is meant here is the Divine's Love. As a cosmic principle, it cannot be far from us. By a turn of mind, one abhors a normal life of indifference and insipidity and wants to be lover and lovable or beloved, and then he finds Love there at hand if he awakens to it. Even in the ordinary life, by taking any action, one can be very fair, good and sweet through an inspiration if one only wants to be so. The same idea is expressed in another passage:

"Were a man to give himself to Love (Jen) but for one day, I have seen no one whose strength would fail him. Such man there may be, but I have not seen one." [52]

(The same passage done by Legge: *"Is any one able for one day to apply his strength to virtue (Jen) ? I have not seen the case in which his strength would*

.

51.   VII, 29
52.   IV, 6.

be insufficient. — Should there possibly be any such case. I have not seen it.")

But even on our human level, it is not a case of "Let there be Light and there was Light" ; tremendous personal effort has to be made to the point of sacrificing of one's life in order to attain to that state of perfection in the Divine's Love. When Confucius was asked "What kind of men were Pê Yi and Sheu Ch'i?" he said they were worthy men of yore, and "they sought Love and found It," so they had nothing to rue. These two worthies simply starved themselves because of seeking that Love (Jen). There could be then no regret nor resentment because the life was offered to that noble and divine cause and the state of inner perfection was reached. They died in perfect peace of mind in a blissful state of fulfilment. And we find in our history innumerable persons who willingly and gladly offered their lives in periods of revolution, especially on occasions of the fall of old dynasties, merely motivated by this single word, Jen. As to the ordinary man with this bit or that of virtue, what could be said then? It is the palm not wrested by every one. We read the following discourses:

Mong Wu Po asked whether Tze-lu had Love (Jen)? (Legge: *"Whether he was perfectly virtuous? "*)

The Master said: "I do not know."

He asked again.

The Master said: "A land of a thousand chariots might give Yao charge of its levies; but whether he have Love (Jen), I do not know."

"And how about Ch'iu?"

"A town of a thousand households, a clan of a hundred chariots might make Ch'iu governor; but whether he have Love (Jen), I do not know."

"And how about Ch'ih?"

"Girt with his sash, erect in the court, Ch'ih might entertain the guests; but whether he have Love (Jen), I do not know." [53]

These are the great disciples of Confucius of many rare virtues and capacities and given the opportunity they could master many things; and as no one knows the pupil better than his master, he does not vouchsafe for their having such a Love or Jen. Only the poverty-stricken disciple Yen Whei who was satisfied with a dish of rice, a gourd of water, living in a low alleyway with his arm bent for a pillow, whose heart never fell from mirth (Ananda), won the praise of his master in these words:

"For three months together Whei's heart never sinned against Love (Jen). The others may hold out for a day, or a month; but no more." [54]

53. V, 7.

54. VI, 5.

Once another poor disciple Yuan Hsien asked:

"When the strife for superiority, boasting, resentments, and covetousness are repressed, may this be called Love (Jen) ?"

The Master said: "This may be regarded as the achievement of what is difficult; but I do not know that it is Love (Jen)." [55]

Tze-chang asked, saying: "The minister Tze-wen thrice took office, and manifested no joy in his countenance. Thrice he retired from office, and manifested no displeasure. He made it a point to inform the new minister of the way in which he had conducted the government ; — what do you say of him?"

The Master replied: "He was loyal."

"But had he Love (Jen) ? (or by Legge: *Was he perfectly virtuous?*")

"I do not know, " said the Master: "how should this amount to Love (Jen) ?" (or *how can he be pronounced perfectly virtuous?*")

"When the officer Ts'ui killed the Prince of Ch'i [56], Chen Wen-tze, though he was the owner of forty horses, abandoned them and left the country. Coming to another state, he said: 'Here they are like our great officer Ts'ui,' and left that state. He came to another state; and said: 'Here they are like our great officer Ts'ui,' and again left it. —What do you say of him?"

The Master replied: "He was pure."

"But had he Love (Jen) ?" (or *Was he perfectly virtuous?*")

"I do not know," said the Master: "how should this amount to Love (Jen)?" (or "*how can he be pronounced perfectly virtuous?*")[57]

Yet in the ancient history there were several great men to whom Confucius attributed such a Love, in the sense that they had manifested It on the earth through their works.

Tze-lu said: "When Duke Huan slew the young duke Chiu, Shao Hu died with him, but not Kuan Chung, was this not want of Love (Jen)?"

The Master said: "The Duke Huan assembled all the princes on nine occasions for peace-conferences, and that without the help of war-chariots, it was all through the policies of Kuan Chung. He had Love indeed, he had Love indeed." (or "*what can love do more?*", doubled; or "*whose beneficence was like this*", doubled.) [58]

Tze-kung said: "Kuan Chung was probably no man of Love (Jen)? When the Duke Huan caused his brother Chiu to be killed, Kuan Chung was not able to die with him. Moreover, he became his prime minister."

.

55.   XIV, 2.
56.   Vide p. 27.
57.   V, 18.
58.   XIV, 17.

The Master said: "Kuan Chung acted as prime minister to the Duke Huan, made him leader of all princes, and rectified universally the whole kingdom. Down to the present day, the people enjoy the fruits of his merits. But for Kuan Chung, we should now be wearing out hair unbound, and the lappets of our coats buttoning on the left side.[59]

"Will you require from his the small fidelity of common men or women, who would commit suicide by hanging themselves along a stream or ditch, no one knowing anything about them?" [60]

Thus we see a statesman who could bring peace to the country was also considered to be a man of such rare virtue judged by his achievements. Tracing ancient history back to the Yin or Shang dynasty, Wei-tze or the Viscount of Wei withdrew from the court. Chi-tze or the Viscount of Chi became a slave of Chau, and Pi Kang remonstrated with the tyrant and died. Confucius said: "The Yin dynasty possessed these three men of Love (Jen)." [61]

Tze-kung said: "Suppose the case of a man extensively conferring benefits on the people, and able to assist all, what would you say of him? Might he be called a man of Love (Jen)?"

The Master said: "What has this to do with Love? Were he not a man of holiness? Then even (both the ancient sagekings) Yao and Shun still yearned for this (deeming this cannot be easily achieved).

"Now the man of Love, wishing to be established himself, seeks also to establish others; wishing to be enlightened himself, he seeks also to enlighten others.

"To be able to judge of others by what is nigh within ourselves, — this may be called the way to Love." [62]

Now, with regard to such a great principle, we may wish to learn how Confucius looked upon himself. With frankness and modesty, he said:

"In exertion, I am equal to other men, but carrying out in his person what a superior man is, is what I have not attained to." [63]

The Master said: "As to Holiness and Love (Jen), how dare I lay claim? It may be simply said of me, that I tirelessly strive to be such, and teach others without weariness." — Kungsi Hua said: "This is just what we disciples cannot imitate you in." [64]

The Master said: "The way of the superior man is threefold, but I

.

59. These were the barbarian customs. Ancient Chinese coats or robes were buttoned either front in the middle or on the right side. Hair was always drawn up and bound.
60. XIV, 18.
61. XVIII, 1.
62. VI, 28.
63. VII, 32.
64. VII, 33.

am not equal to it. As a man of Love (Jen), he is free from anxieties; as a man of wisdom, he is free from doubts; and as a man of courage, he is free from fear."

Tze-kung said: "Master, that is what you yourself say (but we think differently)." [65]

.

65.   XIV, 30.

Chapter V

A CENTRAL PRINCIPLE *(continued)*

Human love is fraught with anxiety. In a negative sense, only when there is no love will there be no anxiety. The avoidance of love is a worldly experience as taught in different systems, a nihilistic tendency which seeks peace in the last resort of a great Void in which both pleasure and pain cease. But what is taught here by Confucius is something positive and absolute. Reviewing all that has been said about it so far, what other adequate term should be put to it except the Divine's Love? It is that in which we all subsist, with or without being conscious of it.

Needless to say, one can be spiritual without being religious. Not only priests or prophets but a great statesman can be a man of Love as well, and in the example of Kuan Chung, he was merely a good political economist [66], a competent diplomat, and a man luxurious in his habits; yet he was considered as a man having such a great virtue because, owing to his effort, peace was brought to the land for a half-century ensuring the preservation of the ancient culture. Equally praised were the three ministers of the Yin dynasty. They all trod a this-worldly way, up to the point of sacrificing their lives. So were also Pê Yi and Sheu Ch'i. Should we here not reflect for a moment on our modern leaders as Abraham Lincoln, Sun Yat-sen and Gandhiji? We would say that they were great men in the sense that each had brought a great Love to the world. Normally to sacrifice one's life may be a large thing or small, as one may take it; it can be as light as a feather or as heavy as a mountain, but the question is: for what purpose? Purposes may differ, but all in all it cannot be for certain personal or egoistic ends. Ultimately it can be no other than for the Divine's Love. So it is said by Confucius:

A man of high aspiration or a man of Love will not seek to live at the cost of Love (Jen). They may even sacrifice their lives in order to fulfill love (Jen).[67]

We may suppose that, as the instinct of self-preservation is born with every human being, so to teach one to voluntarily give up one's life cannot be an easy path. But it is here not a teaching of Death, it is a

---

66. It must be mentioned here that the book called *Kuan Tze* attributed to him was a spurious work.

67. XV, 8.

teaching of Life.

The Master said: "Love (Jen) is more to people than either water or fire. I have seen man die from treading on water or fire, but I have never seen a man die from treading the course of Love (Jen)." [68]

If its importance to life is compared to water or fire, it can be seen at the same time that it is no extraordinary thing but a common path that can be trod by all. One may offer one's life to effect his perfection in the Divine's Love, but the Divine's Love does not demand the destruction of life on Its altar. Quite on the contrary, it is the Divine's Love that preserves life, attaches value to it, and brings it to perfection in an Eternal life. Usually it is compared to the spring season — and we must concede that it is the spring in the temperate zone after the snowy and icy winter, when green plants began to grow and beautiful flowers begin to bud under a bluish sky — as death is sometimes compared to autumn or winter. Can a man's heart be ever so broad and kind and gracious as the clear weather of the spring?

With regard to an Eternal Life, it is a matter of Yoga: a spiritual seeking or other-worldly pursuance, in pursuit of a Paradise after death, or Mukti or emancipation in whatever way. That is than a favorite subject of the Taoists as well as Buddhists. or followers of other religions. But if we take Yoga in a large sense as explained by Sri Aurobindo — that "all Life is Yoga" — then this Way of Confucianism has a say; it can be included. Among the seekers, normally someone feels a natural inclination to the Way of Knowledge and others are more inclined to the Way of Love ; hence there is a distinction of Jnana-Yoga and Bhakti-Yoga, though at the end these two paths must converge into one, and the Jnani can well be a Bhakta and vice versa. Yet in the outward temperament, people may differ. We find certain persons born with high intelligence, sharp or quick wit, and others with less high intelligence but with a loving heart. The latter may find easier access to such a way. We read what Confucius said:

The Master said: "Men of wisdom find pleasure in water, men of Love find pleasure in hills. Men of wisdom are active, men of love are quiet. Men of wisdom are joyful, men of Love are long-lived." [69]

On another occasion, he also said:

"What the mind has won will be lost again, unless Love hold it fast. A mind to understand and Love to hold fast, without dignity of bearing, will go unhonoured...." [70]

.

68.   XV, 34.
69.   VI, 21.
70.   XII, 32. *Harvard Classics.*

The same passage in another translation:

The Master said: "When a man's knowledge is sufficient to attain, and his virtue (Jen) is not sufficient to enable him to hold, whatever he may have attained, he will lose again.

"When his knowledge is sufficient to attain, and he has virtue (Jen) to hold fast, if he cannot govern With dignity, the people will not respect him." (Legge)

Evidently in this teaching it is also shown that the characters of these two types of men are different, corresponding to those taken to these two different paths in ancient India. And Eternal Life is understood to be sought in the divine perfection. Further:

Fan Ch'ih asked, What is Love (Jen) ?
The Master said: "To love mankind."
He asked, What is wisdom?
The Master said: "To know mankind." [71]

The same passage done by Legge:

Fan Ch'ih asked about benevolence (Jen). The Master said: "It is to love all men." He asked about knowledge. The Master said: "It is to know all men."

The reason why we should love mankind is not given. But is Love itself not the reason, or should we attach any arbitrary reason to that spontaneity? In the terminology of Yoga, it is then "to love the Godhead in all men." It is not the human beings or mankind that is to be loved, it is the Self in all these beings that is to be loved. Here we find the turning point of the Vedanta philosophy, in its way inward, and the Confucian, in its way outward. A realization of the Self or Atman can be ascribed to Mencius, a philosopher of the same school, but a grain of doubt remains whether this can also be definitely ascribed to Confucius, so far as the wordly expression shows, if we strictly attach to the historical point of view. The way outward turns towards the field of morals and ethics, and that is extended to the mass on a flat plane. The way further inward or upward turns towards Godhead above, towards the field of metaphysics, and it affords a vertical climbing by the individual. Yet the Confucians would argue "what is the use of personal realization if it is only for one's own salvation and not for all?" In its outward turn we find the effort directed towards the progress of society, the elevation of the mass and, ultimately, the salvation of humanity at large. This reminds us of the Bodhisattva who refuses to enter into Buddhahood if a single soul in hell remains unsaved.

Generally, to the same question diverse answers were given because, as Confucius said himself: "With talented men above mediocrity, high subjects may be discussed. To those below mediocrity, high subjects

71.   XII, 22. *Harvard Classics.*

may not be spoken." [72] The three thousand and more disciples of Confucius naturally could not be of the same calibre, and hence the indications to the Path vary immensely.

Fan Ch'ih asked: "What is wisdom?" (or *knowledge*)

The Master said: "To give oneself earnestly to the duties due to men, and, while respecting spiritual beings, to keep aloof from them, may be called wisdom."

He asked : "What is Love (Jen) ?"

The Master said : "The man of Love (Jen) makes effort his first consideration and merit last; — this may be called Love." [73]

In other words, the desire for fruits has no place in such a great principle, but the "duties due to men" can never be neglected. That, the followers of Gita understand best.

On another occasion the same disciple asked about the same subject.

Fan Chi'ih asked: "What is Love (Jen) ?"

The Master said: "To be respectful at home, reverently attentive at work, strictly sincere to all. Even if one goes to the barbarians, these should not be neglected." [74]

Here we find at once the turn outward.

Usually those who are high in knowledge grasp things by the mind, and those who are devoted to Love comprehend things through the heart. They may be less clever in speech, but all the same, they are none the less intelligent. We read:

The Master said: "Those who are firm, or enduring, or simple or slow in speech , are akin to Love (Jen)." [75]

The Master said: "Fine words and an insinuating appearance are seldom associated with Love." [76]

Ssu-ma Niu asked: "What is Love (Jen) ?"

The Master said: "The man of Love (Jen) is cautious in talking about it."

"If a man is cautious in talking about Love (Jen), does it mean that he had it?"

The Master said: "When a man feels the difficulty in doing it, can he be other than cautious in talking about it?" [77]

.

72. VI, 19.
73. VI, 20.
74. XIII, 19.
75. XIII, 27.
76. I, 3.
77. XII, 3.

Some one said: "Yung has Love (Jen), but he has not a glib tongue."

The Master said: "What is the good of a glib tongue? They who encounter men with smartness of speech all too often procure themselves hatred. I know not whether Love (Jen) be his, but what is the good of a glib tongue? " [78]

Nowadays we see that the art of speech is also a nice thing to be learned, no less important than the art of writing. But ancient China never produced a Demosthenes or a Cicero, because there were no public meetings to be adressed. Logicians and public debators came in at a much later date, only during the period of the Warring-States. In the ordinary life it is deprecated in so far as it sometimes beclouds one's clear conscience by glossing over one's own faults and leaves a bad effect on others. Otherwise, rhetoric stood as one of the four main branches of knowledge in the Confucian school. On one occasion it was remarked:

"A man of worth can always talk, but talkers are not always men of worth. Love (Jen) is always bold, though boldness is found without Love (Jen)." [79]

(The same passage done by Legge:

"*The virtuous will be sure to speak correctly,* [originally "have his words"] *but those whose speech is good may not always be virtuous. Men of principle (Jen) are sure to he bold, but those who are bold may not always be men of principle."*)

Here we find again Legge in a difficult position. The word *"virtuous"* (for the Chinese word "teh") was already used in the first sentence which is correct, and coming to the word Jen which he used to translate as "virtue", he could not but put it as "men of principle" which is no longer exact, in order to avoid repetition.

Boldness is another quality. It is usually referred to the man of action, and the way of Karma-yoga is his. The distinction of these three paths was not made in Confucianism, yet these three prominent characteristics were always separately treated as pertaining to three types of men. Unmistakably we find here a point of concordance among these two ancient systems that had absolutely no reference to each other, a point of coincidence because of the same expression of a universal truth. Nevertheless, the Confucian teaching must be taken as a piece, with all three paths subservient and complimentary to each other in shaping a godlike personality. Thus he whose heart is inclined towards the Divine's love, should still acquire mental knowledge and, whenever action is needed, it should be duly performed. We read:

.

78.   V, 3.

79.   XIV, 5. *Harvard Classics.*

"There is the love of being benevolent (Jen) without the love of learning: the beclouding here leads to a foolish simplicity." [80]

(The same passage in another rendering:

"*The thirst for Love, without love of learning, sinks into fondness.*" But "*foolish simplicity*" is more expressive of the original.)

The Master said: "Let every man consider Love (Jen) as what devolves on himself. He may not yield the performance of it even to his master." [81]

(Another translation reads: "*When love is at stake yield not to an army.*") The word "*army*" here is incorrect though the original word "ssu" has such a sense. "Ssu" means here "master" or "teacher". There has never been any usage in the ancient texts in putting the words "*to yield*" together with the word "army". Otherwise this rendering surpasses others because of its brevity, corresponding to the original of only six words. [82]

It is plain that those who cleave to the path of Love should also resort to knowledge, otherwise a farcical simplicity would be the result. It was once remarked by one of the disciples:

Tsai Ngo asked, saying: "A man of Love, though it be told him,

'There is a man in the well,' will go in after him, I suppose." Confucius said: "Why should he do so? A superior man may be killed, but he cannot be entrapped. He may be imposed upon but he cannot be befooled." [83]

Now the problem seems to be slightly obscure, as it must also be made clear what is a "superior man" (more preferable is the term "gentleman") as compared to such a man of Love. Apparently there is no distinction, as it is said:

"Gentlemen without Love there may be, but the vulgar must ever be strangers to Love." [84]

Without going into a detailed discussion here, it may be said that the "gentleman" is synonymous with such a man of Love. But usually the latter is used in parallel to the man of Wisdom, and the former as the opposite of the mean or vulgar, or the "small man." We read further:

.

80.   XVII, 8.

81.   XV, 35.

82.   Ref. Biography (No. 41. B) of Wang Tan, *History of Sung Dyn.*, fasc. 282.

83.   VI, 24.

84.   XIV, 7.

The Master said: "Love can alone love others, or hate, others." [85]

(In another translation: "*It is only the truly virtuous (Jen) man, who can love, or who can hate, others.*")

Love and hate seem to be used here as contradictory terms, but the sense of the original is "like or dislike."

The Master said: "If the aspiration be set on Love, there will be no practice of evil." [86]

The Master said: "Riches and honours are what men desire. If in any improper way they are obtained, they should not be held. Poverty and lowliness are what men dislike. If in any improper way they are imposed upon one, they should not be forsaken.

"If the superior man (gentleman) abandons Love, how can he be worth the name?

"The superior man (gentleman) does not, even for the space of a single meal, abandon Love. In moments of flurry and haste, he cleaves to it; in moments of stumbling and fall, he cleaves to it." [87]

We can see a trenchant distinction between love in the ordinary sense and Love in this higher sense. If the heart be set on what men normally understand as love, then there is every chance of doing wrong, because one usually still lingers on the vital plane, and if one's love is unreciprocated or contradicted, then every element in our nature opposite to love at once raises its head in rebellion. But what Confucius taught here is the Divine's Love, something absolute and purely psychic in its nature; and for that there is no demand for return (though there may be every reward) and hence there can be no evil because, by itself, it is Freedom from all evil. This psychic love constitutes the essence of "superior-manhood"; and such a man is indeed a "gentil-homme" in the outward appearance but, we should say, inwardly a spiritual seeker par excellence. So ultimately it is the inner effort that matters; and we find that each time a favourite disciple asked the same question, he received a different answer. And this psychic love is not turned towards one or two men, but to everyone and everything in the universe.

Yen Yüan asked about Love:

The Master said: "Love is to conquer self and return to courtesy. If a man can for one day conquer himself and return to courtesy, all under heaven will ascribe Love to him. The practice of Love is from oneself; can it be from others?"

Yen Yüan said: "I beg to know more in detail."

85. IV, 3.
86. IV, 4.
87. IV, 5.

The Master said: "To be ever courteous of eye and ever courteous of ear; to be ever courteous in word and ever courteous in deed."

Yen Yüan said: "Dull as I am, I will practice these words." [88]

In this connection, "courtesy" is here mentioned which is also translated as "propriety", both incomprehensive as an equivalent. But for the time being, we need not go much into detail in that problem of "Li", and let us be content with this rendering, excellent as it is. Otherwise "courtesy" is something quite external and leads one nowhere. The Chinese term "Li" has a much more profound bearing. Three large classical works on this subject alone are now extant, covering the whole of the ancient culture. Further:

Chung-kung asked about Love.

The Master said: "Without the door to behave as though a great guest were come; to treat the people as though we tendered the high sacrifice; not to do unto others what we would not wish done unto ourselves; to breed no murmuring against you in the country, and none in the family."

Chung-kung said: "Dull as I am, I will practice these words." [89]

To receive guests and to perform sacrifices are subjects pertaining to the field of "Li". As such, whether we call this rites or propriety or courtesy, it is intimately connected with music which is always performed during the rites. And both have still the common basis in this Love, as it is once said:

"A man without Love, what is courtesy to him? A man without Love, what is music to him?" [90]

But this fellow-feeling or reciprocity is not so easy a thing to put into practice.

Tze-kung said: "What I do not wish to have done unto me, I likewise wish not to do unto others."
The Master said: "That is still beyond thee, Tz'u!" [91]

On another occasion the same thing was taught to the same disciple:

Tze-kung asked, saying: "Is there one word which may serve as a rule of practice for all one's life?"
The Master said: "Reciprocity (fellow-feeling), perhaps. What you

.

88. XII, 1. *Harvard Calssics,*
89. XII, 2.
90. III, 3.
91. V, 11.

do not want done to yourself, do not do to others." [92]

Here we find then in Confucianism a much broader Shila than that of Buddhism, because the moral precepts can be more extensive, going beyond the limited forms. Not to kill and not to tell a lie are very simple teachings given as commandments by Lord Buddha, yet still they have not reached the root of the problem. Here it is simply said that one should take oneself as a measure. If one does not like to be told a lie, one does not tell one to others, or, if one does not like to be killed, one does not go to kill others. Extending this fellow-feeling to all beings, it becomes compassion. Positively, one should save others from distress if one wishes oneself to be saved. It is the most simple and straight way, and when extended to one's behaviour, it is much more comprehensive than these "Thous shalt not's." Thus, even Tze-kung, equally a sage next to Confucius, was not assured of his attainment in this virtue. Fundamentally it is still grounded in the Divine's Love. When the Divine's Love is brought into full play, reciprocity or considerateness and fellow-feeling will surely be developed, and that to such an extent that all these moral considerations will no longer be needed.

Self-conquest is a universal teaching found in every system of the world since the Delphic inscription "Know thyself." But to say that if one could for one day conquer himself and return to propriety, then all under heaven would ascribe Love to him, this seems to be merely a figure of speech or otherwise an exaggeration. But such a saying must be understood in its historical context. We remember the one who puts these things into practice was supposed to be the "superior man," usually a prince or ruler, and in this sense it is different from the ordinary conception of merely a "gentleman", for this knowledge styles itself as an imperial one.[93] It can be imagined that if rulers who held power in their hands could by a turn of mind tend to such a principle, then their influence would be extended to all, and people all over the world would naturally ascribe such a virtue to them. Be that as it may, much inner effort must be made. And up to a point, after strenuous inner effort has been made, the natural turn is an outward extension. This is a common experience of nearly every spiritual master. In a metaphorical way of speaking, it is like a return to the same point where one had started — and Yen Whei was called in later ages "the Sage of Return" — but actually it is a spiral winding in a cyclic movement; one has only come to the same position but much elevated on a higher plane with the scope of his vision enlarged. Something must be done for all under heaven, it is felt.

Yet it is not an easy task to achieve something positive even if one aspires to it and wins such fame as man of Love or Great Compassion. The general public — usually a mass of inertia which never allows itself to be improved or transformed without great reluctance and yet

.

92.   XV. 23.
93.   p. 60.

at the same time a mass of intelligence more clever than a god which never lets itself be deceived — can only take to this road very gradually after years and years of conversion. Even if a general atmosphere of peace and good-will and harmony — in one word, of Love — were created by anyone with such a high consciousness, it would still take time and much time before the antagonistic elements could be entirely eradicated. So it was said:

The Master said: "'If good men were to govern a country in succession for a hundred years, they would be able to transform the violently bad, and dispense with capital punishments,' true indeed is this saying." [94]

The Master said: "If a truly royal ruler were to arise, it would still require a generation, ere Love would prevail." [95]

According to the ancient interpretation, a generation means a period of thirty years. The truly royal ruler is a man who creates such an atmosphere of Love, but such rulers are not too often met in the whole history. And age-old experience tells us that any such extension of Love cannot be achieved in a short time. At this point we see that Confucianism distinguished itself as a teaching for establishing a Paradise, or, if we prefer, a Utopia in this world, in which the Divine's Love could be extended to every one so that cruelty and death penalty would be entirely vanquished and bliss and happiness alone reign. As such it is then not a teaching of the soul's salvation after death in ascending to a Paradise or in entering into Nirvaṇa. It may or may not be called a religion, but such is the core of its teaching. What Was taught in the Confucian school was this, and what was learnt by the disciples at that time and in later ages was simply this. We read the following passages:

Yu-tze (a disciple) said: "A gentleman nurses the roots: when root has taken, the truth (Tao) will grow. With regard to the duty of son and of brother, are they not the roots of Love (Jen) ?" [96]

The Master said: "The youths should be dutiful at home, modest abroad, heedful and true, full of good-will for the many, close friends with men of Love (Jen) ; and should they have energy to spare, let them spend it upon books." [97]

The Master said:
"Let the will be set on the path (Tao).

.

94. XIII, 11.
95. XIII, 12.
96. I, 2.
97. I, 6.

"Hold to virtue (Teh).

"Rest in Love (Jen).

"Move in art (Yi)." [98]

Tze-kung asked how to practise Love (Jen).

The Master said: "A workman bent on good work will first sharpen his tools. In the land that is thy home, serve the best men in power, and make friends with those men of Love (Jen) among its scholars." [99]

Tseng Tze said: "The scholar had need be broad-minded and firm in endurance, capable of shouldering burdens and covering far distances. Love (Jen) is the burden which he considers it is his to sustain; is it not a heavy one? Only with death does his course end, is it not far?" [100]

The same questions may be asked of a Christian, and further, is the burden not like the cross which Jesus bore?

*

98. VII, 6.
99. XV, 9.
100. VIII, 7.

Chapter VI

SIX ARTS

Jen or Divine's Love is indeed the central principle of what Confucius taught. It was taught perhaps because as a spark of illumination it is within the soul of every human being, capable of being fused with that great Illumination above, and as an open path it could be followed by all. If it were not a *priori* innate in one's being, then it must be something super-imposed *a posteriori*, and every means tending to that would be artificial; then any growth or development or natural flowering from within would be out of the question. At any rate, it could no longer be such an open path. Such an open path must at the end reach that state of Divinity which in itself is still a mystery, but it is a mystery of Sunlight and not of Darkness. And for this very reason we think that Confucius was more aptly titled a spiritual master than a mere ethical teacher. Outwardly it stands as a simple teaching with nothing esoteric in it. The attainment to what is above or at the end, Confucius seldom spoke of. Once he said:

"I would prefer silence."

Tze-kung said: "If you, Master, were silent, what would your disciples have to tell?"

The Master said: "Does Heaven speak? The four seasons revolve, and all things grow. Does Heaven speak?" [101]

On another occasion Tze-kung said:

"Our Master's culture may be heard. But about man's nature and the ways of Heaven his words are denied us." [102]

We must suppose that a good part of his knowledge was not imparted to any of his disciples and the sayings and instructions, of which again only a part, a small part perhaps, was recorded and preserved up to present, dealt only with the spiritual-cultural aspect, while the other aspect was sealed in a permanent silence. Even this exoteric aspect he preferred not to discuss, as such a subject as the

.

101.   XVII, 19.

102.   V, 12. This passage is also explained as "About the Union of his nature with Heaven (or God) cannot be heard." This was also an old interpretation prevalent upto the Han Dynasty.

Divine's Love was one on which he would have kept silent as well had he not been questioned again and again by his disciples. (IX. 1) And we find a full-fledged expatiation on this subject still lacking. However, not to speak of such a great spiritual master, any ordinary man of some inner realization would know how limited the sphere of words is, and a state higher than this sphere is already inexpressible though not untransmissible. Furthermore, upto a certain state it is not only that words are no longer useful, but also not needed. If one could be, let us say, one with Love as Heaven or God, under which everything goes in its, proper routine and grows and multiplies, what is then the use of words? As once Confucius stood by a stream, he said: "Oh, it passes on like this, not ceasing day and night!" Everything in the universe is indeed changing together with the season or Time, and when the point of Nochange is reached, one falls simply into silence. We need not go deeply into Greek philosophy of Heraclitus about the theory of Change, but let us ask if this point could be compared to or identified with what some modern thinkers call the At-one-ment? In the state of an Eternal-Presence, the Time factor simply drops off, not only words.

An external reason for his silence about these high subjects must be that all those disciples were too young to understand their master's deep thoughts. We may count on the average a difference of thirty-five years between the age of the master and the disciple.[103] With such a group of young inexperienced pupils, not much about the decrees of Heaven or Doom, or the nature of man could be discussed. Yen Yüan must have understood his master to a certain extent, yet he did not live to a ripe old age; otherwise he was the one most entitled to the cloak of the master. Usually six general subjects together with four special ones were taught in the Confucian school.

The conditions of the ancient Confucian school can best be understood in the light of the Indian Guruhood. Once the pupil is accepted by the master, he is supposed to he his disciple for his whole life. The master is responsible for his education, for his physical as well as spiritual welfare, for his life and death. The achievements of the pupil increase the glory of the master, but his misconduct or tragic death brings shame, and there were two or three cases of his disciples which Confucius bore as his shame until the end of his life. The pupil must be entirely devoted to the master, and nearly every act or move would be guided by him. He could indeed have his own free will, but on anything of personal importance he must consult his master first. The relationship is like a father and a son, but much closer because a

103. Among the 35 or more most prominent disciples, Kung-sen Lung was younger than the master by 53 years, Pe-chien and several others by 50; Kung-si Hua, by 42; Yen Hing, by 46; Yu-tze, by 43; Fan Ch'i, by 36; Shan Chu, by 29; Fu Tze-tsien, by 49; Tan-tai Me-ming, by 39; Tze-chang, by 48; Tze-hsia, by 44; Tze-kung, by 31; Jan Ch'iu, by 29; Yen Yüan, by 30. Only Tze-lu, the eldest among those famous ones, was nine years younger than Confucius, yet he was almost a military man, and died in a fight for the throne in the Wei state. Actually we can imagine that Confucius was followed by a group of youths in his travels. (*Ancient History*, Vol. 67, Ch. 7, Biographies of the Disciples of Chung Ni.)

Chinese father never teaches his own children though he might be a master himself. Some deep psychology is involved in this phenomenon, and we read such an example by Confucius himself:

Cheng K'ang asked Pê Yu, "Have you heard any lessons (from your father) different (from all that we have heard) ?" [104]

He answered: "No. He was standing alone once, when I passed below the hall with hasty steps, and said to me: 'Have you learned *Poetry*?' I answered, 'Not yet.' 'Who does not learn *Poetry*,' he said, 'has no hold on words. ' I retired and learned *Poetry*.

"Another day, he was in the same way standing alone when I passed by below the hall with hasty steps and said to me: 'Have you learned the *Propriety*?' I answered, 'Not yet.' — 'Who does not learn the *Propriety*,' he said, 'loses all foothold.' I then retired, and learned the *Propriety*.

"These two things I have heard."

Cheng K'ang retired, and quite delighted, said: "I asked one thing, and got three. I hear of *Poetry*, I hear of the *Propriety*, and I hear, too, that the superior man keeps aloof from his son." [105]

Had the boy not passed before him, he was perhaps left to play as he liked. Recently certain European writers began to note the tolerance and indulgence of parents to children among us Chinese, which may or may not be a general fact. The age-old tradition can be traced to this source, that as a father one keeps always a courteous reserve toward his son. Perhaps in this way the natural affection can better be kept, as once explained by Mencius. The teacher could be severe, but the father should not be so. Here is no question of a "second birth," as the same pupil could go to another master according to his own will or the will of his master, and in the latter case, it was again like a father sending his son to a master. One may have several masters in one's life, and in every case the mutual responsibility lasts almost a lifetime.

The greatest pleasure to a man of forestry must be to see the trees he planted grow into large and useful ones, and to an educator, to see the pupils he brought up to become good and useful citizens. Most of the students of Confucius afterwards went into government services in different dukedoms all over the land, and the fame of their master went along with them. In a way we can imagine that the political influence of Confucius was great; and as he travelled much, he often had the assistance of his own disciples whose first duty was to see what they could best do for their master under those circumstances. The Gurus in India in their Vanaprastha stage must have experienced the same emotions if they had many pupils, though the nature of their wanderings might be different. The teacher was usually glad to see the achievements of the pupil in what was learnt from him or, if displeased, could disavow him. We read the following anecdotes:

.

104. Pê Yu was "Fish the eldest," see p. 16.
105. XVI, 13.

As the Master drew near to Wu-cheng, he heard the sound of stringed instruments and singing. Well pleased and smiling, he said: "Why use an ox-knife to kill a fowl?"

Tze-yao (a disciple and the governor of that small district) said: "Master, formerly I have heard you say: 'The nobleman when following the Path will love mankind, the common people when following the Path will be easily subservient.'"

The Master said: "My boys! Yen (Tze-yao) is right. What I formerly said was for fun." [106]

The Lord of Ch'i (i.e. the third House of the Lu state) was richer than the Duke of Chow, and yet (Jan-) Ch'iu increased his wealth by collecting imposts for him.

The Master said: "He is no disciple of mine! Beat your drums and attack him, my boys!" [107]

Such was the relationship between the master and his disciples.

Next, we must enquire what was taught in the school of Confucius. Generally six branches of knowledge were studied in the Chow dynasty, known as the Six Arts, but in the Confucian School, the Six Arts meant the Six Classics which will be discussed in the next chapters. The Six Arts studied and taught were:

1) Li, or Knowledge in the Propriety
2) Music

3) Bowmanship

4) Chariot-driving

5) Writing

6) Arithmetic

Arithmetic in our modern view is a science, but in ancient days it was considered an art. We must suppose that the ancient pupils were not too different from pupils of the modern age in intelligence and elementary things were taught first, thus gradually leading to higher things. But as a practical science it was fairly complicated as it was connected with the building of houses, and the manufacture of all sorts of furniture and vessels, and the measuring of fields, etc. So elements of geometry, both plane and spherical, and trigonometry and a portion of elementary physics must have been included therein. The calculation of dates of the year, such as eclipses and the summer and winter solstices, must also belong to this field, but that was a specialized subject for the advanced students and during the Three Dynasties before Confucius there was a special ministry in the state in charge of the celestial affairs. It may be noted in passing that the ancient people had a much more advanced knowledge in astronomy, unjustly called astrology, than we have nowadays. The peasants, the herdsman knew much more about the stars and the seasons than a citizen in any of our cosmopolitan

106.   XVII, 4.
107.   XI, 16.

cities because their life was more directly connected with nature. For an investigation of the ancient arithmetics, the three classical works on Propriety may be referred to, but the book entitled "Arithmetics in Nine Categories" attributed to the time of Hwang Ti, twenty-seventh century B.C., is a spurious one composed at a much later age.

Writing is indeed an art, now called calligraphy, but as it is concerned with the learning of words, their pronunciation and meaning, the styles of the same words in writing, it must be also considered etymology. To write with lacquer on bamboo slabs slightly heated over fire so that the green colour vanishes, and then to bind them together with leather strips requires much skill and experience. Since that was the only repository of human knowledge, this technique distinguished itself as a separate art.

The third and fourth items belong to the field of physical education nowadays; in ancient times they were not otherwise. Both these arts were accompanied with certain rites which fell out of use long ago. The construction of chariots and carriages differed in later ages and the ancient rites were also no longer held. We still read in ancient texts certain feats in arrow shooting and chariot driving — in the books such as *Djuang Tze*, or *Lien Tze*, or *Lue Lan* — almost fabulous accounts in which it was sometimes shown that the arrow and the bow and the arm and the man formed one mechanical piece, or that the horses and the driver and the chariot formed almost one living body or organic whole. The manufacture of bows and arrows and wheels and cars could be found in *Chow Li*, a classical work now extant, and academic studies in the eighteenth century together with modern findings in archaeological excavations can give us correct information of these things. The technique of driving had to be accompanied by a knowledge of horses and that developed by the Han dynasty into a special study of the physiognomy of good breeds, and then models of the best horses were cast in bronze. But all these things can be only of academic interest to us nowadays. The original idea of these two arts was one of physical education, as for example to draw a strong bow of certain weights — the weight was usually hung on the string and measured — or to drive six horses before a carriage with six reins and a whip required no small physical strength. The practical purposes for which hunting and fighting were practised came to be only of secondary importance, and as a part of ordinary physical education it was not so much aimed at the simple and natural development of muscular strength as athletics in the Greco-Roman world, but was rather aimed at a highly-cultured sportsmanship or knighthood, because so much of Li, or propriety and courtesy, was attached to both.

Unfortunately ancient Chinese music perished with the times. "Ceremonial Propriety decayed and Music died out." These words appeared in a royal mandate during the reign of Wu Ti in the Han dynasty, issued in the sixth month in the year 124 B.C. Ever since then scholars and musicians in every dynasty made efforts to restore ancient music and on every occasion something new was brought to light, but no one could say that the reconstruction was entirely successful. Even nowadays we still have a group of academicians working on this subject, yet perfect results can only be hoped for in the future. The instruments could be reconstructed with the help of ancient models excavated or made according to records in the ancient texts, the theories could be studied (especially those connected with psychology) but could any performance be the same as that of the Chow dynasty?

The fundamental problem is that music, ancient or modern, classical or romantic, is a thing ever changing though not definitely ever progressing. At the beginning of the Chow dynasty, musicians in the court of the Shang emperor had dispersed and fled, taking with them their instruments, so that there was already a great change as the Duke of Chow had to shape the music anew. (Vide *Ana.*, XVIII, 9) This new formation was most probably restricted to the music of the court, performed in palaces on festival occasions or in ancestral temples during sacrifices or otherwise used in the army. This might be called the classical music which suffered the least change for seven to eight hundred years. Parallel to this there was always a current of music of the common people, unrefined perhaps, but nevertheless popular. This popular music called also "vulgar music" was always living, absorbed many foreign elements into itself as time advanced, and is still now existing.

Yet during the time of Confucius, the classical music was still a living thing and this part of education was never neglected. Children were taught singing together with dancing and playing with diverse instruments, usually made of metals, stones, hides, silkstrings, wood, bamboo, and other natural objects. (Vide *Chow Li*) The Director-General of Music was the chancellor of the state university, and he had the duty of general supervision over the educational policies of the state. Usually a scholar or a gentleman did not do away with his string-instruments without special reasons, as for example in the period of mourning over his parents, etc. We have a few records of the life of Confucius connected with music:

"When the Master was in company with a person who was singing, if he sang well, he would make him repeat the song and join in." [108]

"On days when he had been wailing, the Master did not sing." [109]

"Yu Pei wished to see Confucius. Confucius excused himself on the plea of sickness. As the messenger went out at the door, Confucius took a lute and sang to it, so that he should hear." [110]

The first item, Li, was more fortunate. Before the Han dynasty,

108.　VII, 31.
109.　VII, 9.
110.　XVII, 20.

it was in a state of decay and decline, but it was partly restored. In our modern language, this word Li does mean "courtesy", "propriety", "decency" and "politeness", but it is too comprehensive a word, having no exact equivalent in English. Generally speaking, the institutions of festivals in ancient Greece and the church services in our modern world are to be included in this category in our Chinese view. With regard to its contents, three things are to be distinguished: first, the system in theory or the philosophy, second, the practice, which included all ceremonies, formalities, and good manners; and third, the material objects. A most simple example is to send a gift to a friend: there must be first the reason, second the way of presenting it, and third the gift itself. Dealing with its theoretical aspect, deep psychology, ethics, and especially logic are involved in it, because fundamentally it is a knowledge of discrimination, a discrimination of right and wrong, high and low, true and false, beautiful or otherwise, a determination of values of conduct and undertakings and achievements of the individual as well as of the populace.

In ancient days, Li was explained as "nurture" or "culture" (*Hsün Tze*). Aiming at an ideal way of living, what was nurtured or cultured was every part of our being, neglecting not its minutest particle. Subtle emotions, sentiments and feelings are to be carefully nurtured as Music steps in, and aesthesis plays here a large role. Both Li (Propriety) and Yo (Music) always go together with joined hands as twin brothers or sisters. The vital being is never left to dry up, but is regulated with its forces led to right channels, leaving no occasion for any wild outburst of passions without control. Since to do away entirely with desire is a thing impossible among the mass, it is held in leash in a harmonious way so much so that "desire never goes unchecked to its objects, and objects never exhaust themselves for the desire." (*Hsün Tze*)

Outwardly it is a code of good manners and formalities and ceremonies which must be learned in childhood or, to put it in another way, the child is trained in an ideal way of living. Only a great sage, the Duke of Chow could shape such a code, just as only a wise-man like Solon could give laws to the Athenians. In the general populace, a man is punished for having committed any evil; the law, whether vindictive or prohibitive in its purpose, is used. But such a code silently removes the source of any evil are committed and, being transformative in its nature, it precedes the law. But the effect, however tremendous and immense among the people during the time or in later ages when it was still followed, was nevertheless not obvious. In a peaceful and harmonious atmosphere of society, fewer cases of crime could be found, but no one could compile any statistics of how many cases had not come into being because of the salutary effect of such a code. Yet its merit in creating such an atmosphere is undeniable and its influence considerable. Confucius in his late years did not elaborate the law, and this itself shows that he did something much more essential and fundamental.

In comparison to the Buddhist Dharma — understood as also the right way of "holding up" life — there is a great likeness, but Li is more flexible in its nature, and explains and emphasizes more the inner aspect of an ideal way of living than the outward regulations. As times change, this code also varies but its essence never changes. This was the first thing taught in the schools of the Chow dynasty. We find several sayings of Confucius in this connection.

Mong Yi-tze asked the duty of a son.

The Master said: "Obedience."

Soon after, as Fan Ch'ih was driving him, the Master said: "Mongsun (Yi-tze) asked me the duty of a son; I answered 'Obedience'."

"What did you mean?" — said Fan Ch'ih.

"To serve our parents according to propriety (Li) while they live, " said the Master: "to bury them according to propriety (Li) when they die; and to worship them according to propriety (Li)." [111]

Tze-chang asked whether what is to be ten generations after could be known.

The Master said: "The Yin dynasty inherited the manners (Li) of the Hsia, wherein it reduced from or added to them may be known. The Chow dynasty inherited the manners (Li) of the Yin wherein it reduced from or added to them may be known. When others follow Chow, what is to be even a hundred generations hence may be known." [112]

The Master said: "I can speak of the ceremonies (Li) of Hsia, but Khi cannot sufficiently attest my words. I can speak of the ceremonies (Li) of the Yin, but Sung cannot sufficiently attest my words. This is due to their dearth of records and great men. If those were sufficient, I could adduce them in support of my words." [113]

From these three passages we see well that the same word "Li" is differently translated as "propriety", "manners" or "ceremonies". It is a thing ever changing as said before, but its essence does not change. Khi is a district where the descendants of the royal house of the Hsia dynasty ruled because it was again ancient propriety (Li) that the descendants of a fallen dynasty should never be entirely extinguished. They were given a small fief mainly for the worship of their ancestors. Such a custom most decidedly sprang from the motive of Jen, (benevolence or charity) from which the whole construction of Li came into being. The same was the case with the descendants of the Yin dynasty; they were given the district called Sung. Naturally together with the fall of a great empire all its great institutions perished , and records and books were destroyed. Great men who could tell about the past institutions also died out. Hence many things which Confucius

111.　II, 5.
112.　II, 23.
113.　III, 9.

held as true could not be verified. In fact the legal descendants of the Two Kings of Yin and Hsia were always found in later dynasties and charged with the dutiful worship of their ancestors.

The Master said: "After the pouring out of the libation at the Great Sacrifice, I have no wish to see more." [114]

This is also a part of Li. A great sacrifice was a long and complicated process and, after the act of pouring out of the libation to the ground, other items followed which were presumptive in nature, not suited to the rank of a Duke of Lu and hence Confucius thought the rest not worth seeing. Confucius still held the regulations (Li) of the Chow dynasty in which he lived, but the ceremonies were gradually altered in different dukedoms up to his time.

Tze-kung wished to do away with the sheep offering at the announcement of the "first days." The Master said: "Tzu! Thou lovest the sheep, I love the rite (Li)." [115]

At the end of autumn each year, a messenger from the Imperial Court of Chow was sent to different dukedoms to distribute the calendars of the next year and his journey in visiting every state lasted about three months. We do not know about the contents of such calendars, but the intercalary month and days of new moons or the first of each month were in this way made known. To such an officer, sheep were offered for entertainment. This was the ancient Li or "rite". But since the Emperor Ching, [116] no such messengers were sent to the dukedoms and yet in Lu the sheep were still supplied to the Imperial Court each year. Tze-kung thought that, since such a ceremony had become obsolete, the offering should be abandoned; but Confucius thought that in case the sheep were also abandoned, no reminiscence of such an ancient Li would remain.

The Master said: "Treat the king with all courtesy (Li), men call it fawning." [117]

Duke Ting asked how a king should employ his ministers; and how should ministers serve their king?

Confucius answered: "A king should treat his ministers with courtesy (Li), ministers should serve their king faithfully." [118]

The Master said: "What is the difficulty in swaying a kingdom by courteous (Li) yielding? Who cannot by courteous (Li) yielding sway a

.

114.   III, 10.

115.   III, 17.

116.   Since about the 29th year of the Duke Siang, 544 B.C..

117.   III, 18.

118.   III, 19.

kingdom, what can he know of courtesy (Li) ?" [119]

The Master said: "By breadth of reading and the ties of courtesy (Li), a gentleman will also keep from error's path." [120]

(The same passage by Legge:

"The superior man, extensively studying all learning, and keeping himself under the restraint of the rules of propriety (Li), may thus likewise not overstep what is right.")

About this last passage, both translations are correct, but the two words "Chun Tze," translated as *"gentleman"* or *"superior man,"* in the original text is an interpolation, a mistake made by the ancient scribe. The subject is understood to be the common man or any one. (See the same passage in *Analects*, XII, 15)

A judge of Cheng asked whether Duke Chao knew courtesy (Li). Confucius answered: "He knew courtesy (Li)."

After Confucius had left, the judge beckoned Wu-ma Ch'i (a disciple) to his side, and said: "I have heard that the superior men are of no party, but are they too for any party? The prince married a daughter of the state of Wu, of the same family-name as himself, and called her 'the elder lady of Wu.' If the prince knew courtesy (Li), who does not know courtesy (Li) ?"

When Wu-ma Ch'i told this to his Master, he said:

"I am lucky! If I make a slip, people are sure to know it." [121]

The Master said:

"Respectfulness, without propriety (Li), becomes laboriousness; carefulness, without propriety (Li), becomes timidity; courage, without propriety (Li), becomes unruliness; uprightness, without propriety (Li) becomes harshness. When those who are in high stations (Chun Tze) perform well all their duties to their relations, love (Jen) will thrive among the people. When old friends are not neglected by them, the people are preserved from meanness." [122]

The Master said: "It is by Poetry that the mind is aroused. It is by Propriety (Li) that the character is established. It is by Music (Yo) that the divine nature is perfected." [123]

The Master said: "When those above love courtesy (Li), people are easy to lead." [124]

The Master said: "... A mind to understand and Love to hold fast,

119.   IV, 13.
120.   VI, 25.
121.   VII, 30.
122.   VIII, 2.
123.   VIII, 8.
124.   XIV, 44.

without dignity of bearing, will go unhonoured. And mind to understand, Love to hold fast and dignity of bearing are incomplete, without courteous ways (Li)." [125]

(The same by Legge:

"*...When his knowledge is sufficient to attain, and he has virtue enough to hold fast, if he cannot govern with dignity, the people will not respect him.*

"*When his knowledge is sufficient to attain, and he has virtue enough to hold fast; when he governs also with dignity, yet if he try to move the people contrary to the rules of propriety (Li) : full excellence is not reached.*")

The Master said:

"The superior man in everything considers righteousness to be essential. He performs it according to propriety (Li). He brings it forth in humility. He completes it with truthfulness. He, indeed, is a superior man!" [126]

The Master said:

"'It is according to the rules of propriety (Li), ' they say. — 'It is according to the rules of propriety (Li), ' they say. — Are gems and silk all that is meant by propriety (Li) ?

"'It is music (Yo),' they say, — 'It is music (Yo),' they say. — Are bells and drums all that is meant by music?" [127]

Tsai Ngo (a disciple) asked about the three years' mourning for parents, saying the one year was long enough.

"If the superior man, " said he, "abstains for three years from the observances of propriety (Li), those observances (Li) will be quite lost. If for three years he abstains from music (Yo), music (Yo) will be ruined.

"Within a year the old grain is exhausted, and the new grain has sprung up, and, in procuring fire by friction, we go through all the changes of wood for that purpose. After a complete year, the mourning may stop."

The Master said: "If you were, after a year, to eat good rice, and wear embroidered clothes, would you feel at ease?"

"I should feel at ease."

The Master said: "If you feel at ease, do it. But a superior man, during the whole period of mourning, does not enjoy pleasant food which he may eat, nor derive pleasure from music which he may hear. He also does not feel at ease in his home. And so he forsakes these things. But now if you feel at ease, you may do it."

Tsai Ngo went out, and the Master said:

"This shows Yu's lack of Love (Jen). It is not till a child is three

125.   p.71; XV, 32.

126.   XV, 17.

127.   XVII, 11.

years old that it is allowed to leave the arms of its parents. And the three years' mourning is universally observed throughout the empire. Did Yu enjoy for three years a father's and a mother's love?" [128]

From all these quotations above, we can get a general conception of what Li is. A saying of the disciple Yu Yo about this subject is also noteworthy; it is:

Yu-tze said: "In practising the propriety (Li), harmony is to be prized. This was the beauty of the Path of ancient kings, followed by both great and small men. There were cases when it was observed without harmony. (On the other hand,) knowing harmony and entirely led away by harmony in every case without being checked by propriety (Li), this likewise is not to be done." [129]

·

128.   XVII, 21.

129.   I, 12.

Chapter VII

BOOKS OF POETRY, RITES, MUSIC

A sad thing in the world is perhaps to see one's own children passing away in the eve of one's life. After Confucius returned to his native land, he withdrew thenceforth entirely from the political field, and in doing his work afterwards he had his gaze fixed on later generations. As a famous man revered in all the states, he was now surrounded by a group of disciples, among whom were men of great talent, mostly trained and brought up by himself single-handed, and he passed his time in a serene and blissful sagehood. But in the year that he returned, his only son died, survived by his grandson who afterwards became a great philosopher. That was the first great loss. And two years later, his great disciple, the most beloved and hopeful one, Yen Yüan, also died because of a frail constitution emaciated by constant inner austerity and perhaps also due to material poverty. That was even more of a loss. In the next year (481 B.C.), the eldest disciple was killed in a fight during the civil strife in the state of Wei. The tragic end of this disciple had long before been predicted by him, and as soon as he heard of an outbreak of the inner tumult in that state, he said that Tze-lu could not be saved from his voluntary death. How true it proved to be! This was again a great loss. It is said that because of Yen Yüan all the disciples began to have more love of their master and among themselves, and because of Tze-lu, the daring and straightforward gentleman, blasphemies and slanders could scarcely reach the master. On these sad occasions, the sage wept bitterly. We cannot keep from wondering: do sages ever weep? Yes, Confucius bewailed, perhaps even like a child. It was Confucius the man who prevailed.

The school of Confucius was very famous, comparable to that of a Greek philosopher in ancient days, but it was a large one; more similar perhaps would be an ancient Indian Ashram. In spring and autumn, both the ceremonial *Propriety* (Li) and *Music* (Yo) were taught respectively, and in winter and summer, *Poetry* and *History*. Confucius himself did not lecture much, but his disciples were teachers or masters. The school grew gradually to the proportions of a state university, but more illustrious because of this sage. It became even more celebrated after his death.

The six "Arts" taught in this school were the Six Classics. Classics were in existence long before his time, and he merely elaborated them. Some people of the so-called School of the "modern Script" (which will be treated presently) advocated that all classics began first with Confucius, a theory not without its basis but only partly true. All the Six Classics — in fact only Five — preserved upto the present passed through the revision of the sage and his work was limited to their editing and compilation. Thus the work done in the last years of his life consisted of:

1) A compilation of *Poems* and *Histories*

2) Editing of the *Propriety* (Li) and *Music* (Yo)

3) Comments on the *Book of Changes* (*I-Ching*)

4) Work on the *Annals of Lu* (called also *Springs and Autumns*)

Since all these Classics except the *Book of Music* are now extant, they can be referred to without the need of much discussion here. Yet, as the main bulk of Chinese culture consisted in these works with which the race, one third of the whole population of the world, survived through the past twenty-five centuries, it is worthwhile to explore the real nature of such a work, immortal and of endless value as it is, contributed by the sage in his Love for man.

But when we touch upon the Chinese classics, the problem becomes a very complicated one. Nearly all those Confucian classics together with other ancient texts in general were, after the great destruction, only remnants. The first destruction occurred in about 213 B.C. under the tyrannical measures of the First Emperor of Chin. All books preserved by the populace, apart from a certain number of medical, agricultural and horticultural books, and certain books on oracles and divination, were to be handed over to the government and burned. This was indeed a fatal blow to ancient culture, but the effect was not so catastrophic as we suppose. For the first time in history books were burnt, but those kept in the government remained intact. The real tragedy happened in 206 B.C. when the capital Hsien Yang fell, with its most magnificent palace finished just six years before, O-Fang, comparable perhaps to one of the wonders of the world, turned completely into ruins. Before the palace was plundered by the rebellious army and burned, the minister, later the chief minister of the Han dynasty, Hsiao Ho, ransacked the palace, but he took away only the maps and census records of the population. He was too shortsighted or perhaps too much in a hurry to take notice of the library. Shortly afterwards when peace again reigned over the land and the Han dynasty was founded, ancient books were collected and new books written. Then the second destruction came in 23 A.D., and a third in 190 A.D., and fourth between 307–312 A.D. With the exception of the fourth which was somehow purposeful, all the rest were not so planned and schemed as the first one. Three minor destructions occurred afterwards.[130]

Now we see among such a large people that the destruction and reconstruction of its cultural heritage followed one another in succession. Yet China could not claim the monopoly of such a device, if we

---

130. History shows that the negative measure of the proscription of certain undesirable books never proved effective, while the positive measure of the collection and edition of certain series caused the extinction of many books, a totalitarian method adopted in the XVIIIth century by the Manchu emperors.

recollect the burning of the Bible during the Christian persecutions in Europe and the burning of Buddhist books in India, and then the total destruction of the Alexandria library by the orders of Caliph Omar in 642 A.D. Even in the XXth century, Hitler's burning of books gave a last echo to that old practice. Excellent repositories of human knowledge, books, no matter how valuable or useful they might be, could not one day in the eternity of Time escape that fateful doom, so long as the nature of man is not changed. How to avoid any such repetition of history in future is a problem facing mankind.

In the ancient agricultural society in which little material progress or innovation had been made, the factor of Time has never appeared so conspicuous as nowadays, and several hundred years could elapse without much significance; hence upto the time of the first burning of books, the tradition of the different schools of the teaching of Confucius was preserved and suffered no considerable change. The classical texts restored in the beginning of the Han dynasty were partly kept in memory by old scholars so not easily effaced, and they were simply recited and written down. But they were written in a script which was in vogue in that period, and so the texts of the so-called "modern-script" came into being.[131] Yet a very important discovery was made between 156–143 B.C. which has proved to be of great consequence to the history of Chinese culture ever since. In between the walls of a temple of Confucius in the Lu state a large number of ancient texts were exacavated. These were found to be scriptures stored there not long after the time of Confucius, but they were all written in the "ancient script." Since that script was out of use yet still alive and easily decipherable, many of the ancient books in their original form were brought to light and rewritten in the "modern script." These ancient texts agreed mainly with those existent in the "modern script," yet there were differences: differences in the reading, in annotations, in the number of chapters and passages. But there were also certain records altogether indecipherable, so cryptic and obscure that they baffled every great scholar. Henceforth, scholars divided themselves into two main schools, those of the "modern script" and those of the "ancient script," each holding its tradition as the only authority. In fact, each school had its merit and demerit as well, and it was all too natural that quarrels existed between them that have never ended even upto the present age.

The subtle distinctions of the different schools need not be deeply explored by the Sinologists, since the work of making one correct translation of a Chinese work affords already almost superhuman effort and so many other works are not yet translated. But some general idea will surely be helpful. Within the school of the "modern script," subdivisions were made and they differed according to different lineages or lines of tradition. Take for instance the *Analects* so much

.

131. For the history of the Chinese Scripts, a booklet written by the present author entitled *An Analysis of the Chinese Language —an Etymological Approach* may be referred to.

quoted in the previous chapters, which was not included in the Six Classics. It had two schools in the "modern script," that of Ch'i and that of Lu — both being localities to which each belonged and from which they spread with a different tradition — and apart from minor differences in contents, the former had 22 chapters while the latter had only 20 chapters. According to an authentic record, [132] another version of the same in the "ancient script" had previously 100 chapters, and it was condensed into 30 chapters with the obscure and duplicated passages deleted in the Han dynasty. Another version in the "ancient script" current at that time had only 21 chapters. Both the texts of the "ancient script" and the text of the Ch'i school were lost and what we read and translate now is only the Lu text, the only remnant of the school of the "modern script." Yet we can still have glimpses of the lost texts in the commentary written by Cheng Hsuan in the Han dynasty because, when he wrote the annotations and explanations, he made broad references to these texts still existent in his time. A slight difference of one word or two in the original text or in the interpretation sometimes leads to a great divergence in theory and the more the texts were held as sacred and authoritative, as undoubtedly they were, the greater became the discrepancy in their inference.

So the problem is a complex one. We must have first a fairly comprehensive view of the classics in general before we can get a clear conception of what Confucius had built on them. We must know indeed the division of schools, but we must also have some knowledge in discriminating the genuine from the spurious texts — a subject of much research in the past ages — and the conclusions arrived at have been mostly settled now. Ancient spurious texts also have their use, because often historical materials can still be gathered from them, but they must be understood as forgeries. About the life and sayings of Confucius, for example, there are now two works extant, both forged by a scholar named Wang Su in the first quarter of the third century A.D. One is called *Kung Tze Chia Yue*, or *Words of the Confucian School* in 10 fascicles.[133] Another one is entitled *Kung Ts'ung Tze*, or *Collected Works of the Confucian School*, in which talks of the master and disciples have been noted down in 20 chapters together with a supplement. In studying Confucianism these works may be referred to, but they should not be taken as authentic. For many good reasons the false texts came into being and these existed in abundance but, on the whole, the motive of those real authors was not so reprehensible as we suppose. Another book called *Yue Tsueh Shu*, or *A Book on the Forgone State Yue* of which the authorship was attributed to Tze-kung, the disciple of Confucius, was forged by Yuen Kan in the Han dynasty.

132. This is found in *Lung Heng* written by Wang Chung in the Han dynasty. The title of the book may be translated either as "Unbiassed Criticisms" or "Balanced Judgments," a book of much pragmatic reasoning.

133. This book has a German translation done by Richard Wilhelm, but perhaps it may not have been translated into English.

With these taken into consideration, we find the surest and safest way is to rely purely on the authentic texts apart from all commentaries, and, as far as possible, to explain and interpret the classical work by the classical works themselves, — a method followed in this book. The annotations of the Han dynasty come next, because without these a good part of the texts cannot be read at all. Theories held by both the schools of the "ancient" and "modern" scripts should be equally adopted without bias, because both had their excellent points. And these, together with a good knowledge of ancient cultural history helped by the study of ancient geography and philology, can ultimately give us a clear impression of such a great system of teaching in its original form. Further research would lead to the study of texts in stone-inscriptions and written scrolls (as e.g. those discovered in T'un Huang), and the printed editions of the Sung dynasty. But that, as well as the commentaries and sub-commentaries which have grown like jungle forests since the Tang dynasty, come to be only of minor importance to a foreign scholar, in view of the state of Sinology at this moment.

The four works done by Confucius in his old age must be viewed as a whole. According to Lu Hsian Shan, a philosopher in the Sung dynasty, Confucius did these works spontaneously without much thinking, which was probably a fact. Just as poems were connected with music because they were to be sung, and music went hand in hand with the ceremonial propriety, in which dancing was included, so the materials of these three subjects upon which he worked were also of a piece. The work on the *Book of Changes* was metaphysical in nature and the rest pertained merely to history. So the Six Classics came into being

1) The Classic of Poetry
2) The Classic of History
3) The Classic of Changes
4) The Classic of Ceremonial Propriety (Li)
5) The Classic of Music (Yo)
6) The Classic of the *Annals of Spring and Autumn*

We read first the following record:

The Master said: "After I came back from Wei to Lu, the music was set aright, and the verses in the Royal Songs and Praise Poems all found their proper places." [134]

This shows the first work. "Royal songs" and "praise poems" were those sung on ceremonial occasions either in the palace-hall or in ancestral temples, accompanied by music and dancing. "Proper places" meant the right occasions, and their right places of display. These songs — in fact all poems in a high literary sense — were now included in the *Book of Odes*. (There is the English translation done by Legge,

---

134. IX, 14.

included in series of the *S. B. E.*) Since the Duke of Chow first formulated all these songs, rites and ceremonies into a delicate and elaborate system, they were brought into practice, but gradually decayed in the Eastern Chow dynasty. The imperial court declined in its power as the potentates grew gradually stronger, and the old system was in the long run undermined. One historical anecdote will clearly show the case.

In the year 635 B.C. the Duke Wen of the Tsin state succeeded in putting down a rebellion in the imperial court and re-installed the King or "Son of Heaven" to the throne who had fled from the capital. The duke was heavily rewarded, but he requested a privilege which to us nowadays seems to be very peculiar though it was very serious in that age. He requested permission to build an underground tunnel [135] in his tomb after his death, a construction which was only permissible in the mausoleum of a king. And that was Li or Propriety. This favour was not granted, and the King in all courtesy refused this petition, saying:

"It is so in our royal code. Since as yet there is no virtuous one to substitute for myself, and there would appear to be two kings in the empire (if I granted this favour), that would also be disliked by you. Oh! Uncle."

He was then alloted several districts of land for his great merit. (This happened in the 25th year during the reign of Duke Hsi of Lu, see *Tso Chuan*, Vol. 5.)

During the life-time of Confucius, the decay and decline became more manifest. Ancient customs changed and ancient formalities were no longer observed. Degeneration and depravation of both ceremonial propriety and music went along with the decline and fall of imperial power, mutually serving as cause and effect. It was not only so with the nominal central government, it was also the case with the different dukedoms. The prerogatives of those dukes were also usurped by lesser nobilities. We read the following remarks made by Confucius:

Confucius said of the head of the Chi family (i.e. the third and most powerful house in the state of Lu), who had eight rows of pantomime dancers in his court-yard: "If this is to be borne, what is not to be borne?" [136]

According to the proper rites, only the king could have eight rows of dancers, and the duke, six rows, and a minister, four, all with eight handsome boys in a row. Music was played in the hall, while dancing

.

135. Generally, a tunnel with an arch like a Roman architecture was built at a distance from the surface of the ground to the centre of the grave underneath. The huge and heavy coffin of the king could thus slide down through it into the grave without much effort. Afterwards the tunnel was sealed and filled with earth to ground level leaving only the mark of an opening like a closed city-gate. In ordinary burials the coffin was merely sunk into the grave vertically by the use of scaffold and ropes.

136. III, 1.

took place in the open court-yard. The system of ancient Li was such that every ceremony was fixed with every rank of nobility, and nearly everything in life, to the minutest detail such as the small ornaments of the dress and the colour of the robes had distinctions according to ranks. Because of the great merit of the Duke of Chow, his fief, the state of Lu, could alone assume the ceremonial propriety and music of a king, being a special favour granted in the beginning of the dynasty. But how could such a performance be held in the ancestral temple of a minister, however powerful he might be? Further:

At the end of worship, the Three Houses made use of the Yung hymn. The Master said:

"'The dukes and princes assist,

Solemn is the Son of Heaven;'

what sense has this in the hall of the Three Houses?" [137]

The hymn Yung, in which these two lines appeared, now included in the *Book of Poetry* (VIII. ii, 7), was dedicated to King Wen by his grandson, King Chen, and sung at the end of a great sacrifice when the vessels were being removed. Evidently they had nothing to do with dukes, not to say of those ministers. By these and numerous examples we may understand the general condition in that period. Ignorance and presumptive arrogance held sway over the customs of the nobles; so much so that these measures were regarded as traditional and therefore natural, without anyone questioning the matter. The sage expressed his doubts, but practically he could not help much. So, to go to the root of the problem, he began first to edit the poems, including all the odes and hymns, and directed the music and rites to their proper places. This was no radical revolutionary process, yet, as a transformative force, its gradual effect among the people was felt tremendously. Every poem in the *Book of Poetry* was edited in such a way that it could be sung in accord with music. We read a passage like this:

The Master said: "When the music master Chih first entered on his office, the finish of the poem of 'The Osprey' was magnificent; — how it filled the ears!" [138]

"The Osprey" is the first poem in the *Book of Poetry*, a love song. As said before, among the three thousand and more ancient poems, he selected only 305 pieces. In this selection, verses were deleted from a piece, lines from a verse, and words from a line. As said by Confucius himself:

"To sum up the three hundred poems in a word, they are 'free from

137. III, 2.
138. VIII, 15.

evil thought '." [139]

And his own view about the first piece:

"The poem 'The Osprey' is glad, but not wanton; it is sad, but not morbid." [140]

Thus we can conjecture to a great extent the principle he followed in his editing and selection. This was then something like a text-book used in his school; he seemed to be particular about the knowledge of it. We read the following passages:

The Master said: "My boys, why do you not study the *Book of Poetry*? Poetry would inspire you, teach you insight, fellow-feeling, right resentment; show your immediate duty to your father, and then your remote duty to the king; and would teach you the names of many birds and beasts, plants and trees." [141]

The Master said to Pê Yü: "Hast thou conned the Chownam and Shao-nam? Who has not studied the Chow-nam and Shao-nam, is as a man standing with his face to the wall." [142]

Chow-nam and Shao-nam are the two parts of the first volume of the *Book of Poetry*. To stand with the face to the wall means one cannot step forward; that is to say, one would be unable to proceed a step without this means, no matter whatever truth he might have. Moreover, for its use:

The Master said: "Though a man have conned three hundred poems; yet if, when instructed with a governmental charge, he knows not how to act, or if, when sent to the four directions for a mission, he cannot answer for himself, despite their number, of what use is it?" [143]

This was said of its immediate use. A broad knowledge in *Poetry* involves a right cognizance of human nature, familiar acquaintance with the rules of etiquette, correct vision of the right action to be taken in due time, apart from the cultivation of eloquence which affords much tactfulness. But its main purpose is in the building of character. And a man, so it is said, who is deeply versed in this culture, is supposed to be "mild, candid, gentle, generous and full of sympathy towards men." As a special education, when general knowledge divided itself into branches and people were specialized in only one or two Classics, several schools

.

139. II, 2.
140. III, 20.
141. XVII, 9.
142. XVII, 10.
143. XIII, 5.

of learning developed after the time of the Warring States.[144] The contents of those poems were large, and their meaning profound; they could not be taken only at face value. We read the following discourse:

> Tze-hsia asked, saying: "What is the meaning of:
> 'Her gracious smiles,
> Her dimples light,
> Her lovely eyes,
> So clear and bright,
> The ground, not yet
> With color dight?'" [145]
> The Master said: "Colouring follows groundwork."
> "Then do ceremonies (Li) follow after?"
> "It is Shang (Tze-hsia), " said the Master (in addressing other pupils), "who can develop my idea. Now I can talk of Poetry with him." [146]

These six lines had only three in the original. The first two lines can still be found in the *Book of poetry* (I. v, 3, 2), but the third line is only found in this place. The 150 and more citations of the verses from this Book found in *Tso Chuan* — a Commentary on the *Annals of Spring and Autumn* written by Tso Chiu Ming — will show how subtly they were understood, and used in what delicate senses. There was no question of moralizing; but generally, as for example a love-song could not be purely regarded as a love-song, it could mean many things besides and the right understanding depended much upon the circumstances in which it was used. The idea must be grasped from the words and at the same time apart from them. It is altogether a very high and deep learning.

With regard to the history of this Classic, it suffered almost no change in the past ages. Because the verses were recited, and written not only on bamboo-slabs or silk but in the very memory of people, they were not destroyed during the great burning of books. There was practically no difference between the texts of the schools of the "ancient script" and the "modern script." In the school of the "modern script," three divisions could be made: the school of Ch'i, of Lu, and of Han, each having 305 poems in the text with a different line of tradition in the explanation; these had all been sanctioned as "official learnings" by the Former Han dynasty, each with a great master as its custodian. But all these three schools perished through the ages. There is now only one *Extraordinary Commentary on the Book of Poetry of the Han School* [147] in existence which is full of stories and anecdotes that showed

144. Vide The *General Principles of Literature and History* by Chang Hsiu Chen, a book highly recommendable to Sinologists.

145. *Harvard Classics.*

146. III, 8.

147. The true original work of this *Extraordinary Commentary* in VI fasc. was lost since the 11th cent. The present edition in X fasc. seems to be a collected work made by unknown scholars after that period. See Fan Bao's *Collected Works.*

the extensiveness of its application, but it gave no methodical treatment of the contents. The text of the "ancient script" had 311 poems, six pieces more, and they are included in the present text with Mao's Commentary. Mao's Commentary together with its text is classified under the category of the "ancient script," because the historical facts narrated therein agreed with those of *Tso Chuan*, its political system and cultural institutions corresponded with those of *Chow Li* (*Rites of the Chow dynasty*) and the annotations were in common with *Êrh Yah*, an ancient lexicon compiled most probably by the disciples of Confucius but with considerable enlargements and additions in the Han dynasty.

As music was so intimately connected with poetry and musical education so much stressed in the state university, and Confucius himself had good knowledge of it, we have reason to expect a great deal of literature on it. But unfortunately all ancient records were destroyed during or shortly after the first burning of books. Of ancient literature on this subject, from which the Books on Music in the *Ancient History* by Ssu-ma Tsien and in the *History of the Han dynasty* by Pan Kuo must be excluded, what we have now is only a chapter in the Commentary on the *Book of Rites* (*Li Chi*, Ch. XIX), six chapters in *Lue Lan* (V. 2, 3, 4, 5; VI. 2, 3) and several miscellaneous records. Since references were so scanty, scholars began to doubt whether there was actually any such Classic of Music at all. The theory held was that ancient music had no written notes; it was taught orally by musicians in the educational centres, and these musicians were usually blind men with a specially developed auditory faculty and not experts in writing. The songs were preserved in the *Book of Poetry*, and their applications recorded in the *Book of Rites*. So there was originally no special Classic on Music.

Nevertheless the question is not so simple. If there were only five classics in existence, whence and for what reason came the term "six classics" ? This term appeared first in *Djuang Tze*, in a chapter which some people regarded as unauthentic. But in *Li Chi* (Ch. XXVI "Explanations on Classics") a quotation of Confucius was found that "men who are broad, extensive in knowledge and broad-minded, easy-going, good and kind must be men deeply versed in the culture of music," and this passage was contained in the discussion on classics, running parallel to the passages dealing with the other five. Needless to say, in the Han dynasty Ssu-ma Tsien mentioned the "Six Classics" in his Autobiography, and noticed in the Book on Music in his History that "even after Confucius had returned to his native land, and set the music aright, and had written a criticism in five chapters, the customs of his time remained unchanged." Pan Kuo followed the *Ancient History*, adding further that musicians in the beginning of the Han dynasty could record the notes of ancient music but could not explain the meaning. If, according to scholars of the "modern script," everything written by Confucius must be considered as a classical work, then at least there must have been something of five chapters.

Thus far, the question remains unsettled. If any such classic were actually in existence, why do we not find other references to it in the scriptures before the Chin dynasty; if not, what was the purpose of forging the name of a classic that never existed? There was one quotation found in the *Great Commentary of the Book of History*, a very fragmented scripture produced from the school of Fu-shen in the Han dynasty, but that could not serve as a strong evidence. Yet it is not unreasonable to suppose that such a Classic of Music actually existed, including perhaps the five chapters by Confucius, dealing, as most of the later works did, with the psychological aspect of music which was taught by the Grand Master of Music in the state university, and we suppose that the Grand Master had principles and theories to explain to his students also. But that was completely destroyed during the rebellion, even if not prohibited or burned in the Chin dynasty, because the first and second Emperors loved music also, or because music was considered harmless. And a classical work as such treated of the theories (as theories of music could never be simple or understandable by every one whether ancient or modern) so, once lost, it was irretrievable and could never be restored as the *Book of Poetry* through recitation. But all the same, we have now only five in the name of Six Classics.

Li, rites, or propriety was connected with music. Confucius dreamt of a peaceful reign with everything set in good order in a great harmony brought about by Li and Yo — because music is a thing of harmony and equality, parallel to propriety which is indeed also a thing of harmony but of great distinction and discrimination — comparable to the beginning of the Chow dynasty in which culture flourished in its great beauty and splendour. Yet, upto his time, social customs changed, things generally regarded as old-fashioned gradually died out. And what was more, most of the ancient records and documents on this subject preserved in the different states were silently destroyed by the dukes because, since they themselves could not follow such regulations, these things proved to be at least inconvenient, if not vexing or detrimental. What is called *Chow Li*, or *Rites of the Chow dynasty*, now extant, was not written by the Duke of Chow; it was compiled by unknown authors from diverse sources in the beginning of the third century B.C. and discovered in the Han dynasty after the great destruction. It was not established as an "official learning." As a great work included in the series of "Five Classics" we have now also *Yi Li*, or *Book on the Ceremonial Rites* of seventeen chapters which had almost no distinction in the two schools of scripts. Confucius spoke extensively on this subject, and the notes taken down among the seventy and more disciples were afterwards discovered to be 131 fascicles in total; further discoveries in the Han dynasty amounted to 214 fascicles. This was compiled by Tai Têh (the Elder Tai) into a Commentary of 85 fascicles with the duplicated and redundant passages deleted, of which again only 40 are now existent. Another edition was done by the nephew of the same author, Tai Shen (the Younger Tai), whose Commentary had only 49 fascicles, now very much used. Thus we have the three works — *Chow Li*, *Yi Li* and *Li Chi* (49 fasc.) formed into one unit, a study of any one of which could not be separated from the other two. These three works were also considered as three classics in the series of Nine or Thirteen Classics.

Among these three works, *Li Chi* of the Younger Tai is the most important. It contains the descriptions of ancient rites and their changes during the three dynasties, the philosophy of such systems (mostly in the form of discourses between Confucius and his contemporaries) and the discussions among the disciples, which nowadays we may take as a cultural history. Now that nearly all researches in the academic field of the Five Classics have been finished in the past ages, what one could think of as his new discovery might be ultimately found to have been spoken of by someone else before him; yet there is ample room left in this branch for some work to be done. All "the auspicious, the inauspicious, the military, the guest-entertaining and the happy ceremonies" together with their meticulous rites were built upon a very deep human psychology which can still be explored.

Let us just imagine a scene in China in a bitter cold winter before daybreak, with heaps of wood burnt in the spacious courtyard and bright torches lit everywhere. Rows of candles and lamps illuminating the altar thus cast a mystic refraction on everything in the darkness, especially on those geometric sacrificial vessels made of precious metals and stones. Diverse kinds of animals slaughtered and sacrificed, together with all other offerings of food and libations, had been placed there; nobilities and officers of different ranks, all clad in deep-coloured magnificent robes, stood in dead silence, or bowed low to the ground richly covered and decorated. All proceedings were proclaimed aloud by officers in charge, with hymns chanted again and again, praises sung in chorus, instrumental music played at continuous intervals, and dancing performed by boys in uniforms with symbolic weapons in their hands. The King or Son of Heaven was worshipping his ancestors believed to be on the side of God, a ceremony that lasted for hours with every item carried out in a serene and harmonious atmosphere. Was not that grand spectacle comparable to a Catholic mass or any religious worship in the world? On these occasions, the soul of the race seems to have appeared in its full glory and grandeur, and in this way the ancient folk were cultured and transformed into godlike men. That was also a part of the Li of the Chow dynasty.

Chapter VIII

BOOK OF HISTORY AND
ANNALS OF SPRING AND AUTUMN

History was taught in the school of Confucius, and a text-book was edited by him, known as the *Book of History*. Originally there was only a collection of ancient records of history, documents of speeches and orations etc. preserved in the Imperial Court, while their duplicates were stored in the different states, mostly in the dukedom of Lu which had a close relationship with the central government. Scholars wishing to enter into political service must have been equipped with a good knowledge of history, so these records were taught and learned among the people. But they were scattered fragments, without any definite number of chapters in any book form. The first compilation was begun by Confucius, with the contents covering a period of more than seventeen centuries beginning with the Emperor Yao and ending with the Duke Mo in the state of Chin. But what the original form of such a textbook was, we do not know.

The distinction between a text in the "ancient script" and that in the "modern script" of this *Book of History* was the greatest problem among all classics, and the questions involved were numerous and extremely complicated. Two forged texts of the "ancient script" were in existence, one having been lost after a short appearance in the Han dynasty, and another in twenty-five chapters still existing. The forgery was so cleverly done that, in the long run of more than a thousand years, it deceived readers though sharp-sighted scholars continuously offered doubts about it. It was a patch-work of ancient scriptures all gathered from antique sources, and with contents of high moral ideals so nicely interwoven into a piece that it appeared very real. And its commentary, supposed to have been written by Kung An Koo, was equally spurious.

After the first destruction of books, this *Book of History* was reco-vered in the Han dynasty by Fu-shen, an aged scholar more than ninety years old who secretly stored away the book during the destruction when he was young. This branch of knowledge imparted by him was established afterwards as an "official learning" with a disciple of his, O-yang Kao, as the great master. This school together with the school of "ancient script" had flourished for several generations until the fourth destruction, by which both perished. Afterwards the false text mentioned above, together with a second spurious commentary, came into being. Upto the eighteenth century, the authentic text of twenty-eight chapters was finally sorted out and the Great Commentary by Fu-shen was re-collected and edited, but more than half of the original could not be found. After generations of laborious effort in the academic field, the ground was finally cleared of layers and layers of debris accumulated through the ages and the ruins appeared, showing something of the real physiognomy of an ancient architecture. Since this is the most difficult text, cryptic both in phraseology and in style, there still remains something to be done in the improvement of ancient annotations and in new explanations.

Such was the Classic of History. To this part of his work the compilation of *Annals of Spring and Autumn* mentioned in the second chapter belonged also. Three commentaries belonged to this history, all authentic; one by Tso Chiu Ming, a contemporary of the sage or not long after him, another by Kung-Yang Kao, and a third by Ku-liang Chih. About these three authors some questions remain unsolved, but there is no doubt that they all lived before the Han dynasty, and Ku-liang Chih was a disciple of Tze-Hsia. To the latter two authors different names were given in different records, but they were supposed to the fathers and sons following the same line of tradition. Tso's commentary discovered in the Han dynasty was for a very short time established as an "official learning," and then abandoned because of the lack of a master; it aroused much dispute among the scholars of the court when it was first suggested that it might be established as such. The other two commentaries pertained to the school of the "modern script." Both were profound in the elucidation of the principles contained in the *Annals*, especially that of Kuliang which excelled in its just criticisms; Kung-yang was often somehow too unbalanced. Tso's Commentary dealt mainly with the historical facts, written in a very elegant and flourishing style, followed by many fine essayists in later ages. Without this work, much of the facts of what Confucius had written could not be understood because of its brevity; without the other two, the meaning or great principles contained therein would have remained in obscurity because of the same reason. So these three again formed another unit, supporting as the three legs of a tripod the *Annals* written by Confucius.

In the second chapter it was not concluded whether the *Annals* should be classified in the category of classics or of histories. Instead of participating in the ancient disputes, it would be more just to put this question before our modern perspective. As the traditional saying goes, the classics are codes of principles in the universe above Time, mostly codes of morality for the building of character and for maintaining humanity, while the histories are lessons of failures and successes in the past, helping to cultivate the right vision into the achievements of man.[148] In a broad way of classification, one deals with facts and another with theories. The twenty-five or twenty-six Chinese histories are simply cultural and political histories; and the classics, whether in a series of Five or Nine include metaphysics, philosophy, ethics, and in

148. Vide *The New History of the Tang Dynasty*, Biographies No. 27.

Thirteen, also philology. Yet the Six Classics were all taken as Histories according to Chang Hsiu Chen. In a final analysis, the *Annals* is both: it is an historical classic; it is also a classical history. This is still an ambiguous conclusion but there is no better alternative.

By itself the *Annals* is somehow fragmented, but the Three Commentaries are the least mutilated, so textual problems do not come into consideration. Pertaining to its contents, many questions remain unanswered or not justly stressed in past ages. It is interesting to bring one or two into discussion. Why had Confucius begun his *Annals* with the Duke Yin of the Lu state in 722 B.C. and ended it with the incident of a unicorn's appearance in the year 481 B.C. ? And, as "fragmented court-papers," what was the authority of it?

As said before, the original motive of Confucius in compiling the *Annals of Spring and Autumn* has been clearly represented by Ssu-ma Tsien in his Autobiography, the last chapter of his *Ancient History* in 130 chapters. We know that the *Annals*, though a classical history as it was, were in accord with the ideal and central principle of Confucius as a whole, which was also that implicit in his work of the rectification of *Rites* and *Music*, and the edition of *Poetry*. The work in his old age could be divided into several branches, but the stem was one. The *Annals* served also as a permanent example of history-writing, an example which Ssu-ma Tsien secretly followed but openly denied. As the Chinese tradition goes, history-writing in itself was considered as a "creation", and hence the work of a sage. Even Confucius himself ventured not to claim himself a "creator" or "maker" in the sense of shaping things. He spoke of himself as a "teller" and not a "maker", "one who trusts and loves the past" [149] — in other words, a conservator and not an innovator. And nobody in the oriental world would claim himself a sage, except perhaps a fanatic. Ssu-ma Tsien in his Autobiography wrote in the form of a dialogue between himself and a high minister, saying that he was merely compiling some of the historical materials, but that his work was by no means any "creation", adding further, "if you compare my work with the *Annals of Spring and Autumn*, you are wrong." But we would be equally wrong if we believed these words. Let us argue in this way: if he had no such intention of following Confucius, why was this question brought out at all? During the reign of Emperor Wu when he lived and served, the political situation was indeed a different one, yet the authority of a historian was the same as that in former times. Merely out of courtesy and the avoidance of being too presumptive as a court-historian under a jealous sovereign, he refrained from expressing his idea overtly, but he faintly hinted at it in a dialogue which, though not fictitious, might not be based solely on fact. This point will become more clear as we proceed to examine the life of the Duke Yin with whom Confucius began his history.

We must suppose that Confucius could not have chosen any one in

.

149.   *Analects*, VII, 1.

the succession of dukes at random for beginning such a piece of work. The *Book on History* began with the Emperor Yao because previous to that emperor there was no record; there were only legends which could not be taken as history. After the fief of Lu was granted to Pê Chin, a lineage of twelve princes followed upto the father of Duke Yin. Another lineage of twelve princes followed from the Duke Yin to the end of the age of Springs and Autumns. There must have been some reason in the segmentation of such a long period. And we find first noted in Kung-yang's Commentary the following words:

"Why has the *Springs and Autumns* begun with Yin? It is (a history) heard through ancestors in succession. What was seen had differences in writings; what was heard of had differences in reports; what was traditionally heard of had differences in records."

A division into three periods was implied in this passage. But this was no answer to the point at all. This shows only the abundance or divergencies of historical materials and shows also the necessity of such a standardized history. We are tempted to question: how were the periods divided? Was the life-time of Confucius the period of things "seen"? Was the period before the Duke Yin no longer that one called "traditionally heard of"? Above all, through which ancestors is it "heard"? An arbitrary division took the succession of the first five dukes as the period of things "traditionally heard," the next four as the period of things "heard", and of the last three as the period of things "seen". Could that perhaps be the historical truth? All commentators failed to give any definite answer.

The next explanation given by Tu Yue, an annotator on Tso's Commentary who lived at the end of the third century A.D. seems to be more satisfactory; it runs,

"King Ping was the first king of the Eastern Chow dynasty, and Duke Yin, a virtuous ruler who abdicated the throne. Surveying their times, they were in succession; considering the status, the state was a great dukedom; and tracing back in genealogy, the duke was the offspring of the Duke of Chow. If the king could obey and pray Heaven to prolong the life of his kingdom, and create the situation of a renascence, and if the duke Yin could expand and develop the heritage of his ancestors, and largely contribute his services to the house of the king, then the splendour of the Western Chow dynasty could have been revived, and the great achievements of both kings Wen and Wu could have been retraced and never lost." (Preface to the Annotations)

This idea was probably developed from the calculation of time, as King Ping's rule began in 770 B.C. and ended in 722 B.C., in the same year when the reign of the Duke Yin in Lu began. But it touched also the ideal of Confucius which, deduced from all sources, might be partly true. Yet it was no definite answer. We can only take it as an ingenious speculation.

Ku-liang gave no answer to this question, but the criticism of the Duke was sharp. "Duke Yin can be spoken of as a man who could abdicate a state of a thousand chariots, but, with regard to treading the Path (Tao), he was not."

Later scholars in the Sung dynasty (960–1279 A.D.) suggested that there was originally not much meaning in the beginning and ending of such a history. It is the principles contained therein that matter; there is no sense in such a division of time. Some suggested that the materials which the sage could procure began by the Duke Yin, and so he began with that period: both bold and elusive hypotheses cancelled the problem.

We may now scrutinize the life of the Duke Yin. He was the son of a concubine of the Duke Fui, so his birth, though not illegal, was comparatively obscure on the maternal side. As a young prince he was leading an army, and in a certain battle with the Chêng state, he was captured and imprisoned. He succeeded in escaping by bribing his warder and fled with him to his native state. The Duke Fui betrothed him to a girl from the Sung state, but when that girl came her marvellous beauty was discovered and, instead of being married to him, the old duke his father took her as another concubine. A son was born, and afterwards the girl was elevated to a legal duchess. Not long afterwards the old duke died and the throne remained vacant because the crown-prince was still too young. So the people of the Lu state installed him as the prince-Regent. The three Commentaries had the same account that he was not enthroned.

It happened, as the story goes, that in the eleventh year of his Regency, a prince Whei said to him in a flattering and jocular way: "Our people find in you a kind ruler. I will kill the crown-prince for you, and you make me your minister, will you?" To this the De Yin seriously replied: "It is the will of the father. Because my brother is too young. I only act temporarily as the regent. Now has grown up. I am building a chateau in the rural district of Tu-Chiu, and soon I will retire there and enjoy my old age." Being Disappointed, the Prince Whei began to fear that his plot might be revealed, so he offered the same plot in an alternative to the crown-prince, which he approved. So Prince Whei caused him to be assassinated on a certain occasion of sacrifice when the Duke was fasting and making preparations for the worship. The crown-prince then ascended the throne, being known afterwards as the Duke Huan.

In the *Ancient History*, Ssu-ma Tsien omitted an appendix to this drama that was narrated in Tso's Commentary. It was stated that the place where the Duke was stationed was surrounded and thoroughly searched and some persons died, which made the drama more complete; yet the truth in history was still not obscured.

We see that this duke was simply a tragic hero. Grown up under hard circumstances, having had a narrow escape from death as a prisoner, following the will of a villainous father to whom his duty was simply to obey, he declined the throne even when the royal power was transfered into his hands, and he had to sacrifice his life for abdicating in good will. Why was no coronation mentioned in the *Annals*? Because it had not taken place on account of the intended abdication. Thus we may conclude that Confucius began his *Annals* with him, appreciating his virtues. Tu Yue had hit upon the point, but he failed to develop it. The suppositional renascence and expansion of power etc. were somehow exaggerated, because the Eastern Chow dynasty since King Ping had been in a state of decline; threats and menaces from the barbarians outside and disruptions and conflicts inside the empire never ceased. It was then too much to expect that such a duke could accomplish any feat of great unification or enduring peace.

In the opening of the *Book of History*, the Emperor Yao was praised for resigning in his old age his sovereign power to a virtuous ruler, the Emperor Shun, whom he had chosen as his successor. The Emperor Shun has done the same thing and was equally praised in history. In summarizing the accounts of the "Noble Families" in the Autobiography, Ssu-ma Tsien used twenty-one words of "appreciation"; the first was applied to the Family of the Great Count of Wu, whom he placed first. This Great Count was "appreciated" for his abdication in a spirit of self-denial of the royal power. Pê Yi was placed first in the "Biographies" because of the same virtue.[150] In later ages, whenever a new king was about to ascend the throne, he had recourse to a formal resignation. Even if he were the most ambitious hero or a bloody usurper he had usually to decline not only once or twice, but again and again many times before he finally proceeded to perform the rites of worshipping Heaven in proclaiming himself a new king. This was indeed hypocrisy, but the force of this traditional custom could also be seen in such a formality, and no one had ever ventured to seize the crown as did Napoleon, in his straightforwardness and simplicity during the coronation.

Whenever we read histories, eastern or western, we find the royal palace the most unhappy spot in the world, a hotbed for all black plots, intrigues, conspiracies, corruptions and bloodshed, in which overt or secret fights for power, for the rights of heritage, for the favour of the rulers scarcely ceased for a day. And every ruler, if he had some intelligence, was conscious of the sword of Damocles permanently hanging over his head. In a way, the abandonment of royal power inherited by birth was always a wise measure.

It was never an easy task in ancient times (just as it is difficult nowadays for a rich man to abandon his wealth). Such a virtue, if carried out in the right spirit, not out of fear or timidity or faintheartedness, or formally simulated in hypocrisy, ever deserves our high appreciation. In

150. A Sung-edition of the *Ancient History* places the Biography of Lao Tze first; but the arrangement was made in the Tang dynasty owing to the fact that Lao Tze had the same family-name as that of the ruling house and was much venerated in that period. In the original order, the Biography of Pê Yi was placed first.

plain human nature there is always an element of yielding, self-denial and self-sacrifice, which plays no small part in our activities; and even in our ordinary life, it is seen in courtesy and polite manners. This was considered as a line of demarcation between the barbarians and cultured society. If this virtue had been developed to its fullest extent, many conflicts and wars would have been avoided and the past twenty-five Chinese histories might be re-written. This, we suppose, must have been the subtle idea of Confucius when he began to compile the *Annals* by beginning with the Duke Yin. If we search for any great principles contained in this work, this was the first one.

With regard to the ending of this book, it ended with the appearance of a unicorn in the 14th year of the Duke Ai, two years before the death of Confucius. All sorts of speculations came into being based upon superstitious beliefs. The actual story was that, in a hunt in the western fields of the Lu state, a rare animal was hurt and caught, and since nobody knew what it was it was brought before Confucius, who, in his broad knowledge of things in the physical world, recognized it as a "*lin*" or unicorn. Since the appearance of such an animal was very rare, it was rumoured among the populace as an outstanding occurrence. To mark the end of a current history with such a novel occurrence was a natural thing and there was no deep meaning in it, judged by the highly enlightened mind of the sage. All the explanations by later commentators about an ill-omen and a sad feeling that overwhelmed him etc. may be discarded.

As to the authority of such a book, Chinese scholars always followed it in shaping the policies of the state. The Christian Bible has been taken as a guide to personal and social conduct and indeed many battles have been fought over the principles contained in it, or at least under its name, though it is doubtful whether any national policy based thereon was ever formulated. But the *Annals*, instead of serving as a personal guide, served as a guide to the state. At critical moments, such as in a revolt or revolution when people lost their orientation, the Book was consulted and referred to for the building of a new dynasty. It tells nothing of the fortune of a state as do the Sibylline verses, but it offers the right and proper actions, forms, norms and examples to be followed. Every new ruler enthroned relied upon it because justification for being the king had to be found for him and no one else. If he was not the legal or lawful monarch judged by the standards of this Book, but was looked upon as a "usurper of the throne," he had to be ready to use force to suppress the endless revolts initiated and motivated by those who relied on the "great principles." These histories are too numerous to be narrated here.

It is enough to give here just one or two examples with regard to the shaping of a foreign policy based upon the salutary teachings of the *Annals*. The northern and north-western borders of China had never been peaceful for any length of time for many centuries B.C.. For the purpose of self-defence the "Great Wall" was built. During the Han dynasty, several great incursions were made and only after tremendous effort were the invading Huns repelled. It happened that in about 57 B.C. the Huns had certain internal tumults and several tribes fought among themselves. It was suggested in the Chinese court that this opportunity could be seized and forces sent to exterminate those tribes, thus bringing an end to the eternal troubles. A minister, also a great scholar, named Hsiao Wang Chi was consulted and he replied in the following words:

"In the *Annals of Spring and Autumn* it is written:

'Ssu Kai of the Tsin state was leading an army to invade the state Ch'i (554 B.C.), and on approaching the city Ku (in the now Shantung province, bordering the ancient Ch'i state), he heard the news that the Duke of Ch'i had died, so he returned.'

"Superior men praised his return and his cessation in attacking an enemy state during the period of its mourning, holding that in doing so, his kindness could win the hearts of the sons of the dead, and his justice could move the other dukes.

"The former chieftain of the Huns admired Chinese culture, and adopted a policy of goodness and friendship. He had sent messengers for diplomatic relations and all of us within the four seas were glad, and other barbarians had also heard of this. Unfortunately he is killed by his treacherous ministers, without being able to fulfill his agreements. If we attack them on an occasion like the present one, it is that we are taking advantage of their troubles, and that we are rejoicing at the catastrophies of others. And in this way to manoeuvre our forces in injustice, we will probably exhaust ourselves without any success. In fact, they will flee far away.

"On the contrary, I suggest that we send a special messenger to present our condolence, and try to help them out of their troubles. Barbarians of the four directions will also treasure our kindness (Jen) and justice (Yi) if they hear of this. If, by the Grace of His Majesty the lawful chieftain could be restored to his former seat, he will henceforth cultivate a submissive and friendly relationship with us. This, among His Majesty's virtues would be a great one." [151]

This suggestion was followed. A special messenger was sent for the purpose, an army was sent to protect the chieftain, and peace was brought to those fighting tribes. Afterwards when that chief came to the Chinese court he was treated as a king, owing to the good counsel of the same minister.

So a line of mere words in the *Annals* could thus save a neighbouring race from a great calamity a thousand years later. And history repeats itself, as it is often said, for the same thing happened in the Sung dynasty, in 1048 A.D. when King Chao of the Western Hsia tribes died, leaving behind him a young son and the reins of government held by

---

151. Vide *History of the Former Han Dynasty*, Biographies 48.

three powerful generals. It was again suggested in the Chinese court that these three generals should be separately decorated and appointed governors, so that once their power was divided, there would be some peace on the north-western borders. This again opened a debate in the court and a great minister Chen Lin held to the same policy as that toward the Huns given above, for the very same reasons, based upon the passage quoted from the *Annals*. The same policy was followed with good result.[152]

Such were the teachings of Confucius given in concrete historical events and they were followed also in concrete historical facts. These are not legends but authentic histories, though perhaps not so well known to European scholars.

152.   Vide *Collected Works of O-yang Siu*, Vol. 30, Tomb-inscriptions No. IV.

Chapter IX

BOOK OF CHANGES

We come now to the last great piece of work done by Confucius on the *Book of Changes*. This is the first Book in China, of both Confucianism and Taoism; it is perhaps also the first Book in the orient. Confucius was exceedingly fond of it in his late years, and it was said that the leather stripes that bound the book in bamboo-slabs were worn out thrice through constant handling. We can say that since the Christian era there has been at least one book written each year under the title of this work. Commentaries, sub-commentaries, sub-subcommentaries, annotations and dissertations, etc. on the *Book of Changes* amounting to more than two thousand books are now extant, excluding all the miscellaneous pamphlets and short essays. In the past nearly every Chinese scholar worth the name read this Classic and, having once read it, he would have naturally expressed his own ideas about it in long or short essays; these essays must have necessarily occupied the first place in his "collected works," if he had any, since the *Book of Changes* itself occupied the first place among the classics in general. Moreover, this Book was not only used by scholars, it was also used by other classes of society since its metaphysical contents were mostly expressed in the form of realistic images. Statesmen in handling political affairs, military men in executing certain campaigns, physicians in the treatment of diseases, masons in the building of a house or in the laying of a tomb, yogins in their breath-control and exercises, pugilists, fortune-tellers, even the calligraphists found their references in this book, and based their theories upon it. Since it is cosmic in nature, it refers to nearly every branch of human knowledge in the past, and we have reason to treat it here, however briefly, in some detail.

Needless to say the present text of the *Book of Changes* is defective, insofar as we find here and there lacunae in existence, though it is not altogether fragmented. Since the Book was primarily for princes and superior men, how it survived the first great destruction we cannot say definitely. In the age of recovery it was established as an "official learning," with first a scholar named Tien Ho as its grand master from whom afterwards three more-or-less different lines of tradition came into being, all belonging to the school of the "modern script." The school of the "ancient script" had Fei Chih as its grand master and flourished for several centuries since the Eastern Han dynasty. The origin of both schools could be traced back (as could many other schools) to Tze-hsia[153], and ultimately to Confucius.

The work of Confucius on this Book was supposed to be "Ten Wings" or ten different pieces of commentaries. They were:

T'uan Chuan — Commentary on the Decision I, II

Hsiang Chuan — Commentary on the Images I, II

Ta Chuan — Appended Judgments I, II

Wen Yen — Commentary on the words of the text (only in the first two hexagrams)

Shuo Kua — Discussion of the Trigrams

Hsu Kua — Sequence of the Hexagrams

Tsa Kua — Miscellaneous Notes on the Hexagrams

In the chapter "Bibliography of Classics" in the *History of Sui Dynasty* (589–618 A.D.), the true authorship of the last three "wings" was doubted because of their late appearance. Since O-yang Siu of the Sung dynasty, both *Ta Chuan* and *Wen Yen* (the 5th, 6th, 7th wings) were considered as not written by Confucius. *Ta Chuan* or the "Great Commentary" was a name used in the Western Han dynasty and it was called *Hsi T'zu Chuan* or abbreviated as *Hsi Tz'u* in the Eastern Han dynasty that followed. Yet both were produced mainly in the Confucian school, and those passages beginning with "the Master said" were generally taken as authentic quotations made by later lecturers. As the *Book of Changes* was used for divination purposes, the Miscellaneous Notes and the Discussion (8th and 10th wings) were written by the anonymous intelligent fortunetellers. [154]

Since this Book has aroused some interest among the Western readers in recent years through its translations, it is worthwhile to dwell upon it at some length, presenting in broad outlines something of our traditional Chinese view. Both the German translator Richard Wilhelm and the English Cary F. Baynes have done their best; but, as a rule, a translation can only be perfect within its limits. The barriers of language simply do not allow themselves to be transgressed or overstepped, especially between languages which are written horizontally and those running vertically. To fix a round peg in a square hole is an impossibility. Generally speaking, poems and rhythmic prose cannot be translated. The *Book of Changes* contains both; it contains lines accorded in rhyme and nicely worded couplets. This then we can only slur over because we say that it pertains to the outward form and what matters to us most is still the content. But the original text is not too settled

153. There is a slight perplexity here which is often neglected: a scholar in the Western Han dynasty named Han Yin had also another signature, Tze-hsia, a master in the *Book of Poetry* and also taught the *Book of Changes*. Tze-hsia, the disciple of Confucius was Po Shang. Vide *History of Tsing Dynasty*, Vol. VII, Biographies No. 266, p. 5169 a.

154. The most powerful support of the hypothesis that the *Wen Yen* was not written by Confucius was that the first words in its passage on Ch'ien (C. F Baynes' trl., Vol. II, p. 8, a, l; a, 2) were found in Tso's *Commentary of the Annals* as said by the Duchess Mo Chiang, twelve years previous to the birth of Confucius. It is also difficult to take that passage as a later interpolation forced into Tso's Commentary.

in its interpretations. The philological researches on it, especially those done since the eighteenth century, have fairly exhausted the field and they are worth our appreciation. The German translation was merely based upon the annotations of Chu Hsi (1130–1200 A.D.), which was regarded as a sort of standardized work and used for public examinations. The great weakness of Chu Hsi was his ambiguity. Perhaps it was the best way to treat an ancient cryptic text with an ambiguous commentary, thus leaving enough room for researches to be done by future generations, but that shows lack of scholarship, nor was it really a scientific approach. But Chu Hsi was a profound scholar deeply versed in the Classics, and it is impossible to say that he did not rightly understand it. Unfortunately, all the later discoveries after him were not utilized in the translations.

The eighteenth century researches in this work were mainly centred in the philological field or in its literary aspect, one aspect of the four which will be discussed presently. With regard to its metaphysical aspect, it should be left as it is. We hesitate to call it a philosophy, although it is highly metaphysical in nature; it is unwise to systematize it into a philosophy in our modern fashion. Just as the Greek logic represented by Aristotle, the Indian logic by Gaudapada and other shastris, the Chinese logic by Mo Tze and other dialecticians (which has now become almost obsolete) all resembled each other in essence but differed in form, so these systems must be left standing separately as they were, instead of putting the formula of the one upon the other or forcing one into another channel. The same is the case with the *Book of Changes*. So globular in its construction, so multiple and complex in its contents with so many divergencies and contradictions in all directions, it is also impossible to bring it successfully into any new form suited to our modern mentality. We may accept it in total, taking everything in it for granted and come to our own conclusions, or we may neglect or reject it in total. It is still a living knowledge, though originated from the most ancient times, and it has a formula of its own not spoilt by our modern systematization.

Generally metaphysics in China includes three main works: first, this *Book of Changes*; second, *Lao Tze*; and third, *Djuang Tze*. Basing study of Being upon this book as a fundamental, one may proceed to the study of the Non-Being of the other two and, by these three together, one may comprehend the Being and Non-Being in total. To comprehend Being and Non-Being in total means to realize Tao, the Supreme Being or, in our modern language, to embrace God. It is just such a spiritual learning to be approached through the layers of consciousness above the mind. And, it may be remarked, to go from that attainment to any emancipation would be only a side-step.

Tracing the history of this Book, we find it was the composite work of four authors or, if we prefer, of four great minds — all sages, as they were called in China. First, Fu Hsi was supposed to be the original author of the eight trigrams. Three straight lines placed above one another form a trigram. The straight line may be broken in the middle, forming two separate segments still considered a "line", or it is a whole; only eight variations are possible in this arrangement. Two trigrams placed one above another form a hexagram and sixty-four variations are possible. At this point the tradition varied: one saying was that Fu Hsi was also the author of the sixty-four hexagrams[155]; another saying was that he formed only the eight trigrams. Next, it was King Wen who wrote the "judgements" ; then the Duke of Chow wrote the "words on the lines." Fourth, Confucius wrote Commentaries on it, as noted above. About the historicity of the last three authors there is no more doubt, but about the first one, there can be some discussion. It was called a Book of Three Sages, excluding yet the Duke of Chow.

Fu Hsi (otherwise also called Bao Hsi) was merely a legendary hero of the race in primitive times. We cannot be sure whether it was the collective name of a clan or the individual name of a chieftain. It seems reasonable to suppose that the eight trigrams were just signs designed in the primitive society first by someone called Fu Hsi, and their duplication into sixty-four hexagrams a natural turn. There is almost no doubt that the trigrams were intimately connected with the formation of the ancient script, as three of them could be identified with three ancient words. Moreover, it is not too bold to suppose that both the trigrams and hexagrams, because of their simplicity, preceded or were parallel to the use of words. The invention of the written script could be attributed to not only one person, such as Ts'ang Chieh of semi-legendary history, but could only be multiple in its origin, judged by the manifold diversity of the scripts. Even in the organized society of the modern age it would be difficult for any person, however powerful he might be, to force into use a system of language created by him alone. We would suppose rather that it was Ts'ang Chieh who brought the then prevalent diverse and numerous forms of words into a sort of standardization for the convenience of the people, and hence the legend came into being. The same could be the case with the trigrams and hexagrams. They might have been in vogue in the primitive society as abstract symbols or even words before someone, either Fu Hsi or King Wen, brought them to a certain systematization. In the nomad or half-nomad and half-agricultural society, all such hexagrams or symbols such as

"water above thunder, to stay" (3rd),

"water under the mountain, a spring" (4th),

"water above heaven, to wait" (5th),

"water under heaven, conflict" (6th),

"earth above water, the army" (7th),

"water above earth, union" (8th), etc. etc.

could have their practical significance, and any such design made on the earth or on a tree or on the cliff could indicate something significant to the traveller. In the comparatively barren land, the symbol of a

.

155. The author of 64 hexagrams has been attributed to 4 persons according to 4 shools: 1) Fu Hsi. 2) Shèn Lung. 3) Emperor Yü. 4) King Wen.

"well" (48th) found somewhere could indicate the existence of a well nearby, or the symbol of the "abysmal" (29th), a pit-fall. The symbols of "decrease" (41st), and "increase" (42nd), "obstruction" (39th), and "deliverance" (40th), "marriage" (54th), and "the family" (37th), etc. may be assumed to have had sociological value and all trigrams and hexagrams to have preceded their mystic applications in later ages.

As the language developed, these signs gradually fell out of use. Such a system remained and it was directed entirely to the use of divination in the hands of magicians. Two other systems based upon the trigrams existed before the present one, but they were lost and we cannot tell what their contents were as only their names remained. Since the present one was first commented upon by King Wen of the Chow dynasty, and later by the Duke of Chow, it was known as the "System of (instead of the "Book of ") Changes of the Chow Dynasty."

This is then the ancient sociological aspect which may or may not be of great importance. If we believe in the evolution of mankind in general, if we believe in the development from a barbarian society into a civilized one, then the assessment above could be true, and the later explanations — "Discussions of the Trigrams" or the Eighth Wing, (Ch. III, 7, 8, 9, 10, 11; Baynes' trl., pp. 292–300) — could be regarded as remnants of the ancient tradition. Once fallen out of use and retained only as a system of divination in the hands of magicians, these ancient abstract symbols representing material objects or attributes in primitive times had to be re-interpreted, and it was at once the problem of the oracle-consulter to make some real sense from the abstract symbols which he chanced upon. Words of the ancient sages were there which were considered divine, and from those divine words which were said to have great occult power, he could take his advice. Yet we fail to understand the *raison d'être* of such divination based upon the *Book of Changes.*

In the Introduction to the English translation, C. G. Jung, world-famous psychiatrist, when he was more than eighty years of age had written his own experience in consulting this *I Ching* or *Book of Changes*, and hinted upon the notion of causality as a prejudice of the Westerners. "The less one thinks about the theory of the *I Ching*, the more soundly one sleeps," he remarked. The whole Introduction was very trying insofar as the thoughts of the ancient oriental world cannot be forced into a fashion suited to the modern occidental mentality. In our ancient Chinese scholarship causality was not ignored but chance had no place, nor was coincidence taken into consideration. It was only taken for granted that certain circumstances occasioned a certain happening which we call chance, but these circumstances were not known. Coincidence was then entirely explained by events in correspondence; this will be treated a little more in detail later on.

It is certain that a thing on a different plane presents a different prospect or outlook. The division of the "parts of Being" made in the Upanishads found its counterpart in China far back in the Han dynasty. It was more a common belief than a system of philosophy in Chinese history. Causality on the physical plane holds good, but it is less evident on the vital and even less on the mental plane; we still admit causality by itself to be an axiomatic truth with only difference in degrees of manifestation. On planes higher than mind where we tread the paths of mysticism, causality as we normally understand it may or may not exist. It is then a matter not left to the matter-entranced scientists but to highly enlightened souls to pronounce any judgement. If the sticks of Moses and those of the Egyptians could be changed into snakes, or if water could be turned into wine by Jesus, we simply call such events wonders, because these happenings baffle our modern scientists. If anyone takes them seriously, we are inclined to think that he has something wrong in his head, and a treatment by Prof. C. G. Jung would perhaps be recommended. Things pertaining to other spheres we do not think of, and hence we sleep more soundly. Yet we may still assume that causality exists in other spheres; it may be of a different "outlook".

Yet the *Book of Changes* is neither a book of wonders nor a heap of meaningless words under the handsome disguise of mysticism, nor meaningless oracles to be consulted by superstitious persons. If it were so it would have perished long ago, for no code of nonsense used by imposters could have passed the intelligentsia throughout the past ages. On the contrary, endless books were written on it and numerous cases of its wholesome effects in the field of human affairs have been recorded in history. Generally no one ever doubted the authority of its four aspects: the first its literary; the second its metaphysical; the third its artistic; and the fourth its mystic aspect. Only the third aspect remained somehow obscure, and the rest were clear. To quote a passage from its "Great Treatise" :

"The *Book of Changes* contains a fourfold Path (Tao) of the holy sages. In speaking, we should be guided by its judgements; in action by its changes; in making objects, we should be guided by its images; in seeking an oracle, we should be guided by its pronouncements." [156]

This translation is not precise. It is not exactly that "in speaking we should be guided by its judgements," though that can be the verbal sense. It is simply "those who are fond of words appreciate its sayings." In other words, as a piece of literature both in verse and prose, it is of high value, paramount and everlasting. In it are included certain principles which fall short of scientific proofs, yet they are verifiable and we prefer to call them verifiable beliefs if not verifiable truths. Since our universe is a large one — somewhat larger than the reach of our thinking mind — we must suppose that there are in it other than modern scientific truths. These we usually take for granted, so a word of elucidation is needed, and for this we must at once step into the field of metaphysics.

.

156.   Bayne's trl., Vol. I, p. 337.

In the context of the *Book of Changes*, three primal powers constitute the universe: "the Way (Tao) of Heaven is in it, the Way (Tao) of earth is in it, and the Way (Tao) of man is in it." [157] Heaven indeed represents God, but together with Earth it is what we call Nature and Man is an entity that stands between these two. A step further leads to the belief that he is the fulfilment of the two, capable of exercising his influence on these two, and hence he is in a way the master of the universe. It is said:

"When he acts in advance of heaven, heaven does not contradict him. When he follows heaven, he adapts himself to the time of heaven. If heaven itself does not resist him, how much less do men, gods and spirits!" [158]

What is meant here by acting "in advance of heaven" and the man not being contradicted thereby is simply the conquest of nature, just as he cultivates the virgin soil and tames the horse, and develops the natural resources for his own welfare. But he must also adapt himself to the time of heaven in the sense that he must take the right action at the right moment, just as he can plant grain only in spring and not in winter. These things are too plain to need any explanation. But here is a subtle point that stands like a slight deflection in the centre of a circle which, when extended, makes a tremendous difference in distance on the circumference. The Man considers himself an entity between the two primary powers and, being himself also a power and hence the master of them, he is also conscious that whatever fills the space between these two is *he himself*, and so he is everywhere. This can only best be understood in the light of the Indian philosophy of the Self of Atman, and Neo-Confucians had made this point very clear. Furthermore, since he has within him what we call divine nature, he is conscious of himself as being capable of becoming divine. The word "entity" used here is still not the exact equivalent of the original Chinese which means literally"the top-most beam of a roof" or "a pole," just as we speak of the north- or south-pole, representing the extremity in a triad. In other words, he stands supreme between heaven and earth and therefore he is himself *a priori* a God-like being.

To the God-fearing people of Western traditional beliefs such a belief seems to be entirely absurd. Yet if we take what is said in the Book of Genesis — that God made man according to His own image — as a parable, we see that this is the same idea put in another form. If man is the image of God, then he is like God. To be "like God" does not make any sense unless it is further inferred that he is capable of becoming God. This idea was indeed implicit in Genesis, yet the ancient sage who had written this line had the wisdom of stopping just

157. *Ibid*, Vol. I, p. 377.
158. Baynes' trl,, Vol. II, pp. 15—16.

here in order to avoid any misunderstanding, because it was a book written for everyone and not for only the chosen few. There is ever a strain of God-seeking in the history of mankind, from the ancient Egyptian kings to the Greco-Roman world, from the Gymnosophists and Yogins to the desert-hermits and pillar-saints, a strain that, though exposed to much ridicule — such as to dress and decorate the body like the legendary Apollo or Hercules or Isis, or simply to let oneself be worshipped as a god, as Alexander did after he conquered Darius — showed the belief that a possibility existed for the human being to become divine and like God. The story among Chinese was indeed not too different, only perhaps there were fewer fanatics and a purer air in the spiritual field, unclouded by the heavy smoke of frankincense or the hectacombs burned profusely on the altar.

Gradually we see the discrepancy growing more manifest, and the distance increasing. The Chinese mind is never atheistic, of that we may be sure. But the centre of gravity of belief is still in Man, and since he is one of the "poles" in the universe, he is ever conscious that he has his own part to play in this world, and when justice has been done in his proper sphere of society, he regains satisfied and then leaves everything to God. Yet his God still lies somewhat within the field of Man. Extending this concept to the extreme, it is man who created God out of his own imagination, a reverse of the statement in Genesis. In such a pagan religion or belief from the Christian point of view, there is no conception of "original sin," nor fear of the wrath of God, nor special love for Him — and Love as explained in the foregoing chapters is his, is that which he has to realize — nor the aspiration towards a paradise nor the abhorrence of a hell.

This serves as the key to the Chinese mentality, a clear notion of which may lead to a correct understanding of the Book. In seeking the Divine Perfection it is believed to be the utmost perfection within the limits of man, which, as history tells, can be unlimited. Translated into human activities, this gives rise to the expressions of what in Greek is called "megalopsychia" and "megaloprepeia", commonly found among the ancients and their achievements. This explains also why Buddhism had found an easier entrance into China because, apart from numerous points of concordance in its teachings with the Confucian, it emphasized also the self-reliance of man. Christianity (including the religion of the Israelites) was twice introduced into China and failed twice, each trial lasting for only a few decades, and the present missionary campaign is the third experiment which began less than a hundred years ago. An over-emphasis on the adoration of a personal God and the Creator of the universe, or on the glory of the other world after death, or on "original sin" could perhaps find less response among the Chinese; though ultimately, a Chinese, after his own tremendous effort and self-exertion, would also say in his utmost humility: "O God, it is Thy Will that has to be accomplished and not mine."

In the system of the *Book of Changes*, Man is always represented by the middle line in a trigram, with Heaven above and Earth below, or he is represented by the two middle lines in a hexagram, viz. the lower line of the "outer trigram" above, and the upper line of the "inner trigram" below. He is always in the middle or in the centre, a balanced position that finds its importance in every field of human activity. The theory of "medium" together with "harmony" was well exemplified in music, and as a philosophy it developed in the so-called "Doctrine of the Mean," which will be treated in another chapter (Ch. XIV).

Next, in the analogy of Heaven and Earth, two principles are evolved: that which is dark, Yin, and that which is light, Yang. It is what may be called a dualistic-monism, a principle which, in Chinese, is called Tao, variously translated as "the Way," "the Path," or "the Truth." These two ever-increasing and decreasing make up the Change, just as day and night, hot and cold seasons succeed each other. The "old" and "young" stages of both — a theory that held the field for many centuries upto present — was a comparatively late formulation. In the incessant movement of the universe, there could be progress and retrogression of both, but nothing like an "old" or "young" stage of either, as both these terms are relative and undetermined; and as progress does not follow a straight course ad infinitum, but a cyclic one, so either coming to its extreme becomes a reversal of itself and is changed to its opposite. But comprehending and governing and regulating both is Goodness[159], and accomplishing either is the Essence. As yet it is still a cosmic principle, but, when translated in the human plane, "the man of Love sees it and calls it Love, the man of Wisdom sees it and calls it Wisdom. The common people use it daily without being aware of it."

Originally these two principles might refer to the male and female sex. Yang has been translated as the Creative (Das Schöpferische) and Yin, the Receptive (Das Empfangende), both terms being uncomprehensive. The ancient view tells us that neither alone could be productive, and only through a combination of the two could there be a creation. Both are equal in potency and in magnitude and, as independent principles, both are mutually necessary. There is no basis of Chu Hsi's theory that the Yang is always larger than the Yin; his idea came perhaps from the notion that heaven (space) is larger than the earth. Otherwise "large" and "small" must be understood in their German equivalents "*Vergrösserung*" and "*Verkleinerung*" indicating states of waxing or waning of each. As a biune principle it stood originally above morality, until the time of Confucius when the ethical mentality crept into this system and degraded Yin to something evil. Fundamentally this indicated the equality of sexes. Neither could be without its opposite. Even in the human body, whether of man or of woman, in the sound and healthy constitution both are found to be

.

159. This passage has been too literally translated in the German version: "Als Fortsetzender is er gut. Als Vollender ist er das Wesen." (Taschenausgabe, *Das Buch der Wandlungen*, S. 276) And hence in English: "As continuer, it is good. As completer, it is the essence." (The *I Ching*, Vol. I, p. 320) The "Fortsetzender" or "continuer" does not convey any sense.

present in an equilibrium and neither can be dispensed with without causing an end to life.

Next, a word on the conception of Change may be noted. Generally speaking, a verisimilitude can be found in the philosophy of Heraclitus (525–475 B.C.), who sees the cosmos as involved in a constant flux and nothing in it having any permanence. "One cannot descend twice into the same stream," it is said. ('Fr' 41, 81) Or, "All comes from One, and One from All." ('Fr' 59) Or, "God is day and night, summer and winter, war and peace, satiety and hunger." ('Fr' 36) All these theses can be extracted from the *Book of Changes* without descending to scholastic trickery. The same strain of thought appeared in Indian philosophy — let us be cautious in the matter of chronology, and not try to say which preceded or was influenced by which — an over-emphasis on the Anitya or changing aspect of nature developed into a pessimistic view of life, especially in Buddhism, which held it as the first of the Four Uddanam. But in ancient Chinese philosophy, the theory of Changes took a humanistic turn ere it developed into any speculative philosophy. "All" is supposed to be involved in the Changes, but in the Changes there is the Supreme, synonymous to the "One" of Heraclitus, otherwise also translated as the Great Primal Beginning (Tai Chi). It is from the Supreme (Tai Chi) that the two primary forces were generated. Furthermore, all movements in the universe were started by the action of these two forces, and all their movements proceed in expansion or contraction, progress or retrogression, attraction or repulsion, ascent or descent without cessation. A principle of duality is understood, yet it is one.

On the other hand, the static reality of the universe has never been ignored, though changes were often stressed. Once more let us take, for instance, the view of man. In Mahayana Buddhism, a man is a "continuity" of changes and nothing else, and for him there is almost no static condition. That theory has its pragmatic purpose insofar as it enables man to break down his ego, because he has no true individuality, and by means of realizing this he attains to emancipation. But in the Chinese Tao a man is considered as a primal power, he is not without reality, and he has his zenith to achieve which is the God-like Man. This, in a religious sense, may also be his emancipation. Change in the phenomenal world is only one aspect of Tao, while the substratum of all changes, *Tao in itself*, does not change. Nowhere in the *Book of Changes* can we find any teaching that there is no other reality in the universe except a continuity of changes. In every trigram or hexagram, a line represents a fixed condition which is changeable, yet of a definite status, just as Heaven has its position above and Earth below. The positions and order of the lines cannot change. "As the firm and the yielding lines displace one another, change and transformation arise." [160] In other words, change and transformation arise *a posteriori*

·

160. I, p. 310.

to a fixity and definiteness. Furthermore, change does not take place at random, it has its "logos", variously translated as "law" or "reason". Generally speaking, this "logos" can best be understood in the light of the first passage of the Gospel of St. John. Neo-Confucianism in the Sung dynasty is nothing else than a knowledge of this "logos". And the Supreme Logos is none other than the logos in everything. We read the following passage:

"By means of the easy and simple we grasp the reason (logos) of the whole world. When the reason (logos) of the world is grasped, therein lies perfection of the status (of Man)." [161]

The so-called "easy and simple" was originally an attribute derived from a philological explanation of the word Î, meaning "change" but also meaning "easy". Theories on forms of changes such as "interchange," "reciprocal change," "reversal change," "transposing change," "opposite change," etc. were developed in detail in later ages, but the positive side of "change", the "non-change" including "unchange-ability", was contained in the original idea. Thus when we come to the word "Change", three ideas are at once evident: first, changes, implying multiplicity; second, non-change, meaning stability, firmness, and also unchange-ability; and third, easiness, suggesting simplicity. The third idea is indeed an external attribute, yet together with the second item it forms a practical philosophy of life which is exceedingly useful. Any action, taken at the right moment and in a right way, by the measure of its unchange-ability, can be considered perfect. If a perfection is attained which allows no further alternative and being capable of no further change, that must be a state in accord with Divine Perfection. Fundamentally perfection is to be sought in the logos of all states of Being in the universe, and not merely in the external phenomena which are always changing. Furthermore, to take hold of a certain principle or to grasp several main points of a principle in order to meet the multitudinous exigencies and endless vicissitudes of life is a key to supreme success. Reducing this attitude to a very simple formula, it is to confront every change with non-change. There is in it rest and constancy, and there is in it easiness and happiness. "Because of the good in the easy and the simple, it corresponds with the supreme virtue." [162] Further reasoning leads to the philosophy of Lao Tze, which need not be discussed here.

To conclude such a simple exposition, words of Sri Aurobindo — *jurare in verba magistri* — in *Notes on Bergson* may be quoted in helping to elucidate the idea:

161. I, p. 308. This passage has been misunderstood by D. T. Suzuki, and wrongly translated as "Through change (?) and selection (?) is obtained the reason of the universe. When the reason of the universe is obtained, the perfect (?) abides in its midst." (Vide *A Brief History of Early Chinese Philosophy*, p. 17.)

162. I, p. 325.

"In the world of our experience contradictories often complement and are necessary to each other's existence. Change is possible only if there is a status from which to change; but status again exists only as a step that pauses, a step in the continuous passage of change or a step on which change pauses before it passes into another step in its creative passage. And behind this relation is a duality of eternal status and eternal motion and behind this duality is something that is neither status nor change but contains both as its aspects — and That is likely to be the true Reality."

And That ... a Chinese scholar would cry: "Logos!"... "That aspect of it which cannot be fathomed in terms of the light (Yang) and the dark (Yin) is called Spirit." [163] "That" being existent in both and indeed at the same time transcendent to both, is said to be "unfathomable" — as the old commentary goes.

163.   I, p. 323.

Chapter X

BOOK OF CHANGES (continued)

That the *Book of Changes* has drawn much attention to itself in all ages in the East and recently also in the West must be due to, among other reasons, its use in divination. As human beings are totally ignorant of the future, any knowledge that professes itself capable of enlightening them about the future will likely draw the utmost attention and curiosity. But the foreknowledge of anything has never been much appreciated by the intelligentsia in China. However, since the divination of the *Book of Changes* is of a different nature, (and that again is only one of its four aspects) it still maintains the dignified position of a Classic. It was said by Confucius that "those who are pure, silent, very subtle and minute, are those people deeply versed in the *Book of Changes,*" but the defect of such knowledge is that it "tends to make one thievish," and that defect must be obliterated.

People in the West have often found their guidance in times of great doubt or distress in a particular passage in the Bible. The same purpose was served by the *Book of Changes* in the East, only the passage was determined through calculation. Among oracles, this would belong to the category of the "sane" in contrast to the "ecstatic" or "enthusiastic" form of divination, as classified by Plato in his Phaedrus. Predictions, prophecies, oracles of all kinds were found among every race in the past, and great minds like Socrates and Plato, not to say the Graeco-Roman world in general, believed in oracles. Oracles are mostly concerned with events in the future, since the present and the past are somehow already known. But it seems that the inspired words of the priest or priestess, or the magicians or the prophets had no definite code, and their indications had no general characteristics in common, though on the whole they might be considered religious. The Indian Nirgranthas in ancient times with their magic formulas drawn on the ground or the Gipsy fortune-tellers with their cards nowadays may foretell something of the future, and that even with a certain precision but it is doubtful whether they have had any principle in general in any book form apart from their oral traditions and experiences, and a good deal of humbug and imposture. With the *Book of Changes* the case is entirely different. There are definite principles represented by a set of symbols, and the consultation requires definite calculations. It has a system of its own, and we might be inclined to call it almost a "science", if it were not so mystic in nature.

In the *Book of Changes*, numbers are used for calculation. In our modern view, the numbers and figures themselves do not contain any philosophy and thoughts attached to them are quite arbitrary and external. "To attach importance to all sorts of numbers and figures is an innocent amusement," as Hegel says in his *Smaller Logic*, "but it is also a sign of deficiency of intellectual resources." Yet, in the traditional Chinese view, numbers are not without their intrinsic value. 1 is considered a Yang number, or odd number, and 2 a Yin, an even number or dual. But 1 cannot be a number. 2 can not be a number, since it can still be a positive and a negative side of the 1. Yet, when there is already 1, "the 'idea' of the 1 and the 'word' one make 2." (*Djuang Tze*) That "ideas" (translated by Baynes as "thoughts") and "words" were different things was also spoken of by Confucius in his Great Commentary. When 1 and 2 are in existence, 3 is the spontaneous result. Here we have first an "accomplished number" in the strict sense of the word. 5 is a number which contains one primary Yang number, 3, and one primary Yin number, 2. It stands in the middle of the numbers with 1, 2, 3, 4 before, and 6, 7, 8, 9 behind; and it is called the "ancestor of numbers." In the arrangement of a Magic Square which was probably first formed by the inhabitants of the Lo River, a tributary of the Yellow River, it is placed in the middle. The Magic Square has nothing magical in it, it is actually an "innocent amusement." But this "ancestor of numbers" corresponds with the Pythagorean theory of 5 being a number of "marriage", perhaps because of the primary Yin and Yang going together. If this couple is taken as a unit, the first change of 1 begins with 7, because added by 5 it makes 6, but 7 would be 2 plus 5. (*Lieh Tze*) 9 is the end of all numbers, and 10 comes to 1 again. If numbers are arranged in the dualistic principle of Yin and Yang, both having their extreme stages (called also the "old" stages, viz. capable of changing to the opposites), then the primary Yang number, 3, has its extreme stage in 9, and the primary Yin number, 2, has its extreme stage in 6, being both multiplied by the "accomplished number" 3. The multiplication shows a growth to the fullest extent, and that with an equal number shows the equality in magnitude as well as in potency or capacity. In our modern language, in such a relative dualistic view of the cosmos, Yang may represent Space and Yin, Time. 9 is more than 7 in Space, or greater or "older", but 8 is "younger" than 6 in Time, in the sense that the 8th comes after the 6th in the sequence. So, only these two numbers 6 and 9 were used to represent the different lines of the hexagrams, and among the 64 hexagrams, the number of lines was equally divided between these two principles, each having 192. This is then neither real philosophy nor mysticism, but while it is merely a convenient way of numerical representation, it seems to have relation to both.

As we proceed further, we find the process a mechanical one, not without its charm to satisfy our intellectual curiosity, but, in any case, without any delineated philosophy nor any degree of mysticism. In calculation, 50 is used and from that only 49 is employed; be it 49 yarrow stalks, as used in ancient days, or 49 pebbles, or of anything.

These 49 stalks are first divided into two groups at random, and 1 is taken out from the right group. Then each group is counted through by fours, because 4 is taken as a unit. The result is: what remains on the left is 1, or 2, or 3, or 4; then what remains on the right is 3, or 2, or 1, or 4 respectively. This is called the first change. Of the remainder on both sides taken together, with the one already taken out beforehand, the whole number is either 5 or 9. 9 is considered dual because it contains two units; 5 containing only one unit, is single. With these set apart, the two groups are again mixed together, separated at random again and counted again. The same process is repeated thrice. In the second and third changes, what remains on the left is 1, or 2, or 3, or 4; what remains on the right is 2, or 1, or 4, or 3. Together with the one taken out, the number is either 4 or 8, 4 being single and 8, dual. Three changes make one line. By the remainders taken together, only four variations are possible:

a) 3 singles = 13 = Old Yang

b) 2 singles
    = 17 = Young Yin
    1 dual

c) 2 duals
    = 21 = Young Yang
    1 single

d) 3 duals = 25 = Old Yin

In repeating this eighteen times, a hexagram is figured out, drawing from bottom to top in succession. Words found under this hexagram in the *Book of Changes* are referred to for guidance. Since the "great" or "old" Yin and Yang lines change, another hexagram may be drawn from the one already found, and the passages under these lines together with the second hexagram may be referred to. But also two more trigrams can be found within the hexagram; first, the third line to the fifth line, and second, the second line to the fourth line. These must also be taken into consideration, so the range covered is fairly broad.

But with regard to the single and dual numbers, the ancient Chinese view is slightly different from the modern. 3 is considered round, because it corresponds roughly to the π. 4 is considered square, because of its root, 2. We learn that Heaven is round and Earth is square. It is not that a physical heaven is round and the earth globe is square, but rather the *Tao* or *Truth* of Heaven and Earth is "round" (spherical) and "square" (a square cube).[164] In our modern language, Heaven or Spirit is spherical in the sense that It is all-comprehensive and all-pervasive, and in Itself one. Earth refers to the physical Nature, whose multiple and diversified truths or mechanical laws are square and from which Man, also related to it, cannot escape. It implies straight lines, surfaces, edges, and hence limitations. In the calculation, 3 is taken in whole, while 4 is taken of its square root. And thus we come to the figures 6, 7, 8, 9 again. We see the following table:

.

164. Vide Elder Tai's *Commentary on Li.*

No. of remainders				No. of stalks counted		
a) 3s.	= 3 × 3	= 9		36	=	4 × 9
b) 2s.	= 2 × 3					
1d.	+ 2	= 8		32	=	4 × 8
c) 2d.	= 2 × 2					
1s.	+ 3	= 7		28	=	4 × 7
d) 3d.	= 2 × 3	= 6		24	=	4 × 6

At this point we cannot keep from admiring the ingenuity in formulating such a numerical device to represent the progress and retrogression, combination and separation etc. of these two forces already symbolized in abstract figures in lines. A most simple system of trigrams was used to represent all the changes in the universe — if that was a thing impossible, at least it was so intended — and here again we find another simpler method imposed upon the other in numerical representations. Unfortunately such an intelligence in numbers had not developed into any high or scientific mathematics. It ceased there as a primitive device of divination, and when oracles and divinations were highly valued, science could not flourish.

Next, we come to the question of consultation. "Had not the Changes come into use in the period of middle antiquity? Had not those who composed the Changes great care and sorrow?" (Vol. I, p. 370) Traditionally the Book was consulted only in times of doubts. In the oracles on tortoise-shells, it was asked whether it would rain when one went out for hunting, a custom in the Shang dynasty. "Middle antiquity" refers to the period since the beginning of the Chow dynasty. Simple and crude questions were no longer asked and people consulted the Book only on grave occasions. It was the proper guidance for the right action to be found. In life we often find ourselves confronted with a dilemma and we have to make a choice. A doubt means there are at least two ways, equally good or equally bad, and we do not know which to follow. When we have no doubts, this Book is not consulted. When one's direction has already been determined, this Book is also no longer consulted. Two words appear very often in the Book, trans-lated as "good fortune" and "misfortune", which, in a more literal render-ing would be "auspicious" and "inauspicious" or rather "toward" and "untoward". Strictly speaking, fortune-telling is of a different character, and we have no reason to believe that those sages or great minds were so much concerned with the blind fortunes of men as with their proper ways and actions.

Secondly, we must understand that this Book is for "Chun Tze" or "superior men," and not for small men. This term appeared in the first volume 58 times and in the second volume 47 times, and 21 times again in the appended treatises. We can imagine that questions asked by the "superior men" are usually of a different nature, at least they are not so much concerned with personal "good fortune" or "misfortune" and the very same words found as an answer may be understood in another sense than the ordinary interpretation. But, even then, the laymen may go to the professional diviner to ask such questions as whether his or her beloved at a distance will return in near future or whether some person in the family may be cured of a certain disease. These questions are permissible and this Book may be consulted, as the tradition goes. When the diviner is least interested in the matter and the questioner most sincere and earnest, then the answer given is most likely to come true. So it depends much upon the attitude towards divination.

As the tradition goes, it is not considered a sacrilege or profanation to consult the Book even on trifling matters; one may even play with it. But if one has fathomed its depth to a certain extent and is actually capable of telling something of the future with certainty, then one has to pay a heavy price for it. It seems to be one of the mechanical laws in the universe that things in the future should not be revealed if they are known. In the meaningful mythology of ancient Greece — and we take examples from the very distant and different lands to illustrate the same common phenomenon — Laokoon foresaw the trick of the wooden horse and, just at the very moment he was about to proclaim it, he was at once strangled by snakes. The matter known to him was by no means through any of the mystical or occult ways; even then, it was prohibited. Thus we see the ancient Greek wisdom tells of the same thing. In Chinese society, diviners, soothsayers, fortune-tellers are looked down upon as a low class and the most famous and prominent among them usually come to an infamous end, a tragic or catastrophic death. Whether this fact has any truth in it or not can be doubted, but the invariable experience shows that it is true. It seems that the future can only be known to the All-wise and Provident One above, and anyone who attempts to wrest some knowledge of it from His hands will surely "knock his head." But if one is graced with some power of knowing the future, and is sure of the fact (which may or may not be the case with the diviners in general) then the case may be different.

Be that as it may, how can the grass-stalks or pebbles counted have anything to do with events occuring at a distance in space and in time? So the whole system may be discarded as superstition, as factually it was, letting those "superior men" brood over it, or the lower class people bother about it. But occultists would say that it is only mystic calculation. How is it possible? It is possible in the field of mysticism. That, the rationalists would say, is again superstition. Let us take the case a little more objectively from the historical point of view: if such divination were entirely explicable to the thinking mind, then everything could have been explained long, long ago and it would have ceased to be an art as such. If, on the contrary, it were entirely inexplicable to the thinking mind, then so many books on it could not have been written and the Book itself might also have long, long ago gone out of existence. But as an esoteric teaching it always subsisted throughout the ages and the secret teachings were not made known to the public. Some say that when the theories were taught, oaths were taken beforehand by those pupils not to reveal their secrets, except to another generation of students they had chosen, or else they might incur divine vengeance. Modern occultists would say that it is also inadvisable to teach those who are not initiated the manipulation of occult powers, lest those who teach may lose them at once. That is almost the same thing said in another way. But it is also well to suppose that those practioners expert in the art of divination may themselves not know the theories of it, just as a fine pianist may not know the theory of music or the history and construction of the piano. They speak according to this-or-that calculation, the result must be this-or-that; but why should there be this-or-that result, they cannot tell.

With regard to the theories or principles of divination, we must take many things for granted. To a clear thinking mind, these are never scientific truths, they can only be taken as common beliefs. There may be some truth in such beliefs, but they need not be accepted by all. First, we must take for granted that there is such a thing as pre-determinism in the universe. If a stream of water flows on the ground, it will take a definite course and reach its destination as it must, and under those circumstances in which it flows, it cannot be otherwise. Such an analogy is the life of a man. The present is somehow predetermined by the past, and the future by the present. So by the past and present it is not entirely impossible to forecast the future. We must suppose that at the moment of divination, the answer to a question about a future event is already determined. The philosopher may trace the origin of this pre-determination to the First Cause, but here lies just the point of greatness of the *Book of Changes*; it points men to the right action to be taken or the right attitude to be adopted, instead of purely relying upon the fatal doom of Fate with everything foreordained.

Relevant to such a belief is the supposition that all future events and occurrences have already been accomplished on a subtler plane than the physical, but as yet they are only unmanifest. If by this-or-that means one's consciousness can be projected or can penetrate into that plane, then the prognostication of the future is not impossible. Many prophets in the past have done it and their prophecies came true. We do not know through what means they attained to that knowledge, but in the case of the *Book of Changes*, a definite set of symbols was used.

As the tradition goes, to know anything in the future is not the chief problem. We must again take for granted that the factor of Time is taken in another perspective. The fundamental problem is to know a thing in its essence or reality. In mathematics, to calculate dates such as eclipses in the past is the same as to calculate those of the future. Here certain fundamental factors of life are represented, and they are thrown into different equations for determining the results, whether of the past or of future. And, if Time is not taken in our normal view, then the term "a memory of the future" is neither paradoxical in language, nor illogical in reasoning.[165]

Next, we must suppose that all things in the universe, whether objects or happenings, are an organic whole in a well-balanced Harmony. Here lies perhaps a point of the meritorious effects of Chinese culture: people are taught to be ever cautious in their acts and words so as not to disturb the Harmony of the universe.[166] In the ordinary parlance, any harsh word or act considered as "doing harm or injurious to the Harmony of heaven and earth" is condemned, and it is a severe reproach. What constitutes this organic whole is the dualistic-monistic principle of Yin and Yang, and, if they are taken as two separate powers, they are mutually exchangeable and never cease in their movements. If actions and movements cease, then nothing of Harmony can be talked of. No matter how multiple and complex the data of any phenomenon may be, they are supposed to be ultimately regulated by these two forces. We human beings exist within a great Harmony of these two principles without being conscious of it.

Within this conception, everything in the universe is related to every other thing, and every act of ours, however insignificant, has its direct or indirect effect or influence on others and vice versa. This interrelation is thinkable even on the physical plane. An apple dropping from the tree in my garden may have an influence on me, because at the very moment when the fruit is dropped, the inner condition of this atmosphere in which I live is changed, or rather, its inner *balance* is changed, just as the point of gravitation becomes varied. In a sense we may say that nothing is isolated in the world, all are related to, if not strictly dependant upon, each other. We know in general that in the spiritual field. Space can be of another kind and distance in space does not come into consideration as in our normal ken. As is often said, occultists have sometimes achieved certain great things, either constructive or destructive, before they are realized on the physical plane. That is again understandable, because interrelationship involves a complexity of correspondences whether of actions or movements or of static objects. That may be analogous to saying that a change in tune changes its resonance, or the introduction of a new plant or insect alters the destiny of old plants. Actions and reactions of forces never cease in this great Harmony, only in this case they are attended with a human will, and by enlightened souls it is the Divine's Will, because theirs are not different from His. And in this way they shape things. The diviner cannot consider himself excluded from this great Harmony,

.

165. It is worthwhile here to take the definitions given by Sri Autobindo into consideration: "Time, you can say, is consciousness in action working in Eternity and Space is consciousness as being in self-extension, " (*Evening Talks*, p. 98)
Further: "Time presents itself to human effort as an enemy or a friend, as a resistance, a medium or an instrument. But always it is really the instrument of the soul ... To the Divine, an instrument." (*The Synthesis of Yoga* , p. 76)

166. A typical example of this is not to go hunting in the beautiful spring season when birds and animals are reproducing. Even capital punishment of criminals was inflicted only in winter in peaceful times.

and the questioner as well, both being forces at play, as they are playing with forces. His duty is indeed only to know, but "to know" anything is action already taken. He may take further actions, but usually he stops at the point of imparting the required knowledge to others. Thus, in the end it is found that one's fate is changeable.

Thus far it seems that hypotheses are built upon hypotheses like castles in the air without any firm rational foundation. Yet the system is not altogether so irrational as we suppose. The firm ground is still the consciousness. Ultimately it is the psychological condition of the questioner and the diviner, or the psychological atmosphere between both of them at the very moment of divination that is of primary importance. Both must be sincere, and the latter must be specially disinterested, counting the numbers almost automatically without allowing his mind to be occupied by inclinations or disinclinations. In other words, he must not let mental mixtures interfere with the divination, but simply let the higher consciousness point out the answer already determined but not yet found out. On the whole, it is the higher consciousness that is at work in the process, and sincerity involves much concentration and one-pointedness of mind. The rest of the process is merely an intelligent interpretation of those words found in the Book, and that depends much upon the worldly experience and inspiration of the diviner.

Generally speaking, the divination through the *Book of Changes* always had marvellous results. We do not find any evil resulted from it in society or any harm caused to any individual. As "art" always requires genius, we find in every dynasty in the past several great geniuses of this "art" and their achievements were astonishing. As the "official histories" in China are reliable resources, we quote several cases as follows:

The prince of the Tsin state had doubts as to whether he could one day come to the throne. So he himself consulted the *Book of Changes*, and found "perseverance in Chun and remorse in Yü, all being eight in number." (This means that he met the 3rd and the 16th hexagrams.) All the diviners deemed it inauspicious, saying that "the passage has been blocked, the lines wouldn't do."

But the Minister of Works, named Chi Tze said: This indicates good fortune. The Judgements of both hexagrams say: — It furthers (one) to establish (or to "install") dukes.[167]—If the state of Tsin were not obtained in order to offer a strong support to the Royal House, how can a duke be established? The question asked is: Could the Tsin state be obtained? The answer given is: "It favours the establishment of dukes." This means the acquisition of the state. What greater good fortune can there be?

"Chên represents the carriage, K'an, water, K'un, the earth. Chun

167. Translated as "It furthers one to appoint helpers" (p. 16), and "It furthers one to install helpers." — neither being too exact.

means magnanimity and generosity, and Yü means joy and happiness.[168] Carriages are found everywhere, in the outer fields as well as in the cities. To instruct people in a yielding and fitting manner, and to nourish them as the sources of water while they have the generous and fostering earth yielding fruits for their enjoyment — without having obtained the state, what should all these correspond to?

"Chên means thunder and also chariots. K'an means labour, symbolizes water; and also the multitude. The main thing is the thunder and chariots; and importance should be laid upon water and multitude. If the chariots are thundering, that symbolizes the military strength. If the multitude are in a state of docility, that shows civility. Being equipped with both military strength and civility, (a state of) great prosperity is manifest thereby.

"So it is called Chun, and its Judgment says: 'Supreme success. Furthering through perseverence. It behoves one not to go anywhere. It favours the establishment of dukes.' — The main point is Chên, which means the thunder and also the eldest. The eldest is the 'supreme'. A large docile populace shows a beautiful harmony, so it is called 'furthering'. And within this multitude there is contained the great power of the arousing thunder, so 'it furthers through perseverence.'

"Thundering chariots above running like water precipitating downwards foretell supremacy over all states. The blockade refers to failures in small matters, as it is also said: 'It behoves one not to go anywhere.' That refers to the activities of the individual. But since it is a multitude, docile, obedient and equipped with powerful strength, so 'it favours the establishment of dukes.'

"K'un is the mother, and Chen, the eldest son. As an old mother is supported by the powerful son, it is a state of joy and happiness. Its Judgment says 'it favours the establishment of dukes and to set armies marching,' this means abiding in joy and happiness and a display of military strength.

"So, to conclude: 'these two hexagrams show definite acquisition of the state.'"[169]

This divination proved true.

"Nam Kuai (the governor of a small district of the Lu state) intended to start a rebellion, and secretly consulted the *Book of Changes*. He found the 2nd hexagram changed into the 8th hexagram. The words under the 5th line of K'un were: 'A yellow lower garment. Supreme good fortune.' He thought it a very good omen, and showed it to Mong Tsiao (a nobleman of the Mong's family) without revealing his plot. He

.

168. Chên is the inner trigram of the 3rd and the outer trigram of the 16th hexagram. K'an is the outer of the third, and K'un, the inner of the 16th. So three trigrams are here represented.

169. *Kuo Yue*, Tsin Yue —This was the Tsin State which was divided by three noble houses before the Christian era, not to be confounded with the Tsin Dynasty, the history of which is quoted later on.

asked merely: 'If there should be any undertaking, what would this line foretell?'

Mong Tsiao said: "Formerly I learned this thing. If it is connected with acts of loyalty and faithfulness, these words hold good. Otherwise, one is sure of one's failure.

"With a mild and temperate inner being yet with a powerful outward expression, one may act in loyalty. Following a course of constancy and perseverance in harmony, it signifies faithfulness.[170] So it is said : 'A yellow lower garment. Supreme good fortune. '

"'Yellow' is the color of the middle, 'Lower garment' is the decoration of the lower body. 'Supreme' is the sublimity of goodness. If, on the contrary, what is in one's heart is disloyalty, there can be no such color in the outward expression. If people of lower ranks are not subordinate and respectful, there can be no such decoration. If any act has no goodness in itself, its extreme cannot be reached.

"Loyalty can be explained as a state of harmony and integrity among all members inside and outside. Faithfulness in conducting affairs shows respectfulness. Cultivating the three virtues (rectitude, severity and mildness) means goodness. Without having these three characters, words of this line cannot be realized.

"Above all, this line of Changes cannot be used for the divination of dangerous undertakings. What is the attempt? Can it be embellished?

"The inner beauty can be 'brilliant'.[171] Superb beauty can be 'supreme'. Lower beauty refers to a 'lower garment.' If the three characters are perfect, the consultation can be followed. If there is imperfection in any part, then even if one meets such an auspicious line, the words will not come out true." (*Tso Chuan*, The Duke Chao, 12th Year)

These words proved true. The rebellion ended in ultimate defeat.

Many such examples of divination can be found in the literature previous to the Han period as these two cited above. In the *Ancient History* of Ssu-ma Tsien, biographies of famous astrologers and diviners[172] were written because it was the intention of this court-historian to have every line of human activity represented in his History. But upto the Han dynasty it seems that this "art" flourished and ramified through specialists expert in definite branches. According to the *History of the Former Han Dynasty* by Pan Ku, there were thirteen different branches on the *Book of Changes* but they were not all on divination. The philosophy of Yin-Yang established itself as a separate branch which was connected with astrology. The "Records of the Five Natural Movements" of the same History[173] must be referred to if any

170. This description comes from the allusion to "water" and "earth" a combination of the 8th hexagram.
171. "Yellow" means "brilliancy" in most ancient texts.
172. Biog. Nos. 67, 68.
173. Vol. 27, Ch. 1—5.

research is to be made on this subject because it dealt mainly with the relationship between Heaven (God) and Man. Two famous scholars of this dynasty, Tung Chung Shu and Liu Hsiang (together with his son Liu Hsin) were great advocates of the belief in such relationships and the history-writer Pan Ku himself was in no small measure influenced by them. Nevertheless, divination through this Classic was not worshipped as something religiously divine. People played with it, and in the court of Emperor Wu, to use this Book to find out what was hidden in a covered vessel was an amusement and the great scholar Tung-Fan Suo (also a favorite comic) could tell with accuracy the things hidden, in one case, a lizard and in another, some mushrooms.[174] It was not regarded as remarkable or unusual, but was considered quite commonplace. As we know, it leads neither to scientific discovery, nor to any philosophical formulation in our thinking.

In the *History of the later Han Dynasty* by Fang Yeh, biographies of thirty-four such "artists" are collected in one volume (Vol. 82, Ch. 72. a, b), beginning with a wonderful mystic Jên Wên Kung, ending with Wang Ho Ping. But some of them were physicians, magicians, what are called in Indian terminology Hatha-yogins, hermits or men with supernatural powers. Their practices in general were indeed based upon this Book.

In the period of the Three Kingdoms that followed (beginning officially from 220 A.D. upto 265 A.D.) such men were not rare. In the *History of the Kingdom of Wei* by Chen Sheu, several biographies of such wonderful men were compiled in one volume (Vol. 29) and among them a celebrated diviner, named Kuan Lu, had his feats recorded in detail. Another scholar famous for his annotations on the *Book of Changes*, but also expert in divination, Yue Fan had a special biography and it was included in the *History of the Kingdom Wu* (Biog. 12, Vol. 57). Next to these famous Four Histories, in every "official history" of each dynasty that followed, we find literature of this kind in abundance. It would require several volumes to render them into any European language in order to bring them to the reading public for judgment.

Reading these histories in general, an intelligent thinker would well suppose that a certain percentage of fiction might be very natural to these narratives. As a rule, euphemism was tolerated in history-writing but forged stories could find no place *ad libitum*, because the general regulations of every "official history" were usually very strict. Nevertheless, some might still be unauthentic to a certain extent. Yet since so many marvellous feats were centered upon one person and so many such "wise men" were noted, it makes one think that this matter could not be an entire falsehood. It is a general fact that whenever the times were the worst and most unpeaceful, many more such "wise men" appeared; their prophecies through divinations came true most often and they were revered by the common people. It was a common "art" in society and one biography from the *History of the Tsin Dynasty*

---

174. Biography of the same, Pan Ku's *History*, Vol. 35.

(265–420 A.D.) is translated here (Biog. 65, Vol. 95) to show that such divination was by no means held as a monopoly by the "superior men" or aristocratic class.

Wei Chao was a native of Yue Yin district. He was an expert in divination by the *Book of Changes*. When he was about to die, he wrote some words on a wooden board, and gave it to his wife, saying: "After my death there will be famine in this land, and you will be poverty-stricken. But even then, do not sell this house. After five years, on such-and-such a date in the spring, there will be a court-messenger passing through this district and he will stop at the resting-arbour nearby. His surname is Kung. He owed me much money. You should give this board to him asking about his debt. Do not forget or counteract these words of my last will."

After his death, the family became poor and the years became harder and harder. More than once the house was about to be sold but, remembering the last words of the dead father, it was retained. After five years, on the exact date, there actually appeared a messenger whose name was Kung sent from the court passing through that district and he rested in that arbour nearby. The woman went with the board, asking about the debt, but that messenger Kung knew nothing about this matter.

The woman insisted on her claim and assured him repeatedly that they were the words of her husband written on the wooden board and she did not venture to tell a lie.

After meditating for a good while, the messenger asked: "What special knowledge had your honourable husband?"

"He was expert in the divination by the *Book of Changes*, but he never did it for others," she replied.

"Yee-ee! that is now understandable." He ordered his yarrow-stalks to be brought to him and formulated a hexagram. When that was finished, he clapped his hands, sighing in applause: "Oh, how wonderful, this Wei! Living as a hermit, he concealed his brilliance. Mirroring all the ups and downs of life, he penetrated deeply through fortunes and misfortunes."

He then told the woman: "I do not owe to your honourable husband any debt. Your honourable husband had his wealth. He knew that after his death the family would for a time be sunk in poverty, so he stored away the gold he had for you for a more peaceful future. He did not tell you, nor his sons lest, once the gold was exhausted in those first years of famine, the poverty would continue without end. He knew beforehand that I was also expert in divination, so he wrote the words on this board to convey his ideas.

"There is a treasure of his five hundred catties (1 catty= 16 ounces) of gold contained in a large blue urn, covered with a bronze plate. It was buried in earth on the eastern end of the hall, ten feet from the wall and nine feet under the floor."

The woman went home and found the treasure as he said.

Chapter XI

IN PRAISE OF THE MASTER

The last days of Confucius were briefly described in the *Ancient History* by Ssu-ma Tsien (The Noble Family of Kung Tze, No. 17; Vol. 47). This court-historian visited the native place of Confucius during the Han dynasty, about four hundred years after the Master's death, and wrote that he could scarcely leave it. He wrote about Confucius' passing, the main points of his description being summarized as follows:

Confucius fell sick. Tze-kung asked to see him. Supported on his staff, Confucius was pacing at ease in the door-entrance. Seeing this disciple, he said: "Ts'ze! how late have you come!" He sighed and began to sing:

"Is the Great Mount falling?

And are the pillars decaying?

And away the wise men withering?"

With these words, his tears fell. And then he said to Tze-kung: "For a long time there has been no proper way (Tao) under heaven, People cannot follow me... The Hsia people placed the coffin in the eastern steps of the court-yard; the Chow people, in the western steps; and the Yin people, between two pillars. Last night I dreamt of being seated and performed a sacrifice between two pillars, am I perhaps a man of the Yin dynasty?"

After seven days, he died.

Confucius died on the day of "Chi Chiu" in the fourth month of the sixteenth year of the Duke Ai, aged seventy-three. (According to our modern calculation, he was seventy-four and the date given here is not exact.)

The Duke Ai offered an elegy.

Confucius was buried in the northern district of the city Lu, along the banks of the Ssu River.

All the disciples observed a "heart's mourning period" [175] of three

.

175. According to ancient Rites, a disciple had no obligation to observe a mourning period for his master. The three years' mourning — in fact only 25 months after the death — was specially designated as the "heart's mournings," first instituted after Confucius who was revered as a father. It was less obligatory than that to one's parents.

years. After that, they dispersed and, saying good-bye to each other, they all wept bitterly. Some stayed, but only Tze-kung lived near the grave for six years before leaving. More than one hundred families of the disciples and other people of the Lu state settled themselves near the grave, and the district was named Kung's Settlement. For generations, the people of the Lu state worshipped the grave on festival occasions every year, and the scholars also studied various Rites there together with the practice of the Rural Drinking and Shooting ceremonies. The grave itself covered a piece of land of a square Ch'ing (about 15 acres).

The dwelling place in his life-time was turned into a temple in which his hats, robes, musical instruments, books and the carriage were preserved. This was kept for more than two hundred years upto the Han dynasty when the First Emperor passed the Lu state and worshipped (the tomb) with an ox, a sheep and a pig as a sacrifice. All the dukes and ministers always paid their respects to this place before they took office.

This account is authentic as well as authoritative. The Settlement, continually rebuilt and enlarged in the succeeding ages, is still existent, attracting thousands of visitors every year. His teachings were spread far and wide in Asia, wherever the Chinese language was used or partly used. For the reverence of such a sage, we read the following passages from the *Book of Mencius*:

Kung-sun Ch'ou, in a discourse with Mencius, observed:

"Tsai Ngo and Tze-kung were skilful in speaking. Jen Neu, Min Tze, Yen Yüan were distinguished for their virtuous conduct and nice words. Confucius united the qualities of these disciples in himself, but still he said: 'In the matter of speeches, I am not competent.' Then, Master, have you attained to be a sage?"

Mencius said: "O! what words are these? Formerly Tze-kung asked Confucius, saying: 'Master, are you a sage?' Confucius answered him, 'A sage is what I cannot rise to. I learn without satiety and teach without being tired.' Tze-kung said, ' You learn without satiety: that shows your wisdom. You teach without being tired: that shows your benevolence (Jen). Benevolent and wise: Master, you *are* a sage!' Now, since Confucius would not have himself regarded a sage, what words were those?"

(Kung-sun Ch'ou said,) "Formerly, I once heard this: Tze-hsia, Tze-yao, Tze-chang, each embodied one limb of the sage. Jen Neu, Min Tze, Yen Yüan, had all the limbs but in small proportions. I venture to ask, with which of these are you pleased to rank yourself?"

Mencius replied: "Let us drop speaking about these, if you please."

(Kung-sun Ch'ou asked,) "What do you say of Pê Yi and E-yun?"

"Their ways were different from mine," said Mencius. "Not to serve a prince whom he did not esteem, nor command a people whom he did not approve; in a time of good government to take office, and on the

occurrence of confusion to retire; this was the way of Pê Yi. To say —
'Whom may I not serve? My serving him makes him my prince. What
people may I not command? My commanding them makes them my
people.' In a time of good government to take office, and when disorder
prevailed also to take office: that was the way of E-yun. When it was
proper to go into office, then to go into it; when it was proper to retire
from office, then to retire from it; when it was proper to continue in it
long, then to continue in it long; when it was proper to withdraw from
it quickly, then to withdraw quickly: that was the way of Confucius.
These were all sages of antiquity and I have not been able to do what
they did. But what I aspire to do is to learn to be like Confucius."

(Kung-sun Ch'ou said:) "Comparing Pê Yi and E-yun with
Confucius, are they to be placed in the same rank?"

Mencius replied: "No, since there have been living men on earth,
there has never been until now another Confucius."

(Kung-sun Ch'ou said:) "Then, did they have any points of
agreement with him?"

"Yes. If they had been sovereigns over a hundred miles of territory,
they would, all of them, have brought all the princes to attend in their
court and have obtained the empire. And none of them would have
committed one act of unrighteousness or put to death one innocent
person in order to obtain the empire. In those things they agreed with
him."

(Ch'ou said,) "I venture to ask wherein he differed from them."

Mencius replied: "Tsai Ngo, Tse-kung, and Yu Yo had wisdom sufficient to know the sage. Even had they ranked themselves low, they would not have demeaned themselves to flatter their favorite."

"Now, Tsai Ngo said: 'According to my view of our Master, he is far superior to Yao and Shun.'

"Tze-kung said: 'By viewing the ceremonial ordinances of a prince, we know the character of his government. By hearing his music, we know the character of his virtue. From the distance of a hundred ages after, I can arrange, according to their merits, the kings of a hundred ages before; not one of them can escape me. From the birth of mankind till now, there has never been another like our Master.'

"Yu Yo said: 'Is it only among men that it is so? There is the K'e-lin (the auspicious unicorn) among quadrupeds; the Feng-hwang (the phoenix) among birds, the T'ai Mountain among mount and ant hills, and rivers and seas among rain pools. Though different in degree, they are the same in kind. So the sages among mankind are aslo the same in kind. But they stand out from their fellows, and rise above the level, and from the birth of mankind till now, there never has been one so great as Confucius.'" [176]

On another occasion Mencius said:

---

176. *Mencius*, Bk II, Pt. I, Ch. II, 18—28.

"Formerly, when Confucius died, after three years had elapsed, his disciples collected their baggage, and prepared to return to their several homes. But on entering to take their leave of Tze-kung, as they looked towards one another, they wailed, till they all lost their voices. After this they returned to their homes, but Tze-kung went back, and built a house for himself on the altar ground, where he lived along another three years, before he returned home. On another occasion, Tze-hsia, Tze-chang and Tze-yao, thinking that Yu Yo resembled the sage, wished to render to him the same observances which they had rendered to Confucius. They tried to force Tseng Tze to join with them, but he said: 'This may not be done. What has been washed in the waters of the Kiang and Han, and bleached in the autumn sun: how glistening is it! Nothing can be superior to it.'" [177]

About the worship of Confucius in a representative of Yu Yo, the story wad differently told in the *Ancient History*. This disciple was younger than his Master by 43 years and had some physiognomical resemblance. He was actually revered and served by other disciples as an idol of their master. On one occasion, some disciples asked him:

"Formerly, when our Master was about to go out, he ordered us to bring our rain-coverings. Afterwards it actually rained. We asked: 'Master, how do you know that the weather would rain?' He answered: 'Is it not said in the Poetry, that

"When the moon crosses Hyades,

It will cause a heavy rain."

Was not the moon crossing the constellation Hyades last evening?'

On another occasion, the same thing happened, but there was no rain.

Furthermore, Shan Chu was grown up and had no offspring. His mother engaged a girl for him. But Confucius wanted to send him on a mission to the Ch'i state. On this, his mother petitioned not to send him and Confucius said: 'Do not be worried, Chu will have five sons after his fortieth year of age.' We venture to ask how our Master knew all these things beforehand."

Yu Yo fell silent, he could not give an answer. The disciples stood up and said: "Yu Tze! Please vacate, this seat cannot be yours." [178]

It seems that the qualifications of a sage in ancient times included an element of prophecy, especially as a barometer, otherwise he could not be a sage. We read the following anecdote, also an authentic history:

"In the spring of the 22nd year (551 B.C.) Tsan Wu Chung (of the

.

177. *Mencius*, Bk. III, Pt. I, Ch. IV, 13.

178. *Ancient History*, No. 17, Vol. 17.

Lu state, reputed as a sage) was sent on a mission to the state Tsin. On the way it rained. So he dropped in to see Yu Shu who was present in his district and was about to drink wine. Yu Shu said:

'What is the use of being a sage? I will just drink wine. To go in the rain! ... what is that of a sage?'

Mu Shu, having heard of this, said:

'As he himself could not be sent on such a mission, he is yet so haughty towards the delegate. This is the parasite of the state. '

So he ordered him to be doubly taxed (as a penalty for his haughtiness)." [179]

The quotation of the ancient *Poetry* by Confucius was a joke, but not rightly understood by his disciples. The sage had a sense of humor, which was always present in an easy, contented and self-possessed manner in his private life. His conjectures becoming true showed that he had the capacity of prophecy, but he never revealed it, nor had he taught anything about that to his disciples.

A physiognomical likeness tells nothing of any inner resemblance of the man. It was not Yu Tze but Yen Tze (alias Yen Yüan or Yen Whei) who stood supreme among the three thousand and more disciples. Yet through his whole life, Yen Tze was poverty-stricken. With his talents he could have easily rendered some useful service to his native country which was in a state of degeneration and decline — in our modern language, he could have saved the nation — yet he did not do anything in that direction. He could also have easily written some books for the benefit of others, yet he did nothing of that kind. He could also have received some disciples, yet he had none. In spite of all, he was respected by fellow disciples, next only to the master. The following passages may give us some idea about his personality:

The Master said to Tze-kung: "Which do you consider superior, yourself or Whei?"

Tze-kung replied: "How dare I compare myself with Whei! He hears one point and knows all about a subject; I hear one point and know only a second point."

The Master said: "You are not equal to him. I grant you, you are not equal to him." [180]

The Duke Ai asked which of the disciples loved to learn. Confucius replied to him: "There was Yen Whei; he loved to learn. He did not transfer his anger; he did not repeat a fault. Unfortunately, his appointed time was short and he died; and now there is not such another. I have not yet heard of anyone who loves to learn as he did." [181]

.

179. Tso's Commentary, Vol. 22.
180. *Ana.*, V, 8.
181. VI, 2.

Yen Yüan, in admiration of the Master's doctrines sighed and said: "I looked up to them and they seemed to become more high; I tried to penetrate them, and they seemed to become more firm. I looked at them before me, and suddenly they seemed to be behind.

"The Master, by orderly method, skillfully leads men on. He enlarged my mind with learning, and taught me the restraints of propriety.

"When I wish to give up the study of his doctrines, I cannot do so, and having exerted all my ability, there seems something to stand up before me; but though I wish to follow and lay hold of it, I really find no way to do so." [182]

The Master said: "Whei gives me no assistance. There is nothing that I say in which he does not delight." [183]

When Yen Yüan died, the Master said: "Alas! Heaven is destroying me! Heaven is destroying me!" [184]

When Yen Yüan died, the Master bewailed him exceedingly, and the disciples who were with him said: "Master, your grief is excessive!"

"Is it excessive?" said he, "If I am not to mourn bitterly for this man, whom should I mourn?" [185]

When Yen Yüan died, the disciples wished to give him a great funeral, and the Master said, "You may not do so."

The disciples did bury him in great style.

The Master said: "Whei behaved towards me as his father. I have not been able to treat him as my son. The fault is not mine; it belongs to two or three among you, O disciples!" [186]

It is not too bold an assessment to suppose that, had Yen Tze died after Confucius, the cloak of the master could have been handed to him, and the homage paid by the other disciples to Yu Yo could have been more fittingly applied to him. He would have followed in the footsteps of his master, equally giving inspirations to his pupils. A true lineage would have been preserved, narrower in its scope perhaps, but some other beautiful flower could have bloomed in the history of Chinese culture. He was always considered s rare genius of a sage — to learn to be a sage one must also have genius, or, in our modern language, to have special spiritual capacities — in whose presence all the worldly undertakings (as services in government or teaching and the writing of books etc.) lose their importance. He had his inner attainments which only his master knew. It was perhaps due to the loss of a great successor

.

182. IX, 10.

183. XI, 3.

184. XI, 8.

185. XI, 9.

186. XI, 10.

that Confucius mourned so bitterly. The accounts of him given by Djuang Tze might or might not be true, yet the line of teaching of meditation and concentration found in him one of the great exponents. Along with this, self-denial and introspection were none the less taught and cherished in later ages. In the Sung dynasty as Confucius was designated as the Supreme Sage, and Mencius the Next Sage, he was canonized as the Sage of Introspection, referring to his self-denial and "return" to propriety (Li).

As said before, after the mourning and a collective wailing for Confucius was over, most of the disciples dispersed. They went to different countries and worked as officers or teachers, among whom Tze-hsia was the most long-lived, being 101 years of age in 407 B.C. when he discussed ancient music with the Duke of Wei. The Six Classics were mainly taught by him and handed to later generations. It can well be imagined that the works edited by Confucius himself assumed at once a great importance, and the Scriptures beginning with "The Master said ..." gradually came into being. The same was the case with Indian Buddhist texts beginning with *"Evam mayā srutam"* ("Thus have I heard") after the *Parinirvāṇa* of Buddha. And it was all-too-natural that such a great flow of spiritual teachings should have divided itself into different streams, but afterwards streams of philosophy. One current, represented by Tze-yao and Tze Ssu, the grandson of Confucius, climaxed after several generations in Mencius, distinguishing itself as Rationalism though still spiritual in nature.

Another current, represented by Tze-hsia and Tseng Tze, came to a great flowering in Hsün Tze, and is regarded by scholars in modern times as a sort of Empiricism. These two schools laid the foundations of Neo-Confucianism in the Sung dynasty which was again divided into two branches, each having its subsequent divisions into different sects with separate lines of tradition. These great representatives will be treated later on. To conclude the narrative of Confucius himself, the following passages are quoted from the *Analects*:

Kung-sun Ch'ao of Wei asked Tze-kung, saying, "From whom did Chung Ni get his learning?"

Tze-kung replied: "The doctrines (Tao) of King Wen and King Wu have not yet fallen to the ground, and they are to he found among men. Men of talents and virtue remember the greater principles of these, and others, not possessing such talents and virtue, remember the smaller. Thus, all possess the doctrines (Tao) of Wen and Wu. From whom could our Master have not had an opportunity of learning them, and yet what was the necessity of his having any regular master?"

Shu-sun Wu-shu observed to the great officers in the court, "Tze-kung is superior to Chung Ni."

Tze-fu Ching-pê reported the observation to Tze-kung, who said: "Let me use the comparison of a house and its encompassing wall. My wall only reaches to the shoulders. One may peep over it, and see whatever is valuable in the apartments.

"The wall of my Master is several fathoms high. If one does not find the door and enter by it, he cannot see the ancestral temple with its beauties, nor all the officers in their rich array.

"But I may assume that they are few who find the door. Was not the observation of the chief only what might have been expected?"

Shu-sun Wu-shu having spoken revilingly of Chung Ni, Tze-Kung said, "It is of no use doing so. Chung Ni cannot be reviled. The talents and virtue of other men are hillocks and mounts, which may be stepped over. Chung Ni is the sun or moon, which is it not possible to step over. Although a man may wish to cut himself off from the sun or moon, what harm can he do to it? He only shows that he does not have the sense of right proportions."

Ch'en Tze-chin, addressing Tze-Kung, said: "You are too modest. How can Chung Ni be said to be superior to you?"

Tze-Kung said to him: "For one word a man is often deemed to be wise, and for one word he is often deemed to be foolish. We ought to be careful indeed in what we say.

"Our Master cannot be attained to, just in the same as way the heavens cannot be gone up to by the steps of a stair.

"Were our Master in the position of the ruler of a state or its minister, we should find him as in the saying — he would plant the people and forthwith they would be established; he would lead them on, and forthwith they would follow him; he would make them happy, and forthwith multitudes would resort to his dominions; he would inspire them, and forthwith they would be harmonious. While he lived, he would be glorious. When he died, he would be bitterly lamented. How is it possible for him to be attained to?" [187]

187. XIX, 22–25.

Chapter XII

YEN TZE AND TSENG TZE

To understand Confucianism in its essence, one must have a fairly clear notion of the life of Confucius, a life of endless failures, but also of monumental achievements, together with the general political situation of his time as broadly sketched in the previous chapters. His teachings indeed exercised a tremendous influence in all dynasties and shaped the destiny of the Chinese race. The hereditary knowledge imparted from one generation to another was variously developed, emphasizing this or that point through this or that disciple; but the main principles remained the same throughout the ages. It was like a piece of large and lofty architecture, always repaired and extended here and there, thus preserved from falling into decrepitude, but the basic plan was never altered. Perhaps that could not be. The original grandeur and beauty were still kept undemolished, like the towering pyramids breaking the monotony of the horizon in deserts, serene and everlasting.

A study of the doctrines developed in the Confucian school involves the lives of those disciples and followers of several generations. This may be a subject of lesser importance as compared to the life of the sage himself, because his whole life was integral and every act, large or small, taken as a norm or standard afterwards. People in later ages taught mostly by speech, while this ancient master taught with his whole being. Yet as exponents of certain principles, his disciples and other followers were sincere enough to live according to their principles without much self-contradiction.

Confucianism was divided into eight schools after the death of the Master. These schools represented different developments of the same teachings in different aspects; ancient literature on this subject, though scanty, is still available for research purposes. For the present, we can only limit ourselves to four great masters who had their influence upto the present day. In other words, only the greatest among the great are taken into consideration.

Of the first, the "Sage of Introspection" or Yen Yüan, we know still too little. Everything about his life that could be gathered from authentic sources would fill only a page or two. Apart from the few passages given before, a few more quotations may be added as follows:

The Master said: "Admirable indeed is Whei! With a single bamboo dish of food, a hollow gourd of drink, and living in a poor alley, while others would not have kept from grief, he did not sway from his joy. Admirable is indeed Whei!" [188]

The Master said: "Never flagging when I set forth anything to him; — ah! that is Whei." [189]

And then after his death, the Master said something in lamentation:
"Alas! I saw his constant advance. I never saw him stop in his progress." [190]

It seems that Yen Tze was always in a happy mood, though he was materially very poor. He was delighted in Truth, and so was in a state of constant ecstasy. Once such a question was asked in the Sung dynasty: What was the knowledge that Yen Tze delighted in? Scholars were asked to write essays on this subject in a public examination. We still find it a very difficult question and, unless one has actually realized that constant ecstasy, it would not be easy to give an appropriate answer. How to attain that realization is a even more difficult question. But, anyway, one thing seems to stand for certain: even without having taught many disciples, without having written 101 volumes or having delivered 1,001 lectures, one could also have established one's fame for more than two-thousand five-hundred years, provided one had the true inner realization. That realization brings with it the nectar of Joy, and in that Joy, riches and fame both pale into insignificance. Let us question: if the disciple was so, how much more was the master?

We cannot definitely say the famous Taoists Djuang Tze and others were exactly influenced by Yen Tze, but that they followed more-or-less the same path was unmistakable. If one makes a constant and earnest inner effort, gradually one can attain to a certain degree of enlightenment without the need of much external learning or book-knowledge, although the greatest Enlightenment still depends upon the Grace. Books must be read indeed, but this was an ancient question: what books were read by those saints and sages in times of Yao and Shun when our history just began? The example of Yen Tze opened the way for many scholars in later generations who were outwardly perfect in the virtues of a Confucian, but inwardly Taoist in all simplicity. It seems that knowledge by them could be self-revealed as they remain "in constant communication with the Spirit of heaven and earth." (*Djuang Tze*) Then all these external discriminations in religions fall away; we are at a loss to ascertain whether they belong to the category of Taoists or Confucians when we write a history.

The next was Tseng Tze, another disciple of Confucius. In the fourth passage of the first chapter of the *Analects*, we find already his words:

·

188.   VI, 9.
189.   IX, 19.
190.   IX, 20.

Tseng Tze said: "I daily examine myself on three points: whether in giving counsels to others, I may have been not loyal; whether in intercourse with friends, I may have been not faithful; whether I may have not practised the knowledge in which I was specialized?" [191]

But Confucius regarded him as "dull" (XI, 17). "Dull" is a polite description of stupidity, and stupidity is synonymous with foolishness. Yet nobody can ignore the great use of this dullness which, metaphorically, is capable of carrying heavy loads over long distances. Sharpness of wit and alertness in action are usually praised in our daily life, but dullness is equally praiseworthy in so far as when it is applied to the right path, it may mean perseverance and one-pointedness and long endurance. As we see in life, most of those men of great achievements were not sharp in every aspect, and those people who were too intelligent or quickwitted achieved much less or nothing at the end. The chief reason may be that the nerve-energy of those quick-witted can be easily exhausted through their intense reactions, while the stubbornness of Nature must be dealt with by a tremendous momentum, not of great velocity but of heavy mass, if one wishes to gain a final victory. Tseng Sen was "dull" in the eyes of Confucius, but he became a sage.

There are only several passages connected with him in the *Analects*, and apart from the passage quoted above (end of Ch. VI), the others are worth reading:

The Master said: "He who is not in any particular position, should not meditate upon its administration." (Upon this,) Tseng Tze said: "The superior man does not permit his thoughts to go beyond his situation." [192] (This passage was one, while in Legge's translation, it was taken as two.)

What Tseng Tze said on this occasion was quoted from the Image of the Ken, the 52nd hexagram in the *Book of Changes*.[193] This shows the mental energy directed to the proper channel without waste, a matter sometimes difficult for very intelligent persons.

The Master said: "Sen, my doctrine is that of an all pervading unity." Tseng Tze said: "Yes."

The Master went out, and the (other) disciples asked, saying: "What do his words mean?"

Tseng Tze said: "The doctrine of our master is faithfulness and forgiveness — this and nothing more." [194]

The same thing was said by Confucius to Tze-kung. On this occasion

.

191. I, 4.
192. XIV, 27.
193. Baynes' trl., Vol. I, p. 215.
194. XV, 1—2

it was understood by Tseng Tze as "faithfulness and forgiveness." Evidently it was only his explanation. The original words of "an all-pervading unity" meant "the oneness all-penetrating or thorough-going in comprehensiveness" in a more literal rendering. This meant integrity and unity in One. Explanations on this One never come to an end but, simply taken in an ordinary sense, point to the integrity of all one's being without self-contradiction in one's words and acts. Legge has translated the last sentence as "The doctrine (in fact, 'the Path') of our master is to be true to the principles of our nature and the benevolent exercise of them to others — this and nothing more." That was how again it was understood by Legge. "Faithfulness" can be more fittingly translated as "loyalty" or "truthfulness", and "forgiveness" also as "considerateness". Yet the latter has a larger beating. It means something like pardoning and forgiving all the faults and wrongs done by others to oneself and, taking oneself as a measure, not doing to others what one dislikes. Yet this applies only to a negative side. In a more positive sense, it means an extension of love and kindness to others, such as revering aged persons as one loves one's parents or to be forbearing to children just as to be compassionate to one's own children.

Because the Tao (Path) of Confucius was broad, we do not venture to say that this interpretation about Oneness was final or that it could have no other interpretation. When Yen Tze was asked the same question, he might have given another answer. But in ordinary life, these two words, faithfulness and forgiveness, would suffice as a guide to one's normal actions. Strictly speaking, it is an enormous task to have them carried out, especially the latter which requires great compassion or Love. The Path is indeed broad, but also difficult.

Among a few other sayings of Tseng Tze we read the following:

Tseng Tze said: "Gifted with ability, and yet putting questions to those who were not so; possessed of much (knowledge), and yet putting questions to those possessed of little (knowledge); having, as though he had not; full, and yet counting himself as empty; offended against, and yet entering into no altercation; formerly I had a friend who pursued this style of conduct." [195]

The friend referred to was no other than Yen Tze. This was Ma Yung's annotation, but it could be proved by a passage in the Elder Tai's *Commentary on Rites*; Yen Tze was very much revered by him.

Tseng Tze said: "He who can be entrusted with the care of an orphan less than fifteen years of age, and can be commissioned with authority over a state of a hundred miles, and whom no force can drive from his great principles: is he not a superior man? ... a superior man indeed." [196]

.

195. VIII, 5.
196. VIII, 6.

Tseng Tze said: "A scholar should not be without broadness of mind and great determination, capable of carrying a heavy burden in going a long distance.

"Divine's Iove (Jen) he considers his to sustain; is it not heavy? Only with death does his course stop; is it not long?" [197]

Furthermore, the dying words of this philosopher were instructive:

Tseng Tze being ill, Mong Ching Tze went to ask how he was.

Tseng Tze said to him: "When a bird is about to die, its notes are mournful; when a man is about to die, his words are good.

"There are three things which the superior man treasures of the Path: acting in accord with it in his deportment and manners, he keeps from violence and heedlessness; regulating in accord with it his countenance, he keeps near to trustfulness; and uttering in accord with it his words and tones, he keeps far from lowliness and impropriety. As to such matters as attending to the sacrificial vessels, there are proper officers for them." [198]

Tseng Tze being ill, he called to him the disciples of his school, and said: "Stretch my feet and unfold my hands ...

"It is said in the *Book of Poetry*:

'Be apprehensive and cautious,

As if on the brink of a deep gulf,

As if treading on thin ice.'...
Now and hereafter, I know I have peace, O children!"[199]

This last passage has been somehow misunderstood by certain annotators. On the death-bed, he asked his pupils beforehand to place his limbs properly after his death, as that was a part of the ceremony. Moreover, it was customary to have oneself surrounded by men when one breathed his last because women could sometimes not rightly understand the last words of a man, or else they could falsify the last will. There was no question of asking his pupils to "uncover" his bed-sheet, as pedants interpret the above passage, to examine that his hands and feet were not injured during the life-time. The physical body, as the teaching goes, is wholly inherited from parents, therefore it should be well cared for lest any injury or disease could cause grief or sorrow to parents. That was considered as "filial piety." The quotation from the *Book of Poetry* shows his attitude towards life in general.

With regard to the love of one's parents, there has been some mis-understanding since the original Chinese word has been traditionally rendered as "filial piety." Westerners love their parents no less than Easterners, but in the East there has been much discussion on this

197. VIII, 7.
198. VIII, 4.
199. VIII, 3.

subject since ancient times. Fundamentally, culture of mankind springs from two sources: one from the heart, as emotion, and one from the mind, as reason. The great splendour of buildings as the first Mausoleum and Taj Mahal has its fountainhead in love, and the facility of the Grand Canal is purely an achievement of reason. All our human institutions are built upon these two primary forces. But love in itself is sacred and above reason, and, if improperly consigned to reason on the human level, it will degrade into something commonplace or change into its opposite. The most elementary form of love in a human being is that toward one's parents, especially to the mother. There is in it an intrinsic and instinctive force that, when directed to the right channels, will develop into a tremendous power. Ancient Chinese education made use of this initial motive, so much so that it flourished into a great culture. Needless to say, this developed into the worship of the Virgin. Maria in Catholicism and the cult of the Divine Mother in India.

Since Tseng Tze was specially learned on this subject, we will read some of his sayings before entering into any discussion:

Tseng Tze said: "I heard this from our Master: 'Men may not have exerted themselves to the utmost, except, perhaps, on occasions of mourning for parents.'" [200]

Tseng Tze said: "I heard this from our Master: 'The filial piety of Mong Djuang Tze, in other matters, was what other men are capable of, but, as seen in his not changing the ministers of his father nor his father's mode of government, it is difficult to attain to. "' [201]

Tseng Tze said: "Let there be a careful attention to obsequies of parents and sacrifices to ancestors; then the virtue of people will assume corpulence." [202]

To arrive at a clear understanding of these teachings the cultural background of ancient China must be explored. In ancient Chinese society a great-family system predominated and many members of the same family for at least three generations (sometimes five and, in rare cases, seven generations) lived together, forming a sort of small clan. This system had its great demerits and defects which could not be placed in the background, but it had its great merits and good points as well. In our modern view, this was a sort of socialistic commune in a nuclear form, in which each member, man or woman, young or old, did the best for the common weal; it produced a great economy with regard to board, food, clothing and other comforts impossible to the same number of individuals living separately. The organization was naturally hierarchical and the one the most advanced in age and in

---

200.   XIX, 17.
201.   XIX, 18.
202.   I, 8.

seniority (with regard to the rank in the lineage) was the final authority in great decisions. If the family was well to do, the aged ones enjoyed a comfortable life rarely found in modern society. The regulating principle of such an organization is simple enough; it is: one should be filial towards one's parents. And that is all.

To be filial to one's parents means that the duty of a son or daughter is well fulfilled, and the duty is not any complicated matter nor any difficult task. There are only several essential things to be done: the first is to be respectful and obedient to one's parents, to remonstrate gently on their faults and to take good care of them when they become aged and weak or sick. This is the natural result of love, the primary instinctive force. The next is that one must be married at a mature age— the legal age is thirty for men and twenty for women — and give birth to at least one son so that the lineage of the family may not be broken. Finally, the observance of a period of mourning for twenty-five months after the death of the parents is obligatory and, in that period, one is supposed to lead a humble life in purity, preferably to keep aloof from all luxurious enjoyments, and to meditate on oneself. This seems to be the sanest institution, in so far as it gives an ample space of time for one to return to himself from his grief and sorrow. As a rule, no matter how important a work one was engaged in, even in military service or in the court (as a general just about to deploy a certain campaign or as a minister just making great decisions) on hearing of the death of his father or mother, he at once had to resign from all posts and hasten home to perform the funeral rites and to build the grave. This is a powerful brake on one's progress, something that must happen at least twice in one's life, but it gives an occasion for one to step back amidst all the bustle and flurry of life in order to reflect objectively on everything of the past and to determine anew a course for the future. A period of twenty-five months crosses the border of three years, so it is called a "three-years' mourning." It is no short period, but also not a long one. After this, only the annual sacrifices must be duly performed according to proper Rites.

The main point of this principle is exalting one's love of parents into an ethical code so as to build the character of man. The individuality of man is slightly hampered for the good of a family, but never ignored nor annihilated as in a totalitarian state of the modern world. Somehow the family served as a stronghold of society, and if fine individuals were produced from a family they became fine members of society. Unlike ancient Greece where the state was given first consideration and where individuals could only rank next, the state in China came second and separate families first where individuals still were considered first. Loyalty to the king assumed an equal importance since the Middle Ages; if anyone fails to fight bravely as a soldier in the battlefield, he is considered an "infilial son." A good citizen brings honor to his parents and his motive in being a good citizen is to be a dutiful son. In this way not only the large family but also the large nation was consolidated.

Psychologically, the well-being of a family lies not so much in its material wealth as in the harmony that is prevalent within the blood-relationship. Such an ethical principle oversteps richness or poverty because a poor man may be delighted in his loving son no less than a rich man in his. Detailed discussion need not be entered into here, since we have a *Classic on Filial Love*, a dialogue between Confucius and Tseng Tze on this subject. The discourse deals mainly with the governing of the state through this principle and an expatiation extends from the obligations of a prince to those of a common man. This has the merit of filling up the loop-holes where the legalists have failed. Cultured societies must undoubtedly be governed by laws, but laws, however perfect, have their shortcomings and deficiencies. The ancient comparison of the laws to a cobweb capable of catching only small insects is well known. A Utopian state was always fancied by ancient scholars in which all lived as in a large family where laws, apart from a few very fundamental ones, were no longer needed.

This Classic had two editions, one of the "ancient script" with 22 chapters and one of the "modern script" with only 18 chapters. Both had nice annotations in the Han dynasty, but in 722 A.D. the Emperor of the Tang dynasty published an edition of the "modern script" with annotations of his own, and gradually the old works fell out of use. In the Sung dynasty, Chu Hsi made his "Corrections" of this Classic in the "ancient script"; he omitted 222 words, and separated a text of one chapter from a commentary of 14 chapters. A standardized edition made in the Yuan dynasty by Wu Chen was again based upon that of the "modern script," he separated the main text from a commentary of 12 chapters. A work of annotations supposed to be written by Chêng Hsüan prevalent in the Tang dynasty was a forged one, as it was doubted by the famous historian Liu Chi Ghih and other scholars, but it was lost. Strangely enough, another work of the same author was found in the eighteenth century in Japan, another spurious work built upon an old spurious one.

Another very important work on Confucianism owes its authorship to this philosopher; it is the so-called The *Great Learning*. Originally it was included in *Li Chi* as a chapter (Vol. X, Ch. 42), but after the Sung dynasty it was separated from it as an individual work and regarded as one of the Four Books. What Confucius taught and repeated by Tseng Tze was preserved as the main text; the remaining ten chapters were explanations made by Tseng Tze and recorded by his disciples. There were three editions of this work: the "ancient edition" which seemed to lack coherence in the arrangement of passages, but this seeming discontinuity appeared in words and not in ideas; the edition of the "stone-scriptures" had differences in the arrangement, but also had interpolations evidently jotted down from the *Analects*; the "standaidized edition" made in the Sung dynasty by the two brothers Ch'eng Hao (1032–1085 A.D.) and Ch'eng I (1033–1107 A.D.) and annotated by Chu Hsi. This is the edition most prevalent upto the present. Apart from these, Wang Yang Ming (1442–1529 A.D.), a famous master in Neo-Confucianism, made another edition that differed slightly from the standardized one. The book had given rise to endless discussions since the Sung dynasty and to the present day scholars are not agreed in their explanations of certain very simple terms. The main text consisted in only 207 words of Confucius in total, and they are translated as follows:

"The Path (Tao) of the Great Learning lies in manifesting illustrious virtue, in endearing oneself to the people, and in resting in supreme Perfection.

"The point of rest being known, there can be determination; and, being determined, there can be silence; being silent, there can be peace of mind; and having peace of mind, there can be careful deliberation; and careful deliberation will be followed by attainment.

"Things have their root and their branches. Affairs have their end and beginning. To know what is first and what is next, one may approach near to the Path.

"The ancients who wished to manifest illustrious virtue to all under Heaven, first ordered their states well. Wishing to order their states well, they first regulated their families. Wishing to regulate their families, they first cultivated their persons. Wishing to cultivate their persons, they first rectified their hearts. Wishing to rectify their hearts, they first sought to be sincere in their thoughts. Wishing to be sincere in their thoughts, they first acquired their knowledge. The acquisition of knowledge lies in warding off (the desire for) things.

" (The desire for) things being warded off, knowledge came. Knowledge being there, thoughts were sincere. Thoughts being sincere, hearts were rectified. Hearts being rectified, persons were cultivated. Persons being cultivated, families were regulated. Families being regulated, states were well-ordered. States being well-ordered, peace was brought to all under Heaven.

"From the Son of Heaven down to the mass of people, all without exception, must take the cultivation of the person as a basis.

"When the basis is in disorder, what is built upon it cannot be in good order. It has never been the case that what is important can be slighted, and that what is being slighted can assume great importance."

Here we have come to almost a spherical view of Confucianism. A practical philosophy originates from the cultivation of an integral personality extending to a peaceful reign all over the world, a system of eight items or eight gradations. It can only be imagined as an eight-layered globe, with one contained in the other like a set of carved ivory balls. The inmost being of the individual is at its very centre with its rays of light radiating forth, penetrating through the mind and heart and body, shining upon the external circumstance, be it the family, the state or all under Heaven. To a modern thinker, this cannot be a practical philosophy, because the gulf between the individual and society is too broad to be easily overpassed. But we understand that there is another link between them, the family, and unless the family is understood as the sort of clan described above, the chain cannot be properly comprehended.

But the difficulty lies in the correct interpretation of the first item called in Chinese "Kê Wu," and rendered here as "to ward off the desire of things." No less than eighteen different explanations could be found of this single term. The original sense became obsolete, and Tseng Tze did not annotate on it, perhaps in ancient times it was too plain to need any explanation. Moreover, we cannot definitely say that the original term was so multiple in its meaning as to tolerate eighteen different interpretations. It could have only one single idea: "Wu" means simply "things", and "Kê" means "to ward off," "to measure," "to let something come," "to arrive at," etc.

We need only take three explanations into consideration: first, the most ancient and authoritative; the second, the most prevalent and widely adopted, and the third, the translation given above. First, according to Chêng Hsüan, the famous annotator in the Han dynasty on Classics, "Kê" means "to let come" and "Wu" means "affairs" or "things". In his opinion, if one knows goodness in profundity, then good things will come or be attracted to oneself; the same with evil. This corresponds with the teaching of Confucius in that "If I want Love, and lo! Love is there"; and it can be equally inferred that "If I want evil, and evil will also be there." This is the most ancient explanation, but its weakness lies in that the knowledge of things good or evil must be there before these things could be attracted to oneself. The process is the reverse of that stated in the text which points plainly to a way of acquiring knowledge; otherwise as a worldly experience of life, this is profoundly true.

Next, we come to Chu Hsi's interpretation of "Kê Wu" as the "investigation of things." We quote his words:

"The meaning of the expression, 'The perfecting of knowledge depends on the investigation of things,' is this: If we wish to carry our knowledge to the utmost, we must investigate the principles of all things we come into contact with, for the intelligent mind of man is certainly formed to know, and there is not a single thing in which its principles do not inhere. But so long as all principles are not investigated, man's knowledge is incomplete. On this account, the *Great Learning*, at the outset of its lessons, instructs the learner, in regard to all things in the world, to proceed from what knowledge he has of their principles, and pursue his investigation of them, till he reaches the extreme point. After exerting himself in this way for a long time, he will suddenly find himself possessed of a wide and far-reaching penetration. Then, the qualities of all things, whether external or internal, the subtle or the coarse, will all be apprehended, and the mind, in its entire substance and its relations to things, will be perfectly informed. This is called the investigation of things. This is called the perfection of knowledge." [203]

In our modern view, this is the work of a scientist and a philosopher combined. Could one by this process of investigation of things become sincere in thoughts and rectified in heart? There seems to be a lack of psychological necessity for this change, and also lack of logical sequence. Moreover, we doubt that the knowledge of things can be exhausted by "investigating one thing today, and another thing tomorrow," as Chu Hsi said. The famous scholar Wang Yang Ming experimented with this process himself by sitting before a bamboo and "investigating" it. Perhaps he concentrated his thoughts on it, he meditated on it, but after three days he fell sick and gave up this "investigation".

The third explanation upon which the translation above was based, was given by Ssu-ma Kuan, a statesman and historian in the Sung dynasty. "Things", according to his explanation, refer to the external objects, all desirable things as music, women, hunting, etc. "To ward off" these things means subjectively to avoid the desire for them. In other words, the vital urge must be somehow silenced before even ordinary knowledge can be acquired; yet this still lingers on the mental plane. As taught in every religion of the world, true knowledge descends into a clean receptacle only when it is entirely purified of vital desires. This applies to modern times just as to olden times.

The opposing view is that the *Great Learning* was meant to be taught to young scholars of the state, mostly princes and specially talented students from all over the land. It was not meant for the training of recluses, hermits or Sannyasins, but we must remember that, just because they were to hold power in their hands afterwards, they were given such an education in youth. The same idea was adopted by countries in south-eastern Asia; even nowadays the youths of noble families are initiated as Buddhist monks and lead an austere life for a certain period before they are called back to secular life to enter office. The "mysteries" of ancient Greece had perhaps some sort of similar discipline. In any case, it was a sound principle to check the desire for things in the luxurious environment to which the young noble princes were accustomed, so that when the reins of government were held by them later, fewer dangers would accrue to themselves and to the common people. Yet there was no rigorous training nor religious discipline of any kind; youths were taught to ward off desire for external things so that knowledge could be acquired. It was a medium path without any radical measure, so that vitality was still carefully fostered for the cultivation of personality.

.

203.   Commentary on *The Great Learning* by Chu Hsi; trl. by Legge. *The Four Books*, pp. 322–323, Shanghai ed.

Chapter XIII

TZE SSU

Other discourses between the Master and this disciple can be found in the Elder and Younger Tai's *Commentaries on Rites*, from which a collected work entitled "Tseng Tze" came into being. This work had originally (during the Han dynasty) 18 chapters, but eight chapters were lost and the present edition has only 10 chapters. This book was annotated by Yüan Yuan (1764–1849 A.D.) but as an independent work it was not much read, in spite of its famous annotator.

Confucianism, from the viewpoint of its philosophy, especially in its psychological training, has another very important work which was read by every scholar. It comprises mostly sayings of Confucius, composed by Tze Ssu, his grandson. Originally it was included in *Li Chi* as its 31st chapter, but singled out in the Sung dynasty as an independent work included in the series of Four Books. The title of this book is in Chinese *Chung Yung*, variously translated as "Juste Milieu," or

"L'invariable Milieu," or "Medium constans vel sempiternum," or "The Constant Medium," or "The State of Equilibrium and Harmony," or "The Doctrine of the Mean," etc. etc.

Etymologically the word "chung" has the idea of "just hitting the mark," as in shooting. The target is hit just at its centre, and so it is "right" or "correct". All those secondary ideas as "centre", "medium", "mean", etc. are deduced therefrom. "Yung" means the "use" or "constancy". These two words taken together have been interpreted as a principle "not inclined towards any side" and hence of keeping to the middle, and of a constancy which means unchange-ability. What is described as constant and unchangeable is the Path (Tao or Truth); superficially it may be rendered as "The Doctrine of the Right and Constant Path."

Before entering into any discussion of this book, there is the need of explaining certain unnecessary if not entirely false conceptions of this doctrine. Usually we say that we are taking a middle path in our daily life, not going to either extreme, and thus we keep a normal standard. We try to maintain ourselves on the average level, being neither too good nor too bad, but that was not meant by this doctrine. Another misunderstanding is the going only half way and leaving something unfinished, not persevering to the final degree, and hence to rest in some slight imperfection. We often see cases in fine arts when the artist intentionally leaves something unfinished, and by that imperfection the reader or observer is pointed towards a higher perfection which can be imagined, but that was not meant here. We can only take the imperfection in arts as an unexpressed perfection, and the thing unfinished as already finished. If the doctrine is of the right and constant path, that artistic imperfection pertains to the "right" as well.

In our daily life, we see it is always advisable not to go to extremes. And it is said in the *Book of Changes* on the "nine at the top" of the first hexagram: "Arrogant dragon will have cause to repent," Someone who goes to extremes meets with misfortune. In time he exhausts himself. Arrogance refers to one who "knows how to press forward but not how to draw back, one who knows existence but not annihilation, knows something about winning but nothing about losing." This seems to be the basis of such a proposition. But it is further said: "It is only the holy man who understands how to press forward and how to draw back, who knows existence and annihilation as well, without losing the right Path. The holy man alone can do this." [204]

But it can also be easily seen that a half-way solution or compromise may or may not be the right way. If we build a dike of ten thousand feet, as one of our modern scholars argued, we must go to the extreme of not leaving an anthole unstopped, lest the water may pierce through it and, gradually enlarging it, ultimately destroy the whole dike. In that case then, we cannot allow any slight imperfection leaving the complete perfection to be imagined. The question is therefore not one of going to the extreme or not, but one of the right thing to be done in the right way at the right time, and just to the point. This Book treats of such a subject.

It must once again be remarked here that the general method adopted in this pamphlet in treating all the subjects is "to explain Classics by Classics." There was a noted master in the Sung dynasty who said: "All the six Classics are foot-notes to my philosophy." We do not doubt his boldness in making such a statement. Evidently it was a reaction to that pedantry in his times that never enabled anyone to withdraw from endless, valueless and senseless hairsplitting work of erudite exegeses which, having exhausted the vitality of a scholar for a whole life, ultimately led him nowhere. Nevertheless, we doubt whether his was the right attitude towards the Classics. It seems that one must first have had his enlightenment from elsewhere, or have established his own philosophy before one can successfully utilize the ancient texts as footnotes. In fact, many eminent scholars have done the same thing, but refrained from being so outspoken and straightforward. Most of the Classics (if not all) are sufficiently capacious, generous and inexhaustible in their resources so as to let any one draw upon them for his own benefit. But injustice must not be done to them by reading different meanings into the text, or twisting the original idea to suit one's own purpose. Correct interpretations are limited, but far-fetched explanations and theories are endless. So we venture to put all the commentaries aside and make a direct approach to the text itself.

·

204.   *I Ching*, Baynes' trl., Vol. II, p. 16, with a slight adjustment of wording.

This is a comparatively higher method, for it presupposes a correct understanding of a good number of texts, yet it is a surer one.

The text opens with these words:

"What Heaven has conferred (upon man) is called the Nature, and accordance with this Nature is called the Path (Tao), and the following of this Path is called culture."

Here we see a real, orthodox Confucian teaching that man's nature is something conferred upon or ordained by Heaven (or God) and this nature is purely good. As a human being endowed with this nature, it is therefore his duty to develop this goodness to the fullest extent. It is a simple teaching that persisted through all the ages. We cannot but conclude that this is the description of the psychic nature, the divinity in man, as inferred from not only this passage, but also from Mencius. But it cannot be denied that human nature can be divided into the higher and the lower, or the sattvic, rajasic and tamasic according to Indian philosophy; apart from the higher or the sattvic, the rest may not be necessarily good. But in Confucianism there is a correlative to nature known as habit. Man is born good *a priori*, but his habits may be bad *a posteriori*. Hsün Tze, also a Confucian during the period of the Warring States, held the theory that human nature is fundamentally bad; goodness is artificial and therefore must be cultivated. Yang Tze in the Han dynasty held that human nature is mixed with both good and bad elements co-existent in it. In these three theories, we see only a difference in the point of emphasis on one single aspect: the last refers to simple human nature in various degrees of goodness; the second emphasizes the lower nature which is called habit by orthodox Confucians, and the first points to the psychic nature of those highly developed souls or "superior men." Nearly the entire ancient education was aimed at the development of superior men.

Tao or Path is sometimes translated as the Truth[205]. A path that is in accordance with this Truth is to be followed in the sense that this Truth is to be discovered and revealed and cultivated. So the passage above is immediately followed by the next below:

"With regard to this Path, it cannot be left for an instant. If it could be left, it would not be the Path."

In reading this passage, a Vedantin would perhaps say: this sounds very much like our Atman. What else in the world cannot be left for an instant other than Atman or Brahman? We are all That, and we are all in That, and how is it possible to leave That for an instant as an instant is also That? A Taoist would also claim that this is exactly the description of his Tao, no longer the monopoly of a Confucian. A Neo-

---

205.   The interpolation made by Legge as "the Path (of duty)" is quite irrelevant.

Confucian in the Sung and Ming dynasties would also say that this is simply "logos" ; and it should be again remarked that this "logos" means something else other than its original verbal sense. Furthermore, what would those enlightened people say who see God in everything? It is no parody to say that God cannot be left for an instant. And we read further:

"On this account, the superior man is ever cautious and careful of that which he does not see, and fearful and apprehensive to that which he does not hear.

"There is nothing more visible than what is hidden, and nothing more manifest than what is minute. Therefore the superior man is watchful over himself when he is alone." [206]

"That which" one does not see or hear refers to That above, which is beyond the reach of our sensory faculties of seeing and hearing, yet not on this account being hidden or unmanifest. A right attitude towards That is therefore to be vigilant and apprehensive, to be devoted in a silent reverence as in state of constant prayer or meditation. If we say That, it seems to be impersonal, something of neuter gender, yet it makes little difference whether it is to That or to Her or to Him that a prayer is addressed or the meditation and concentration are directed. Again, if we say "above", it is also a way of speaking. Traditionally it is said "as if He (or She or That) is above, and as if He (or She or That) is on the right and on the left." In this way one is ever watchful over oneself when alone, because the "as if" or Divine Presence is there, and one is no longer alone. Understood in this context, the passages above are never inexplicable. In our modern language, these first three passages deal with the divine Nature in man, and the ubiquity of God, and the right attitude of worshipping God in a manner of consecration.

Here follows a passage of psychology which deals with equilibrium and harmony in the microcosm, the man, who is related to and corresponds with the Macrocosm, the Universe. We read:

"While there are no stirrings of pleasure, anger, sorrow, or joy, it is said to be a state of equilibrium. When those feelings have been expressed with proper accentuation under control, that may be called the state of harmony. This equilibrium is the great fundament of all under Heaven, and this Harmony is the universal Path.

"Let this state of equilibrium and Harmony be attained, and heaven and earth will find their correct places, and everything will be nourished and fostered."

Here ends the first chapter of this Book. The next ten chapters are quotations from the sayings of Confucius to explain this first one. The

---

206. This is the literal rendering which Legge made, considering it unintelligible to an English reader, which the author thinks otherwise.

twelfth chapter contains the words of Tze Ssu. The next eight chapters which follow are partly his own illustrations and partly quotations of Confucius. The twenty-first to the thirty-third (or final) chapters contain his own words with sporadic quotations from the Sage, but mostly from the *Book of Poetry*.

It is noteworthy in the passage above that "anger" and "sorrow" were mentioned together with "pleasure" and "joy". It seems that "anger" and "sorrow" were not considered totally bad emotions that had to be abolished or eradicated from one's reactions. Later scholars said the children of Kung's family knew not how to be angry, and the children of Yen's family knew not how to blame or to quarrel, but that was probably a later invention. Only a clause here needs perhaps a little explanation: viz. "expressed with proper accentuation under control." Literally the original means "in accordance with the time-beating," as in music. This does not mean any wild outburst of feelings, but the natural and right expression of the feeling with moderation and temperance, or as Legge puts it: "in due degree." Time-beating in music analogizes hitting the point at the right time. It was not taught to entirely eliminate anger and sorrow, though they had to be held under control; history teaches us that anger is in a certain way healthy, for when rightly expressed it can cure certain diseases. Sorrow proved always hurtful, but to a certain extent it could maintain a state of sobriety and have a purifying effect on vital upsurges and help growth. In any case, they were not considered as too detrimental to one's progress on the spiritual path. (Here we can also mark a subtle point of difference between this system and Buddhism in which anger is entirely ruled out as one of the "Three Poisons.")

With regard to "joy" or "happiness", the approach is slightly different. It has been calculated that the Chinese word for "joy" has appeared in the *Analects* 45 times, and there was no single word for "distress" or "suffering". A spiritual ecstasy was meant and experienced by the disciples. In an enigmatic way, it was said by the scholars in the Sung dynasty "to learn this joy and be joyful over this learning" or "to learn is to learn this, and to be happy and joyful is to be happy and joyful over this." Now, the Vedantin would perhaps again say that this "This" is "That", and the "Joy" is no other than Brahmananda. Indeed, in essence the truth must be the same, but being represented by different systems the outward aspects may be entirely different. On the other hand, "distress" or "world-suffering" was a later introduction into the consciousness of ancient Chinese people by Buddhism. It cannot be said that ancient Chinese where happier than later generations, but what was taught emphasized the more positive aspect of life that tended to increase vitality and lead to a greater Joy and Enlightenment, rather than the negative tendency which pointed towards Nirvana and Emancipation.

The psychological state of "equilibrium" cannot be easily attained. In Chinese language, both "mind" and "heart" were represented by the same word. "Equilibrium" in the original sense meant "resting at the centre." It is a state of clarity or enlightenment in which one feels both the mind and heart at rest in the centre of one's whole being, inexpressibly pure and limpid and full of light. The traditional description of such a state is the "that logos — reasonably misinterpreted as Reason — has manifested" in such a person; and the keen observer, usually one's Guru, can discern this very well through the eyes, the doors of one's soul. We usually say that the psychic being of such a person has come to the front, and there can be no mistake in the right recognition of such a psychic state by others. In this, there can be no stirring of passions and feelings such as the waves of pleasure, anger, sorrow and joy that toss about merely on the surface. Instead, there is only the Joy or Delight of the Infinite, much more deep and placid and serene, which may be called Ananda.

"Harmony" refers to activity. There must be activity and outward expression before Harmony can be talked of. This can easily be grasped in music. There can be indeed silent music, but music itself has harmony as its soul. Without harmony music is but a number of disorganized sounds and notes, and no longer music. But then even a single note has its harmony with regard to the number of its vibrations. The same is the case with the activities of man. A highly developed mind may conduct a person to act according to certain principles, but other parts of his being may or may not follow. Thus he may still not be free from self-contradiction or incongruity; in any case there is still lacking of harmony in his whole being. But once the psychic being has come to the front, the condition will be otherwise. He cannot fail to have his whole being integralized and act according to certain principles involuntarily and spontaneously without much mental effort. Sometimes the psychic being might be obscured when it has drawn back, or when the said "equilibrium" is lost; nevertheless, that obscurity can be obliterated, just as the sun cannot be permanently veiled by clouds. It is just this function of the divinity in man, the Nature of supreme goodness, and expressed in such a way that there can be no more fitting description for it than "harmony". Here we find almost the exact concordance of the spiritual philosophy of Sri Aurobindo and this ancient Chinese system.

Harmony is found everywhere. It is in man; it is in the universe. A baby may cry for the whole day without becoming hoarse, because there is in it the supreme harmony, as Lao Tze says. Furthermore, if such a state of equilibrium and harmony is reached in oneself, it can be extended to one's external environment, so that everything above and below can find its proper place and both heaven and earth are at peace. It is no longer merely a subjective quality, it is directly an objective influence. This influence, large or small, exercised far or near, depends upon the power at its radiating centre, or the degree of revelation. If the person is in disequilibrium or in disharmony with himself, then no external situation can be controlled by him. It is even doubtful whether he can live at all. It is equally doubtful whether or not any object, animate or inanimate, can ever exist in the universe without equilibrium and harmony. The crow parliament may raise a noise disconcerting to our ears, yet amongst these crows themselves there must still be a harmony. It is a universal truth. A stone will go on incessantly falling if it loses its equilibrium, until it recovers its ground again somewhere and becomes static. It is no mystical teaching but a plain psychological fact that such a state must be attained before one can successfully cultivate his person, regulate his family and, finally, govern a state. The process is one which starts at the centre of a globe, as it were, and step-by-step enlarges itself, until its influence is extended in all directions.

To illustrate such a principle, several passages of the sayings of Confucius as quoted in this Book may be sufficient:

Chung Ni said: "The superior man acts according to the Right and the Constant, the small man acts contrary to the Right and Constant. The superior man in acting according to the Right and Constant, keeps a timely right course. The small man in acting contrary to the Right and Constant, is reckless and mannerless."

The Master said: "The Path of the Right and Constant is perhaps supreme! People have long been unable to follow it."

The Master said: "Men all say, 'We are wise'; but being driven forward and taken in a net, a trap, or a pitfall, they know not how to escape. Men all say, 'We are wise'; but having chosen the course of the Right and Constant, they are not able to keep it for a month."

The Master said: "With regard to the character of (Yen) Whei, he made choice of the Right and Constant, and whenever he got hold of one virtue, he cultivated it diligently in his bosom, and did not lose it."

The Master said: "All states under heaven may be perfectly ruled; dignities and emoluments may be declined; naked spearedges may be trampled under feet; but to be perfectly right and constant is impossible."

The question of the Right and Constant is a philosophical one. In ancient times this was entirely relegated to the field of Propriety and in it there was always a meticulous treatment of the exact thing to be done on a certain occasion, that being considered as right. Tze Ssu must have understood this quite well, but he illustrated it in an ingenious yet general way. In his interpretation it is to act in accord with one's position or situation or environment. There is a contentment in one's lot and yet it is no blind submission of one's fate because, above all, the appointment of Heaven (or God) is to be waited for. Here one acts with regularity and steadfastness in a state of cheerfulness, yet with much self-retrospection and self-restraint. It is conformism in a deeper sense, but carried out with firmer assurance of the soul. We read:

"The superior man does what is proper to the station in which he is; he does not desire to go beyond this.

"In a position of wealth and honour, he does what is proper to a position of wealth and honour. In a poor and low position, he does what is proper to a poor and low position. Situated among barbarous tribes, he does what is proper to a situation among barbarous tribes. In a position of sorrow and difficulty, he does what is proper to a position of sorrow and difficulty. The superior man can find himself in no situation in which he is not himself.

"In a high position, he does not treat with contempt his inferiors. In a low position, he does not court the favour of his superiors. He rectifies himself, and seeks for nothing from others, so that he has no dissatisfactions. He does not murmur against Heaven above, nor grumble against men below.

"Thus it is that the superior man abides in peace, waiting for the appointment of Heaven, while the small man walks in dangerous paths, looking for lucky occurrences.

"The Master said: 'In archery, we have something like the way of the superior man. When the archer misses the centre of the target, he turns round and seeks for the cause of his failure in himself.'" [207]

What is meant by Chung Yung is best explained in this passage. The example of archery shows that it is a central Path hitting just at the point. This has little to do with the "Mean" or mediocrity. Moreover, to do what is proper to one's station means to keep a constancy in conformity with the prevalent mode. The idea is broader than merely to keep to one's duty which may not be the destiny of the man. But what is the right thing to be done by the superior man? It was outlined in hind items by governing of a state, as the superior men were trained for such work, such as the "honouring of virtue and talents," "affection towards relatives," "indulgent treatment of men from a distance," etc. etc. together with their causes and effects. But these are problems pertaining to the field of political philosophy which need not be treated here. Yet there was a psychological basis with regard to the cultivation of the person which we find nowhere in ancient literature so excellently elucidated as in this Book, i.e. sincerity. And we read the following passages:

"Sincerity is the way of Heaven. The attainment of sincerity (or 'to be sincere') is the way of Man. Sincerity involves hitting at what is right without an effort, an apprehension without thinking. He who follows easily and leisurely the right way must be a sage. He who attains to sincerity is he who chooses what is good, and holds it fast.

" (To this attainment there are requisite) the extensive study of it, accurate inquiry about it, careful reflection on it, clear discrimination of it, and the earnest practice of it.

"The superior man, while there is anything he had not studied, or

207.   Based on Legge's translation, with certain adjustments of wording.

while in what he has studied there is anything he has not mastered, will not abandon his effort. While there is anything he has not inquired about or anything in what he has inquired about which he does not know, will not abandon his effort. While there is anything which he has not reflected on, or anything in what he has reflected on which he does not apprehend, he will not abandon his effort. While there is anything which he has not discriminated, or his discrimination is not clear, he will not abandon his effort. If there be anything which he has not practised, or his practice fails in earnestness, he will not abandon his effort. If another man succeed by one effort, he will make a hundred efforts. If another man succeed by ten efforts, he will make a thousand.

"If a man is actually capable of proceeding in this way, though dull he will surely become intelligent; though weak he will surely become strong."

"To be enlightened through sincerity can be ascribed to nature. To be sincere through enlightenment can be ascribed to culture. With sincerity, one shall be enlightened, with enlightenment, one shall be sincere."

"Sincerity is that whereby self-perfection is effected, and the Path is that to which one must direct himself.

"Sincerity is the end and beginning of things; without sincerity there would be nothing. On this account, the superior man treasures the attainment of sincerity (as the most excellent thing).

"Sincerity does not stop at one's self-perfection, it is also for the perfection of others. Self-perfection involves the embodiment of Divine's Love (Jen), and the perfection of others shows wisdom. (Both these are) virtues of man's nature; it is a way by which a union of the external and internal is effected. Therefore it is right (or 'fit') when duly carried out in time."

"It is he who is possessed of the utmost sincerity under heaven, who can have the fullest development of his nature. Capable of developing his nature to the fullest extent, he is also capable of doing the same to the nature of other men. Capable of developing to the fullest extent the nature of other men, he can do the same to the nature of everything. Capable of developing to the fullest extent the nature of everything, he can assist the evolution and foster everything between Heaven and Earth. Able to assist the evolution and to foster everything between Heaven and Earth, he may with Heaven and Earth form a ternion."

"Next would be the cultivation of perfection. In perfection there must be sincerity. Whatever is sincere will take an external form. Taking a form, it will become manifest. Being manifest, it will become illuminating. Illuminating, it will be inspiring. Inspiring others, they will be changed by it. Changed by it, they are transformed. It is only the utmost sincerity under heaven that can transform."

"By the Path of the utmost sincerity, foreknowledge is possible. When a state or family is about to flourish there must be certain auspicious omens; and when it is about to perish, there must be unlucky omens. These are seen in the divinations through milfoils and tortoises, and appear in the movements of the four limbs. When a calamity or a blessing is about to come, the good shall certainly be foreknown by him, and the evil also. Therefore possessed of the utmost sincerity, one is like God."

"Therefore in the utmost sincerity there is no cessation. Not ceasing, it continues long. Continuing long, it evidences itself. Evidencing itself, it reaches far and wide. Reaching far and wide, it becomes large and substantial. Being large and substantial, it becomes high and brilliant.

"Being large and substantial, so it supports all things. Being high and brilliant, so it covers all things. Reaching far and continuing long, so it accomplishes all things.

"Largeness and substantiality par with Earth. Height and brilliancy par with Heaven. Far-reaching and long-continuity have no bounds.

"In this way, without display, it becomes manifest; without movement, it transforms; and without effort, it accomplishes things."

"It is only he who, possessed of the utmost sincerity, can manipulate the great principles under heaven, and establish the great fundamentals of mankind, and understand the transforming and nurturing processes of Heaven and Earth. And thus, there is the thing to depend upon."

"A man of Love (Jen), how honest is he! And as an abyss, how deep is he! And like Heaven, how vast is he!

"Who can know this, but he who is intelligent and wise as a sage, acquainted with the virtue of Heaven?" [208]

This is a very simple and plain exposition which starts from a factual statement that nothing can exist in the universe without sincerity. When sincerity has reached its utmost degree in the individual, and when one has penetrated into the realm of sagehood, then it is possible for him to transform things. In the present world situation, we cannot expect any such sincerity to exist in the diplomatic relationship between nations, yet this is the only remedy and does exist to a certain extent at certain times; but on the Path of Yoga, as the Divine Mother more than once remarked, it is the only Protection. And how utterly true we find that it constitutes the first condition of psychological perfection in the individual! We marvel with what concord this universal truth is taught whether in the East or in the West, in ancient or in modern times. With regard to the transformation, She has also said: "When you are truly changed, everything around you will also be changed." [209]

·

208.   *ditto.*
209.   Vide *Words of the Mother*, III, p. 98.

Chapter XIV

MENCIUS

The rest of the *Book Chung Yung* treats of the highest attainments of Man, or the "superior man," and the establishment of a divine sovereignty over the earth. Traditionally, ever since the Han dynasty, this was called a knowledge that is "a link between Heaven and Man." No paradise is promised in the other world or this, but the ideal of a spiritual rule that brings peace and happiness, culture and transformation to all beings in a well-organized humanity is set before later generations. This ideal is the Path (Tao) that "...set up between heaven and earth, there is no malediction; presented before gods and spirits, doubts do not arise; and waiting for the sanction of sages of a hundred generations after, there will be no misgivings." (*Chung Yung*, XXIX, 3, 4) Before such an ideal, honorable values held high in later ages such as theism, heroism, charity, philanthropy, humanitarianism etc., naturally fell away. It is not a Kingdom of God, it is a kingdom of the godlike Man, the highest transformed being in the universe.

With regard to the material phase of such an ideal we read the following passage from *Li Chi*, the chapter on Great Unity, too often quoted in recent times:

"When the Great Way (Tao) prevails, all under Heaven is for the common benefit. Select the virtuous and the able in the service of the government. Observe the principle of faithfulness and cultivate cordiality in the general intercourse of man. Therefore, one will not only reverence one's own parents and love one's own children, but do the same to those of others. The aged shall die in peace, the young shall render service for the welfare of the community. The infant shall be well cared for and brought up. Widowers, widows, orphans and the invalid shall be under the protection of the government. Each man shall have his share in the general development of the community, in accordance with his ability, and each woman shall have a happy married life. It is deplorable that natural resources should be unexploited, yet it does not follow that wealth should be privately owned for selfish ends. It is deplorable that human efforts should not be well utilized, yet these efforts should not be directed toward the fulfilment of selfish interests. In a community as such, tricks and intrigues will be obliterated, and robbery, larceny and all kinds of grossness will be eliminated. It will be unnecessary to bolt the gate, for no one will think of stealing. This is called 'The Great Unity.'" [210]

Much dreamt of yet never promised by anyone, a Utopian state as such would be something like a happier world than our present one. Yet it is only on this basis that human culture may begin to flourish and rare geniuses may soar high. It would be vain to talk about the salvation of mankind or the improvement of society if the great unity is neglected and welfare to be brought to a special class or only to a chosen few. The unity of mankind is an ideal which everyone cherishes in our modern civilized world. We wonder how modern these thoughts appear, though they were formulated four centuries before Christ. The question is: has such an ideal state ever been realized? History tells that there were "Minor Comfortable Ages" in which this ideal had been partially realized. It was restricted only to districts and states, large or small, for longer or shorter periods, especially when the place was inhabited by some spiritual personage who might not necessarily be in any political position, but with high inner and outer accomplishments, whose influence extended far and wide. But a nation-wide realization of such a "Great Unity" has never taken place. It has remained until the present an ideal, yet, however large or broad, it is not of insurmountable height. As it pertains still to the physical world, it can ultimately be materialized some day in the infinite future as a final victory of a universal Truth, we believe.

After Tze Ssu, we come to Mong Tze, latinized as Mencius. In the

Sung dynasty, he was canonized as the fourth great Philosopher after Yen Tze, Tseng Tze, and Tze Ssu, and was called also the "next Sage," meaning next only to Confucius. To know about him we must reflect again on the ancient history of his times.

After the death of Confucius, China entered into a period of the Warring States (circa 479–246 B.C.). The once most powerful state in the north, the dukedom of Tsin, was divided by three Houses, and the once equally powerful state in the northeast, the dukedom of Ch'i, was usurped by a minister Tien. The state Ch'u in the south which had formerly annexed all the small fiefs along the Han River, still retained its power, but became also gradually weakened and had to align itself with all the other states to cope with the new power arisen in the north-west, Ch'in. In the southeast, two large states were in constant battle which ended with the annexation of Wu by Yue. It was a period of endless fighting in which each warlord of a state styled himself as King, and those kings were used as toys in the hands of a class of dark politicians, called "wandering sophists." In spite of all that, it was also a period of philosophy in which the "hundred schools" arose, ending with the unification of all the states into a great empire by military force, the formation of the Ch'in dynasty. Its first ruler or the First Emperor (246–210 B.C.) had left an immortal stigma on the history of Chinese culture by the burning of books and persecution of scholars;

.

210. *The Essence of Chinese Culture* by Chi-Tun Chang, pp. 10–13

that subject has been treated before.

In such a period Mencicus was born, for his date was supposed to be 372 or 371 to 289 B.C. He was a descendant of the first noble House of the Lu state, and his mother was a talented lady whose name was in the "Biographies of Distinguished Women" by Lin Hsian. That she changed her residence thrice for the education of her child is a story very well known. But whether Mencius was a disciple of Tze Ssu or a disciple of his disciple, is still a question not settled. Certain dates recorded in the *Ancient History* by Ssu-ma Tsien proved to be inconsistent according to modern calculation, hence unreliable. Tze Ssu probably lived twenty years longer than the traditional record of sixty-two, but that Mencius was a disciple of his disciple seems to be nearer to the truth. There is no doubt that his knowledge was directly received from the lineage of Confucius through the school of the sage's grandson.

The life of Mencius had almost the same fate as that of Confucius. He travelled to different states for employment in order to realize his high ideals — a Royal Path of Peace in contrast to the then prevalent Heroic Path of Might — but he failed just as surely as did his predecessor. He went to the courts of Ch'i and Liang, had constant audiences with those kings, but his words were not adopted though his person was respected. In his old age as in Confucius' he had no alternative but to work as a philosopher in holding discussions with a group of disciples, his words being recorded and preserved as books; at the same time he was reputed to be a great mathmatician and, as we see from his works, he was actually also an expert philologist.

The present work of Mencius, supposed to be a work written in his late years, was actually not. There are a number of evidences on this: the most powerful one is that a number of disciples in this book were called "Tze" or "master", which was not the customary way for a teacher to address his pupils. Furthermore, in the opening chapter, King Whei of the Liang State was mentioned, and in Part I, Mencius called him "Your Majesty" no less than ten times. But during the life-time of King Whei, he had never styled himself a king; he was only posthumously honoured so. If the Book was written by Mencius himself, he could not have been so inexact. Moreover, the story of the state Yen being smitten and taken possession by Ch'i during the reign of King Seuen actually happened many years later. The perplexity shows that this book was not even written by his disciples, but by the third generation after him, or the disciples of his disciples.

This work is probably familiar to every scholar even nowadays because, ever since the Sung dynasty, it was included in the Four Books and these were used as text-books in grammar schools, hence also used in the first public examinations. The text is in plain and clear prose without any difficult reading, though the meaning in a few passages remains obscure. It contains seven fascicles, each being divided into two parts, comprising altogether 259 chapters with 35,226 words. But the text used by Chao Chi in the second century A.D., when he annotated this Book, had 261 chapters with 34,685 words, as noted in his Introduction. The three chapters lacking might be due to a difference of division, and the surplus number of words due to later interpolations. It was also mentioned in Chao Chi's "Introduction" that apart from these seven fascicles, there were another four fascicles in existence, which he refrained from annotating because they seemed to be definitely spurious works, judged both by the style and the contents; these four fascicles were also lost. There are still other sporadic and miscellaneous quotations from Mencius in several books written in the Han dynasty not found in the present text, but they are of minor importance, so they need not be discussed here.

With regard to the contents of this work, it treated mainly of political philosophy. His ideals were the same as those taught in the Confucian school. When the rulers made their fiefs independent states and styled themselves kings, a system of absolute monarchy generally prevailed, and conflicts between them naturally arose. Amidst these, what Mencius propounded was a Royal Path of Peace, with historical evidences showing that it was also an easy path judged by the circumstances of his times; "with half of the merit of ancients, double their achievements could surely be realized." (Bk. II, Part I) His doctrine was exceedingly democratic in our modern view. We quote only a few passages:

(Mencius) said: "The ruler of a state advances to office a man of talents and virtue as a matter of provisionary exigency, thereby causing the low to overstep the honorable, and strangers to overstep his acquaintances; should he not be careful in this?

"When all those about you say, — 'This is a man of talents and virtue,' you may not for that believe it. When your great officers all say, — 'This is a man of talents and virtue,' neither may you for that believe it. When all the people of the state say, — 'This is a man of talents and virtue,' then examine into the case, and when you find that the man is such, employ him. When all those about you say, — 'This man won't do,' don't listen to them. When all your great officers say, — 'This man won't do,' don't listen to them. When all the people of the state say, — 'This man won't do,' then examine into the case, and when you find that the man won't do, send him away.

"When all those about you say, — 'This man deserves death,' don't listen to them. When all your great officers say, — 'This man deserves death,' don't listen to them. When all the people of the state say, — 'This man deserves death,' then inquire into the case, and when you see that the man deserves death, put him to death. So it can be said that he is killed by all of the people in the state." [211]

Mencius said: "The people are the most important; the gods of the land and grain come next; the sovereign is the last and least." [212]

211. *Mencius*, Bk. I, Pt. II, Ch. VII, 3—5.
212. *Ibid*, Bk. VII, Pt. II, Ch. XIV, 1.

Mencius said to the king Seuen of Chi: "When the prince regards his ministers as his hands and feet, his ministers regard their prince as their belly and heart; when he regards them as his dogs and horses, they regard him as any other man; when he regards them as earth-clods or as grass, they regard him as a robber or an enemy." [213]

According to these passages, a system monarchical in form but democratic in spirit was promulgated by Mencius. But ultimately to whom does a scholar owe his allegiance? It was certainly not to a prince or a king, and even not to the people or state. It was rather to the Tao or Path (or Truth) that he should be permanently loyal and devoted. His Path to his conviction was the divine Decree of Heaven or God, a broad and even road carved and trodden by ancient sages before him, and that the same road would be followed by sages of later generations he had no doubts. Just as Confucius not only served his native country but travelled to other states, Mencius did the same. Both we sure of the Truth they held, and later generations had never considered them as disloyal or unpatriotic in any sense. On the contrary, nearly every act of theirs was taken as a standard.

We know that the central principle of the teachings of Confucius was Divine's Love. What was taught by the "Next Sage" was the same thing but with another principle next to and closely connected with it. It was Righteousness, which was indeed taught in the Confucian school, but formerly it gained no special prominence because it was included in the domain of Rites or Propriety in which it was taken as a matter of course and afterwards included in the Doctrine of the Right and Constant. It had never been so separately and emphatically stressed as was done by Mencius. The traditional illustration of these two principles forms a cross with the Divine's Love, a line descending vertically, and Righteousness extending to both sides in another line. In the psychic field the descent is a thing of cosmic nature, of which an identification can be found between the very depth of one's being and that in the universe, the so-called "heart of Heaven and Earth," while the extension is on the human level and especially on the mental plane. Righteousness implies reason, but this Reason is not purely intellectual; a grasp of Reality by the emotional nature is included. From very ancient to modern times, the Chinese mentality is never merely that of a logician or a legalist, it is largely that of a Confucian of which the humanist has his claim and it was with this teaching of Righteousness that Confucianism became the more complete and perfect, flourished exuberantly and was honestly glorified; as with warp and woof, it was woven into a piece.

Righteousness is a moral value nowadays known to everybody, but we must examine how Mencius understood it. In his exposition it was something diametrically opposed to another principle current in

.

213. *Mencius*, Bk. IV, Pt. II, Ch. III, 1.

his times, that of "profit" or "benefit". In his first interview with King Whei of the Liang state, he confronted this subject, and we read in the opening chapter of the book the following words:

Mencius went to see King Whei of Liang.

The king said: "Venerable Sir! since you have not counted a thousand miles too far to come here, could there be anything perhaps to profit my kingdom?"

Mencius replied: "Why must Your Majesty talk about profit? There must be only the principles of Love (Jen) and Righteousness (Yi).

"If Your Majesty say, 'What is to be done to profit my kingdom?' the great officers will say, 'What is to be done to profit our families?' and the inferior officers and the common people will say, 'What is to be done to profit our person? ' Superiors and inferiors will try to snatch this profit the one from the other, and the kingdom will be endangered... If Righteousness be put last and profit first, then (ultimately) people will not he satisfied without having snatched (the crown).

"There has never been a man of Love who neglected his parents. There has never been a man of Righteousness who left behind his king. Your Majesty can just say: Let there only be Love and Righteousness, and that would be all. Why must you talk about profit?" [214]

Wang Chung, a famous scholar in the Han dynasty, argued about this point saying that while "profit" as we normally understand it could be meant by the king, in another sense "benefit" could also have been meant, so there was no mistake in asking what might be beneficial to his state. But what Mencius emphasized was the two principles of Love and Righteousness, and material "profit" or "benefit" he placed beyond the scope of his consideration. We read further:

"Love is the comfortable habitation of man, and Righteousness is his right path.

"It is lamentable that such a comfortable dwelling should be left empty and uninhabitated, and the right path should be abandoned and not taken to." [215]

Mencius said: "Love is man's heart, and Righteousness is man's path.

"How lamentable is it to neglect the path and not pursue it, to lose this heart and not know enough to seek it again.

"When man's fowls and dogs are lost, they know to seek for them again, but they lose their heart, and do not know to seek for it.

"The means to learning is nothing else but to seek for the lost

---

214.   Bk. I, Pt. I, Ch. I, 1—6

215.   Bk. IV, Pt. I, Ch. X, 2—3.

heart." [216]

Sung Kên, being about to go to Ch'u, Mencius met him in Shih Kiu. "Master, where are you going?" asked Mencius.

"I have heard that the states Ch'in and Ch'u are fighting together," he replied, "so I am going to see the king of Ch'u and persuade him to cease hostilities. If he is not pleased, I shall go to see the king of Ch'in, and persuade him in the same way. Of the two kings I shall receive an assent from one of them."

Mencius said: "I myself venture not to ask about the particulars, but I should like to hear the general idea with which you are going to persuade them."

"I will tell them that it is unprofitable."

"Sir," said Mencius, "Your aim is great, but your argument, Sir, is no good.

"Sir, if you by reason of their own 'profit' advise the kings of Ch'in and Ch'u, and if the kings of Ch'in and Ch'u are pleased with the consideration of that profit so as to stop the movements of their armies, then all the soldiers of these armies will rejoice in the cessation of war, and find their pleasure in (the pursuit of) profit. Ministers will serve their sovereign for the profit of which they cherish and thought, sons, will serve their fathers, and younger brothers will serve their elder brothers, all for the profit they cherish — then sovereign and ministers, fathers and sons, younger and elder brothers, will all totally abandon

Love and Righteousness, and all contact each other with the idea of profit cherished in their breasts. There has never been such a society which has not fallen into ruins.

"Sir, if you use Love and Righteousness to persuade the kings of Ch'in and Ch'u, and if the kings of Ch'in and Ch'u are pleased with the consideration of Love and Righteousness so as to stop the movements of their armies, then all the soldiers of these armies will rejoice in the cessation of war, and find their pleasure in Love and Righteousness. Ministers will serve their sovereign with Love and Righteousness cherished in their bosoms, sons will serve their fathers, and younger brothers will serve their elder brothers, all with Love and Righteousness they cherish — and so, sovereign and ministers, fathers and sons, elder and younger brothers, will abandon the thought of 'profit' and cherish Love and Righteousness in their intercourse. There has never been such a state which has not risen to imperial sway. Why must you use the word 'profit'? " [217]

216. Bk. VI, Pt. I, Ch. XI, 1—4.

  Legge had rendered the word "heart" as "mind", which is permissible, and the "means" as "the great end." The difference seems to be small but, in inference, the discrepancy is evident. What is meant by "tao" in the original here is the "means" and not the "end"; the object of learning is something else. This would lead otherwise to a state of concentration on the Void which was taught in Taoism but not by Mencius.

217. Bk. VI, Pt. II, Ch. IV, 1—6.

Sung Kên was a great philosopher in the age of the Warring States, and was probably older than Mencius. Mencius addressed him as "Sir" or "Master" showing his respect, a case not common with Mencius. In our modern view, Sung Kên might be considered a pacifist, and his doctrines in brief can be found in the last chapter of *Djuang Tze*. His general principle of using persuasion on these two kings was perhaps a realistic one, showing the material losses and destructions which would ensue to both states etc., and could be interpreted as "unprofitable" or "unbeneficial". What Mencius held was something of a permanent truth, more idealistic, and considered as "a circuitous route," impractical and therefore unappreciated by those kings. Perhaps there was also no better way to spread a gospel of Peace among the warlords than to argue in a pragmatic spirit, foretelling the immediate consequence of ruin and destruction etc. But Mencius was not a pure pacifist. Even of ordinary values he held a different view. We read:

Mencius said: "Those who nowadays serve their sovereigns say, 'We can for our sovereign enlarge our territories and fill his treasuries and arsenals.' Such persons nowadays called 'good ministers' were in ancient times called 'robbers of the people.' If a sovereign does not follow the Path, nor has his mind bent on Love, to seek to enrich him is to enrich (the tyrant) King.

"Or (they will say,) 'We can for our sovereign form alliances with other states, so that our battles will be victorious.' Such persons are nowadays called 'good ministers,' but they were in ancient times called 'robbers of the people.' If a sovereign does not follow the Path, nor has his mind bent on Love, to seek to fight successful battles for him is to assist (the tyrant) King.

"Pursuing the path of the present day without changing its practices, a prince cannot remain in (the throne) for one morning, even if the whole empire were given to him." [218]

If these ancient views were taken too seriously, this would lead to a revaluation of all values. Further:

Mencius said: "There are men who say, 'I am skilful at marshalling troops, I am skilful at conducting a battle!' They ae great criminals.

"If the sovereign of a state love Benevolence (Jen), he will have no match all under heaven. ..." [219]

Mencius said: "Ch'iu acted as the chief officer to the head of the House of Chi, whose (evil) ways he was unable to change, while he exacted from the people double the grain formerly paid. Confucius said: 'He is no disciple of mine! Beat your drums and attack him, my boys!'

218.   Bk. VII Pt II, Ch. XI, 1—3.
219.   Bk. VI, Pt. II, Ch. IV, 1—2.

"In view of this fact, if a prince does not practise benevolent (Jen) policies, all those who enriched him were rejected by Confucius: How much more would he have rejected those who tried forcibly to fight for him? Fighting for the contention of territory, people are slaughtered till the fields are filled with them. Fighting caused by the contention of a city, people are slaughtered till the city is filled with them. This is what is called 'leading on the land to devour human flesh.' Death is not enough for such a crime.

"Therefore, those who are skilful to fight should suffer the highest punishment. Those who unite the princes (for warfare) should receive the secondary punishment. And those who exploit grassy fields and make compulsory divisions of land come next (as they do these things for assisting the warfare)." [220]

Such were the thoughts in the teachings of Confucius as understood and developed by Mencius. Compared with other schools of thought in his times, they were not less radical though very much contradictory to the prevailing current. We see plainly that these thoughts contained a very evident truth which has proved infallible through all ages and which could be testified to by historical facts. Its influence could not be ignored; that explains to a certain extent why the Chinese *as a race* remained unwarlike and peaceful.

According to this train of thought, a good government consists in the employment of the right men, but it depends ultimately on the prince himself. It is said that "virtue alone cannot be sufficient for the exercise of government; laws alone cannot put themselves into practice." [221]

"Therefore only the men of Love ought to be in high stations. When a man destitute of benevolence (Jen) is in a high station, he thereby disseminates his wickedness among all.

"When the prince has no principles (of Truth) with which he measures (Heaven's Will) [222], and all under him have no laws which they observe (in the discharge of their duties), when officers in the court have no faith in principles, and all workers and artisans have no belief in measurements, and when the superiors do not keep themselves to Righteousness, and inferiors violate the penal code, then it would be a sheer chance that any such state is preserved from destruction.

"Therefore it is said: 'It is not the exterior and interior walls being imperfectly built, or the supply of weapons offensive and defensive not being abundant, which constitutes the calamity of a kingdom. It is not the cultivable area not being extended, and stores and wealth not being accumulated , which occasions the ruin of a kingdom.' When superiors

.

220.   Bk. IV, Pt. I, Ch. XIV, 1—3.

221.   Bk. IV, Pt, 1, Ch. I, 3.

222.   This is based upon Chao Chi's annotation, which is reliable. Legge has rendered it "when the prince has no principles by which he examines (his administration)," understanding it as such.

do not observe the rules of propriety, and inferiors do not learn, then seditious people spring up, and that kingdom will perish in no time." [223]

Mencius said: "It is not worth while to slander those in offices, nor to blame governmental policies. It is only the great man who can rectify what is wrong in the sovereign's mind. If the ruler were benevolent (Jen), then all would be benevolent. If the ruler were righteous (Yi), then all would be righteous. If the ruler were correct, then all would be correct. Once the ruler being rectified, the kingdom will be (firmly) settled." [224]

In reviewing the history of the period of "Spring and Autumn," Mencius expressed his criticisms in the following words:

Mencius said: "The five lords of the princes were sinners against the three kings.[225] The princes of the present day are sinners against the five lords.[226] The great officers of the present day are sinners against the princes.

"The emperor visited the princes, which was called 'a tour of inspection.' The princes attended at the court of the emperor, which was called 'giving a report of office,' (as was a custom) in the spring to examine the ploughing, and supply the deficiency (of seed), and in autumn to examine the reaping, and assist where there was a deficiency (of the crop). On entering the boundaries of a state, when it was found that (new) ground was being reclaimed, and the fields well cultivated; if the old were nourished and the worthy honored; and if men of distinguished talents were placed in office: then the (prince) was rewarded with an addition to his territory. (On the other hand,) if, on entering a state, the ground was found left wild or overrun with weeds; if the old were neglected and the worthy unhonored; and if the offices were filled with harsh and braggart persons, then the (prince) was reprimanded. If (a prince) once omitted his attendance at court, he was punished by degradation of rank; if he did so a second time, he was deprived of a portion of his territory; if he did so a third time, then the six armies (of the imperial forces) were set in motion. Thus the emperor commanded the correction, but did not inflict any attack, while the princes inflicted an attack, but did not command any correction.

"Among the five lords the most glorious was the Duke Huan. At the assembly of princes in Kwei Chiu, the ox was bound but not slain to smear (the corners of their mouths) with the blood, and the articles of agreement were written in documents and buried. The first injunction in their agreement was, — 'Punish the unfilial; change not

223.   Bk. IV, Pt. I, Ch. I, 7—9.

224.   Bk. IV, Pt. I, Ch. XX, 1.

225.   The Three Kings were Yue of the Hsia dynasty, Tang of the Yin dynasty, Wen of the Chow dynasty.

226.   The Five lords of the princes were, Duke Huan of Ch'i, Duke Wen of Tsin, Duke Mo of Ch'in, Duke Siang of Sung, Duke Djuang of Ch'u.

the son who has been appointed legal heir; exalt not a concubine to the rank of wife.' The second was, — 'Honor the worthy, and maintain (lit. "nourish" or "cultivate") the talented, in order to give distinction to the virtuous.' The third was, — 'Respect the old, and be kind to the young. Be not forgetful of strangers and travellers.' The fourth was, — 'Let not offices be hereditary, nor let officers have multiple offices. In the selection of officers let the consideration only be the right men. Let not a ruler take it on himself to put to death a great officer.' The fifth was, — 'Follow no crooked policy in making rules. Impose no restriction on the sale of grain (to other states in years of famine). Let there be no donations of land (in forming states) without (first) announcing them (to the emperor). ' It was then proclaimed 'All we who have united in this agreement shall hereafter maintain amicable relations.' The princes of the present day all violate these five regulations, and therefore I say that the princes of the present day are sinners against the five lords.

"The crime of him who enlarges the wicked (order) of the prince is small, but the crime of him who anticipates and aids that wickedness is great. The officers of the present day all anticipate and aid their sovereign's wickedness, and therefore I say that the great officers of the present day are sinners against the princes." [227]

227.   Bk. IV, Pt. II, Ch. VII, 1—4.

Chapter XV

MENCIUS *(continued)*

Thus far we have seen in brief the ideal of a sovereignty no longer limited to a state but spread all over the earth through peaceful means, a rule of Love (Jen) and Righteousness (Yi). It was also the ideal cherished in the Confucian school long before Mencius, and continued to flourish after him right up to the present day. As mentioned before, in the political philosophy of ancient Greece the state comes first and the individual last, while in the Confucian teaching the opposite seems to be the case. Nowadays we are inclined to think that if the society is well organized under a sound political system, the individuals would naturally develop their best and contribute to the common welfare, and hence lead a happy collective life. It is therefore the good social system that should be our first consideration.

It must be noted in passing that what Mencius taught had nothing to do with what we understand as individualism. As a philosophy, individualism, or rather "egotism" also existed among the "hundred schools" propounded by Yang Tze. His doctrines were generally known through the quotations and refutations made by his contemporaries, though he himself left behind him no writings. He was perhaps too true to his own principles of egotism or else too selfish to benefit others by his writings. But in the end, we see that even a good social system depends upon the right persons to put it into practice and these fit persons must rely upon the corresponding states of consciousness to hold themselves true to certain principles. As in ancient times government was conducted by princes or kings, so their "hearts" were to be "rectified" first, and then, according to Mencius, everything good would result. In our modern democratic systems, we no longer have so many princes or kings, we have leaders in their stead. Put in a more metaphysical way, it is still the higher states of consciousness of those individuals serving as leaders which can exercise their beneficial influence on those whom they lead and hence secure to some extent a harmonious collective life.

Endless evidences in history show that whatever sound and healthy codes of laws and constitutions (in recent times "plans") and whatever excellent systems were adopted, they necessarily declined and gradually fell into decadence if they were not constantly maintained, renovated and improved by superior minds with far-sight and, more important, good-will. Good-will, termed in ancient times "good-heartedness", abides in Divine's Love (Jen). There is in this Love an immense power of life-giving and preservation, which, when rightly realized, can be an inexhaustible source of felicity and blissfulness to the individual as well as to society. This life-giving and life-preserving force was considered as "a great virtue of Heaven and Earth," which is, in our terminology, the Grace. There is the "comfortable home in which human beings should dwell" and that is the aim to which every scholar should aspire. We read:

> The king's son of the Ch'i state, Tien, asked Mencius, saying:
> "What is the business of a scholar?"
> Mencius replied: "To exalt his aspirations!"
> "What is meant by 'to exalt his aspirations'?" — Tien asked.
> Mencius replied: "Towards Divine's Love and Righteousness and nothing else. (For example,) to put a single innocent person to death is contrary to Divine's Love; to take what he has not a right to is contrary to Righteousness. Where should one dwell? — In Divine's Love. Where is his Path? — In Righteousness. Dwelling in Divine's Love in following the Path of Righteousness, the business of a great man is complete." [228]

The Divine's Love is never unaccompanied by Righteousness. "To put a single innocent person to death" refers to the saying "in order to obtain an empire," as it was commonly understood. "Not to take what one has not a right to" means not to steal, an equivalent to the second commandment in Buddhism. But here it is included in a greater and more positive principle of Righteousness that is to be followed. Further:

Mencius said: "Under an over-lord of might, the people look brisk and cheerful. Under a true sovereign of peace, they have an air of broad and deep contentment. Even if he slay them, they do not murmur. When he benefits them, they do not think of his merit. From day to day they make progress towards what is good, without knowing who makes them do so.

"Wherever the superior man passes through, transformation follows. Wherever he abides, his influence is of a spiritual nature (or lit. 'godlike'). It flows abroad above and beneath, like that of Heaven and Earth. How can it be said that he helps (society) but in a small way!" [229]

By this, we understand that there is an influence of transformation which is easily explained in the light of a transmission of higher states of consciousness. Extending what is meant here, we find certain sayings in Taoism such as "a teaching without words," or "an accomplishment by non-action" can be utterly true. But emphasis here has been laid on individuals, the few leaders or rulers, and in case they could be

228.   Bk. VII, Pt. I, Ch. XXXIII, 1—3.
229.   Bk. VII, Pt. I, Ch. XIII, 1—3. This trl. by Legge is excellent, given with only very slight adjustment of wording.

converted into great men of Love and Righteousness then the policies or principles handled by them in a state would naturally adopt a right and proper course and progress and prosperity of the society would be achieved knowingly or unknowingly to the contentment of all. The work to be done is always at the centre, so that whenever a slight deflection of the angle were made the difference on the circumference would be great. The problem, so to say, is tackled at its root.

Mencius said: "People have the common saying, — 'All under heaven, the state and the family.' The root of all under heaven is in the state. The root of the state is in the family. The root of the family is in the person." [230]

We may examine further the conception of the "great man" as taught by Mencius:

"To dwell in the large dwelling of the universe, to stand in the correct position in the world, and to walk on the Great Path under heaven; when he obtains the right occasion for realizing his ideals, to practice them with the people; and when that chance is not given, to pursue his Path alone; riches and honors cannot make him dissolute, poverty and mean condition cannot move him, and might and power cannot make him bend, — such is called a great man." [231]

Mencius said: "With regard to the great man — his words may not be true, his acts may not be resolute — he (speaks and does) only what is right." [232]

Mencius said: "The great man is he who does not lose his child's-heart." [233]

The "child's-heart" represents a state of innocence, simplicity, purity and sincerity, the only basis upon which great things can be built. This has a correspondence with what Jesus taught, "Except ye be converted and become as little children, ye shall not enter into the Kingdom of Heaven."

The problem resolves back to the nature of man, which was always considered to be good.

Mencius said: "The ability possessed by men acquired without learning is intuitive (lit. 'good') ability, and the knowledge possessed by them without the exercise of thought is their intuitive (lit. 'good') knowledge.

.

230.   Bk. VI, Pt. I, Ch. V.
231.   Bk. III, Pt. II, Ch. II, 3.
232.   Bk. IV, Pt. II, Ch. XI.
233.   Bk. IV, Pt. II, Ch. XII.

"Children carried in the arms all know to love their parents, and when they are grown up, they all know to respect their elder brothers.

"Filial affection for parents is Divine's Love (Jen). Respect for elders is Righteousness (Yi). (The Path therefore lies in) nothing else than to extend these to all under heaven." [234]

The "intuitive knowledge" mentioned here, otherwise called also "good conscience" developed later in the Ming dynasty into a great philosophy. This passage above has given rise to much discussion, because ultimately it can only be said that the good elements are latent in human nature and they can be fully developed by education. The child carried in arms loves his mother because he has been fed by her and his love can be shifted to any other foster-nurse. When a child grows up, he respects his elders, but if the teachers are too severe his respect could be shifted to someone else. Thus both the intuitive knowledge and ability mentioned here do not count for much without further development, as certain scholars argued.

As mentioned before, the nature of man was always a subject of discussion and debate in philosophy. A contemporary of Mencius, a speculatist named Kaou Tze, held that the nature of man cannot be spoken of as either good or bad. We read in this book refutations made by Mencius to his theories:

Kaou Tze said: "Man's nature is like willow-wood, and righteousness is like a cup or a bowl. The fashioning Benevolence (Jen) and Righteousness (Yi) out of man's nature is like the making cups and bowls from the willow-wood."

Mencius replied: "Can you, leaving untouched the nature of the willow-wood, make with it cups and bowls? Or must you do violence and injury to the willow-wood, before you can make cups and bowls with it? If you must do violence and injury to the willow-wood in order to make cups and bowls with it, then must you in the same way do violence and injury to humanity in order to fashion from it Benevolence (Jen) and Righteousness (Yi) ? Leading all men under heaven to do injustice to Benevolence and Righteousness must be your words." [235]

Kaou Tze said: "Human nature is like water whirling round (in a corner). Open a passage for it to the east, and it will flow to the east; open a passage for it to the west, and it will flow to the west. Man's nature is indifferent to good and evil, just as the water is indifferent to the east and west."

Mencius replied: "Water indeed will flow indifferently to the east or west, but will it flow indifferently up or down? The tendency of man's nature to good is like the tendency of water to flow downwards. There are none but have this tendency to good, (just as) all water flows

.

234   Bk. VII, Pt. I, Ch. XV, 1—3.

235.   Bk. VI, Pt. I, Ch. I, 1—2.

downwards.

"Now by striking water and causing it to leap up, you may make it go over your forehead, and, by damming and leading it, you may force it up a hill; — but are such movements according to the nature of water? It is the force applied which causes them. When men are made to do what is not good, their nature is dealt with in this way." [236]

Kaou Tze said: "Life is what is to be understood by nature."

Mencius asked him: "Do you say that by nature you mean life, just as you say that white is white?"

"Yes, I do," was the reply.

Mencius added: "Is the whiteness of a white feather like that of white snow, and the whiteness of white snow like that of a white gem?"

Kaou Tze again said: "Yes."

"Very well, " pursued Mencius: "Is the nature of a dog like the nature of an ox, and the nature of an ox like the nature of a man?" [237]

Kaou Tze said: "Food and sex both are man's nature. Benevolence (Jen) is internal and not external; Righteousness (Yi) is external and not internal."

Mencius asked him: "What is meant by saying Benevolence being internal and Righteousness external?"

He replied: "There is a man older than I, and I give honor to his age. It is not that there is the old age in me which I give honor to. It is just as when there is a white man, and I consider him white; — according as he is so externally to me (In the same way,) I say (Righteousness is) external."

Mencius said: "It is different. (You may say that) the whiteness of a white horse is the same as the whiteness of a white man. But I do not know whether (you mean) between the respect to an old horse and the respect to an old man there is no difference? And what is it which is called Righteousness? —the fact man's being old? or the fact of our giving honor to his age?"

Kaou Tze said: "There is my younger brother; — I love him. But the younger brother of a man of Ch'in I do not love; that is, the feeling is determined by myself, and therefore I say that love is internal. But I give honor to an old man of Ch'u, and I also give honor to an old man of my own people; that is, the feeling is determined by the age, and therefore I say that Righteousness is external."

Mencius answered him: "Our enjoyment of meat roasted by a man of Ch'in does not differ from our enjoyment of meat roasted by ourselves. With regard to things there are also cases (as you say), and will you say likewise that our enjoyment of a roast is external?" [238]

.

236.   Bk. VI, Pt. I, Ch. II, 1—3.
237.   Bk. VI, Pt. I, Ch. III, 1—3.
238.   Bk. VI, Pt. I, Ch. IV, 1—5.

Kung-too Tze said: "Kaou Tze says, 'Man's nature is neither good nor bad.'

"Some say, 'Man's nature may be made to practise good, and it may be made to practise evil,' and accordingly, under (the rule of) King Wen and Wu, the people loved what was good, while under (the tyrants) Yew and Le, they loved what was cruel.

"Some say, 'The nature of some is good, and the nature of others is bad.' 'Hence it was that under such a (benevolent) sovereign as Yao, there yet appeared Siang'[239]; that with such a father as Koosow, there yet appeared Shun; and that with Chou (the tyrant) for their sovereign, and the son of their elder brother besides, there were Ki, the Viscount of Wei, and the prince Pi-kan.[240]

"And now you say: 'The nature is good.' Then are all those wrong?"

Mencius said: "Following the reality of it, it is constituted for the practice of what is good. This is what I mean in saying that (the nature) is good.

"If men do what is not good, the blame cannot be imputed to their natural gifts.

"The feeling of commiseration belongs to all men; so does that of shame and dislike; and that of reverence and respect; and that of approving and disapproving (lit. 'right and wrong'). The feeling of commiseration (implies the principle of) Benevolence; that of shame and dislike, the principle of Righteousness ; that of reverence and respect, the principle of Propriety; and that of approving and disapproving, the principle of Knowledge. Benevolence, Righteousness, Propriety and Knowledge are not decorations on us from without; we are internally furnished with them. Only you do not reflect on them. Hence it is said: 'Seek and you will find them. Neglect and you will lose them.' Men differ from one another in regard to them; — some as much again as others, some five times as much, and some to an incalculable amount; — it is because they cannot carry out fully their natural gifts ..." [241]

All these thoughts in such analogous forms might have led to the development of a school or schools of speculative philosophy, which, however, did not take place. Mencius was a spiritual master to whom a philosophy founded purely on mental reasoning could only be a quite secondary consideration. His teachings were all practical in nature, dealing with the right ways (or Tao) of being a man in serving God. We read:

"Though a man may be wicked, yet if he properly adjust his thoughts and fast and bathe, he may do sacrifices to God." [242]

239. Siang was the younger brother of Shun who always conspired against his life. Koosow was their father, an ignorant and obstinate man.

240. Chou was the tyrant, but the Viscount of Wei and the prince Pi-kan were both virtuous men.

241. Bk. VI, Pt. I, Ch. VI, 1—9.

242. Bk. IV, Pt. II, Ch. XXV, 2.

Mencius said: "To act in accord with the Conscience to the utmost presupposes of the knowledge of his nature. Knowing his nature, he knows God-conscience (lit. 'Heaven').

"Preserve one's Conscience, and cultivate one's nature, — this is the way to serve God (lit. 'Heaven').

"When life, whether short or long, could not change his determination, he waits for the Ordinance of God (lit. 'Heaven') in the cultivation of his personal character; — this is the way in which he establishes himself as a human being (as ordained by God)." [243]

"Nature" here must be understood as that expressed in the opening passage of *Chung Yung*; in other words, man's divine Nature. What Kaou Tze and others said referred to human nature in general. Their arguments cannot be taken as definitely wrong, but they did not point to this aspect of divinity. The arguments could not meet so as to come to a definite conclusion because, strictly speaking, the subjects spoken of were different.

Here a little philological explanation may be helpful to a clearer understanding. The same terms used in Taoist texts may have a slightly different bearing, but since we are temporarily concerned with Confucian texts, we may leave that aside. In Chinese, the word for "heart" means also "mind" and hence the whole mental being; and in a higher sense it means also "conscience". "Heaven" means the physical nature, but being always used in a higher sense means God, or God-

Conscience, and also as an abbreviated term for Heaven's Ordinance. Heaven's Ordinance is sometimes rendered as Heaven's Decree or Appointment, or more commonly, the Ordinance of God; literally it means "Heaven's Command" and, taken in a narrower sense, it means one's fate or destiny. The word for "life" in Chinese is a compound, meaning literally "living" and "command" and since the Han dynasty it is traditionally defined as "that in which Heaven commands the existence and growth of men." With the exception of a very few enlightened souls perhaps, this appointment of Heaven upon oneself is scarcely known; even Confucius knew this only when he was about fifty years of age. Yet somehow one must be vaguely conscious of a definite form of destiny. One is subject to the command from Above and his fate, shaped or "commanded" by God, must be obeyed. But this is in no sense a blind submission to a dark and unwitting fate. One acts in accord with his Conscience which, on the highest level, is the same with God-Conscience and he should leave no room for compunction, resentment or any uneasiness whatever. The meaning of the word for "Blessing" in Chinese is defined as "the condition in which one's virtue

.

243. Bk. VII, Pt. I, Ch. I, 1—3.
Comparing this translation with that done by Legge, one may see how different they are. Legge followed faithfully and almost painfully the original text, and went so far as to attach translations of different commentaries on these passages in the footnote, yet the result was cryptic though not unintelligible, when certain terms are made clear the passages are easily understandable.

is perfect." One should not even crave any extraordinary good luck from Heaven. In other words, he must have exerted and made himself perfect to the utmost and, as for the rest, he waits for the Ordinance of Heaven, or, in a very familiar expression, he leaves himself in the hands of God. This is the orthodox Confucian attitude towards life, and one is not supposed to swerve from such a proper course whatever vicissitudes he may encounter as his fate, whether he be short- or long-lived, going through fortune or misfortune. Fundamentally this attitude springs from the faith in the intrinsic goodness of human nature, and one should act in its accord.

But to cultivate or to nourish one's basically divine nature is not so simple a task as to believe that one's nature is originally good. We are tempted to ask how? and by what means? We find here first the term "to nourish one's heart" which means none other than to maintain a high state of consciousness. That is easily understandable, because what is taught on this point was taught by sages of all ages, both in the East and in the West. We read:

Mencius said: "To nourish the heart there is nothing better than to make the desires few. As a man with only few desires, though he may cease to exist, (such cases are) rare. As a man with many desires, though he may exist, (such cases are) rare." [244]

This applies still to the negative side, being devoid of something.

Positively, it is the conscience or goodness of mind and heart that is to be nourished. We read the following elucidation:

Mencius said: "The trees of the Nyu Mountain were once beautiful. Being situated, however, in the outskirts of a large state, they were hewn down with axes and bills; could they retain their beauty? Still, through the activity of vegetative life day and night, and the nourishing influence of the rain and dew, they were not without buds and sprouts which sprang forth, but then came the cattle and goats who browsed upon them. To these things is owing the bare and stripped appearance of the mountain which, when seen by people, is thought never to have been finely wooded. But is this the nature of the mountain?

"And so also of what properly belongs to man; shall it be said that the man is without Love (Jen) in his heart and Righteousness (Yi) in his mind? The way in which he loses the proper goodness of his mental being is as the way in which the trees are denuded by axes and bills. (Similarly) hewn down day after day, can it retain its beauty? There is a development of man's life day and night. In the poise of one's inner being just at day-break there is every goodness, and within that inner poise there is almost no distinction between the likes or dislikes of all

---

244.   Bk. VII, Pt. II, Ch. XXXV.

Legge has translated this passage differently; though not exactly wrong, it is inappropriate to the original sense.

men. But this poise has been fettered and destroyed by his activities during the day. This fettering taking place again and again, then the poise at daybreak can no longer be maintained. When that poise is no longer maintained, then the man becomes not too distant from birds and animals. When people see that the man is like a bird or animal, they think that he is not possessed of the powers (of man's nature with all its goodness). Can that be the reality of a man?

"Therefore, if it receive its proper nourishment, there is nothing which will not grow. If it lose its proper nourishment, there is nothing which will not decay.

"Confucius said: 'Hold it fast, and it remains with you. Let it go, and you lose it. Its outgoing and incoming cannot be defined as to time or place.' It is the mind of which this is said!" [245]

The importance of "nourishment" is clearly explained above. But here we meet a term which causes much perplexity, i.e. "chi" or literally "air" or "breath". There is a state of the inner being just at daybreak, at the juncture of night and day when, after a night of rest, the man feels himself fresh and restored of his bodily strength. It is translated here as the "poise", which is the same as what is called verbally the "nocturnal (diurnal) air" in the text. It is a common experience to all men, and in the Yogic way of speaking, it is the moment when Agni flames up; in it there is indeed every goodness.

A story may serve as an example of this cultivation or nourishment of one's inner being which gives a spontaneous expression in one's "chi" or "air".

Mencius, going from Fan to Ch'i, saw the son of the king at a distance, and said with a sigh: "One's position alters the style and deportment (chi) just as the nourishment affects the body. Great is the influence of position! Are not we all men's sons?"

Mencius said (to his disciples) : "The residence, the carriages and horses, and the dress of the king's son, are mostly the same as those of other men. That he looks so is occasioned by his position. How much more by one whose position is in the wide house of the world!

"When the prince of Lu went to Sung, he spoke aloud at the Deetzoe Gate. The keeper said: 'This is not our prince. How is it that his voice is so like that of our prince?' This was occasioned by nothing but the correspondence of their positions." [246]

This "nourishment" or "nurture" of one's inner being depends upon how one is poised. The "position" means in the original text the "dwelling" or, in another form of expression, "living". The external circumstances can influence the inner being, but ultimately it is the inner being that conditions the outward life. It would be ridiculous to

245.   Bk. VI, Pt. I, Ch. VIII, 1—4.
246.   Bk. VII, Pt. I, Ch. XXXVI, 1—3.

say that to live majestically should make the man like a king, but there is certainly an inner grandeur or greatness of the soul in which one can dwell.

Here we come to the most difficult subject in the whole teaching of Mencius. To put it into adequate words is still possible, even if the equivalents are lacking, but the subject itself is somehow pliant enough for diverse interpretations and it can only be made clear in a round-about way. It has to do with the inner attainment of the sage. The whole problem hinges upon the Chinese word "chi", which has been put as "air" above. It means also the "vital breath," corresponding to the Sanskrit word Prana, which is a physiological entity. There is in our body the vital current running through all the systems which is different from the inhaled or exhaled air. First we begin with the physical being or form, which, according to Mencius, can scarcely be "fulfilled" except by a sage. The passage runs:

Mencius said: "The (bodily) form and its beauty belong to our Heaven-conferred nature. But a man must be a sage before he can realize (lit. 'fulfil') such a form." [247]

"To realize such a form" means that there must not only be an empty external form of a man, whether ugly or handsome; there must be the inner content to fill such a form; in our view, the content of truth or goodness or beauty. The functions of all the organs of the body in such a human form are, under normal conditions in themselves, good and perfect and the aims to which they are applied must be worth that goodness and perfection. The complete realization of form in such context gives rise to what is called *brahmavarcasam* in Vedanta philosophy. Otherwise, this outward form or physiognomy is the least reliable datum in the observation of a man. We need not be reminded of the physiognomy of Socrates. Even Confucius said once that he lost the correct observation of a man by judging from his outward appearance.

Next, the inner being of a man is constituted of such a "chi", which Legge has put as "the passion nature." We read:

(Mencius said:) "... The Will is the leader of the passion nature. The passion nature pervades and animates the body. The Will is (first and) chief, and the passion nature is subordinate to it. Therefore I say, — 'Maintain firm the Will, and do not violence to the passion nature.'" [248]

That "passion nature" which pervades or animates the body is none other than the vital being. It is also called "chi", yet, there is a very slight difference in emphasis, because "chi" conveys the idea more of the movement of the being than the being itself. So, to interpret it as the "movements of the vital" would be nearer to the original. As a

247. Bk. VII, Pt. I, Ch. XXXVIII.
248. Bk. II, Pt. I, Ch. II, 9 end.

rule, rigorous religious disciplines of the world have always a strong tendency to modest, reduce, weaken, or to suppress the movements of the vital being, but that, in the Confucian view, should not be done. On the other hand, to indulge and allow the vital being to be wildly rampant would be equally wrong. It has only to be well guided by a firm Will. This needs further explanation, and we read:

(Kung-sun Ch'ou observed:) "Since you say, — 'The Will is chief, and the passion nature is subordinate,' and again you say, 'Maintain firm the Will, and do no violence to the passion nature,' what do you mean?"

Mencius replied: "When the Will is concentrated, it moves the passion nature. When the passion nature is concentrated, it moves the Will. For instance, now, in the case of a man falling or running, — that is from the passion nature, and yet it moves the mind."

The meaning of the question is that if the Will is chief, then there need only be attention paid to the Will, why should there be further concern about the vital movements? The answer is that there is no doubt that the Will can lead all the vital movements, but there are cases when the vital movements affect the Will. The example given is of when a man stumbles or falls; at that moment his mind may have been disturbed or a fear aroused, and he may start to run. This example is not a happy one; but we understand that it is a common phenomenon that the vital movements do affect the Will, debasing or transforming it into a desire; this is observable by everyone in our ordinary life. A fit of anger (chi) may change the mind and heart (sim) and move one from his original determination or proper course.

Then the question was asked with regard to the inner attainment of the sage; it runs:

"I venture to ask, " (said again Kung-sun Ch'ou,) "Master, wherein do you excel? "

(Mencius told him:) "I understand words. I am skilful in nourishing my vast, flowing passion nature." [249]

Here we have come to a critical point where the term "passion nature" for "chi" no longer holds good at all. The description of "vast" and "flowing" is correct, though more exact would be "vast-like". But this "Chi" of the nature of a Proteus should be here transformed into "atmosphere". The desperate translator would render the last sentence as: "I am skilful in maintaining my vast-like Spiritual Atmosphere."

First, we see what was meant by his understanding of words. There are words and *words*. If they are inspired words, then it requires a sage to understand them, but what Mencius was skilled in still pertained to

.

249. *Ibid*, II.

the mental plane. He meant chiefly the different theories held by those philosophers of his age, His own answer to this question is:

"When words are one-sided, I know (how the mind of the speaker) is clouded. When words are extravagant, I know how (the mind) is fallen and sunk. When words are all-depraved, I know how (the mind) has departed (from principle). When words are evasive, I know (the mind) is at its wit's end. (These evils) growing in the mind, do injury to government, and, displayed in the government, are hurtful to the conduct of affairs. When a sage shall again arise, he will certainly follow my words." [250]

We pass no comment on this passage, because it is a general fact that through words one can read meanings into the thoughts and sentiments of the speaker or writer, no matter how feigned or camouflaged they be.

Next, we must enquire into that "as if vast" or vast-like atmosphere.

(Kung-sun Ch'ou pursued:) "I venture to ask what you mean by your vast Spiritual Atmosphere?"

(Mencius said:) "It is difficult to describe it.

"As a movement of the spirit, it is exceedingly vast and great, and exceedingly strong and powerful. Being nourished by rectitude, and sustaining no injury, it fills up all between heaven and earth.

"As a movement of the spirit, it is coupled with Righteousness (Yi) and Truth (Tao). Without these, it would be emaciating.

"It is produced together with Righteousness (and Truth). It is not being obtained or seized by any act of Righteousness (from outside). If any act leaves some uneasiness in the heart, then it shrinks." [251]

If Mencius himself finds it difficult to describe it, how much more do we? Though brief as the description is, it gives some concrete idea of such an atmosphere. What is called "rectitude" and "righteousness" could be all-inclusive in the large terminus "Tao" which means Truth. "Shrinking" and "emaciation" were both denoted in the original by a word meaning "being hungry," hence Legge has put it as "in a state of starvation." Thus we may conclude that such an atmosphere is produced in a spontaneous growth from Truth and, coupled with Truth, it must always be maintained by Truth — so to say, to be "nourished" by It and so kept from sinking into a state of starvation, That such an atmosphere can pervade the universe is no figure of speech; it is a spiritual fact, recognized by nearly every master of inner realization, A man feels himself identified with Truth pervading the universe. What then is this Truth? ... Ultimately it comes to an inner experience which can only be proved by similar inner experience or even greater ones;

.

250.   *Ibid*, 17.
251.   *Ibid*, 12—15.

more than this we do not venture to say. Our Chinese scholars from ancient to modern times have always taken this passage as a guide to their personal cultivation.

As to the other teachings of Mencius, those in exact conformity with what was taught before him need not be repeated here. Moral problems such as the proper attitude of a father to his son, or the gifted to those ungifted, or a Guru to the questioners; social problems such as the general economic welfare of the agricultural community and the ideal condition under a peaceful sovereign; philosophical problems such as his refutations on the altruism of Mo Tze and the egotism of Yang Tze, upto the importance of sacrificing life for Truth and the use of hardships for training personality in order to receive the "great office" conferred by Heaven, etc. are all famous discourses known to nearly every scholar. For the most part they are plainly stated in the text and do not need any separate discussion here; to elucidate them at any length would require a volume. In concluding this chapter, it is enough just to quote one single passage that reveals something of the inner realization of the sage. To this, perhaps not only a Christian prophet but also a Hindu Rishi would nod his head in assent. It runs:

Mencius said: "All things are already complete in Me (Atman).

"There is no greater delight (Ananda) than to find oneself in self-introspection in perfect sincerity.

"If one acts with a vigorous effort at (considerateness or) forgiveness, when he seeks for Divine's Iove (Jen), nothing can be closer than his approximation to It." [252]

252.   Bk. VII, Pt. I, Ch. IV, 1—3.

CONCLUSION

After Mencius, ancient Confucianism ceased in its further development; it had no great representative until new shoots of the Sung and Ming dynasties sprang up and flourished in diverse directions, forming the so-called Neo-Confucianism. But that is a subject in itself.

Upto this point, the learned reader may well have formed some impression of the teachings of this Sage and of those masters who followed the same path. But he may also have realized how large and broad such a subject is and how many difficulties arose owing to the barrier of language. When adequate equivalent expressions were lacking, only approximate substitutes could be used, and hence every now and then unavoidable philological explanations were necessitated for a clearer understanding. Moreover, it is not only the language which offers a barrier but also the formulation of the thoughts themselves which are not in keeping with our modern mentality, especially the

Western mind. Just as in simple arithmetic, the Chinese with his abacus and mnemonic verses may swiftly reach the same conclusion as any one using the Arabic numerals in calculation, yet his system is different. With the increase of knowledge in science we no longer think in terms of the ancient formula. Things obsolete have simply lost their appeal to most of us and we do not find them interesting; there is a difference in method as well as a difference in taste.

The qualification to attempt such a large piece of work by such a humble scholar has always been doubted, not by others, but by the author himself. Fundamentally speaking, to talk about a sage, one must have certain inner attainments approximate to that sage, which the author does not venture to assume. The old parable is that a poor man destitute of means talks broadly about gold. His description may be correct, it is yellow, it is heavy, etc. but the whole thing is a farce. This has prompted the shrewd saving of that Taoist: "Those who know (the Tao) do not talk about it, and those who talk about it do not know it."

Yet the whole question is more simple than it seems. If we enjoy a piece of work in fine-arts, we need not consider the artist. When all wise men perish, their words remain. From the standpoint of the reader what matters most is that the information here afforded is correct and worth consideration. For that the author has tried to gather from the most authentic and authoritative sources with careful selection, and as far as possible to give the original words in faithful translations with the fewest explanations by himself so as to leave the thoughts to be developed by the reader. Moreover, the author is of the opinion that if any one can make ample and real use of one or two lines in the quotations or even one word or two, the entire purpose of this volume is served, and his labours fully rewarded. Invariably it should be an anthology.

In the Preface to a book called "The Italian Painters of the Renaissance" Bernard Berenson remarked: "We must look and look till we live the painting and for a fleeting moment become identified with it. If we do not succeed in loving what through the ages has been loved, it is useless to lie to ourselves into believing that we do." If this is true of paintings, how much more so to the truths propounded by those ancient sages! One may be expected to live these truths, and not only for a fleeting moment but always to become identified with them. This seems to be the only sincere approach to noble appreciation.

But to any sagacious reader, a further requirement must be made with regard to his approach, i.e. it must be free mental construction. A very clear illustration was given by the Divine Mother, and we quote Her words:

"Take, for example, the very universal superstition, prevalent all over the world, that asceticism and spirituality are one and the same thing. If you describe someone as a spiritual man or a spiritual woman, people at once think of one who does not eat or sits all day without moving, one who lives in a hut in great poverty, one who has given away all he had and keeps nothing for himself. This is the picture that immediately arises in the minds of ninety-nine people out of a hundred, when you speak of a spiritual man; the one proof of spirituality for them is poverty and abstinence from everything that is pleasant or comfortable. This is a mental construction which must be thrown down if you are to be free to see and follow the spiritual truth. For you come to the spiritual life with a sincere aspiration and you want to meet the Divine and realize the Divine in your consciousness and in your life; and then what happens is that you arrive in a place which is not at all a hut and meet a Divine One who is living a comfortable life, eating freely, surrounded by beautiful or luxurious things, not distributing what he has to the poor, but accepting and enjoying all that people give him. At once with your fixed mental rule you are bewildered and cry, 'Why, what is this? I thought I was to meet a spiritual man.' This false conception has to be broken down and disappear. Once it is gone, you find something that is much higher than your narrow ascetic rule, a complete openness that leaves the *being* free. ..." [253]

This "freedom from mental constructions" corresponds exactly with one of the four characters of Confucius, on a negative side. "There were four things from which the Master was entirely free." [254] First,

.

253. *Words of the Mother*, Vol. I, pp. 114—115.

254. *Ana.*, IX, 4.

"He had no foregone conclusions," which does not mean that he had no logical reasoning or imagination; on the contrary, it shows his Wisdom. Second, "He had no arbitrary predeterminations," but this does not mean that he had no great opinions or decisions. Third, "He had no obstinacy," but this does not mean that he had no perseverance on the right Path. This tenacity and the second trait confirm his hold to Righteousness and Propriety, and consequently he was styled a "Timeous Sage" [255] a sage capable of progressing with the flux of time. Fourth, "He had no ego," from which grew his Love and Compassion, but this does not mean that he had no "self" in self-cultivation. The first characteristic includes also certain biases and prejudices from which perhaps no one can be perfectly free. So long as this freedom is not attained, our scope of vision will never be enlarged. And the bit of mental knowledge which we treasure for ourselves is sometimes no more than a heap of opinions, prejudices and biases —so much so that it often hampers the influx of new knowledge. Faced by obstinacy, progress is often wellnigh impossible. As a remedy, the Confucian as well as the Taoist always emphasized the importance of a "voidness", in the sense that one should keep the bosom or heart and mind free in order to accept not only the opinion of others but also new knowledge in general.

Confucius was outwardly just such a spiritual man as the example given above. He did not live in poverty, but as a matter of fact led a fairly luxurious life suited to the rank of his nobility. Detailed descriptions of life were found in the *Analects* (Bk. X) which the author considers superfluous to this small volume. His was in general a very healthy and comfortable life in accord with ancient Propriety. As to his end, he died a natural death at a ripe old age. He was not like Jesus crucified, nor like Buddha immersed in Nirvaṇa, nor like Lao Tze did he perish in an unknown land as an Indian Vanaprastha. Was he then less of a Spiritual Master?

In the Indian mythology, Lord Buddha turned his gaze back to mankind when he was about to enter the door of Parinirvana; thus he was called the Great Compassionate One. Is Maitri something essentially different from Karuna and these again different from love? But Confucius had his gaze always fixed on mankind and on future generations and on this world, yet with his inner vision always turned toward Heaven or God. "My praying has been for a long time," he once remarked. In his life, he had never taught anything about the cessation and total annihilation of pain and suffering. He had never held any pessimistic view of life. We can imagine that in his school the boys were filled with a joy of life in an exceedingly harmonious atmosphere where natures were silently and gradually transformed. Above all, what do we mean by calling him a Sage? We find the answer given by Mencius very instructive:

255. *Mencius*, Bk. V, Pt. II, Ch. I, 5.

"A man who commands our liking is what is a good man.

"He whose goodness is part of himself is what is called a real man.

"He whose goodness has been filled up is what is called a beautiful man.

"He whose perfect goodness, so filled up and brightly displayed is called a great man.

"When this great man exercises a transforming influence, he is what is called a Sage.

"The Sage (exercising his transforming influence) beyond our knowledge is a Spiritual Man." [256]

256. *Mencius*, Bk. VII, Pt. II, Ch. XXV, 3—8.

Discussions on Man afford too large a subject with plenty of materials in ancient literature for research. Modern thinkers may find those given in *Djuang Tze* quite interesting. This work has a recent translation done by James R. Ware: *The Sayings of Chuang Chou*, publ. by the New American Library, 1962. Pan Ku in his History has categorized all famous historical personages into Nine Gradations. *Records of Man* by Liu Shou is also highly noteworthy.

附录一

周子《通书》

Appendix I

The Book of Universality

—A Supplement to the *Book of Changes*

序 [1]

　　湖南是中国南部大省，有湖名为洞庭，纳归四河之水。省内土壤因富含铁质而呈红棕色，森林覆盖其上，红棕绿翠，相衬鲜明。源自南部山脉的河水纯净清澈，蓝天倒映，偶有黄色沙洲散落其间，自成一片悦目的风光。

　　在历史上，这是一片伟人迭出的土地。百年以来的革命领袖大多来自湖南。境内最长的河流自古名为湘江，因此湖南亦简称"湘"。《通书》作者周敦颐于公元 11 世纪开创湘学，在过去九百多年间，湘学对中国的影响堪称巨大。

　　周敦颐（1017—1073）是宋学或新儒家宗祖。在晚唐五代长期动乱之后，宋朝（960—1279）建立，权力稳固，始有和平的环境，于是，学者得以转向古代经典的研究。在这个文化已然高度繁荣的时代，学者们对待经典文献的态度迥然不同于前辈了，学者治学不再仅为求学识，或求仕途，而是为求启示，求真理。求之不舍，终亦得之。这些儒家学者大多深研《周易》，以及子思的《中庸》。佛教此时早已衰败，如鲜花绽放过后，继而凋落。道教也在颓废之中。新事物的产生是历史之必然，于是儒学中出现了新的发展，古学得以新生。

　　儒学复兴始于五位大儒。为首者是创作《通书》的周敦颐；其次是师从周敦颐的二程兄弟，程颢（1032—1085）和程颐（1033—1107）；再次是张载

---

1. 周敦颐所撰《通书》经徐梵澄先生译成英文，并以英文作序。今按中文在前、英文在后的顺序附录于此，方便读者对照阅读。"序"由李文彬译成中文。——编者注

（1020—1077）；最后是朱熹（1130—1200），朱熹的《四书集注》及后人所辑《朱子语类》，时至今日仍使朱子之名家喻户晓。

五位大儒的教义在本质上皆属形而上学，然而从根本上说，能否称之为哲学，则有待讨论，因其教义主要源自内中的觉悟，并非全部出自心思之域。在社会中，他们皆是学者、师者、政治人物，更是能力出众的管理者。他们之中没有宗教领袖，也无人自称宗教领袖。他们有弟子，弟子再有其弟子。其教义凭借此种方式，传承延续七百年之久。师徒传承皆有清晰的记录，追溯源头则止于周敦颐。设若读者以西方哲学概念批判地审视这些教义，则很难冠以哲学之名。不可否认，相较于孔子之后的晚周诸子，五位大儒稍显逊色，他们缺少晚周诸子的原创性。然而，如果思及印度的瑜伽，尤其是室利·阿罗频多的整全瑜伽，则可见到许多相同之点。他们无一例外都将"诚"作为寻求"真理（道）"的起点，"无欲"作为入道之门径，"无我"作为进阶，"转化"作为终阶。值得注意的是，他们之中没有人知道印度的瑜伽。[1] 我们只能惊叹，这些分隔于喜马拉雅山脉两侧的学者或圣贤，虽然彼此不知，竟然在许多方面，沿着相似的路径，寻求相同的目的。

于此可略作说明。我们通常将张载列于五位大儒之末。相较而言，他的形而上学体系更为简明。张载的《西铭》，全文仅353字，开篇有言："故天地之塞，吾其体；天地之帅，吾其性。"这不正是《薄伽梵歌》中的"我"吗？又言："民，吾同胞；物，吾与也。"进而言及"责任"，这正是《薄伽梵歌》详细讨论的主题。《西铭》结尾有言："存，吾顺事；殁，吾宁也。"而此时之中国并不知晓《奥义书》和《薄伽梵歌》。[2]

《通书》虽有取于《易经》，但是不可简单地将《通书》视为《易经》的注解或续篇。《通书》是一部独立的著作。《易经·乾卦九五文言》，有孔子之言：

夫大人者，与天地合其德，与日月合其明，与四时合其序，与鬼神合其吉凶，

先天而天弗违，后天而奉天时，天且弗违，而况于人乎？况于鬼神乎？[3]

这段描述"大人"品质的文字与印度大瑜伽师的观念十分契合。中国人通常含糊地将这段文字看作是对统治者的赞颂。然而，"合"字的原初义与梵文"瑜伽"的词根"yuj"（结合）完全相同。或者可以更直接地说为"与神同一"。张载在其《西铭》中也曾提及此点，并归之于圣人。邵雍（1011—1077）不在五位宗师之列，他基于《易经》而作"先天易学"，著作流传至今，读者甚众，所作诗歌多有脍炙人口者。《宋史·邵雍传》记载，邵雍有超常的听觉，遇事能前知，有超诣之识。从印度传统看，邵雍实乃一成就非凡的瑜伽师或圣人。

此外，程颢教授弟子，有一简明原则，即"敬"。以"诚"为根基，培育内中之"敬"，依此消除内中有体之诸多负面活动。这与"敬爱瑜伽"极为相似。"敬"的对象正是"神圣者"。长久的内中自律甚至可以强健身体。如此或致于行事严毅、不谙俗世，但并不为病，因为与神圣者之接近是一绝大的补偿。虽然此处并未强调"敬爱瑜伽"中的"爱"，但程子却时常教导弟子，观看鸡雏亦可体"仁"。

在新儒学与韦檀多学之间，还可找到许多相似之处。然而"转化"一词的中文含义则略为宽广，并非只表个人变化，还表大众的变化。其所指涉，是教育与学校，而非宗教与寺庙。

《宋史·周敦颐传》记载，周敦颐出生在道州营道县，现位于湖南省的西南

.

1. 宋儒定然听过"瑜伽"一词，因为公元7世纪已有《瑜伽师地论》的中译本。然而此论只流行于佛教某派之中，而新儒家学者则大多反时佛教的义理和实践。

2. 《薄伽梵歌》中译本首次出版于1957年，捧地舍利室利·阿罗频多修道院印制。除《伊莎书》和《由谁书》出版于1957年外，《五十奥义书》中译版还没有出版。直至本书第二版时（1983），才有《五十奥义书》中译版之出版。

3. 英译文参见贝恩斯的英译本。

部。传记继而言其曾任主簿、司理参军等各类职务，历迁各地职位七八处，皆有治绩。周敦颐不惮劳苦，力避拖延、腐败，落实善政，洗冤泽物，果行不懈，渐受民众的爱戴。周敦颐一生所为，表明他的成就既在学问，亦在行业。传记记载周敦颐晚年居于庐山莲花峰下，室前有溪水汇入溢江，因家乡有河名为濂溪，遂名室前之水为濂溪。周敦颐移居庐山后不久，因病去世，终年 57 岁。学者宗之，称其"濂溪先生"，其学称"濂学"。

《周敦颐传》叙事简略，对于我们关心的许多重要史实，例如周敦颐的成长环境和师承授受，都没有记载。传记提及《通书》和《太极图说》，并简述《太极图说》要义，然而《太极图说》是否为周敦颐所作，仍可存疑。我们可从传记记载的若干逸事中，见到周敦颐的真实品格，似更有教益，略述如下：

周敦颐的舅父郑向曾任龙图阁学士，因郑向推举，周敦颐初入政坛，任分宁县主簿，职责为辅佐长官、掌管文书。当时有一桩久而未决的复杂案件，周敦颐接手后，经过一次审讯，辨明情况，立下判决。当地民众无不惊叹，经验丰富的老吏也没有他这样的能力。

周敦颐在南安军任司理参军时，遇一罪犯被判死刑，他检视后，发现罪不当死。转运使王逵是周敦颐的上司，王逵为人粗暴严酷，无人敢反对他的决定，唯独周敦颐与之争辩，但无济于事。于是周敦颐丢下手版，准备辞官而去，说道："既然如此，还做官干什么？我决不会为了讨好人而杀人。"王逵由此醒悟，罪犯幸免一死。

周敦颐在郴州桂阳县（今属湖南省）担任县令时，治绩尤著。郡守李初平非常敬佩周敦颐，他问周敦颐："我想读些书，你有何建议？"敦颐说："您现在年岁大，太迟了。我说给您听吧。"两年之后，郡守果然有其内中所得。

周敦颐在南安做属官时，程颢和程颐的父亲程珦任通判。程珦见周敦颐气貌非常，遂使二子受教于周敦颐。周敦颐教程氏兄弟孔子和颜子所乐何事，令寻孔颜乐处。二程之学即受启于此。程颢曾说："再次拜见周先生，归家途中，有吟风弄月之感。"由此可知，亲炙精神人物，心中是怎样的欢喜（阿难陀）呵。

侯师圣曾求学于程颐，不得其要，于是拜访周敦颐。敦颐对他说："我老了，不得不详细地说给你听了。"三日后，侯师圣大有明悟，返回程颐处。程颐惊异于侯师圣的变化，问他："你是去见了周先生吗？"

程颢年少时喜欢打猎，见到周敦颐后，自以为不再有此喜好。但是敦颐对他说："这么容易就断定自己不再有此喜好了？这只是暂时潜藏在心里而已，将来萌动起来，就又如从前了。"十二年后，程颢偶遇猎人打猎，又觉心喜如旧。

北宋诗人、学者黄庭坚称赞周敦颐："人品甚高，胸中洒落，如光风霁月。廉于取名，锐于求志，薄于徼福而厚于得民，菲于奉身而燕及茕嫠，陋于希世而尚友千古。"

朱熹曾作《濂溪先生像赞》：

> 道丧千载，圣远言湮；
>
> 不有先觉，孰开后人；
>
> 书不尽言，图不尽意；
>
> 风月无边，庭草交翠。

现存的周敦颐著作，几乎只有《通书》，其学术精华全在此书。周敦颐的文字简洁、扼要，或许他本无意著书，或许他是在效仿古代经典。译者不得不在《通书》的英译文中添加一些文字，以使英语读者更易理解。这是一部无法依照文字直译的著作，若直译，则无法阅读。

现在，可以总括地说一下新儒家了。我们可说，新儒家始于周敦颐，延续至清代（1644—1911）初年。新儒家在明代（1368—1644）有起于王阳明（1472—

1529) 的大发展和大繁荣。自 17 世纪末，新儒学遇到新兴历史哲学的反对，同时遭遇新进的西方科学，如天文学和数学，逐渐没落了。最初的攻击指向某派后学的举止行为，身着宽袍，头戴高帽，踱步缓行，不合时宜地大谈心性天理，这样的学究形象成为戏剧和讽刺文学经常嘲弄奚落的对象。严肃学者指责他们未能挽救宋朝的危亡，亦是明朝陷落的间接原因。清代中叶的诗人文士和历史学家都痛斥新儒学。

虽然有这些批评，新儒学的潜流仍强力地涌入现代社会。太平天国运动（1850—1864）席卷了大半中国，覆灭该运动者正是一批新儒家的忠实追随者。其政治和军事领袖曾国藩，临终时（1872）手中仍握着张载的著作。此外，成功推翻清朝、建立共和的革命党人都受到新儒学的极大影响，这些革命党人大多来自湖南。甚至在第二次世界大战的炮火中，著名学者马一浮和熊十力仍然如九百年前的儒学宗师一样，在四川向弟子讲授新儒学，出版其《答问》。因此，新儒学或宋学之长短仍（亦应）值得好学深思者留心品读。

INTRODUCTION

Hunan is a large province in the southern part of China where four rivers flow into the Tung Ting lake. The soil, rich in ferric compounds, is reddish brown in colour, and when covered with green forests, presents an impressive contrast. The pure and limpid waters from the rocky mountain ranges in the south refract the blue sky, and, together with sporadic yellow sand-eyots, form very beautiful landscapes.

This is the land where great men in Chinese history were born. Most of the revolutionary leaders of the last hundred years came from this province. It is also called the Siang province because its longest river has been called Siang since ancient times. Chow Tun Yi, the author of the *Book of Universality* founded the Siang school of philosophy in the eleventh century A.D. For the past nine hundred or more years this Siang school has exercised tremendous influence throughout China.

Chow Tun Yi (1017–1073) was the first patriach of the Sung dynasty Philosophy or Neo-Confucianism. When the power of the Sung empire (960–1279) was finally consolidated after a long period of turmoil, Chinese scholars turned their efforts to the ancient classics, since the time had become peaceful and circumstances favorable for their studies. In the new period which was already far advanced in cultural prosperity, they approached the classical works in a different spirit from that of their predecessors in that they no longer worked merely for scholarship or for employment in government services.

Instead, they sought for revelation, for Truth. And as assiduously as they sought for it, so they found it. Most of them studied the *Book of Changes* in depth, and the *Doctrine of the Mean* which had been written by the grandson of Confucius. By that period Buddhism had long been in a state of deterioration. Like a flower whose blooming stage was over, it was about to whither away. Taoism as a religion had also sunk into decadence. Out of historical necessity something new had to arise. Hence a new development took place in Confucianism, rejuvenating the ancient system.

Five great masters brought about this renaissance. The first was Chow Tun Yi, the author of the *Book of Universality*, the next were two brothers, Ch'êng Hao (1032–1085) and Ch'êng Yi (1033–1107), both of whom were disciples of Tun Yi. The fourth was Chang Tsai (1020–1077), and the fifth Chu Hsi (1130–1200) whose annotations on the Four Books and *Thoughts and Dialogues* made him popular to the present time.

Fundamentally it can be argued whether the teachings of these masters, though metaphysical in nature, can be called philosophy at all, because mainly they are the knowledge of inner realisations and not mere thoughts on the mental plane. In society these philosophers were all scholars, educators, political leaders, and what was more, all competent and able administrators. No one of them was a religious leader, nor did any one of them profess to be so. Each had disciples, and these disciples in turn had other disciples. In this way continuity of the teaching was established for seven hundred years. These successive generations of disciples were clearly recorded and could be traced back to Chow Tun Yi but no further. If one bears the Western conception of philosophy in mind and views the doctrines critically, they can scarcely be termed philosophy. It cannot be denied that these masters were less brilliant than those Sophists in the Late Chow Dynasty shortly after Confucius. They lacked the originality which the Sophists (*"Tze"*) had. But if one takes Indian Yoga into consideration, especially the Integral Yoga of Sri Aurobindo, one can see many points in common. Without exception every one taught "Sincerity" as the starting point for seeking the "Truth" (Tao), "Freedom from desire" as the means by which it is entered, "Freedom from ego" as a step forward, and "Transformation" as its end. Yet it must be noted that none of them had any idea of Indian Yoga.[1] It is left to us to marvel how in many respects learned men or sages who, separated by the Himmalayan ranges and without knowing of each other, strove for the same end along similar paths.

To illustrate briefly this point: Chang Tze (Tsai), usually considered as the last of the Five Great Masters, formed a metaphysical system of his own which was a little more concise than the others. In the first few lines of his masterpiece, the *Inscription of the Western Hall*, a short composition of only 353 words, we meet expressions like these: "That which fills the universe has myself as its being. That which is supreme in the universe has myself as its nature." Is this not the Atma of the *Bhagavad Gita*? Further: "People are my brothers and sisters, and things my companions." Then it goes on with a description of "duty" which is clearly expounded in the Gita. It ends by saying: "While I am alive, I serve and surrender to the Divine; while I die, I die in peace." Yet the *Bhagavad Gita* was unknown in China as were the *Upanishads*.[2]

The *Book of Universality*, though it had drawn from the *Book of Changes* as its source, was

---

1. The term Yoga must have been heard of, because there was a translation of the *Yogacarabhumi-sastra* made in the middle of the seventh century A.D. But that book was current only in one sect of Buddhism. Neo-Confucians were mostly opposed to Buddhism both in theory and in practice.

2. The first Chinese translation of the *Bhagavad Gita* appeared in 1957, printed by Sri Aurobindo Ashram Press, Pondicherry. A *Collection of Fifty Upanishads* in Chinese has not yet been published, except the *Isha* and *Kena* (1957). It has come to daylight by the time of this 2nd edition (1983).

not meant to be merely a commentary on it nor its supplement. It stood as an independent work. In the *Book of Changes* we note a very important comment made by Confucius on the fifth line of the first hexagram. It reads:

"The great man accords in his character with heaven and earth; in his light, with the sun and moon; in his consistency, with the four seasons; in the good and evil fortune that he creates, with gods and spirits. When he acts in advance of heaven, heaven does not contradict him. When he follows heaven, he adapts himself to the time of heaven. If heaven itself does not resist him, how much less do men, gods and spirits." [3]

The description of the character of the "great man" here fits remarkably well with the Indian conception of a great Yogi. In Chinese tradition, the passage is often vaguely taken as a eulogistic representation of the ruler. The original Chinese term of "in accord with" (*"ho"*) means exactly "yuj" in Sanskrit or "to join." Expressed in a less metaphorical way, it is simply "to be one with the Divine." Chang Tze mentioned this point in his *Inscription* and attributed it to the sage. Shao Tze (Yung, 1011–1077), who was not included among the Five Great Masters, formed a separate system on the *Book of Changes* called *Sien T'ien I Hseuh* or a "System in advance of Heaven." His writings are now extant, still widely read, and some of his poems are very popular. He had clairaudience, foreknowledge and other occult powers as recorded in his Biography in the *History of the Sung Dynasty*. From the perspective of the Indian tradition, he can be regarded as a great accomplished Yogi or Rishi.

Furthermore, Ch'êng Tze (Hao) taught his disciples one simple principle: Reverence. On the basis of sincerity, the inner attitude of respect and reverence is to be cultivated. This excludes many negative movements in one's inner being. There is a great similarity between this and Bhakti Yoga. The object of this reverence is none other than the Divine. When this inner discipline has been followed for a long time, it leads even to the strengthening of the body. A certain sternness in one's behaviour or an aloofness from ordinary human relations sometimes results, but that is not a fault. It is greatly compensated by closeness with the Divine. But the element of love in Bhakti Yoga is not emphasized here. Yet Ch'êng Tze always taught his disciples to realize the Divine's Love (*Jen*) even in observing young chickens.

Many such parallels may be drawn between the teachings of Neo-Confucianism and the teachings of Vedanta. But the term "transformation" has a slightly broader sense in Chinese, it denotes not only the change of individuals but also of the masses, It suggests more education and schools than religion and temples.

The life of Chow Tun Yi is narrated in his biography in the *History of the Sung Dynasty* (Vol. 427). It states that his birth place was the Ying Tao county in Tao chow, now in the south western part of Hunan. It goes on to describe him as an able administrator who served in various positions in the government as, for example, the magistrate of a county or a minister in charge of the prisoners in a province. He passed through seven or eight such offices, and in every one he performed superbly. He gradually became very popular among the people as he was assiduous in bringing into effect good policies which might have suffered from procrastination or corruption. He immediately rectified whatever wrong may have been done to any individual through inapt jurisprudence. All his accomplishments show that, while being a scholar, he was at the same time a man of action. The Biography further states that as he was about to enter his old age, he settled with his family under the

---

3.   See Baynes' translation.

Lotus Cliff of the Lu Mountain, a famous landscape in the northern part of Kiang-si. A brook in front of his house ran into the River Pan. He named it Lien Hsi or Brook Lien, the same name as a similar one in his native land. Soon afterwards he died at the age of 57. In the academic field people called him the Master of Lien Hsi, and his school, the Lien Hsi School.

The Biography falls short of many important facts which we would like to know such as under what circumstances he was brought up or under whose guidance he had acquired and developed his knowledge. It mentions the *Book of Universality*, and examines the gist of a thesis entitled "An Explanation of the Diagram of the Absolute," which, however, might or might not be an authentic work of his. What reveals his true character and seems to be more instructive to us are the anecdotes about him. To mention a few:

When Tun Yi began his service in the government, he acted as an assistant magistrate and at the same time was in charge of the official documents of a small county, Fen Ning. This position was obtained through the recommendation of his maternal uncle who was a great minister close to the emperor. There was a law case in which the verdict had long been delayed owing to its complexities. Tun Yi swiftly cleared up the case, pronouncing the correct judgement. The people of that county were amazed, saying that even an old and very experienced judge could not be likened to him.

While he was serving as a counsellor in the martial court in Nan An province, a prisoner was sentenced to death. He examined the case and found that the prisoner did not deserve such a penality. The chief justice, named Wang Kuei, was a harsh and rude and abrasive man. None of the officers dared to oppose hime. Tun Yi argued with him, but in vain. Then Tun Yi gave up his badge of office and wanted to resign, saying: "How can one serve in the government in this way? To kill someone in order to please someone is something that I cannot do." Finally Kuei was convinced, and the prisoner's life was spared.

While he was acting as a magistrate in Kwei-yang in Chen-chow (now in Hunan), he was very popular among the people. The governor of the district respected him very much. He said to him: "I want to begin to read books. What do you think?" Tun Yi said: "Lord, you are old now. It is too late. I will carry on discussions with you instead." After two years the governor attained his inner realization which he had aspired to.

The father of Ch'êng Hao and Chêng Yi was a high official in Nan An where Tun Yi worked as a counsellor. He noticed that Tun Yi was not an ordinary man. So he sent his two sons to him to be his disciples. Tun Yi taught them to understand why Confucius and Yen Whei were so joyous and also to seek for this joy. Thus the philosophy which these two brothers later on taught originated with him. Ch'êng Hao once said: "Having met Master Chow for the second time, I came home singing with the wind and playing with the moon!" This shows that upon coming into contact with such a spiritual master, one could be filled with ecstasy (Ananda).

When Ch'êng Yi began to receive disciples, a scholar named Hou went to him to learn, but he could not understand. So he took leave and went to Tun Yi. Tun Yi said: "I am old now, and cannot but explain things slowly in detail." Hou was greatly enlightened and returned. Ch'êng Yi wondered at Hou's change and asked him: "Have you come from Master Chow?"

When Ch'êng Hao was young, he liked hunting. After he met Tun Yi he thought that he no longer had this inclination. But Tun Yi told him: "How can this be so easily concluded? Your propensity is only hidden now. Once it rises up in you again, you will be your former self." Twelve years later, Hao met some hunters and felt the old enthusiasm of the hunt. Then he realised that Tun Yi had spoken truly.

Huang Ting Chien, a poet and scholar of the same dynasty, praised Tun Yi with these words: "The grade of his personality is very high. He harbours nothing in his bosom. He is like the gentle breeze in spring and the bright moon after a rain. He is timid in seeking after fame but courageous in carrying out his will. He cares not for blessings for himself but works hard for the welfare of the people. He is very frugal as regards his own comfort, but his generosity extends to widows and orphans. He transcends his times and is befriended by the sages in all eternity."

Chu Hsi, in a eulogy written on his portrait, wrote thus:

For a thousand years
The Path (Tao) has been lost.
Sages are rare and remote,
Their sayings sunk in oblivion.
If it were not for this pioneer,
An awakened soul,
Who could enlighten.
The generations that follow?
Words cannot exhaust his sayings,
Figures cannot exhaust his ideas.
Boundless are the wind and the moon-light,
Even the grass in his courtyard appears rereshining.

The essence of Tun Yi's philosophy is presented here in the *Book of Universality*, almost the only work of his left to us. His style is pithy, terse and brief. Perhaps he had originally no idea of writing a book, or perhaps he tried to imitate the ancient classical writers. In translation some words had to be added in order to make the meaning clear to English readers. This work could not be rendered literally and at the same time be readable, unfortunately.

Now a word may be said about Neo-Confucianism in general. We may say that it began with this master and lasted till the beginning of the Ching dynasty (1644−1911). It experienced great development and flourishing during the Ming dynasty (1368−1643) brought about by Wang Yang Ming (1472−1526). From the end of the seventeenth century on it was opposed by a new school of historical philosophy and at the same time confronted by the then newly introduced Western sciences such as astronomy and mathematics. It gradually declined. At first attacks were directed at the behavior of certain groups of followers. The scholar wearing a high hat or out moded turban and a large robe, pacing slowly and talking grandly about the Absolute, Nature, and Mind, and Heavenly Reason etc. under unseeming circumstances, became a constant object of ridicule in drama or in satire. Serious thinkers blamed them for being unable to save the Sung dynasty from its doom and for having indirectly brought about the downfall of the Ming empire. Refutations on their doctrines burst forth profusely in the middle of the Ching dynasty, made by historians as well as by poets and men of literature.

In spite of all this opposition, a strong undercurrent of Neo-Confucianism flowed on into the modern age. The Tai Ping agrarian revolution (1850−1864) which devastated a large part of China was put down by devout followers of this philosophy. Their great leader, both political and military, the Duke Tseng (Kuo Fang) held a book of Chang Tze in his hand when he died (1872). Furthermore, the successful revolutionaries, mostly natives of Hunan, who had overthrown the Ching empire and founded the Republic, were all greatly influenced by this philosophy. Even under the rain of bombs of the Second World War, famous scholars such as Ma I Hou and Hsiung Shih Li propounded these same doctrines in Szechwan to groups of disciples and published their *Dialogues* as the ancient masters had done nine hundred years before. Thus the merits and demerits of Neo-Confucianism or Sung philosophy remained and should remain worthy of the consideration of deep-thinking men.

诚上第一

诚者，圣人之本。

"大哉乾元，万物资始。"[1] 诚之源也。

"乾道变化，各正性命。"诚斯立焉。纯粹至善者也。

故曰："一阴一阳谓之道，继之者善也，成之者性也。"[2]

元亨，诚之通。[3]

利贞，诚之复。[4]

大哉易也，性命之源乎！[5]

诚下第二

圣，诚而已矣。诚，五常之本，百行之源也。静无而动有，至正而明达也。

五常百行，非诚，非也，邪暗塞也。故诚则无事矣。

至易而行难，果而确。无难焉。故曰："一日克己复礼，天下归仁焉。"[6]

诚几德第三

诚，无为。

几，善恶。

·

1. 《周易·乾卦彖传》。英译文取自贝恩斯译《周易》，卷二，第 2 页，并依照原文略有调整。

2. 同上，卷二，第 4 页。

3. 同上，卷一，第 319—320 页。亦见徐梵澄英义著作《孔学古微》，第 138 页（编者按：见本书第 454 页）。

4. 同上，卷一，第 2 页。文王之言。

5. 同上。

6. 《孔学古微》，第 77 页（编者按：见本书第 339 页）。

德，爱曰仁，宜曰义，理曰礼，通曰智，守曰信。[7]

性焉、安焉之谓圣。

复焉、执焉之谓贤。

发微不可见，充周不可穷之谓神。

圣第四

寂然不动者，诚也。

感而遂通者，[8]神也。

动而未形、有无之间者，几也。

诚精故明。

神应故妙。

几微故幽。

诚、神、几，曰圣人。

慎动第五

动而正，曰道。

用而和，曰德。

匪仁，匪义，匪礼，匪智，匪信，悉邪矣。邪动，辱也，甚焉，害也。故君子慎动。

道第六

圣人之道，仁义中正而已矣。

守之贵。

行之利。

廓之配天地。

岂不易简？岂为难知？不守，不行，不廓尔。

师第七

或问曰："曷为天下善？"

曰："师。"

曰："何谓也？"

曰："性者，刚柔、善恶，中而已矣。"

不达。

曰："刚善，为义，为直，为断，为严毅，为干固。恶，为猛，为隘，为强梁。

柔善，为慈，为顺，为巽。恶，为懦弱，为无断，为邪佞。

惟中也者，和也，中节也，天下之达道也，圣人之事也。

故圣人立教，俾人自易其恶，自至其中而止矣。故'先觉觉后觉'⁹，暗者求于明，而师道立矣。

师道立，则善人多。善人多，则朝廷正，而天下治矣。"

幸第八

人之生，不幸不闻过，大不幸无耻。必有耻则可教，闻过则可贤。

---

7. 此为五德。

8. "寂然不动""感而遂通"语出《易大传》。英译文参见贝恩斯译《易大传》，卷一，第一部分，第十章，4；第339页。

9. 语出《孟子》，英译文参见理雅各译《孟子》第五篇上，第七章，第五段。

思 第 九

《洪范》[10]曰:"思曰睿,睿作圣。"

无思,本也;思通,用也。几动于彼,诚动于此。

无思而无不通为圣人。

不思则不能通微。

不睿则不能无不通。

是则无不通生于通微,通微生于思。

故思者,圣功之本,而吉凶之几也。

《易》曰:"君子见几而作,不俟终日。"又曰:"知几,其神乎!"[11]

志 第 十

圣希天。

贤希圣。

士希贤。

伊尹、颜渊,大贤也。伊尹耻其君不为尧、舜,一夫不得其所,若挞于市。[12]颜渊不迁怒,不贰过,[13]三月不违仁。[14]

志伊尹之所志,学颜子之所学,过则圣,及则贤,不及则亦不失于令名。

顺 化 第 十 一

天以阳生万物,以阴成万物。生,仁也;成,义也。

故圣人在上,以仁育万物,以义正万民。

天道行而万物顺,圣德修而万民化。大顺大化,不见其迹,莫知其然,之谓神。

故天下之众,本在一人。道岂远乎哉?术岂多乎哉?

治第十二

十室之邑，人人提耳而教，且不及，况天下之广，兆民之众哉？

曰：纯其心而已矣。

仁、义、礼、智四者，动静、言貌、视听无违之谓纯。

心纯则贤才辅，贤才辅则天下治。

纯心要矣，用贤急焉。

礼乐第十三

礼，理也。

乐，和也。

阴阳理而后和。

君君臣臣，父父子子，兄兄弟弟，夫夫妇妇，各得其理然后和。

故礼先而乐后。

务实第十四

实胜，善也。名胜，耻也。故君子进德修业，[15] 孳孳不息，务实胜也。德业有未着，则恐恐然畏人知，远耻也。

·

10. 《洪范》出自《尚书·周书》。

11. 语出《易大传》，英译文参见贝恩斯译《周易》第二部分，第五章，第十一段。

12. "若挞于市"语出《孟子》，第二篇上，第二章，第四段。

13. "不迁怒，不贰过"语出《论语》，第四篇，第二章，第二段。

14. 同上，第六篇，第五章。

15. "君子进德修业"是孔子之言，语出《周易》，英译文见贝恩斯英译本《周易》，第一卷，第13页。

小人则伪而已。故君子日休，小人日忧。

爱敬第十五

"有善不及。"

曰："不及则学焉。"

问曰："有不善。"

曰："不善则告之不善，且劝曰：'庶几有改乎，斯为君子。'

有善一，不善二，则学其一，劝其二。

有语曰：'斯人有是之不善，非大恶也。'

则曰：'孰无过？焉知其不能改。改则为君子矣；不改，为恶。'

恶者天恶之。彼岂无畏耶？乌知其不能改？"

故君子悉有众善，无弗爱且敬焉。

动静第十六

动而无静，静而无动，物也。

动而无动，静而无静，神也。

动而无动，静而无静，非不动不静也。

物则不通，神妙万物。

水阴根阳。

火阳根阴。

五行阴阳，阴阳太极，四时运行，万物终始。

混兮辟兮，其无穷兮。

乐上第十七

古者，圣王制礼法，修教化。三纲正，九畴叙。[16] 百姓大和，万物咸若。

乃作乐以宣八风[17]之气，以平天下之情。故乐声淡而不伤，和而不淫。入其耳，感其心，莫不淡且和焉。淡则欲心平，和则燥心释。优柔平中，德之盛也。天下化中，治之至也。是谓道配天地。古之极也。[18]

后世礼法不修，政刑苛紊，纵欲败度，下民困苦。谓古乐不足听也，代变新声，妖淫愁怨，导欲增悲，不能自止。

故有贼君弃父，轻生败伦，不可禁者矣。

呜呼！乐者，古以平心，今以助欲。古以宣化，今以长怨。

不复古礼，不变今乐，而欲至治者，远矣。

乐中第十八

乐者，本乎政也。政善民安，则天下之心和。故圣人作乐，以宣畅其和心，达于天地。天地之气，感而大和焉。天地和则万物顺，故神祇格，鸟兽驯。

乐下第十九

乐声淡，则听心平。乐辞善，则歌者慕。故风移而俗易矣。

妖声艳辞之化也，亦然。

---

16. "三纲"有英译为"Three Duties（责任）"，亦有译为"Three Bonds（纽带）"，即君臣、父子、夫妇之间的纽带。"九畴"出自《尚书·洪范》。
17. "八风"指八方之风。
18. 最后两句语出《老子》。

圣学第二十

"圣可学乎?"

曰:"可。"

曰:"有要乎?"

曰:"有。"

"请问焉。"

曰:"一为要。一者,无欲也。无欲则静虚动直。静虚则明。明则通。动直则公。公则溥。

明通公溥。庶矣乎!"

公明第二十一

公于己者公于人,未有不公于己而能公于人也。

明不至,则疑生。明,无疑也。谓能疑为明,何啻千里。

理性命第二十二

阙彰阙微;匪灵弗莹。

刚善刚恶,柔亦如之。中焉止矣。

二气五行,化生万物。

五殊二实,二本则一。

是万为一,一实为万。

万一各正,大小有定。

颜子第二十三

颜子,"一箪食,一瓢饮,在陋巷,人不堪其忧,而不改其乐。"

夫富贵，人所爱也，颜子不爱不求，而乐乎贫者，独何心哉？

天地间有至贵至爱可求而异乎彼者。见其大而忘其小焉尔。见其大则心泰，心泰则无不足。无不足则富贵贫贱处之一也。处之一，则能化而齐。故颜子亚圣。

师友上第二十四

天地间，至尊者道，至贵者德而已矣。至难得者人。人而至难得者，道德有于身而已矣。求人至难得者有于身，非师友则不可得也已。

师友下第二十五

道义者，身有之，则贵且尊。人生而蒙，长无师友则愚。是道义由师友有之。而得贵且尊，其义不亦重乎？其聚不亦乐乎？

过第二十六

仲由喜闻过，令名无穷焉。今人有过，不喜人规，如护疾而忌医，宁灭其身而无悟也。噫！

势第二十七

天下，势而已矣。势，轻重也。极重不可反。识其重而亟反之，可也。反之，力也。识不早，力不易也。力而不竞，天也。不识不力，人也。天乎？人也，何尤？

文辞第二十八

文，所以载道也。轮辕饰而人弗庸，徒饰也，况虚车乎？

文辞，艺也。道德，实也。笃其实，而艺者书之。美，则爱；爱，则传焉。

贤者得以学而至之，是为教。故曰："言之无文，行之不远。"[19]

然不贤者，虽父兄临之，师保勉之，不学也。强之，不从也。[20]

不知务道德，而第以文辞为能者，艺焉而已。

噫！弊也久矣。

圣蕴第二十九

"不愤不启，不悱不发。"

"举一隅不以三隅反，则不复也。"[21]

子曰："予欲无言，天何言哉？四时行焉，百物生焉。"[22]

然则圣人之蕴，微颜子殆不可见。发圣人之蕴，教万世无穷者，颜子也。

圣同天。不亦深乎？常人有一闻知，恐人不速知其有也。急人知而名也。薄亦甚矣！

精蕴第三十

圣人之精，画卦以示。圣人之蕴，因卦以发。卦不画，圣人之精不可得而见，微卦，圣人之蕴殆不可悉得而闻。《易》何止五经之源，其天地鬼神之奥乎！

乾损益动第三十一

"君子乾乾，[23]不息于诚。"然必"惩忿窒欲"，[24]"迁善改过"[25]而后至。乾之用其善是，损益之大莫是过，圣人之旨深哉！

"吉凶悔吝生乎动。"[26]噫！吉一而已。动可不慎乎？

家人睽复无妄第三十二

治天下有本，身之谓也。治天下有则，家之谓也。本必端，端本，诚心而已矣。则必善，善则，和亲而已矣。家难而天下易，家亲而天下疏也。

家人离，必起于妇人。故"睽"次"家人"。以"二女同居而志不同行"[27]也。

尧所以厘降二女于妫汭。[28]舜可禅乎？吾兹试矣。是治天下观于家，治家观身而已矣。

身端，心诚之谓也。诚心复其不善之动而已矣。不善之动，妄也。妄复则无妄矣。无妄则诚矣。故"无妄"次"复"。而曰"先王以茂对时育万物。"[29]深哉！

富贵第三十三

君子以道充为贵，身安为富。故常泰无不足。而铢视轩冕，尘视金玉，其重无加焉尔。

陋第三十四

圣人之道，入乎耳，存乎心，蕴之为德行，行之为事业。彼以文辞而已者，陋矣！

．

19. 此为孔子引言。参见《春秋左传·襄公二十五年》。

20. 此处涉及教育问题。我们需要知道，古代教育的主要内容是诵读最具文学性的经典著作。

21. 语出《论语》，英译文见理雅各译《论语》，第七篇，第八章。

22. 同上，第十七篇，第十九章。

23. 英译文参见贝恩斯译《周易》，第一卷，第7页。

24. 同上，第一卷，第170页。

25. 同上，第一卷，第174页。

26. 同上，第一卷，第350页。

27. 同上，第二卷，第220页。

28. 引自《尚书》。

29. 英译《周易》，第二卷，第152页。

拟议第三十五

至诚则动，动则变，变则化。

故曰："拟之而后言，议之而后动，拟议以成其变化。"[30]

刑第三十六

天以春生万物，止之以秋。物之生也，既成矣，不止则过焉，故得秋以成。

圣人之法天，以政养万民，肃之以刑。

民之盛也，欲动情胜。利害相攻，不止则贼灭无伦焉。故得刑以治。

情伪微暧，其变千状。苟非中正、明达、果断者，不能治也。

"讼"卦曰："利见大人"，以刚得中也。"噬嗑"曰："利用狱。"以"动而明"也。

呜呼！天下之广！主刑者，民之司命也。任用可不慎乎？

公第三十七

圣人之道，至公而已矣。或曰："何谓也？"

曰"天地至公而已矣。"

孔子上第三十八

《春秋》正王道，明大法也。孔子为后世王者而修也。乱臣贼子，诛死者于前，所以惧生者于后也。

宜乎万世无穷，王祀夫子，报德报功之无尽焉。

孔子下第三十九

道德高厚，教化无穷，实与天地参而四时同，其惟孔子乎！

蒙艮第四十

"童蒙求我"，我正果行。如筮焉。筮，叩神也，再三则渎矣。渎则不告也。

"山下出泉"，静而清也。汩则乱，乱不决也。

慎哉，其惟时中乎！

"艮其背"，背非见也。静则止，止非为也，为不止矣。

其道也深乎！

---

30. 英译《周易》，《易大传》，第一篇，第八章，4。

1 Sincerity (a)

Sincerity is the foundation of sagehood.

"Great indeed is the sublimity of the Creative to which all beings owe their beginning."[1]

This is the source of sincerity.

"The Truth (Tao) of the Creative works through change and transformation so that each thing develops properly its true Nature and Destiny."

This is where sincerity is established. It is quintessential in supreme goodness.

Therefore it is said (by Confucius) :

"That which is Ying and Yang is called Tao; comprehending and governing and regulating both is Goodness, and accomplishing either is the Essence."[2]

"Sublime Success"[3] is the result of sincerity.

"Furthering through perseverance"[4] is the return to sincerity.

Great indeed is the (principle of) Change! Is it not the source of Nature and Destiny? [5]

2 Sincerity (b)

Sagehood is in essence merely sincerity. Sincerity is the foundation of all the five common virtues and the source of all activities. Whilst in non-action, it appears to be non-existent; whilst in action, it emerges as the existent. It is what is proper and correct and what permits clear and thorough discernment.

Without sincerity, all the five virtues and all activities go wrong. There would be obstruction by evil and darkness. When sincerity prevails, troubles cease.

This is very easy to carry out but difficult to fructify, though the result is sure. There is no difficulty. Hence it is said (by Confucius):

"If a man for one day conquer himself and return to propriety, all under heaven will ascribe Love (*Jen*) to him." [6]

3   Sincerity approximates Virtue

Sincerity is non-action (in action).

Germinal activity bifurcates into good and evil, and sincerity approximates that of goodness.

Benevolence (*Jen*) means love. Righteousness (*Yi*) means appropriateness. Propriety (*Li*) means reasonableness. Wisdom (*Chih*) means penetration by one's knowledge. Trustfulness (*Hsin*) means assiduity. [7]

To be one with them in one's own nature and to live comfortably in accordance with them is the work of a sage.

To return to them constantly and to have them firmly in grasp is the work of a wise and able man.

The development from the infinitesimal which is initially imperceptible to an all-

1.   Commentary written by Confucius on the first hexagram in the *Book of Changes*.
     Vide C. F. Baynes, *The I Ching* or *Book of Changes*, Vol. II, p. 2. By quoting from Baynes, often some adjustment of the wording is made according to the original Chinese text.

2.   *Ibid*, Vol. II, p. 4.

3.   *Ibid*, Vol. I, pp. 319—320. See also *Confucianism* by the present translator, p.138.

4.   *Ibid*, Vol. I, p. 2. Words of King Wen.

5.   *ditto.*

6.   *Confucianism*, p. 77.

7.   These are the five common virtues.

pervasive and infinite extension in the universe is the action of a spiritual man.

4   On being a Sage

"Silence without action" — that is sincerity.

"Through sympathy it pervades" [8] — that is the spirit.

Motion that has not yet been formed, that lies between the existent and non-existent, — that is the germinal.

Sincerity is quintessential, therefore it enlightens.

Spirit is responsive, therefore it is subtle.

The germinal is infinitesimal, therefore it is obscure.

He who comprehends sincerity, spirit, and the germinal is called a Sage.

5   On being careful in Action

To move in the proper way is Tao (the Path).

To act in harmony is Teh (Virtue).

All that is not benevolent, not righteous, not decorous, not wise and not trustworthy is errant. To be errant is disgraceful, and if carried to an extreme, it is detrimental. Therefore the superior man is ever careful in his action.

6   Tao

The Tao (Truth, Way, Path) of sages is in essence benevolence (*Jen*) and righteousness (*Yi*), pertinence and correctness.

To hold to this is noble.

To put this into action is beneficial.

To expand this into infinite is to form a trinity with heaven and earth.

Is it not easy and simple? Is it difficult to understand? — It is merely that this is not held to, not put into practice and not expanded.

7   Mastership (Guruvada)

Someone once asked: "What is the universal good?"

The answer: "Mastership."

"What does this mean?"

"With regard to human nature, it is either firmly or softly good and evil, but it is the correct point which must be reached."

The questioner did not understand.

"Firm goodness consists of righteousness, uprightness, determination, solemnity and perseverance, competency and strength, while its evil is audacity, narrow-mindedness and stubbornness.

"Soft goodness consists of compassion, obedience and modesty; while its evil is weakness, indecision and treacherous sycophancy.

"Only to reach the correct point involves harmony and tactfulness. It is the right path of the world and the work of sages.

"The sage establishes his teachings in this manner. He makes man change spontaneously his evil nature and thus attain spontaneously to the correct point. His work ends there. Those who are enlightened should enlighten their followers." [9] Those who are in the

---

8.   The two quotations are from the *Great Treatise*. Cf. Baynes, trans., Vol. I, Pt. 1, Ch. X, 4; p. 339.

9.   Quoted from *Mencius*, see Legge's trans., Bk V, Pt. I, Ch. VII, Sec. 5.

darkness seek for light. Hence mastership is established.

"Wherever mastership is established, there good people will be numerous. When good people are numerous, the court will be in proper order and peace will reign everywhere under heaven."

8 On Fortune

It is unfortunate in life that one does not hear criticisms about one's faults. It is most unfortunate to become shameless. One must have a sense of shame before he can be taught. If one listens to criticisms of his faults, he may become a worthy man.

9 Contemplation

In the *Great Law* [10] it is written that "Contemplation means wisdom. Through wisdom one becomes a sage."

Thoughtlessness is the basis. Comprehension through contemplation is the action. As the (obscure) germinal movement is started somewhere there, it is perceived by sincerity here (through its enlightenment).

A universal comprehension without thought — that is (the knowledge of) a sage.

Without contemplation one cannot penetrate into subtleties.

Without wisdom one cannot acquire universal comprehension.

Hence it is that the universal comprehension is effected by penetration into subtleties. Penetration into subtleties is brought about by contemplation.

Therefore contemplation is the basic effort to becoming a sage. It is also the turning point of a fortune or misfortune.

It is said in the *Book of Changes*: "The superior man perceives the germinal movement and immediately takes action. He does not wait even a single while." Again: "To know the germinal movement, that is divine indeed." [11]

10   On Aspiration for Knowledge

A sage aspires to be heavenly.

An able and wise man aspires to be a sage.

A scholar aspires to be an able and wise man.

E Yin and Yen Yuan were both great able and wise men. E Yin felt ashamed that his lord could not be as the emperors Yao and Shun had been. If there was a single person who was not rightly placed in his position, he felt "as if he himself was being beaten before the crowds in the public place."[12] Yen Yuan "did not transfer his anger; he did not repeat a fault."[13] "For three months there would be nothing in his mind contrary to Love."[14]

Now, if one were to aspire as E Yin aspired and learn what Yen Yuan learned, one could be, if one surpassed him in these things, a sage; if one attained his level, an able and wise man; and even if one failed to reach his height, nothing would be lost of one's good fame.

11   On Submission to the Process of Transformation

Heaven gives birth to every being in the universe by the principle of Yang and

.

10.   The *Great Law* is a chapter in the *Book of History — Book of the Chow Dynasty*.

11.   Quotations from the Great Treatise in the *Book of Changes*. Cf. Baynes' trans., Pt. II, Ch. V, 11.

12   Quoted from *Mencius*, Bk. II, Pt. I, Ch. II, 4.

13   Quoted from the *Analects* of Confucius, Bk. IV, Ch. II, 2.

14   *Ibid*, Bk. VI, Ch. V.

accomplishes every being by the principle of Yin. To give birth is Love (*Jen*), to accomplish is Righteousness (*Yi*).

Therefore, when a sage rules, he fosters every being with Love and guides all people along the proper way by Righteousness.

Hence, the Truth (Tao) of Heaven prevails, and every being becomes submissive to it. Sacred virtues are cultivated, and all people become transformed. Great submission and great transformation occur without there being any visible trace of them and without the people themselves understanding the process. This, then, is spiritual.

Ultimately, the foundation of the multitudinous people under Heaven lies in a single person. Is then the Way (Tao) too far from us, and is the means toward this end too complicated?

12   On Government

In a hamlet of ten families, even if every one is taught individually, the results of the education will be inconsequential. What can be said then, of the immensity which exists under heaven and the countless millions of people?

It is said that perfection can be achieved simply by the purification of one's inner being.

Love, righteousness, propriety and knowledge — if one's action, non-action, speaking, doing, seeing, and hearing are not contrary to any of these four principles, he may be called pure.

If a man's inner being is pure, all virtuous and talented men will come to his aid. With the assistance of virtuous and talented men, everything under heaven can be rightly governed.

Purification of both mind and heart is essential, and the need for employment of virtuous and talented men is urgent.

13   On Propriety and Music

Propriety means order.

Music means harmony.

After both the Yin and Yang principles have been established in good order, harmony issues forth.

If the prince be the prince, the minister the minister, the father the father, the son the son, the elder brother the elder brother, the younger brother the younger brother, the husband the husband, the wife the wife, if everything is in right order, then harmony will prevail.

So propriety comes first, music follows after.

14   On Striving after Reality

If the reality surpasses its fame, it is good. If the fame surpasses its reality, it is disgrace. Therefore the superior man improves his character and labors at his task[15] earnestly without cessation, because he is striving for the perfection of his reality. If his character and work have not yet become prominent, he is timidly fearful of attaining fame so as to avoid the possibility of disgrace.

Small men are hypocritical. Just as the superior man is always at peace, so the small man is increasingly sorrowful.

---

15.   A saying of Confucius, quoted from the *Book of Changes*, see Baynes' trans., Vol. I, p.13.

15 On Love and Respect

"There is the goodness, but one cannot reach it."

"Well, if it has not been reached, then one must learn how to reach it."

Questioner: "There is a wrong."

"Well, if there is a wrong, then inform the man that it is a wrong. And in exhorting him, you may say: 'If this can be corrected, you will become a superior man.'

"If there is one point of goodness in him, and two points of wrong, learn the one and correct the two.

"Someone may say: 'This man has a type of wrong which is not a great evil.'

"Then it may be said: 'Who is without fault? It is known, and yet it is not being corrected. If it is corrected, he becomes a superior man; if not, then it is an evil.'

"Evil is disliked by Heaven. Can he be without fear for Heaven? And how do you know that he cannot correct it?...'"

The superior man will thus attain to all goodness, and everyone will love and respect him.

16 On Motion and Rest

Moving without rest, resting without motion — that is Matter.

Moving without motion, resting without rest — that is the Spirit.

Motion without moving and rest without resting — this does mot mean that it does not move nor rest.

Matter does not pervade. The Spirit is subtly present in everything. (It does pervade.)

Water which pertains to the Yin principle yet has its root in the Yang.

Fire which pertains to the Yang principle yet has its root in the Yin.

The Five Movements pertain to Yin and Yang principles. Both principles pertain to the Supreme. The four seasons move in cycles, bringing an end and a beginning to everything.

Ah! how chaotic, how greatly expanded, and how infinite!

17 On Music (a)

In ancient times sage-kings formulated rules of conduct and propriety and advanced cultural ideals and principles of transformation. The three duties were rightly observed, and the nine categories (of relationships) were established in good order.[16] All people lived in supreme harmony, and everything was prosperous.

Then music was created in order to promote the current of the eight winds [17] and to pacify the emotions of all under heaven. The tone of the music was pure and without sorrow. It was harmonious and without excess. What entered the ear and touched the heart was nothing except that which was pure and sweet. Because of its purity, desires dissolved into calmness; and because of its harmony, both the mind and heart were freed from vexation and anxiety. Free and leisured, peaceful and composed, it was conducive to a glorious state of virtue. All under heaven felt its transforming effect, and it achieved the highest success in government. It is said that then the Tao prevailed equally in conformity with heaven and earth. That marked the apogee of the culture of ancient humanity.[18]

---

16. Three Duties is also translated as the "Three Bonds", viz. the relation between prince and minister, father and son, husband and wife. Nine categories are mentioned in the *Great Law* in the *Book of History*.

17. Eight winds refer to the winds in the eight directions.

18. The last two sentences are adopted from a line in *Lao Tze*.

In later ages propriety and rules of conduct were no longer cultivated. Laws and codes of punishment became uniformly harsh, complex and confused. People indulged in their desires and violated every proper measure. The lower people suffered the more from privation. Assuming that classical music was not worth hearing, people developed new forms. Weird, lewd, mournful and melancholic, that music was conducive to sensual gratification and indulgence in grief, both going beyond self-control.

Hence, the assassinations of kings, desertions of fathers, disregard for life and the decay of morals prevailed unchecked.

Alas, in ancient times, music was created to bring peace to the mind and heart, whereas in modern times, it promoted the growth of desire. While in ancient times it was a means to promote culture, in modern times it only brought about the increase of hatred.

Without the restoration of ancient propriety and without changing modern music, it would be too much to expect peace to reign sovereign in the world.

18 On Music (b)

Music is based upon politics. When political administrations are good and people satisfied, then the soul of the world lives in harmony. So the sages created music in order to clear our impediments to the flourishing of this harmonious soul and to let it extend to heaven and earth. The atmosphere of heaven and earth being thus affected, also becomes harmonious. When heaven and earth have become harmonious, then all that lies between them tend to become submissive. Therefore the gods descend. And birds and animals become tame.

19   On Music (c)

When the sound of music is calm, then the mind of the audience becomes peaceful. When the words of songs are beautiful, then the singers begin aspiring. Hence the conventions and customs of people are transformed.

The effect of fantastic music and voluptuous songs is precisely the opposite, though the processes are the same.

20   Sacred Learning

"Can one learn to be a sage?"

Answer: "One can."

"Is there any essential point that must be learned?"

Answer: "There is."

"I beg to know it."

Answer: "One thing is essential. The one thing is to be without desires. When a man is free from desire, then he can be unoccupied in quietitude and upright in action. Unoccupied in quietitude, he can be clear in vision. This clarity in vision brings forth penetration in understanding. Uprightness in action brings justice. Justice results in an all-embracing universality.

"With clarity in vision, penetration in understanding, and with justice and universality in action, one may aspire to be a sage."

21   Justice and Light

He who is just to himself must be just toward others. There can never be a man unjust to himself yet capable of being just toward others.

If the light comes not then doubts arise. Light is without doubt. If anyone says that the capacity to cast doubts means light, that would be thousands of miles from the truth.

22 On Reason, Nature, and Destiny

What looms large is subtle;

What cannot be resplendent is without a soul.

Adamancy may be good or bad. As may be pliancy also.

In pursuing the golden mean one attains the end.

Two principles, five movements.

Bring forth everything in the universe.

The five are diversified, the two real.

The root of the two is One.

Many are contained in One, and One diversified into Many.

With the Many and the One in place, Largeness and Smallness are ascertained.

23 Yen Tze (Master Yen, or Yen Whei)

Master Yen, "with a single round box for food, a hallow gourd for drink, living in a hovel in a poor alley, could not be swayed from his joy while others could not have been stayed from grief."

While richness and honour were valued by all, Master Yen neither valued nor strove after them. Furthermore, he was joyful in his poverty. What mentality did this represent?

There is, between heaven and earth, something which is the most lovely and most honourable, worth of seeking and different from these things which are apparent. Master Yen saw this great thing and forgot other small things. Having seen this greatness, both his mind and heart were at peace. Being at peace within himself, there was nothing with which he could not be satisfied. When there remained nothing with which to be dissatisfied, whether to dwell in richness and honour or in humbleness and poverty made no difference to him. With such equanimity, transformation and equality could be achieved among the people. So Master Yen was honoured as the Next Sage after Confucius.

24 On Teachers and Friends (a)

That which is supreme in the universe is the Truth (Tao), and that which represents the highest dignity is Virtue (Teh). The most difficult thing is to be a Man. And the most difficult task a man can undertake is to bring about the embodiment of Truth and Virtue. The effort to accomplish this most difficult task cannot be successful without the help of teachers and friends.

25 On Teachers and Friends (b)

If a man embodies both Love and Righteousness, he becomes honourable and dignified. Man is born undeveloped in his consciousness. If he grows up without the guidance of teachers and friends, he will remain in ignorance. That he possesses virtue and right conduct is due to his teachers and friends, and that makes him honorable and dignified. Is this not of great significance? Is it not delightful to be in such company?

26 On Faults

Chung Yao (otherwise known as Tze-lu) was happy to hear of his faults, hence his fame endured. Men of the modern age do not like to be remonstrated for their faults. It is as if they preferred to conceal their disease and avoid the doctor. They would rather let themselves be destroyed without being enlightened. Alas!

27 On Power

Power constitutes the universe. Power means weight. If a thing becomes too heavy, it cannot be overturned. If, however, it is seen that it will become too heavy, the situation can easily be changed. To change it means to apply force. Without foresight, force cannot be easily applied. If force is applied correctly without success, it can be blamed on Fate. But the lack of prevision and force is the fault of man. Can this be blamed on Fate? — Is it determined by Fate? What is the fault of man?

28 Words

Words are meant to convey the Truth (Tao). The wheels and shafts of a carriage may be ornately decorated, and yet it may remain unused. Of what use is it if it is merely decorative, and, what is more, empty?

Words by themselves represent a fine art. Truth and virtue are the realities behind them. Attach importance to the realities and express them artfully. If something is beautifully written, it will be enjoyed by readers; and what is enjoyed will be spread far and wide.

A wise and able man may learn through this means and thus attain his end. This, then, is teaching. Thus it is said: "If the words have no elegance, they cannot be spread afar." [19]

But this is otherwise with the opposite sort of man. Even though his parents instruct him, and even though his teachers and tutors encourage him, he will not learn. To try to compel him would be in vain, as he would not be heedful. [20]

To emphasize only the skill involved in manipulating words without using them as a means of striving after truth and virtue is merely art.

Alas! the decadence has reigned for a long time.

29   On the Treasure of the Sage

"I do not reveal the truth to one who is not eager to receive knowledge, nor help anyone who is not anxious to understand himself."

"When I have presented one corner of a subject to someone, and he cannot from it learn the other three, I do not repeat my lesson." [21]

The Master said: "I would prefer not speaking — Does heaven speak? The four seasons pursue their courses, and all things are being produced." [22]

Therefore the inner treasure of Confucius might have not been discovered if it were not for Yen Tze. It was Yen Tze who unveiled the treasure of the Sage and taught for ten thousand generations without end.

A sage is like heaven. Is this not unfathomable? If an ordinary man has a certain kind of knowledge, he is impatient for people to become aware of his possession. He is anxious to be known and to become famous. How shallow this is!

---

19. An ancient saying quoted by Confucius. Vide Tso's Commentary on the *Annals of Spring and Autumn*, 25th year of Duke Siang.

20. A problem of education is here involved. But we must remember that in ancient times learning was a matter of reading classical works which had the best literary expressions.

21. *Analects*, Legge's trans., Bk. VII, Ch. VIII.

22. *Ibid*, Bk. XVII, Ch. XIX.

30 On Spiritual Essence

The essence of sagehood is demonstrated in the drawing of trigrams and hexagrams. The treasures of the ancient sages were displayed by this means. Without the drawing of these trigrams and hexagrams the essence of sagehood could not be discerned, and the treasures of the ancient sages could not be completely known. Is not the *Book of Changes* the source of the Five Classics? Moreover, is it not the mythical archives of heaven and earth and of the spirits and gods?

31 "On Creativity"..."Decrease"..."Increase"...&Activities

"All day long the superior man is creatively active [23] without there being a cessation in his sincerity." Yet this can only be achieved if he "controls his anger and restrains his desires,"[24] and "imitates the good when he sees it, and rids himself of any faults he may have." [25] The action of the Creative produces goodness. Neither Decrease nor Increase can be greater than this. Profound indeed is the concept of the Sage!

"Both good fortune and misfortune, remorse and humiliation come about through action." [26] Yee! good fortune is only one. Should one not then be very careful in his activities?

32 The Family (XXXVIIth)... Opposition (XXXVIIIth)... Return (XXIVth)... Innocence (XXVth hexagram)

The government of the world has as its basis the man. The government of the world has as its model the family. The basis must be correct. How can a correct basis be established? It is done simply by being sincere in one's mind and heart. The model must be good. To form a good model all relationships must exist harmoniously together. In a family this is difficult, while in the world it is easier; because the relationships in a family are close, while in the world they are less so.

The separation of the members of a (joint) family must have been caused by women. Hence "Opposition" comes next to "Family" . This is symbolically expressed as "two daughters live together, but their minds are not directed towards common concerns." [27]

Emperor Yao ordered his two daughters to be married to Shun on the banks of the Kuei River. [28] Emperor Yao meant: "Can he succeed the throne after my abdication? Through this he can be tested." Thus the government of the world can be microcosmically observed in the family, as the government of the family can be microcosmically observed in man.

Rectitude means sincerity. Sincerity in one's inner being means simply turning away from negative movements. Negative movements are falsehood. When falsehood is abandoned, one returns to "Innocence". In a state of innocence one can be sincere. Thus the hexagram "Innocence" is arranged next to the hexagram "Return". Moreover, it is said: "Thus the kings of old exerted themselves in harmony with their time and fostered and nourished all beings." [29] Deep indeed is this!

.

23. Vide *Book of Changes*, trans. by Baynes, Vol. I, p.7.

24. *Ibid*, Vol. I, p. 170.

25. *Ibid*, Vol. I, p. 174.

26. *Ibid*, Vol. I, p. 350.

27. *Ibid*, Vol. II, p. 220.

28. A quotation from the *Book of History*, Ch. I.

29. *Ibid*, Vol. II, p. 152.

33 On Wealth and Honour

The superior man considers the fulfilment of Truth (Tao) to be his honour and the comfort of his inner being his wealth. Thus he is constantly peaceful without being dissatisfied. Hence he regards royal carriages and crowns as insignificant and gold and jade as dust, because his inner worth is unsurpassed.

34 On Meanness

The Truth (Tao) of the sages is received by the ear, preserved in the mind and heart, stored as virtue and developed as enterprise. Those who stop at mere words are mean.

35 Consideration

The utmost sincerity moves. Motion instigates change. Change brings about transformation.

So it is said: "They pondered before they spoke and considered before they moved. Through movement and consideration they created change and transformation." [30]

36 On Penalty

Heaven makes everything grow in spring and stops its growth in autumn. Everything which is born will grow, and if it is unchecked by limitations, it will exceed its proper proportions. Thus everything attains perfection in autumn.

Sages adopt Nature as their model. They foster the people with cultural principles and restrain them with penal codes.

When the people live in a state of prosperity, their desires are aroused and passions predominate. They fight against each other for benefits, if this were unchecked, destruction would come about leaving nothing in order. Therefore punishment must be used as a means of maintaining the right government.

Yet the truth and falsehood in law cases are often subtle and assume a thousand different forms. They can only be handled by people possessed with perfect uprightness, justice, wisdom, sympathy and decision.

In "Conflict" (the VIth hexagram) it is said: "It is favorable to see the great man," —because "the firm comes and attains the middle." In "Biting Through" (the XXIst hexagram) it is said: "It is favorable to let justice be administered, "— because "the action is undertaken with clarity."

Alas, the immensity of all under heaven! Those who take charge of punishments are arbiters of human destiny. Should they not be chosen and employed with the greatest care?

37   On being open to All

The Way (Tao) of the sage is none other than being open to all. Someone asks: "What does this mean?"

The answer: "Heaven and earth are unreservedly open to all."

38   Confucius (a)

The *Annals of Spring and Autumn* was meant to point out the right path and to elucidate the great Laws. Confucius edited this history for princes of later generations. Rebellious ministers and disobedient sons were even censured posthumously in order to instill fearfulness in those who were still living.

·

30.   *Ibid*, The Great Treatise, Bk. I, Ch. VIII, 4.

It is appropriate therefore that for the last thousand years people have worshipped Confucius as the Master and uncrowned King with the sense of gratitude for his boundless virtue and merit. This should be so in the endless future.

39 Confucius (b)

As a sage who attained to both the heights and depths of Truth and Virtue, whose teachings and transformative influence have eternal value, who truly formed a triad with heaven and earth, and who acted like the four seasons, — there has probably never been one equal to Confucius.

40 Adolescence (the IVth hexagram) ... Standstill (the LIInd)

"The youths seek me," — so I should be upright and act with determination. It is like consulting the oracle which is something divine. But if one were to ask two or three times, it would be importunate. Through importunity no answer will be attained.

"The spring wells up at the foot of the mountain," — The water is silent and pure. If it is contaminated, it becomes murky. Murkiness signifies indecision.

Therefore, be careful! One must teach at the right time under the right circumstances.

"Keeping one's back still." — The back does not see. Stillness brings one to a stop. Stopping means non-action. Yet the action continues ceaselessly.

This truth (Tao) is deep indeed!

附 录 二

《易 大 传》
——新 儒 家 之 入 门

Appendix II
An Entrance into Neo-Confucianism
—The Great Treatise

时间之轮飞驰，即将引至我们跨越新千年的世纪门槛，这门槛衔接着古老永恒的过去和无限的未来。"车轮"或许是变化机制的最佳象征，因为当车轮以恒久持续的旋转跨越一段路程之时，其自身则是周而复始的。人类在天体运动和四季轮转中察觉到了这种恒定性。我们发现，宇宙中的一切事物都随着时间不停地变化，如果有刹那间的停止，那么整个宇宙就将毁灭。《易大传》明确表述了这一观念。

古代中国思想家通过观察自然，产生了一种观念，即恒久持续的"变化"或"有体变易"。凭借极深之推理，或说极深之洞见，他们明悟了宇宙中一切"变易"之主宰，乃是一切变化之核心，一切变化皆是其外部功能或活动。人能看到的只是事物或静或动的外部表象，而有限表象的内部一定有一无限者，是为真实存在，即与本体论常言之现象相对的本相，无论先秦儒家还是新儒家，对此都有区分。

不同民族都曾经在文明初始之时探讨过现象世界的短暂无常。公元前 5 世纪左右，伟大的希腊哲学家赫拉克利特曾写道：

当你踏入同一条河，遇到的是不同的水流。

或有转述为：

人不能两次踏入同一条河流。

即是说，当你踏入一条河时，下一刻触碰到的水流已经不是第一刻的水流了。这是对宇宙间一切事物之发展过程的生动说明。与此惊人相似的是，孔夫子曾临川而叹：

逝者如斯夫，不舍昼夜！

这表示，世界上没有任何事物是静止的，我们的躯体、情命和心思，每一刻都在变化，我们与片刻之前已然不同。

遗憾的是，这位以弗所的"晦涩"哲学家留给我们的只有一百多条睿智的箴言。他说过，"斗争（或战争）乃万物之父（或王）"，《易经》中相反相成的"阴""阳"原则是对这一格言的最好注解。希腊和中国的哲学家通过观察自然而寻求实在之真理，他们都注意到了相同的现象，并且有相似的言论。

在继续讨论之前，有必要简略地介绍一下《易经》及其注释《易大传》。对于这部堪称中国文化基石的经典，西方人早已十分熟悉。基督教在 17 世纪传入中国时，罗马天主教徒就曾经在北京研究《易经》。《易经》的第一个英译本由法政牧师麦格基（Rev. Canon McClatchie）翻译，题为"A Translation of the Confucian Yi King, or the Classic of Changes, with notes and appendix"，于 1876 年在欧洲出版。随后有拉丁文、英文和德文诸译本相继问世。直至德国汉学家卫礼贤的德译本出版之前，至少存在七个《易经》译本。卫礼贤在著名中国学者劳乃宣（1843—1921）的指导下将《易经》译成德文，出版于 1923 年，这是最后可能也是最好的《易经》译本（最新版为德得利出版社黄皮系列 1987 版）。贝恩斯将卫礼贤的德译本翻译为英文，于 1949 年出版。这个译本的措辞、思维形式（Denkform）和内容安排更符合西方知识界的心思结构，因此对西方知识界来说，更具可读性，更能产生一些影响。然而，对于中国人来说，不可能有完美的迻译，因为除了语言的障碍之外，这部被研究了两千五百多年的经典著作仍然有探索的余地。《易经》之源似乎不可穷尽，亦不可思量。

顺便提及一点，"交易""转易""对易"和"移易"乃易学中相对晚出的概念，是由清初经学家毛奇龄（1623—1716）从《周易》中抽绎而出。毛奇龄博学多识，以敢于挑战学界定论的怀疑精神而闻名，一生著书 130 多卷，多为阐释经学的著作。毛奇龄或有开宗立派之意，如汉代学者所为。然而他又十分谦逊，隐去自己的姓名，以名气稍逊于己的兄长之名发表著作。毛奇龄所作《易经》注释之价值若非最后，则是最近值得留意者。

《易大传》尝言："一阴一阳之谓道。"又言："是故，易有太极。是生两仪。两仪生四象。四象生八卦。"

我们首先谈一下"太极"。"太极"英译为"the Great Primal Beginning"（伟大的原初之始），德文译为"der Grosse Uranfang"（伟大之始），相应于《约翰福音》开篇的希腊文"Logos"（道／逻各斯）。此处术语翻译，在准确性上略有不妥。"Beginning"（开始）通常指"时间"，而"太极"亦表"空间"。我们可以视之为时间与空间尚未分离的原初之混沌。然而在中国人的宇宙生成论中，"太极"不是混沌，而是极具理性者，或可视为逻各斯／理性自身。传统上，用一个分割成黑白两半的圆形表示"太极"，画面好似两只蝌蚪游走在一个圆形之中，这一图示极具误导性。（太极图的画法是将两个半圆反向连接，大圆的半径是小圆的直径。）"太极"不应在平面上表现，我们必须视其为一个难以表象的球形。"太极"的原初义是"栋梁"，即屋顶最高处的横梁。（《庄子》中亦曾提及这一术语。）在更高的意义上，"太极"可以指任何至高无上的事物，如空间中的顶点，皇宫中的大殿，甚至可以指称一种拳术。为什么不用一个点，而是用一条线来表示最高呢？这源于经卦（三线）和重卦（六线）是由画线而成。一条线不仅指一个位置，也指一个平面、一个圆球和一个整体。在占卜中，也指一个数、一个事实、一次事件或一件事。我们可以说"太极"在经卦或重卦之中，但是在所有卦划之上，有一未画出且不可见的"太极"。

有一种中国人进行的体育运动，名为"太极拳"，英文错误地称之为"shadow boxing"（空拳或影拳）。太极拳肢体动作舒缓，能够促进体内生气流动。练习太极拳几乎不需要肌肉用力，所以是老年人喜爱的运动。然而，如果坚持练习，则可以平静心思，有助于保持身体的健康。如果太极拳只是影子戏，那么可以称之为"影拳"了，然而从来没有过这样的称谓。正确的英文翻译应该是"supreme pugilism"（顶级拳术）。太极拳并不用于攻击，只善于自身防卫。

"太极"作为宇宙之最高本体，在新儒家中是"绝对者"的同义词。"太极"还等同于印度哲学中《薄伽梵歌》之"Atman"（我），等同于曾受叔本华猛烈批评的现代哲学之"绝对"。"太极"首次出现于《易大传》后，很快传入道家，反而被儒家学者忽略了。没有人认真对待这一观念，它与古代形而上学一同被遗忘了将近十五个世纪。再次关注"太极"的是新儒学宗祖、伟大的精神导师周敦颐（1017—1073）。然而"太极"观念并没有被完全展开，周敦颐的《通书》（笔者前几年曾将《通书》译为英文）没有详细讨论"太极"，另一本归于周敦颐名下的小书并非其真作。但是自此之后，绝对之"太极"不再是道家独有的观念，进而在宋明儒学中占有重要地位。

接下来，我们谈一谈"阴阳"。对于中国人来说，这是两个似乎无需任何解释的简单原则。在中文语法中，阴阳这两个字既是形容词，也是形容词性名词，还可以用作副词。作为一个复合词，阴阳代表一个整体的两半，也是表现极性的单一对应原则。英文分别称之为"创造性"和"接纳性"。阴阳代表相反的两方，如暗与明，夜与昼，雌与雄，反与正，恶与善，山之北与南，门之阖与开，等等。奇数属阳，偶数属阴。占卜时计算蓍草，数字"六"视为老阴，数字"九"视为老阳。老阴则变为阳，老阳则变为阴。时至今日，我们不再相信神秘数术，即使遇到困境，也不会祈求神谕，此类问题大可搁置不论。我们只须知道，宇宙内的一切事物都处在永恒的相互变易之中。

现在，我们来看一个似乎有些模糊却又十分真实的问题。当我们说"阴阳"是形容词时，其所修饰的对象是什么呢？是"气"，我们说"阴气""阳气"。从字源上说，"气"这个字的形象是表示上升气流的三条曲线。"气"的含义是空气、气息、风，以及任何气态的事物，大气，任何情绪，能量的振动，等等。贝恩斯将"气"译为"force"（力），也是正确的。在宏观中，"气"是无所不在的生命能量，在微观中，"气"是人的生命气息。"气"等同于梵文词"Prana"（般纳），《奥义书》详细讨论了十种般纳，但是般纳只限于人身之内。如上文所引《易大传》原文，阴阳生于太极，阴阳分老少，从而生四象。四象再生八卦，八卦相错，再生六十四卦。原文使用了"生"字，表明这一过程并不是分割，而是一创造和繁育，与生命或生命之气紧密相关。

我们再来看"道"，英文中没有"道"的对应词。由于找不到更合适的词，卫礼贤用德文"SINN"（思想）翻译"道"。然而，"Sinn"这个德文词不足以涵盖"道"的含义，而且在卫礼贤之前普遍接受的译名"Taoismus"会被误称为"Sinnismus"。在汉语中，"道"的原初义是道路、路径，引申为方法、真理、存在的理由和依据。例如，如果我们说所有系统都有其"道"，相当于说所有系统都有其方法、原则和真理。在先验哲学中，我们认为"道"是无所不在、无所不包、无所不成、即刻为多为一的宇宙实体。因此，"太极"是"道"。《易大传》说，天道在上，地道在下，人道在中。分别表之以经卦中的三爻，此三爻还表示所有事物的开始、中间和结束。在生命层度，表示出生、成长及其完成。换一种说法，"道"包含"太极"的三个实体，每一个实体亦有其"道"。

如果将房屋最高处的横梁想象为一点，进而仅为一抽象物，则成为道家的"无"。老子认为，"道"是世界的本体，是"无"。同时，老子的"无"是产生一切的"空"。庄子进一步说明，"道"无处不在，甚至在蝼蚁中，在瓦砾中。如果不能正确理解老子和庄子，必将落入可悲的失败主义的虚无之中。老庄之学如此着重地强调柔弱者之于刚强，足以克胜而不欲强求。老庄二圣皆兴起于孔子之后，本质上几乎相同，同源于此。而儒学则没有这一弊端。

　　对于不熟悉古代中国哲学的读者而言，以上所论或显怪异荒谬。我们可以尝试从现代哲学视角予以解说。严格地说，除佛教以外，中国哲学探究生命和宇宙真理的方法皆非神秘路径。当然，生命和宇宙的秘密终究不是任何学说所能揭示的，总有某些神秘在。中国哲学的主要兴趣是自然，在精神上是自然和世俗的。德国哲学家费希特将所有对立（即中国哲学所言之阴阳）消减为一个基本的统一。这一基本的统一与绝对之太极有何不同吗？论及黑格尔哲学，则更明显。黑格尔所言之"绝对"是内在和能动的，这一点非常重要，此"绝对"即是《易大传》所言之"绝对"。"太极"是不断运动的"绝对者"，太极动则阳生，静则阴生。这就是所谓创造与接纳原则的产生方式。绝对之太极不是位于最高处的抽象的死寂之点，因为阴阳两者处在一巨大的循环运动中。我们必须将"太极"看作为一个永恒持续的进化，实现内收与外演的实体，然而"太极"不是任何人格化的神或上帝。例如，在一昼夜中，太阳在正午时，阴气产生，不断增长，直到第二天中午终结。阳气产生于午夜零时，在正午达到顶点，然后渐渐衰竭，直到午夜告终。季节循环亦是如此。一年之中，阳气起于冬至，阴气起于夏至。因此，阴阳相互包含，一者内在于另一者，二者之一不能独存。宇宙间的任何其他变化莫不如是。二者共同构成一有机整体，即为"绝对"。于此，还有比黑格尔的"能动"更好的描述吗？

　　此外，黑格尔哲学认为，有限者的限度并非来自外部，其本性即是其自身消解的原因，其自身活动使其走向自己的反面。于阴阳原则，还能有比这更清晰的阐释吗？黑格尔于此举例，生命自身含有死亡的种子，有限者因其极度的自我矛盾而内含其自我限制。这也可以作为太极阴阳体系的说明。

　　黑格尔将矛盾的内在性置于其辩证法中，他如此推论：绝对者即是存在，也是非存在。"存在"与"非存在"相互矛盾，二者互为反题。因此需要一个综合，即"变易"。这里涉及赫拉克利特哲学。"存在"是一抽象物，只有通过遍在的"变易"才能认识"存在",而"存在"只有通过"变易"才能显现。此处即是"本体",即"太极"之同义词。黑格尔的能动性即是指向本体的活动。新儒家基于阴阳学说的教义即与此相同。

或有疑问：黑格尔的辩证法由正题至反题，最后走向必然之合题，与此相较，阴阳走向何处？答案是：走向和谐。"和"之教义始于孔子，散播于其弟子，详细阐述于子思之《中庸》。我们知道，"和"意味着将"多"综合于"一"，将特殊者包含于普遍者，同时不失其特殊性，又不扰其普遍性。同时，因永恒普遍之法则和秩序的存在，此结合或集合之获得旨在维护人类之福祉。在传统上，此和谐的反面，即不和谐的例证，在天是彗星、陨石、狂风暴雨之类，在地是地震、火山爆发、洪水、耕地沙漠化之类，在人是饥荒、瘟疫、战争、冲突和暴力之类，总而言之，是一切破坏和阻碍文明进程的事物。由此可以想见与此一切不和谐相对的伟大和谐。作为宇宙始终的伟大和谐的实现，凭借全体而实现于全体之中。

笔者无法在这篇短文中充分讨论如此广大的题目。以上所论，只是对易学进行了浅显的概述，清除了一些概念上的误解。如果读者能够深入地思考这些观念，或可对自己的生命产生某些新的信念，安心于确信二元之相互的内在性，以及二元之上的超越。如果纯粹以研究为目的，读者依此正确知识，可得以进入新儒学囿苑，或可发现自己犹如久别家乡的游子重归故居，那房屋和家具已然重新修缮，却毫无陌生之感。

The turning of the wheel-of-time will soon lead us to the threshold of another century of a new millenium connecting the old immemorial past with infinite future. The wheel is perhaps the best symbol of the mechanism of change as it repeats itself in covering a distance with constancy and continuity in rotation. The constancy is noticed in the movement of luminaries in sky and the recurrence of the seasons in a year. We see everything in the universe changing with time without cessation, and, should it ever have ceased for any infinitesimal point of time, universal destruction would have taken place. This idea is well noted in the Great Treatise of the *Book of Changes*.

By observation of Nature, ancient Chinese thinkers have come to the notion of changes or Becoming of Being in constancy and continuity. By deep and very deep reasoning, or rather by profound insight, they began to realize a mastery of all Becoming in the universe that remained at the core of changes by which all changes were its external functions or working. What one sees can only be the outward appearance of any object, either static or mobile, and within the finite appearance there must be the infinite which is its real being. It is the noumenon as opposed to phenomenon commonly discussed in ontology, and this distinction is made in Confucianism, both old and new.

The transience of the phenomenal world has been severally explored by different peoples at the dawn of civilization. The great Greek philosopher Heracleitus who flourished about five centuries B. C. wrote thus:

"By stepping into the same river, what one encounters is not the same current."

As someone put it in another way:

"One cannot step twice into the same river."

This means as one steps into a river, it is no longer the same water at the next moment as the water he touched at the first moment. This is a very vivid illustration of the procession in the development of everything in the universe. In a remarkable resemblance Confucius said about the same thing as he stood once by a stream thus:

"Oh! Things passing are like this, — flowing on and on without pause day and night!"

This symbolizes that nothing is still or static in the world, and we change physically, vitally, and mentally at every moment; we are not the same as we were a moment ago.

Unfortunately, not much has been left to us by the "obscure" philosopher of Epheseus apart from a hundred and more apophthegms of profound wisdom. His saying "Struggle (or War) is the father (or king) of everything" can best be explained in terms of the two contradictory yet complementary principles of *Yin* and *Yang* in the *Book of Changes*, By observation of Nature in search for the truth of reality, both Greek and Chinese philosophers have noticed the same phenomenon and made similar remarks.

Before we proceed in our discussion, it is necessary to look into, however fleetingly, the Classic and its Commentary or the Great Treatise. As the corner-stone of Chinese culture the classic is well known to the West. In the 17th century when Christianity was introduced to China, Roman Catholics studied this book in Beijing. Its English translation done by Rev. Canon McClatchie entitled *A Translation of the Confucian Yi King, or the Classic of Changes, with notes and appendix* appeared for the first time in Europe in 1876. Various translations into Latin, French, English, and German followed, and there were at least seven translations in existence before the eminent German sinologist Richard Wilhelm, under the guidance of a famous Chinese scholar, Lao Nai Xuan (1838–1917) made the last and perhaps the best one in 1923 (latest edition: Diedrichs Gelbe Reihe 1987). This work was rendered into English by C. F. Baynes and published in 1949. This one might have made some impression on Western intelligentsia which should have deemed it more readable as it befitted more comfortably to their mentality in its wording and form of thought (Denkform) and rearrangement of contents. Yet, as Chinese, we do not think any perfect rendering possible, because apart from the barriers of language, it is still a book that permits further explorations after the studies of more than 25 centuries. Its resources seem to be inexhaustible and unfathomable as well.

It may be noted here in passing that such concepts as exchange, interchange, transposing change, transforming change etc. became more clarified in the field at a relatively later date. These were extracted from the contents of the Book, and formulated by *Mao Ji Ling* (1625–1715), an erudite scholar who wrote more than 130 fascicles mostly on ancient classics, who was famous for his daring spirit in challenging the firmly established authorities in the academic field. Probably he had the intention of forming an independent school of his own, like one of those in the Han Dynasty (202 B.C.–220 A.D.), yet he had the humility of presenting his work in the name of his elder brother, a scholar less famous than he was, thus effacing his own name. His commentary may be the latest if not the last worthy of consideration.

In the Great Treatise it is stated:

"That which lets now the dark, now the light appear, is *Tao*." (VII. v, 1)

(Was einmal das Dunkel und einmal das Licht hervortreten lässt, das ist der SINN. —

German trl. by R. Wilhelm)

And again,

"Therefore there is in the Changes the Great Primal Beginning. This generates the two primary forces. The two primary forces generate the four images. The four images generate the eight trigrams." (I. xi, 5)

(Darum gibt es in den Wandlungen den grossen Uranfang. Dieser erzeugt die zwei Grundkräfte. Die zwei Grundkräfte erzeugen die vier Bilder. Die vier Bilder erzeugen die acht Zeichen. — do.)

First, we begin with the Great Primal Beginning. It is called *Tai Ji* in Chinese, *der Grosse Uranfang* in German, and corresponds to *Logos* in Greek as mentioned in the Gospel of John. Now there is a slight scruple here with regard to the exactitude in terminology, since beginning is generally understood in terms of time, and *Tai Ji* refers also to space. We may take it as the primeval chaos in which time and space were not yet separated. Yet *Tai Ji* in Chinese cosmogony is not a chaos, it is supreme rational one, somewhat like *Logos* the Reason itself. The traditional symbol of a circle including two halves, one black and one white, drawn like two tadpoles running in a circle is quite misleading. (It is drawn by connecting two semicircles in reverse orders with the radius of the large circle as diameter.) It is not on a flat plane, it must be thought of as a sphere which is difficult to represent. The term originally meant the ridgepole or the highest horizontal beam of a roof. (This was also mentioned in *Zhuang Zi.*) In a higher sense it came to mean anything supreme, such as the apex in space, the grand hall in the Royal Palace, or even a kind of boxing. Why is the highest not represented by a point but by a horizontal line instead? This comes from the habit of drawing lines in the formation of trigrams or hexagrams. A line indicated not only a position, but also a plane, a sphere, a whole, and in divination, a number, a fact, an event or a happening. It may be said that a *Tai Ji* is in a trigram or hexagram, but above all the lines there is the great *Tai Ji* that is undrawn and invisible.

Nowadays Chinese athletes practice a kind of physical exercise called *Tai Ji Quan* which is wrongly called "shadow boxing." It consists in very gentle movements of the limbs in order to facilitate the flow of vital currents (*Qi*) in the body. It is very much liked by old people because it requires almost no exertion of muscles. Yet if it is constantly practiced, it tranquilizes the mind and helps maintain one's health in good condition. If it were just like the play of a shadow, it would be called "*Ying Quan*," a term that never existed. A correct interpretation should be "supreme pugilism." It cannot be used for attack in a fight between two persons, it is excellent only as a means for defending oneself.

As the universal supreme, *Tai Ji* in Neo-Confucianism is synonymous with the Absolute. It corresponds also to the Atman of the *Bhagavat Gita* in Indian philosophy, it is also the Absolute in modern philosophy so fiercely attacked by Schopenhauer. Ever since it first appeared in the Great Commentary it was soon adopted by Taoists, and neglected by Confucians. Nobody was serious about it, and together with ancient metaphysics it sank into oblivion for nearly 15 centuries. It was the great spiritual master named Zhou Dun Yi (1017–1073), the first patriarch of Neo-Confucianism, who brought it again to light. Nevertheless the idea was not developed to the full extent, and Zhou's *Book of Universality* — a booklet which the present writer made an English translation years ago — gave no detailed discussion ,and a certain pamphlet on this subject attributed to him was not his. But since then, the conception of *Tai Ji* the Absolute was no longer the monopoly of

Taoists, it occupied a prominent place in the philosophy of the Song and Ming dynasties.

Next, we come to the principles of *Yin* and *Yang* which seem to us too simple to need any explanation. In Chinese grammar, both words are adjectives, adjectival nouns, and used also as adverbs. As a compound they stand as halves of a whole, a biunique principle that shows also polarity. In the English translation they are separately called the creative (*yang*) and the receptive (*yin*). They represent two opposites, such as darkness (*yin*) and light (*yang*), night and day, female and male, negative and positive sides, badness and goodness, north of a mountain and south of a mountain, closing of a door and opening of a door, etc. Odd numbers pertain to yang and even number to yin. By counting the yellow sticks in divinations, the number six is considered as an old *yin*, and the number nine as an old *yang*. Old ones must change to their opposites. Since nowadays we no longer believe in any mystic numerology, nor do we resort to any oracle consultation even in difficult situations, we may leave these things as they were. For our purpose we may just bear in mind that everything in the universe is in a perennial reciprocal mutability.

Next, we come to a problem which seems to be somewhat vague yet real. When we say *yin* and *yang*, we understand them as adjectives, but what is actually qualified? It is *Qi*, we say *yin qi* and *yang qi*. In etymology, the word is a pictography indicating a current of air ascending upwards represented by three curved lines. It means air, breath, wind, anything in its gaseous state, atmosphere, any mood of feeling, vibrations of energy, etc., and in Baynes' translation it is rendered as force, also correct. In macrocosmos it is the allpervading life energy, and in a microcosmos, in man, it is his life breath. It corresponds to the Sanskrit word *Prana* which is of ten kinds mentioned in the *Upanishads*, and discussed there somewhat in detail, but only limited to the human being. As quoted above, both forces are generated from *Tai Ji*, and by a division into the old and young ones, four images are produced. By a further reproduction, eight trigrams are formed and by a further multiplication, 64 hexagrams come into being. We see in the original text the word "generate" is used, it shows that the process is not in the sense of a bisection, but rather in the sense of creation and procreation intimately connected with life or life-breath.

Next, we come to the word *Tao* which has no exact equivalent in English. In German it is SINN, a word newly coded by Richard Wilhelm for lack of a better one. But Sinn is too small to cover the meaning of *Tao*, and Taoismus, a name generally accepted before him can ill be called "Sinnismus". In Chinese *Tao* originally means way, path, and a higher sense method, truth, *raison d'être* or justification for existence. If we say, for instance, every system has its *Tao*, it is the same as to say every system has its method, its principle and its truth. In the transcendental theory we understand it as the cosmic entity all pervading, all involving and all evolving, at once the one and the many. Therefore *Tai Ji* is *Tao*. In the Great Treatise it is said that there is the celestial path (*Tao*) above, the terrestrial path (*Tao*) below, and the human path (*Tao*) in between. They are represented by the three lines in a trigram, indicating also the beginning, the middle, and the end of any event, and on the plane of life, the birth, the growth, and its completion. Put in another way, *Tao* encompasses the three entities as *Tai Ji*, and each entity has its own path, *Tao*, as well.

The highest beam of a roof being imagined as a point goes to a mere abstraction and becomes the Void of Taoism. According to Lao Zi, *Tao* is the noumenon of the world that is the Void, yet his Void is an emptiness that gives place to everything. Zhuang Zi expounded the same doctrine, saying that *Tao* existed everywhere, even in an ant, even in a pebble. If both sages were misunderstood, people would certainly come to a lamentable nihilism of defeatism. And their theories insisting upon the strength of the weak and hardness of the soft were drastic enough to bring to successful yet undesirable consequences. Both sages flourished after Confucius, and their philosophy, almost identical in essence, was derived from this source. Confucianism had no such defect.

For readers less familiar with ancient Chinese philosophy, all what is said above may appear eerie or absurd. We may try to interpret it in the light of modern philosophy. Strictly speaking, in Chinese philosophy, with the exception of Buddhist theories, the approach to life and universal truths is not mystical, though in the end the mystery of life and universe does not let itself be unveiled by any one system, and certain fractions of mysticism must always remain. It is chiefly interested in problems of nature, and naturalistic and secular in spirit. In Germany, Fichte tried to reduce all opposition (*yin* and *yang* in Chinese terminology) to a basic unity. Can that basic unity be different from *Tai Ji* the Absolute? By Hegel it is more evident. The Absolute which Hegel held is immanent and dynamic — and this is very important — it is the Absolute of the Great Treatise. *Tai Ji* is taken as the Absolute that is constantly in motion, and as it moves, *Yang* is generated, and as it remains still, *Yin* comes into being; that is to say, the creative and receptive principles are in this way produced. *Tai Ji* the Absolute is not any dead point of abstraction that stands supreme, as both *yin* and *yang* are in a great cyclic movement. It must be understood as an entity eternally and continuously progressive that affords both involution and evolution, yet not any god or God anthropomorphized. In a day and night, for instance, the *yin* breathe (*qi*) is produced when the sun stands at zenith at noon, and it grows and grows until it comes to an end at noon the next day. The *yang* breath (*qi*) starts to grow at zero hour in midnight, comes to its highest tide in midday, and gradually fades out till midnight. The same it is with the seasons. In a year the starting point of *yang* is the winter solstice, and that of *yin*, the summer solstice. Thus both are mutually inclusive, one exists immanently in the other, and neither can exist without the other. So are all other changes in the universe.

Both constitute an organic whole that is the Absolute. What can be a better than Hegel's description by calling it dynamic?

Moreover, Hegel says in his philosophy that limitations of the finite do not come from without, that its own nature is the cause of its own abrogation, and that by its own act it passes into its counterpart — can there be a better elucidation of the doctrine of *yin-yang* than this? As an example he says that life involves the germ of death, and that the finite, being radically self-contradictory, involves its own self-suppression. That may serve as an illustration of this system as well.

The immanence of the opposite Hegel planted in his dialectics, and he reasoned it out in this way: the Absolute is Being and also Not-Being. Since both terms contradict each other, they are antithetical. Hence a synthesis is needed which is found in Becoming. The philosophy of Heracleitus is here referred to. The Being is an abstraction, it is recognized only through Becoming which is universal, and Being cannot show its existence except through Becoming. And here we come to the Noumenon itself which is synonymous with *Tai Ji*. Hegel's dynamism points to its activity. This corresponds to what is taught in Neo-Confucianism based upon this doctrine of *Yin* and *Yang*.

It may be questioned: Hegel's dialectics proceeds from thesis to antithesis and finally to its necessary synthesis, where does this system of *yin* and *yang* in comparison lead to? The answer is: it leads to harmony. A Great Harmony is taught by Confucius, inculcated by his disciples, and a nice exposition of it is included in the *Doctrine of the Mean* written by his grandson. As we understand it, the Great Harmony means the combination of Many into One, the inclusion of particulars in the general, without losing particularity and without disturbing generality and, as there is the constant and universal law and order, the combination or congregation is achieved in such a manner as to have them maintained to the welfare of humanity. According to traditional description, the examples of its opposite, Disharmony, are given as in sky, the appearance of comets, collision of celestial bodies, devastating hurricanes and violent thunder storms etc., and on earth, earthquakes, eruption of volcanoes, great floods, desertification of arable lands, etc., and in-between among human beings, famines, epidemic diseases, wars and fightings and violence of all kinds — in one word everything destructive and obstructive to the progress of civilization. The Great Harmony as opposed to all these can be imagined. And it is the Great Harmony as the alpha and omega of the universe that is to be achieved in all, and by all.

It is impossible to treat this subject at full length in this small article. What has been discussed above offers only a superficial view of the philosophy of changes, with certain misconceptions cleared off. If one contemplated extensively on these ideas, he may come to certain new convictions in his view of life, rest assured of the reciprocal immanence by dualities, and above them the transcendence. And, purely for the purpose of reasearch, if one enters into Neo-Confucianism in this right knowledge, one may find himself as if he returns home after a long departure, finding the house renovated, the furnitures refurbished, but nothing unfamiliar.

初版译者后记

我生也晚，未尝与徐梵澄先生（1909—2000）谋面；我生也幸，竟与他老人家共事于一个研究所。因此之故，冥冥中心里总是有一种说不出的联系，那就是我想为他做一点事，或确切地说，为着喜爱他的读者们做一点事。现在，由孙波老师委托我翻译的这本小书《孔学古微》完成了，可我心里漾起些许轻松感之时，瞬间又多了几分不安之虞，因为我不敢确定我的工作效果究竟如何。况且，我在读译这本书的过程中，时常有一种奇妙的感受，那就是：我开卷时，仿佛走近了他；我掩卷时，他却又隐去了。也许，我对他的熟悉程度还远远不够，然而即便是与他稔熟了，就能真正了解他吗？他曾谈到鲁迅，说："没有人能窥透那渊深无底的心灵！"（《星花旧影》）也就是说，"渊默"是不可企及的，它是形上之"真实"。由此想到黑格尔的那句话："熟知并非真知"。这么来看，我对他的了解才刚刚开始。

我于徐先生学问的"介入"，是在 2009 年上半年，其时为孙波老师校改《徐梵澄传》做些辅助工作。我不止一次地问自己：现世中还有这等人物（"精神巨子"）？历史上还有这般生活（"神圣生活"）？回答是：有的！我已经听到了他们的声音，见到了他们的容貌。那么温蔼，和平，自信，从容。

徐先生在《跋旧作版画》中说："孔子学琴，久之从曲中见到了作者的面貌，那不是神话和附会之说。""大致只答'用志不分，乃凝于神'，由读其书，知其世，长时心领神会，久亦仿佛取像，如见其人。"我在翻译的过程中也有过这样的

"际遇",比如《徐梵澄传》曾谈到他老人家在陷入昏迷之前,对护理说:"待我睡过去以后,请帮我擦拭一下腿和脚,让它们保持清洁。"(第454页)孙波老师在另一篇文章中也谈到这一情节,他援引了康德的例子加以衬托——康德在殁世前的第九天,医生来访,他时已风烛,双目几近失明。康德颤抖着从椅子上站了起来,口中喃喃自语。有顷,康德的朋友才明白,他坚持要客人先入座。过了一会儿,康德积蓄了些力气,对朋友说:"人道之情现在还没有离我而去呢!"——我理解,孙老师在此解读为"尊严"。不错,但还有一个维度,是"孝"。因为他自知不久人世,要干干净净地去见父母了。《孔学古微》第十二章谈道:"曾子有疾,召门弟子曰:'启于足!启于手!'"徐先生解释说,物理身体得之于父母,应当仔细看护,否则任何不适都会引起父母的伤痛。人们以此为"孝",这是人的根本之爱,即对父母的爱,尤其是对母亲的爱。"其中有一内在的本能力量,如果导向正确之通道,可成为巨大的权能。中国古代教育利用这一原初动力,成就了一系伟大的文化。"那么父母在哪里呢?在"上帝(天)"之侧。徐先生说,这不是可证的"真理",而是可证的"信仰"。于此,我算不算看到了他的"心思"呢?或者,"如见其人"呢?

写作《孔学古微》这本书,是在为纪念印度近世圣哲室利·阿罗频多(Sri Aurobindo,1872—1950)逝世十周年之讲演以后。彼时,身处南印度的徐先生已经完成了印度经典的大宗译事,开始向西方介绍中国传统思想菁华了。既然要向英语世界介绍中国思想之菁华,就要顾及西方读者的心理期待和理解方式,而徐先生深谙其心思结构。可想而知,他的演讲获得了很大的成功,并受到"神圣母亲"的赞扬,而且几年后,是书甫一问世,立刻售罄。至于读者对这本小书的反响呢,徐先生本人谦虚地说:"似评价不恶。"何以如此?因为他们读懂了。比如,他讲"仁"这概念,说为"神圣之爱",印度人和西方人则易明了,即是"大梵之爱"和"上帝之爱"。也许在我们,或觉"神圣之爱"稍显空泛,其实一经推阐，便知确实不诬："仁"是一"全德"概念，以"感通为性，润物为用"（牟宗三语），即是说，"仁"是真生命（精神）之所在，亦是生命之大宗（宇宙），亦即"神圣知觉性（天地之心）"的全般伸展（弥漫，无处不在）。"仁者，爱人"，这"爱"就是精神之爱，各种善行、美德全部包含在内，如此，"仁"就是宇宙存在的根柢。于是，这"精神之爱"岂不"神圣"吗？

阅读这本小书，预先了解一些韦檀多学的基本概念，会对理解有所帮助，皆依阿罗频多的说法为定准。如视宇宙为一大生命的充满与润泽。如知"大梵"一"动"一"静"，分"彼""此"两个半球，彼面有"真""智""乐"三观念，此面有"物质""情命""心思"三观念，贯通两界者为"超（上）心思"，此乃为七条河流或七条原则，彻上彻下，实为一"神圣力"或"神圣知觉性"或"神圣精神"。阿罗频多又分瑜伽为三途（智识瑜伽、行业瑜伽、敬爱瑜伽），自性为两层（高等自性、低等自性）。而瑜伽之目的，无非就是要有生之人类"变低等自性为高等自性"，最终与"至上者"合契。这与宋儒孜孜以求的"变化气质"，以至"与天地合其德"（孔子语）的企向，并无区别。读徐先生引《论语》句："子曰：'有德者必有言，有言者不必有德。仁者必有勇，勇者不必有仁。'"此中有三种德性——"仁"（爱）、"智"（言）、"勇"（行），分别对应三类人，或三条瑜伽之途。仁爱对应敬爱瑜伽，智言对应智识瑜伽，勇行对应行业瑜伽。我们看，"两宗完全未曾交会的古代学问正是在此处契合，两者对一普遍真理有着完全相同的表述。然而在儒家，这教导不能分开领受，此三种道路必须协和互补，以塑成一神圣人格。"（本书第五章）

中西，尤其是中印，看待圣人的眼光不同，我们更注重德行，他们多看重神通。若果阿罗频多未有什么"先见"之明和"升举"之功，即精神改变物质或时势的能力，那么他在印度可能不会有那么大的声誉。以中国古人为例，他们并不以"傲异之士"为然，"二十五史"把这种人归于方技列传，如北宋邵雍，史书记载他有过人的预知力和其他超自然能力，但后人并不视其在宋诸子之列，王船山批评"邵康节志大而好游于公卿之间"。然而在印度人看来，邵雍就是一位大瑜伽师。那么，中印何以相通？相通处在道家，似乎到了这一层，他们便止步不前了。徐先生为照顾印度读者之感受，故而娓娓道来时，叙述有"笼统"之处，如谈到颜子，"颜子为后世学者开辟了一条道路：从外部来看，他具备完好的儒家德性；然而，在内中，却是简朴至极的道家境界。"（本书第十二章）我想他一定是在"境界"意义上讲，故加上"境界"二字，意思是去除私欲境（夫子绝四：毋意、毋必、毋固、毋我），在这里，儒道两家相通无疑，但"境界"并非"根柢"。所谓"根柢"，究竟是"有"（Being），而道家是关乎"非有"（Non-Being）的哲学。虽然，从宇宙论上说，老子仍然是"有"者，然而他并未落实在"仁"（人）上。

另外，有一个通常的观点，说中国传统讲集体，西方传统讲个人。徐先生以古人三年守丧（实为25个月）为例，说这一习俗的主要用意，在于将个人对父母的爱提升为伦理规范，以期塑造良好的人格，"为了家族利益，个体性会受到些许抑制，但绝不同于现代极权国家忽略或抹杀个体性。在某种程度上，家族是社会的堡垒，如果家族培养出良好的成员，他在社会中就是良好的个体。这不同于古希腊，国家第一位，个人第二位（以斯巴达为典型）。在中国，国家第二位，家族第一位（这里主要是指春秋战国时期）。在家族中，个人仍然是第一位。"（本书第十二章）无独有偶，德国哲学家哈贝马斯也持相同的观点，2001年，哈贝马斯访问中国社会科学院时，曾以李铁映院长谈到他来之前读了一点东西，按照他的印象，似乎孟子是承认个人地位的。哈贝马斯的"印象"是有来由的。我们当然不可把孟子的相关思想和现代相关思想等同看待，但我们也不能认为两者之间存在一条鸿沟，因为孟子也将个人视为基础，在他那里，离开了个人也就谈不上什么集体。《孟子》离娄章句中，对空洞片面地强调集体地位的惯常说法明确无疑地表示异议，他说："人有恒言，皆曰天下国家。天下之本在国，国之本在

家，家之本在身。"(参考薛华:《简谈共同精神》，2006 年)

徐先生关于儒学的研究，还有另一本小书《陆王学述——一系精神哲学》(上海远东出版社，1994 年)。初时结稿，大约也只有十万字，编辑以为字数太少，遂请他再作补充，他行一方便法门，辑出"教言摘录"，整整占了 37 页。这就是他的作风，话不肯多说，字宁愿少写，干净利落得惊人，这或许符合"真理"的气质，因为真理皆简单或简易。"易简之善配至德"(《易大传》)，这其中的安宁、幸福与永恒，是宇宙人生真实生命的全部悦乐之体验，可表之于韦檀多学的大"乐"(Ananda)。这"乐"是"学者学此，乐者乐此"之乐，是"仁"的震动，是"神圣之爱"。

读者一定不需要译者这么啰唆，因为译者的转述不及原文之十一。一如徐先生的汉语文章，其英文风格亦属雅言，明净无比而又富于节奏。为了少出错误，也为避免与他的风格相去太远，在中文经典译回时，仍取原典之文。这本小书的翻译，是在孙波和王建二位老师的耐心督促下完成的，译文又经孙波老师的认真校读，以期更贴近徐先生本人的謦欬与气息。当然，疏漏误译之处仍所不免，诚望博达君子予以悉心教正。

李 文 彬　2014 年 10 月 1 日

再版译者赘言

对于《孔学古微》中译本，中文读者可能会有疑问，这样一本写给英语世界的书，是否适合甚或值得中国读者阅读。

答案是肯定的，这是一本同样适合中文读者阅读的书。因为，如今我们与英语读者一样，同处现代世界，同样怀疑一切，欲以科学精神检验并重估一切旧物，对于书中所述之经典文字，我们不说完全陌生，也渐有疏离之感，徐梵澄先生为西方读者之心思结构所作的若干解说，正可为中文读者提供一种参照，在比较中显露出中国思想文化的特点和价值所在。

这同样是一本值得中文读者阅读的小书。徐梵澄先生写作《孔学古微》的基本方法是"以经解经"，这种写作方法的切入点相对较高，需要解说者对经典文字已经有了妥当的理解，而徐先生正是具备这种能力的解说者。他仔细撷取经典文字，做最少的解释，将思考留给读者。读者尽可参考徐先生的解说，循着引文阅读原典，抉择其他注释书籍，做出自己的判断。

《孔学古微》是一部儒家思想断代简史，但是读者不可仅视其为一部横向的思想概念史，因为其中还有个体精神纵向提升之维度。徐先生提示，阅读经典文字，应如欣赏经典画作，必须仔细端详，直至融入其中，有一瞬间与之相合。画作如此，古圣之言更是如此。要在切身体会，不仅在一瞬间与之相合，更在永远与之相合。译者以为，徐先生对经典的解说文字，亦可怀有如此态度阅读。《孔学古微》的英文书写有一完整的精神气象，内中节律起伏平和而有深意，译文难

650

得十一，甚或百一，幸而此次出版附有英文原文，有心读者可自行翻检体会。

徐梵澄先生自述，如果读者能从《孔学古微》中的一两行引文，甚或一两个字之中得到足够真实的益处，那么这本书的全部目的就达到了，作者的劳作也就有了收获。而对于译者来说，如果有读者能循着译文，转而直接阅读徐先生之原文，而不必隔阂于译者拙劣的转述，则是更好的事情了。

《孔学古微》英文本 1966 年首次在印度出版时，书后附有关键词索引。2006 年，国内出版《徐梵澄文集》，收有英文本《孔学古微》，并缩减了索引词条。考虑到这是一部小书，易于翻检，而且此次出版中英文对照本，更易比对阅读，故而不再保留索引。《孔学古微》中译本首次出版于 2015 年，此次再版，译者仔细阅读核对了译文，改正若干错译、遗漏以及译述不当之处，但仍有若干译文或有不妥，只能寄望于将来，对经典文字以及徐梵澄思想有更深切的理解后，再为补益。

李 文 彬　2020 年 7 月 12 日